READINGS IN FAMILY PLANNING
A challenge to the health professions

TIMES MIRROR

THE C. V. MOSBY COMPANY
11830 WESTLINE INDUSTRIAL DRIVE
ST. LOUIS, MISSOURI 63141

For prompt service, call (314) 872-8370

Instructor's Copy

This text is sent to you with the compliments of The C. V. Mosby Company. Examine it at your leisure and see how effectively it can fulfill your course requirements. We would greatly appreciate any comments you may have.

READINGS IN FAMILY PLANNING by McCalister et al

COMMENTS:

Name _____

Course _____ Enrollment _____

School _____

City _____ State _____

FF-371

Readings in
FAMILY PLANNING
A challenge to the health professions

DONALD V. McCALISTER
B.A., Ph.D.

Associate Professor of Sociology,
Department of Sociology, Case Western Reserve University,
Cleveland, Ohio

VICTOR THIESSEN
B.A., M.A., Ph.D.

Associate Professor of Sociology,
Department of Sociology and Anthropology,
Dalhousie University, Halifax, Nova Scotia, Canada

MARGARET McDERMOTT
R.N., B.S.N., M.S.N., Ph.D. (Candidate)

Department of Sociology, Case Western Reserve University,
Cleveland, Ohio

THE C. V. MOSBY COMPANY
SAINT LOUIS 1973

PREFACE

The purpose of this book is to provide a context within which the student may gain an appreciation of the nature of family planning and the challenges it poses for him both as a health professional and as an individual likely to engage in reproductive behavior. The areas of challenge are to *increase* the involvement of health professionals in family planning and to enhance the *effectiveness* of their involvement. Our position is that family planning represents a necessary part of comprehensive health services, one for which there are increasing demands from diverse quarters, and one that we are only beginning to learn how to deliver effectively. Although family planning has implications for population growth and composition, our main focus is upon the problems and prospects of family planning at the level of individuals.

Family planning refers to the intricate process by which persons, if they wish, can determine for themselves the timing, spacing, and number of children to be born to them. To understand this complex process, it is necessary to distinguish between the *ability,* the *desire,* and the *practice* of conception control.

The *ability* to control the timing and number of pregnancies presumes a modicum of intelligence and awareness that such control is possible; not all have this awareness. It also presumes a rudimentary knowledge of reproductive physiology, of the ovulatory cycle, and of the availability of treatment for infertility as well as the availability and proper use of natural, surgical, chemical, or mechanical means of avoiding or terminating conception. Even college graduates frequently lack the minimum level of necessary knowledge.

The *desire* to control when and how large a family is formed is also necessary. Relatively few persons proceed from the outset to make and implement deliberate plans; our concerns and desires change as a result of altered circumstances and of new experiences. Few events in life are as critical as is reproduction in influencing our subsequent life style, physical health, and emotional well-being; yet, few events are as casually, mistakenly, or accidentally caused.

Family planning *services* are health services, but family planning *practices* do not necessarily depend upon the health practitioner. Further, the current strategies for delivering services tend to be the same as those used in the treatment of illness. These may be less than appropriate, given the non–health-related attitudes and behaviors that are central to human sexuality and to reproduction. For example, the oral contraceptive pill and the intrauterine contraceptive device are at the present the most effective medically approved methods, but the condom is one of the most frequently used methods to avert conception. Individuals frequently express a desire to have small families but may proceed to have large ones. Family planning clinics exist in health centers, in hospitals, and in free-standing facilities, but they are often underutilized by the population. The health professional may regard family planning as a health issue, whereas the patient may define it as an integral part of his or her sexuality and thus too intimate to be a proper concern of anyone other than self or mate. The practitioner may "know" that he is per-

v

ceived as being the most informed source of knowledge about family planning. At the same time, he may be unable to respond to patients' needs because of inadequate knowledge, difficulty in communication, personal anxieties, ethical ambivalencies, or inability to separate himself as a person from himself as a professional.

Family planning means many things to many people, whether they support it, oppose it, or are ambivalent. The same may be said of organ transplant, fluoridation of water supplies, environmental pollution, public housing, and numerous other areas of health-related concerns and activities. Different as these examples seem, they share two basic similarities. Each involves health but goes far beyond the traditional domains and conventional resources of the health practitioner. Each draws sharp reactions, pro and con, from the health professional as well as from the public; however, health per se frequently is not the dominant concern. In family planning, the result is that our ability to deliver services is less than ideal. Why?

The issues sketched in the preceding examples illustrate an additional challenge to the health professional in family planning. This challenge is for students of nursing, medicine, and social work to broaden their orientations to the point of viewing the patient as an *active* biological, psychological, and social being. Thus seen, the patient is not a passive recipient of either preventive or curative care. Rather, he is an active participant in a social interaction sequence to which he and the professional may bring similar or radically divergent definitions and expectations of the problem and of legitimate, feasible treatment. The likelihood of dissimilar expectations is high in family planning. Why this is so and how the health professional might cope more effectively with it is the focus of our attention.

The content of Part I provides a general framework in terms of what is meant by family planning, why it is needed, with what cautions, and what appear to be the specific rea-

sons for the health professional to adopt the broader orientation alluded to earlier. Part II presents position statements from different points of view on the question of who needs family planning, points of view that are not necessarily in agreement. In turn, Part III is devoted to descriptive research reports from different parts of the United States. These provide information on who uses what in the way of family planning. The focus of Part IV is upon examining the disparity between who "needs" family planning and who practices it, plausible reasons for the differences, and their implications for the health professional. The final section, Part V, treats specifically the roles of the various health professions in delivering family planning services.

The articles we have included range from those written originally for different professional audiences to several written specifically for this reader. This range inevitably poses problems of balance, of differences in style, and of terminology. We have attempted to minimize these differences in selecting articles and by writing explanatory introductions to each section. If this has been successful, it is largely because of the extent to which the editors have been able to pool within a behavioral science perspective their variety of experiences from basic and applied research in family planning and from clinical practice.

Perhaps this book will raise more questions than it can provide answers; we will not be unhappy with this situation if the right questions have been raised. It may be that a major problem in the delivery of family planning services is that we have been more willing to assume ready answers than to formulate the relevant questions.

• • •

We wish to thank Mrs. Geraldine Mink of the Health Sciences Library at Case Western Reserve University for her invaluable assistance in locating and assembling the several hundred references from which the selections were chosen.

Miss Kathie Tyno has completely typed all the original papers and editorial comment, maintaining a cheerful imperturbability under the stress of revisions and the meeting of deadlines.

We thank the authors and publishers who permitted us to reprint articles, and especially those who prepared original material for this volume.

We fondly acknowledge the contribution of Nancy McCalister without whom this book could not have been completed. Finally, we wish to thank Janice Daniel and Noel McCalister for their superb and uncomplaining efforts in the tedious task of proofreading the final manuscript.

Donald V. McCalister
Victor Thiessen
Margaret McDermott

CONTENTS

READINGS IN FAMILY PLANNING
A challenge to the health professions

PART I
THE BACKGROUND OF FAMILY PLANNING

The purpose of this book and the explicit challenges posed to the health professions are stated in summary form in the preface. These are expanded upon in the introductions to the subsequent sections as well as in the content of the articles that are presented. The aim in Part I is to provide an orientation for the book and to introduce the reader to the background considerations that are necessary to appreciation of the specific problems and prospects for the health professional in family planning.

"Family planning" is defined for our purposes as the intricate process by which persons, if they wish, can determine for themselves the timing, spacing, and number of children to be born to them. Few would disagree with the immediate goal of family planning, thus approached, particularly when it is regarded as basic to implementing the value of responsible parenthood.

There is often objection, however, to the *means* by which this end is pursued (that is, the means by which conception is controlled, averted, or terminated). The sources of these objections have ranged from personal ethics to religious or moral tenets. More recently, political considerations have been voiced by militant minority groups concerned with genocide on the one hand and political power through quantity (rather than quality) of numbers on the other. Detailed consideration of many of these issues goes beyond the scope of this book; therefore we have focused on those issues that we deem central to the preparation of health professionals for more effective direct delivery of family planning services.

A number of writers have addressed the ethical and social controversies raised by family planning in its various forms; however few have addressed directly the question of concern here: How may the delivery of service by the health professions be made more readily and acceptably available to persons desiring it? The background framework that is suggested as necessary in answering this question is outlined below by McDermott and others: What is needed is insightful analysis and improvement of the procedures by which family planning care is provided in medical and nonmedical settings and adaptation of those procedures to the behavioral patterns of patients and clients.

1

The article by Ketchel provides additional background of a different sort in clearly and perceptively discussing the potentials of family planning at the general level of the world's population problem. The focus of the book is at the level of individual fertility; however both the health professional and the layman benefit from exposure to the broader implications of the need and possible consequences of family planning.

Hellman ("Family Planning Comes of Age," Reading 3) traces recent changes at the state and federal levels that have led a more enlightened context for delivering family planning services in the United States. This includes changes in laws, in policy concerning the use of tax revenues, and in policies in favor of family planning formulated by professional associations in the health field. The current policy statements of major health associations are presented immediately after Hellman's article.

Finally, Smith ("Techniques of Conception Control," Reading 4) presents a sensitive, knowledgeable treatment of currently used methods of contraception, their advantages, and their disadvantages. This is written from the perspective of an experienced private practitioner and reflects many of the human considerations vital to good patient care. These considerations are amplified in subsequent portions of the book.

1 Medical and behavioral perspectives on family planning services

Margaret McDermott
Donald McCalister
Victor Thiessen

Family planning services in the United States tend to be regarded at present as being essentially the prerogative of the health professions. As the preface to this volume indicates, this prerogative is a sufficient but not necessary condition for the provision of means by which most individuals may determine their fertility and, in general, plan their families. The health professions command enormous respect in this society and are in possession of the technical know-how to provide family planning care. Despite these advantages, the contents of this volume attest to a number of ways in which the current delivery of care has fallen short of meeting the needs and demands for it.

Why have medically oriented and controlled approaches to providing family planning services fallen short in meeting human needs? How might the delivery of this important element of care be improved? The answers appear to reside in the disparity between the approaches of current models of medical service and the behavioral characteristics and practices of those in need of such services. From what sources does this disparity arise? First, as will be discussed in more detail, family planning is not entirely a matter of health and illness. Second, the inclusion of family planning within the broad rubric of health care practices appears problematic because health practitioners and the general public do not necessarily share the same definitions of health and ill-

ness. Delivery patterns which fail to account for this divergence thus fail to attract those for whom the conduct of sexual behavior is essentially a private matter to be decided between the individual and his or her sexual partner. Third, communication barriers between practitioner and patient frequently act as a deterrent to the free and full exchange of relevant information that would ultimately enhance optimal use of a contraceptive method by the patient. Finally, there are religious, ethnic, socioeconomic, and personality factors that effectively prevent access to the services currently available in many communities.

That individuals desire to control fertility is beyond dispute. From the time of preliterate man, attempts to accomplish this goal have existed in all societies. The early use of contraceptive agents has been documented from ancient papyri that record the sprinkling of crocodile dung in the vulva. The use of seeds and potions and the practice of coitus interruptus by the male were known during the early centuries of the Christian era.[1] Advances in the basic sciences and subsequent technological applications have provided modern man with a variety of more precise and effective methods for fertility control. But, as is frequently the case with new technology, it is not yet available to and used by the total population of those who are eligible.

Along with the advances in contraceptive technology have come complex problems engendered by human factors involved in the diffusion of information about technological advances, as well as in the acceptance, availability, and use of these improved agents. The problems are posed by the characteristics of individuals and interest groups and by government bodies. The solution of these problems has been a matter of interest and concern for many groups within society. In addition to the health professions, members of such diverse disciplines as demography, economics, psychology, sociology, and anthropology, as well as government officials, have been involved in efforts to plan and to deliver family planning services. Understanding of such a complex process as the regulation of human fertility requires integration of the insights of these and perhaps other disciplines. Even so, it is likely that if it were possible to instantly integrate and apply all currently relevant knowledge to the provision of family planning services, the future of technology would ultimately outmode our best efforts.

The balance of this discussion is an examination in greater detail of what we shall label as medical and behavioral perspectives toward family planning care, integration of which is seen as a potential means of improving the present situation. The reader is cautioned that although the two perspectives are counterposed in the discussion, the intent is neither to imply the current existence of an absolute dichotomy in the delivery of care nor to suggest artificial distinctions. Conscious awareness of the merits of each point of view, and the necessary distinctions between them will, we hope, help the health professional to assess current programs and proposals in a more realistic and constructive fashion.

The disparity between the medical and behavioral perspectives seems to arise from the fact that family planning is partly a medical enterprise and partly a matter for individual action and social concern. It is our thesis that the public will be better served when both perspectives are appropriately incorporated into evolving models for the delivery of family planning services and other facets of health care.

ORGANIZATION OF SERVICES

Family planning services in the United States are currently organized largely within the health care system. Facilities exist in hospitals, comprehensive health centers, and independent clinics such as those operated by the Planned Parenthood World Federation. Additional medical sources of care include the private physician and the various forms of group practice.

The historical roots of this type of sponsorship lie in the medical management of the total female reproductive sequence, with its stress on reduction of maternal and infant morbidity and mortality. Although it is true that medical risk exists with pregnancy for some women, the majority of actual and potential users of contraceptives *are not ill.* Nonetheless, the logical emphasis within the medical setting stresses the identification of pathological conditions and the treatment of the sufferer. It is true that prevention of illness is an important aspect of medical management, but the prevention of pregnancy cannot be readily equated with the avoidance of illness for most women.

Within this "health-illness" context, family planning programs appear to have taken on the characteristics of a disease or disease-prevention model. The recipient of service is defined as a patient, with all of the connotations that this label conveys to health practitioners. Compliance with a regimen is expected on the basis of the expertise of the professional who prescribes for the patient according to the tenets of acceptable medical practice. The source of the criteria used in the provision of service may be largely independent of patient choice, or of characteristics of the individual other than those that are explicitly medical in nature.

From a behavioral perspective, the seeker of service is a client in need of information and advice who ultimately decides on whether and what method to adopt and use after alternatives have been presented and considered. The client is free to reject the service, or to sequence her or his acceptance so that the information-seeking stage may occur much earlier than the final decision to adopt a specific method. Postponement of adoption of a service may reflect a need for information to be put to use in the future, rather than disinterest or rejection of the service currently offered. The practitioner needs to recognize and accept the fact of individualized patterns caused by differences in motivation, in present circumstances, and in time orientation of each potential adopter.

In service settings today the patient frequently comes to adopt a family planning method *after* a pregnancy has occurred. In fact, many family planning programs are hospital postpartum services, appointments for which are made prior to release from the obstetrical service after delivery. The recency of the childbirth experience may enhance the salience of family planning at this time for the postpartal patient, but the approach does not include those women who have not yet experienced a pregnancy. Nonhospital facilities tend to recruit from diverse sources in the community and to attract the younger, the never-pregnant, and the unmarried woman. The paper by Rothenberg and McCalister (Reading 13) describing the recent experience in nonhospital clinics in Cleveland notes the increase of never-pregnant women seen when the age and marital status criteria for clinic eligibility were modified and evening and weekend clinics were opened. This, in turn, raises question as to the means by which private practitioners might enhance the effective delivery of care to their patients.

Within the medical perspective, services are understandably administered in a manner that promotes the efficient management of the system. However, appointment systems and hours of operation frequently con-

flict with the time and activity schedules of potential clients. The inflexible hours of many service settings may well be an especially effective barrier to increased utilization of contraception by the young, working male. The paper by Arnold cites the appeal of a program that routinely offered condoms to males during both daytime and evenings in nonmedical locations. This experiment reflects a behavioral perspective that takes into account the preferences of the individual; it provides scheduling patterns and settings accessible, convenient, and familiar to the client. Evening hours and walk-in arrangements in clinics and private physicians' offices could permit more open access to services for *both* male and female users.

METHOD ADOPTION AND CONTINUED USE

Two of the most effective contraceptive methods, the pill and the intrauterine device (IUD), are currently prescription controlled in this country; their initiation and continued use must be carried out under medical surveillance. Less effective methods are often available in clinic settings, as well as in drug stores and other commercial outlets. However, when the patient in a medically-oriented setting is instructed about contraceptive methods, personnel tend to emphasize the effectiveness criterion and to neglect the personal factors important to the individual.

The paper by Smith (Reading 4) points out the fallacy of regarding any single method as the "perfect contraceptive" and adds the warning that no contraceptive method is effective unless it is used regularly and properly. Health practitioners frequently describe the discomforts attributable to pill use as "minor"; however, from the viewpoint of the obese user, the weight gain that may ensue is not uncommonly a sufficient reason for discontinuation. Similarly, the woman who cannot forget the presence of the IUD and regards it as an unwelcome bodily intrusion may request its removal. The practicing Catholic woman who requests instruction in the rhythm method (but reluctantly accepts the pill if rhythm is derogated as a less effective method) may soon discontinue the pill because of guilt feelings. Perceptive listening to patient reports might result in change to a less effective but more personally acceptable method for such women. Individuals who discontinue contraceptive use are often described as unintelligent, unmotivated, and uncooperative. Such labeling seems unwarranted until more is known about the meaning of human sexuality and its implications for decision-making in relation to the utilization of family planning services.

There is a tendency on the part of the health professionals to regard the adoption of a medically effective method as a permanent commitment to continued use unless additional children are desired at some future time. From the behavioral perspective, the individual is always subject to pressures for change from his or her personal and interpersonal worlds. Little is known of the motivational states that produce stability or variation in one's attitudes and behaviors. Contraceptive use may be more wisely

viewed as an intervening event in a series of related, yet quite distinct stages of reproductive behavior, of family building, and, ideally, of family planning. These stages extend over a period of several decades for most men and women. There is every reason to expect that changes in attitudes toward contraceptive behavior will occur during this prolonged period within the human life-span.

These brief comments contain the essential elements of both the medical and behavioral perspectives toward the provision of family planning services. They should serve to orient the reader toward the content of this book, portions of which are written from an exclusively medical or behavioral perspective and portions of which represent an attempt at desirable integration of the two views. More importantly, it is hoped that these comments will serve to sensitize the health professional to some basic considerations involved in the service of their patients who are at the same time their clientele.

REFERENCE
1. Noonan, J.: Contraception, Cambridge, Mass., 1965, Harvard University Press.

2 Fertility control agents as a possible solution to the world population problem

Melvin M. Ketchel*

The world is now facing a severe problem of human overpopulation because the birth rate has generally remained high while the death rate has been dramatically reduced. Plans to lower the birth rate have almost invariably centered upon the concept of family planning. It is the purpose of this paper to point out that even if family planning methods become widely used they may not necessarily lower the birth rate sufficiently to provide a solution to the population problem and that other methods can and probably will be developed which could solve the population problem without relying on family planning. The use of such methods will raise moral and political questions of great importance, however, and it is my hope that this essay will provide a basis upon which a discussion of these issues can begin. Such a discussion would prepare us for making decisions concerning the implementation of these methods when they become available and may, if sufficient support for their use emerges, encourage the development of such methods.

FAMILY PLANNING AS A SOLUTION TO THE POPULATION PROBLEM

The pioneers in the family planning movement were primarily concerned with aiding

*Department of Physiology, Tufts University School of Medicine, 136 Harrison Avenue, Boston, Massachusetts, 02111.

Reprinted from *Perspectives in Biology and Medicine* 11:687-703, summer 1968, Dwight J. Ingle, editor. Copyright University of Chicago Press.

families. When the natural fertility of the parents resulted in too many children for the family's welfare, family planning methods were provided to prevent unwanted pregnancies. Somewhat later the family planning movement was strengthened by the inclusion of many people whose major interest was in solving the population problem by lowering the birth rate. It was reasoned that, as more and more couples learned the techniques of limiting the size of their families, they would do so, and eventually a large percentage of the world's population would practice family planning with the result that the reduction in the number of children born to them would significantly lower the world's birth rate. No other acceptable means of solving the population problem have been available, and even partial success of the family planning approach has been of value.

Some hope has been provided by history that family planning methods might eventually dramatically lower the world's birth rate. The term "demographic revolution" has been applied to the transition of a population with a high death rate and a high birth rate to a population with a low death rate and a low birth rate. It appears that the reduction in the infant death rate which occurs as a country becomes developed makes it unnecessary for each couple to have many babies in order to raise children to maturity, that children become an economic liability rather than an economic asset, and that the aspirations of people to provide more education and other advantages for their children encourages them to have fewer children on which to concentrate their efforts. These factors, plus many others, lead to the development of the "small family ideal." The decision to have fewer children is implemented primarily by the utilization of contraceptive techniques. A demographic revolution occurred in Europe and North America following the Industrial Revolution, and in Japan following World War II, and people concerned about the growth rate of the population of the rest of the world hope that the dramatic world-wide reduction in the death rate during the past twenty-five years is the first step in a demographic revolution that will result in a rapid reduction in the world's birth rate.

Whether the conditions under which a demographic revolution can complete itself now exist in the underdeveloped countries of the world is a matter of considerable controversy. Up to the present, demographic revolutions have occurred only when a gradually declining death rate was accompanied by considerable economic and social development. It may be that the levels of education, living standard, and motivation required if family planning is to be successful cannot be attained in underdeveloped countries precisely because their high birth rates prevent the necessary economic development. On the other hand, the demographic revolution which occurred in Europe and North America took place essentially without governmental or organizational influence, whereas at present strong organizations and some governments are working strenuously to lower birth rates. How successful these efforts will be is of course a matter of conjecture, but it cannot be assumed that the demographic revolution will complete itself in the absence of considerable economic development, and it seems unlikely that the necessary economic development will occur without a decrease in the birth rate.

Even if we assume that a demographic revolution is taking place, we must also question how rapidly it will progress. The absolute numbers of people produced during a gradual reduction of the annual growth rate may provoke catastrophic upheavals as the essentials of life become increasingly scarce. Some reliable experts now believe that widespread famine will occur in the underdeveloped countries within ten years [1, 2]. Of course the growth and effectiveness of the family planning movement should, like the growth of populations, be exponential, and we should be optimistic about the future of family planning. But a look at the most recent ten-year period for which data are available shows that the death rate is falling more rapidly than the birth rate, so that the annual rate of growth of the world's population is increasing. We simply do not know how rapidly the people in countries with high birth rates will accept family planning, but the slow rate at which such acceptance has occurred in the past by no means excludes the possibility that overpopulation will become overwhelming before the birth rate can be significantly lowered.

Family planning has already lowered the world's birth rate to some extent, and undoubtedly further effort will improve the results. How much improvement is required if family planning is to solve the population problem? To solve it permanently, of course, the birth rate must be lowered to the level of the death rate, for the exponential nature of the growth curve dictates that, if births exceed deaths by any amount, astronomical numbers of people will eventually be produced. For practical purposes, however, we probably ought to be satisfied if the birth rate can be lowered enough to alleviate the problems caused by overpopulation during the next three or four generations. It would be difficult to obtain agreement among experts on how much the birth rate should be lowered, but one might ask how much the birth rate would have to be lowered if the world's population were to double only once during the next 100 years, or about four generations. The present annual growth rate of the world's population of about 1.7 per cent would then have to be reduced to about 0.7 per cent. In large parts of the world, particularly those in which the introduction of family planning is proving most difficult, the average annual growth rate now exceeds 2 per cent. The only major area of the world in which the annual growth rate is below 1 per cent is Europe.

What would be required to bring the annual growth rate of the rest of the world to below 1 per cent? Assuming that there will be no further drastic changes in the death rate, we would have to reduce the birth rate by about one-third. While at present this could not be done without family planning techniques, we must realize that even if family planning were used by everyone, the birth rate might not be sufficiently reduced. Enough people may simply choose to have large families to keep the growth rate above 1 per cent. While it is obvious that family planning can reduce only the number of unwanted children, it seems to me that discussions of family planning in relation to the population problem always have implicit in them the assumption that if we could only get enough people to use family planning techniques the population problem would be solved. This assumption cannot be accepted until we know how many children people will wish to have when they achieve the ability to regulate the numbers.

How many children could each family have if the annual growth rate is not to exceed 0.7 per cent? It is not possible to translate an annual growth rate directly into an average number of children per family, but if certain assumptions are made, a rough approximation may be calculated. For example, suppose that the average generation time, or average age of parents when their children are born, is twenty years and that all children born reach reproductive age. The average generation time varies widely

and would probably be higher than twenty years in some cultures and lower in others. While all children born do not reach reproductive age, the numbers who do not are small enough to be neglected in these rough calculations. Let us assume further that 10 per cent of the couples in the population are infertile and that another 10 per cent of the population does not marry. Most estimates of infertility put the number of infertile couples at about 10 per cent, but many of these people are treatable, and probably this number could be reduced. The number of people who do not marry would probably be more than 10 per cent in some populations and less in others. Using these admittedly hypothetical conditions, a zero growth rate could be maintained if each fertile couple had an average of 2.5 children. If each fertile couple had three children, the annual growth rate would be slightly less than 1 per cent, and the population would double every eighty years. An average of 3.5 children per fertile couple would reduce the doubling time of the population to thirty-nine years. In any population in which 80 per cent of the people born marry and have children at a young age, family planning would have to reduce the average number of births to considerably less than three per family if the population were to double only once every 100 years. But an average of one-half child more or less per fertile couple makes the difference between an acceptable growth rate and a growth rate of serious consequences.

We do not have adequate information to predict how many children the average couple will want when family planning is available to everyone. It may well be less than three in some cultures, but it may also be more than three in others. In general, we have assumed that as the standard of living, educational level, and motivation of a population are increased—conditions under which family planning would be most successful—the desire of couples for large families will be decreased. But will it be decreased enough? While no statistics are available, many readers will share with me the impression that there were large numbers of couples in the United States who graduated from college and married in the years following World War II, and who used family planning methods but still had large families. Is it not possible that, even when they can easily control the size of their families, the desire for children will lead people to have more children than the earth can support?

Thus, while it is obvious that the family planning movement has been of tremendous value to the people who have used it, has lowered the birth rate when it is used, and will become increasingly valuable as the movement expands, it seems to me that the following statements should be accepted as possibilities. *The reduction in the world's death rate may not, in fact, indicate that a world-wide demographic revolution will continue to completion. If a demographic revolution is occurring, it may proceed so slowly that the increases in population which occur before its completion may be so large that they cannot be supported. And even if the demographic revolution does complete itself rapidly, the desire for children in the world's population may still be strong enough to produce an annual growth rate which will soon result in overwhelming numbers of people.*

FERTILITY CONTROL AGENTS

The great interest in recent years in the study of the physiology of reproduction and in methods of contraception makes it appear to me very likely that in a relatively few years efficient methods by which the fertility of populations can be reduced without dependence upon the practice of contraception by individual couples will become available.

For the purpose of discussion, let us suppose that a compound has become available which, when administered in small doses, has no significant physiological effect ex-

cept to raise the threshold requirement of some substance involved in the implantation of blastocysts. This would mean that while some blastocysts would implant in women given the compound, a percentage of blastocysts which would otherwise have implanted would not now do so. Let us further suppose that the dosage of this compound could be varied so that the reduction in the birth rate could be established at from 5 to 75 per cent less than the present birth rate. Although many problems would remain even if such an ideal compound could be found, the use of such a compound would enable a government to control the rate of growth of its population without depending upon the voluntary action of individual couples. Although a number of colleagues with whom I have discussed this differ with me in speculation about when such compounds will be developed, I believe such compounds should be available for field testing in a relatively short time, perhaps five to fifteen years.

I differentiate, then, between two methods of reducing the birth rate. One is the family planning method in which participation is voluntary. The other, which I have designated "fertility control" measures, would be carried out by governments to lower the fertility of their populations without requiring action by individual couples. Thus, part of a population may be using family planning techniques, but all of the population would be affected by fertility control measures.

EFFECTS OF FERTILITY CONTROL MEASURES

One of the principal requirements for a contraceptive method, if it is to be useful in the family planning approach to population control, is that it be virtually 100 per cent effective. In contrast, any method developed for fertility control must not have 100 per cent effectiveness, or the population would stop having births. What would be required, then, is a method which is capable

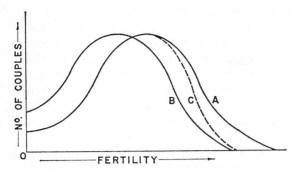

Fig. I.—Curve A: Probable shape of the distribution curve for fertility within a population. No data are available. It would be expected that the curve would be similar to a normal distribution curve, except that since there are a number of infertile couples in the population, the curve does not become asymptotic at the left. Curve B: The effect of fertility control measure which decreased the fertility of all couples in the population to an equal degree. Curve C: The effect of a fertility control agent which reduced the fertility of the most fertile couples in the population.

of reducing the births to any desired level.

The nature of the curve which would be obtained if a survey were made of the fertility* of couples in a population is unknown, since the data have not been collected. I have drawn curve *A* in Figure I as my guess as to the nature of that curve, without designating absolute units. The curve for fertility of a population would probably resemble a normal distribution curve, except that, since some couples are infertile, the curve would not become asymptotic at the left. If a compound such as the one I have hypothesized were administered to a population, it might act by slightly reducing the fertility of each couple in the population, so that there would be a shift to a lower average fertility, as shown by curve *B*. Perhaps there would be advantages if such a compound had the effect of selectively reducing the fertility of the most fertile couples in the population, an effect

*"Fertility" is used here to represent the relative capability to reproduce, not the amount of reproduction which actually occurs.

represented by curve *C*. Other possibilities exist, however, which would have to be guarded against as such agents were developed and tested. For example, some agents might selectively lower the fertility of those whose fertility is already among the lowest in the population, so that the number of infertile couples would be increased without affecting the fertility of the most fertile couples. Such an agent would deprive people of relatively low fertility of having any children at all and would not be satisfactory. Another possible effect of such a compound which would probably make it unusable is that, because of inherent variability from couple to couple of the factor affected by the agent, some couples would become completely infertile while the fertility of other couples would be unaffected. I believe that the goal in the development of fertility control agents should be to reduce the fertility of everyone equally.

It should be strongly emphasized that, although fertility control agents would be used to cause a reduction of the fertility of the population as a whole, there would still be considerable freedom of action for individual couples. Family planning methods could still be used for the purpose of limiting and spacing children within the family. Well-motivated people could probably circumvent the action of any fertility control measures that could be developed by acting to increase their chances of establishing a pregnancy, much as many couples of low fertility do at present. If too many couples circumvented the action of the fertility control agent, it would no longer be useful. However, the necessity of taking positive action would probably make such circumvention relatively unimportant.

Fertility control agents such as the hypothetical one I described would have no effect in reducing the number of unwanted children, legitimate or illegitimate, except insofar as they reduce the fertility of the population as a whole. One can, however, visualize a fertility control agent which would render everyone infertile until its action was reversed by an act of the individuals involved. Such a method might require an individual to take a pill to become pregnant, rather than to take a pill to prevent pregnancy, and would virtually eliminate the serious problem of unwanted children.

SOME REQUIREMENTS FOR A SATISFACTORY FERTILITY CONTROL AGENT

In order to be usable, a fertility control agent would need to have the following characteristics: (1) It should lend itself to being easily and unobtrusively included in the intake of everyone in the population; requiring people to receive injections, to take the agent themselves, or to submit to direct physical treatment would be unsatisfactory. In highly organized urban areas an agent might be included in the water supply, but other methods would be required in less developed areas and in areas with low population density. (2) It must be harmless. There must be no danger to the health of anyone receiving it, or to the development of fetuses or children. (3) It should be inexpensive. (4) Its effect should be easily reversible. The agent should disappear and have to be replaced fairly rapidly so that, if the fertility of the population becomes too low, there would not be too great a time lag between cessation of administration and cessation of its effect on the fertility of the population. (5) It should not interfere with the family planning activities of individual couples. (6) It should not act by affecting in any way the sexual activity of the individuals in the population.

FERTILITY CONTROL AS A FUNCTION OF GOVERNMENT

A primary question involved in the decision to use fertility control agents is whether the control of the rate of growth of its population is a proper function of government. A recurrent theme in science fiction is the plight of couples who wish to have children but are forbidden by their government (or its computer) from doing so. Governmental intervention in the lives of individuals is often characterized either by an inflexibility which neglects individual circumstances or by a flexibility which permits discrimination and injustice. Ingle, in a discussion of the ethics of governmental intervention in reproduction, concludes that such matters should not be undertaken by governments [3]. In 1967, U Thant, secretary-general of the United Nations, issued an important statement signed by thirty heads of state in which the decision to have as many children as one desires is called a "basic human right" [4]. Yet the rate of growth of the population profoundly affects the lives of all individuals within the population as well as the members of future generations. No couple may reasonably maintain that the number of children born within the family is strictly a family matter, for the quality of life of every individual in the population is changed simply by the increase in the number of people competing for the necessities of life. Few people would now maintain that the control of air pollution is outside the responsibility of government, and I would argue that allowing population growth to go unchecked is at least as serious a hazard to the welfare of people as the exhaust from automobiles and factories.

Governments already can and do influence fertility rates, although at the present time their ability to do so is primitive, and therefore the degree of control is probably small. However, governmental support or prevention of family planning activities may make it easier or more difficult for people to practice family planning. Propaganda is often used by governments to encourage people to have children. Such governmental action as giving financial rewards to couples with large numbers of children, providing housing allotments for families, giving income tax deductions for dependents, and establishing child care centers for the children of working mothers may not have as their primary purpose the encouragement of people to have children, but such actions probably tend to raise the birth rate to some degree by relieving people of some of the financial burden associated with parenthood. Traditionally, most governments, when they have acted at all, have acted to encourage a higher birth rate, but more recently some countries have made it governmental policy to encourage family planning in order to reduce the birth rate.

The function of the government in regulating the rate of growth of its population should be clearly differentiated from governmental involvement in decisions concerning who may and who may not reproduce. It would be possible for a government using fertility control agents to reduce statistically the birth rate of the population without making decisions concerning individuals, and therefore strict impartiality could be maintained. However, there would probably be great pressures exerted on the government to couple the use of fertility control agents with programs aimed at preventing reproduction among people considered "unfit" for parenthood or among geographic, racial, economic, or political groups. Such proposals would undoubtedly be made in the name of "positive eugenics." The role of government in a eugenics program should be argued on its own meirts, however, because it poses a threat to individual liberty that is not involved in a program to lower statistically the birth rate of the whole population by a method that would affect everyone equally.

I believe that the question of whether the control of the rate of growth of its population is a proper function of government ultimately comes down to the question of whether it is necessary. If the rate of growth of the population presents no serious problems, the government ought not to intrude in this matter. But if the growth rate of the population is seriously affecting the welfare of the population, as a rapid growth rate

surely does, and the growth rate cannot be lowered by any voluntary means, then it is, I believe, a necessary and proper function of the government to take action to slow the rate of growth.

POSSIBLE ALTERNATIVES TO FERTILITY CONTROL AGENTS

If the control of the rate of growth of its population is a proper function of government, then a decision must be made concerning how to exercise that control. Obviously, the method of choice would be the one which is capable of accomplishing the objective of lowering the birth rate but which least interferes with the lives of the people.

It seems obvious that any government contemplating the use of involuntary methods of fertility control should lower its birth rate as much as possible by supporting family planning programs. If it becomes necessary to prevent some people from having children they want, it would be ridiculous not to try to prevent the births of children that were not specifically wanted. Also, the more the birth rate was lowered by voluntary means, the less the population would have to be affected by the use of involuntary means.

Aside from family planning programs, how can governments lower birth rates? The suggestion has often been made that there be a reversal of economic policies which encourage people to have large families. For example, dependency allowances on income taxes might be eliminated or changed to tax surcharges for each child over a specified number. Direct financial allotments to large families could be stopped. Free or inexpensive child care centers could be eliminated. Such proposals must be judged as alternatives to fertility control agents on two counts. First, how effective they would be, and second, whether they would be more onerous than fertility control agents.

Financial pressures against large families would probably be effective only in developed counties in which there are large numbers of middle-class people. In underdeveloped countries partically no financial inducements to have children now exist to be reversed, and the imposition of further taxes upon the many poor people would depress their living standards even further and probably only succeed in raising the death rates. In developed countries people in higher economic groups could still afford to have as many children as they wished, so the economic pinch associated with having children would be felt mainly by middle-class and lower-middle-class people, to whom the cost of having children, though somewhat eased by government economic favors, is still relatively high. In order to be effective, economic pressures would probably have to be severe enough to be quite painful, and when they reached a level of painfulness at which they were effective, they would probably seriously affect the welfare of the children who were born in spite of the pressures. It seems to me that the same arguments apply to the use of economic pressures to lower the birth rate as are used to argue against the issue of suppressing illegitimacy by cutting off aid to dependent children. If children become a financial burden, there will be fewer of them, but those that are born will be punished by being deprived of precisely those economic advantages they should have, both for humanitarian reasons and for their growth and development into worthwhile citizens. The same objection applies to the use of financial rewards to induce people not to have children because such programs would make the families with children the poorer families. A further objection to the use of economic pressures or rewards is that, since they would be primarily effective against certain economic groups, such methods are discriminatory.

Since there is a substantial decrease in fertility among couples as they advance in age, a delay in the age of marriage has been proposed as a means of reducing the size of families. To be effective in keeping the average family size between two and three chil-

dren, the average age of marriage would probably have to be advanced by a sizable number of years. The age at which people marry is largely determined by slowly changing cultural and economic factors, however, and could probably be changed quickly in a population only by rather drastic measures. How might this be done? One can visualize raising substantially the legal age of marriage, but an inordinately severe punishment for violaters would be required. Denying housing or other requirements for married life to people below a certain age could also be used to prevent marriages. But neither of these alternatives seems attractive to me when compared to a situation in which people are allowed to marry at an age consistent with their cultural and biological desires and to have their families while they are young, and in which there is no other interference with their marriages except that the number of children they will have is reduced statistically by a fertility control agent.

A policy of allowing couples to have only a certain number of children would, of course, be effective in solving the population problem, but any conceivable way in which this could be done would, I think, be more objectionable than the use of fertility control agents. Statutory regulations of family size would be unenforceable unless the punishment for exceeding the limit was so harsh that it would cause harm to the lives of the existing children and their parents. Such possible procedures as vasectomizing the father or implanting long-acting contraceptives in the mother would require a direct physical assault by a government agent on the body of an individual that, in my opinion, would be worse to contemplate than fertility control agents. It may be argued that philosophically there is little difference between the direct physical asault of sterilization and the remote physical asault of administering a fertility control agent, but in practical terms there is obviously a great difference.

I think that, once family planning has

been exploited to the degree that it can be to reduce births, further reduction, if necessary, could be accomplished only by a choice of unpleasant methods. It is my opinion that fertility control agents would be less objectionable than other solutions that can be visualized at this time.

MORAL ASPECTS OF FERTILITY CONTROL AGENTS

Surely the most controversial aspects of fertility control agents would be the moral issues. Is it possible to justify the affront to human dignity and privacy of forcing people to take a drug which they do not want but which may be necessary for the welfare of the society? I believe that justification for the use of fertility control agents comes from an analysis of what will happen if they are not used.

If voluntary methods of population control are not sufficiently effective, then we must either impose some involuntary method of fertility control or accept the consequences of excessive population. I attempted earlier in this paper to show that any workable involuntary methods would be more objectionable and would probably require a greater infringement on human liberty than fertilty control agents. If my analysis is correct, then, we may ultimately be forced to make a moral choice between fertility control agents and excessive numbers of people.

During the 1950's, discussions of the population problem often included projections of exponential growth curves which showed that the world's population would eventually become ridiculously large. One of my favorites was a projection which calculated that, if population growth were not curbed, at some future time the layer of human protoplasm which would by then be covering the surface of the earth would be expanding at the speed of light. Such dramatic projections made the problem seem so remote, however, that many people felt that population problems were really no concern of the present generation and that the relatively few children more or less that

the present generation had would not be a problem. Also, such unrealistic projections invited speculation in a similar vein for dealing with the problem. For example, many people suggested that our excess population could be shipped off to other planets. More recently, when discussions have centered about problems of feeding and caring for the people that are projected for the near future, unrealistic projections of technological advances were still suggested as solutions to the problem. Farming of the sea and desert, greater utilization of farm land, and mass culture of microorganisms were proposed as solutions to the problem of feeding large numbers of people. Let the population grow, people seemed to think, somehow they will be taken care of, and we might as well have as many children as we want because what difference would our few children make in the millions that will be born.

It now appears, however, that the race between technological advances and population growth is favoring population growth and that starvation will be a major problem in the world in about ten years [1, 2]. Most food surpluses in the world have been used up, and there is no indication that food production can be increased quickly enough to prevent this starvation. Laissez faire will apparently solve the population problem, therefore, simply by raising the death rate, through starvation and malnutrition, to the level of the birth rate. Large numbers of births will still occur, but so many people will die that there will be no increase in the world population until technological improvements produce a larger food supply. There seems little that can be done now to prevent starvation for millions of people in the next decade, but if we had been able to curb population growth in the last decade, this suffering probably would not be in prospect.

Massive hunger in the world, then, seems to be one alternative to reducing the birth rate. If the reduction of the birth rate requires the use of fertility control agents by governments, then the moral justification for their use must certainly be in the prevention of the agony of hunger and slow death for millions of people and a miserable level of existence for millions of others.

A laissez faire attitude toward population growth presents another prospect which seems to me to be equal in seriousness to the starvation that will occur. Unless some new technological approach to fertility control is utilized, a solution to its problem of overpopulation would require a massive effort on the part of the government of an underdeveloped country which such governments may be unable or unwilling to undertake. It would probably be far easier for a large underdeveloped country to develop a nuclear capability than it would to solve its population problem. As more and more countries acquire nuclear capability, their attempts to obtain the essentials of life may cause catastrophic upheavals in the world which will result in even greater danger and suffering than the starvation itself.

The moral question, then, resolves itself for me into a choice of alternatives. A laissez faire attitude is unthinkable because of the amount of suffering that will result. Voluntary methods are to be preferred if they will work, but if they do not, then involuntary methods must be used. Fertility control agents would seem to be the most effective and least objectionable of any methods that can be visualized.

POLITICAL ASPECTS OF FERTILITY CONTROL AGENTS

If a perfected fertility control agent were available now, I am certain that it would not be utilized in any democratic country, for no population would be likely to vote to have such agents used on itself. This means that the effects of overpopulation are not yet acute enough for people to accept an unpleasant alternative. It seems ironic to me that, when the problems of overpopulation do become acute enough to make people willing to accept fertility control, it will only be after subjecting many individuals to great suffering which need never have occurred.

Thus, any attempt to lessen by fertility control agents the problems that will eventually occur as a result of overpopulation requires an analysis of the distastefulness of fertility control agents. The understanding gained from such an analysis would be useful in implementing governmental action.

One level of resistance to the acceptance of fertility control agents would probably be psychological. The benefits of fluorides in alleviating dental disease seem clearly to be worth the risk involved in its use, yet the acceptance of fluoride treatment of public water supplies has met extreme political resistance. Even though a primary requirement of any fertility control agent would obviously be that it have no significant effect on any physiological function other than fertility, I am sure that public resistance to fertility control agents would be far greater than the resistance to fluoride. Also, I have been surprised at the number of sophisticated and educated people who mention "saltpeter" when I suggest the possibility of using fertility control agents. They were obviously confusing the control of fertility with the control of sexual activity.

Fertility control agents will ultimately become politically acceptable when they become politically necessary. If population growth continues, people will probably be willing to accept fertility control agents as the lesser of evils. It will help people to accept them, however, if they are informed of the degree to which starvation, poverty, and other problems which ensue are related to overpopulation.

SUMMARY AND DISCUSSION

The rate at which humans can reproduce is an evolutionary vestige remaining from an era in human history in which large numbers of offspring were required for the survival of the species, and probably includes a substantial safety factor of reproductive potential as well. The full reproductive potential of the human is probably not expressed because a variety of social, cultural, economic, and biological forces have tended to limit childbirth. These limiting forces tend to evolve very slowly, but over a sufficient period of time they can be effective in adjusting the birth rate of the population to any change in circumstances. Thus, as the death rate was gradually reduced in Europe and North America following the Industrial Revolution, a reduction in the birth rate gradually followed.

Modern technology has recently had a dramatic effect in reducing the death rate throughout the world, and it now appears that the forces which can lower the birth rate will not evolve rapidly enough to prevent widespread overpopulation and an eventual re-establishment of a high death rate. What would be required to prevent this is another significant technological advance, one which will dramatically increase the ability of the world to support the population, or one which will limit the number of people being born.

We should be actively seeking a technological advance which will increase the number of people that the earth can support, for such an advance will help us to cope with the numbers of people who will be born despite any humane action that can now be taken. However, even if such an advance were made, it could only act as a palliative because ultimately a reduction in the birth rate must occur. It is possible, however, that a technological advance which would increase greatly the food supply would provide the necessary time for the further evolution of forces which would decrease the birth rate.

Meanwhile, we should be actively seeking a revolutionary break-through in methodology for reducing the birth rate. Improve-ments in the technology of contraception, though helpful, may not suffice, because the birth rate would still depend upon how many children people wanted rather than how many were required to stabilize the growth of the population. What is required is a method which would allow a population to control its rate of growth. I have suggested that fertility control agents would provide a practical solution to the problem. I have also attempted to show that the advantages of using fertility control agents would more than offset the considerable objections to them.

It seems clear that no single, simplistic solution to the population problem is available. Family planning has already had an effect in reducing the birth rate of the world, and our goal should be to extend its use as rapidly as is possible to the point that the only children born are those that are specifically wanted. Improved methods of contraception are important, but ways of motivating people to use them must be developed further. Food production must immediately be increased as much as is humanly possible to prevent the suffering and starvation that will inevitably occur in the next decade. But I believe we should also begin to develop and test fertility control agents seriously, to develop methods of introducing them into the intake of populations, and to arrive at a consensus which will dictate whether such agents will be utilized when they are developed.

REFERENCES

1. William Paddock, and Paul Paddock. Famine—1975! America's decision: who will survive? Boston: Little, Brown, 1967.
2. James Bonner. Science, **157:**914, 1967.
3. Dwight J. Ingle. Med. Opinion and Rev., 3:54, 1967.
4. U Thant. Studies in Family Planning, no. 26, January, 1968.

3 Family planning comes of age

Louis M. Hellman, M.D.*

No discussion of fertility control can be complete without acknowledgment of the role played by Dr. Howard C. Taylor, Jr. For many years he has served in the forefront of those who saw the problems of unbridled fertility and were willing to become activists in its control.

His devotion to the cause of family planning in the broadest sense is exemplified by his citation for a Lasker Award in 1955, years before family planning was considered "safe" or "respectable." The citation reads:

> To Howard Canning Taylor—physician, scientist, teacher. As Chairman of the Committee on Human Reproduction of the National Research Council, he has taken a leading role in futhering knowledge of human fertility. As an educator, he has taught the care of childbearing women to a generation of physicians. Long a friend of Planned Parenthood, his active participation in the councils of the Federation has added wisdom and dignity to its program and achievements. His work as a research investigator has advanced the science of medicine and contributed immeasurably to the reduction of maternal mortality and illness. He has taken important factors of fear and chance from the precious task of having babies, permitting parents to build their families less on anguish and accident, more on love and reason.

Technically and philosophically, birth control and a woman's right to control her

*Deputy Assistant Secretary for Population Affairs, Department of Health, Education and Welfare, Washington, D. C.

Reprinted from *American Journal of Obstetrics and Gynecology* 109(2):214-224, January 1971. Copyright The C. V. Mosby Company. *A portion of the section on abortion is taken from the author's writing in Hellman, L. M., and Pritchard, J. A., editors: Williams Obstetrics, ed. 14, chap. 39, New York, 1971, Appleton-Century-Crofts, Inc.*

fertility have come of age in the past 10 to 15 years. Before that time, these subjects were not considered matters fit for public policy or discussion. Statements of policy are now common on both federal and local levels. All states have removed ancient statutory restrictions concerning birth control, and many have adopted positive regulations. In 1967 the Congress approved several proposals designed to initiate federal leadership in this field.

This shift in policy and the mobilization of public opinion in favor of tax-supported contraception for all people without regard to social or economic status can be said to have begun in 1957 to 1958 in New York City. At that time there was initiated a campaign to reverse the long-standing ban on contraceptive prescription in the city's municipal hospitals. Birth control was then offered in maternal health programs of public health departments in only seven states: Alabama, Florida, North and South Carolina, Georgia, Mississippi, and Virginia. The New York campaign has been the subject of many reviews.[1,13,15] Briefly, the challenge occurred when the Medical Board of the Kings County Hospital of Brooklyn sent a resolution to the Commissioner of Hospitals indicating that the doctors of the hospital had a right under the laws of the state to give patients contraceptive devices as a part of medical care. The Commissioner took the position that the traditional ban against contraceptive practice fell within his jurisdiction. The confrontation occurred when an attempt was made to give a diaphragm to a severely diabetic postpartum patient. The doctors complied with the Commissioner's telephoned prohibition of the procedure but gave the story to a prepared and alerted press. This incident had the proper ingredients to secure victory: a just cause, a victim, and a biased prosecutor.

For two months the situation occupied the front pages of all the city's newspapers and received increasing attention in national news media. Spread upon the record was a more comprehensive picture of the current political and religious status of contraception than had ever been seen. As expected, the Commissioner's position was defended by the chancery office of the archdiocese, which issued a statement reiterating traditional Roman Catholic positions. Further support was forthcoming from Catholic medical and lay groups, which felt that public monies should not be spent for services they believed "immoral." Unexpected, however, was the near unanimity of the rest of the community.

Vigorous denunciation of the Commissioner's prohibition was spearheaded by the Council of Protestant Churches, the Board of Rabbis, and the American Civil Liberties Union, as well as the Planned Parenthood Federation and nearly every other public-spirited organization in the city. The staid New York Times summarized public opinion in an editorial that characterized as "astonishing" any doubt that "birth control, which is regarded by many medical authorities . . . as an important element in preventive medicine, can be prescribed in city hospitals . . . . Birth control is profoundly objectionable to many persons, and, whether as patients or nurses or doctors, their views must be fully respected. These views cannot be controlling in regard to other persons in the community who also use the city hospitals and to whom medical prescription of contraceptive devices presents no moral or religious problem. Freedom of religion works both ways."

As the New York controversy reached this stage, many thoughtful Catholics were embarrassed and saddened to find their Church placed in the undemocratic position of attempting to impose its views on others.

An unusual editorial by James Finn in *The Commonweal*,[7] a Catholic publication, reflects this concern. On the issue, he wrote:

> It is evident that beliefs, teachings, attitudes, and opinions have changed greatly for many people during the past several decades. Where consensus once existed, it no longer does. Or more correctly, it has shifted ground. Other citizens cannot expect Catholics to change their beliefs or their practices merely to conform to this new consensus. But neither can Catholics expect to control the beliefs and practices of others concerning these measures. . . . There are many sound and compelling reasons why Catholics should not strive for legislation which clashes with the beliefs of a large portion of society. In so doing, they do not only strain the limits of the community and considerably lessen the persuasive force of their teachings, but they almost inevitably strengthen, in the minds of non-Catholics, the already present worries about Catholic power.

This editorial was singularly effective, expressing a basic concept of democracy deeply held by our people and soon to be clearly enunciated by a young man destined to become our first Roman Catholic president. It is entirely possible that without solution of the New York controversy, and without Mr. Kennedy's unequivocal stand on the matter, he might not have become President of the United States. In any case, in face of an unmistakable public attitude, the ban was no longer tenable. Keenly aware of this situation, Mayor Wagner stated that, despite his personal Catholic view, the issue was a medical matter to be decided by the Board of Hospitals. Their decision, written largely by a Catholic member, Dr. Charles Gordon, was a statesmanlike approach, "When there are clearly defined conditions in which the health of a woman may be jeopardized by pregnancy, it is generally recognized by the medical profession that contraceptive measures are proper medical practice. Municipal hospitals should provide such needed advice, preventive measures and devices for female patients under their care, whose life and health, in the opinion of the medical staff, may be jeopardized by pregnancy and who also wish to avail themselves of such services."

The New York controversy is noteworthy because it proved that established tenets of neither the laity nor clergy necessarily pose serious obstacles to the control of fertility in a population well informed and fully cognizant of the perils of unimpeded fertility.

Although the action of the New York Board of Hospitals was repeated to one degree or another in many municipalities, federal policy was slow to follow. In 1959, Draper[4] published a presidential report that urged incorporation into foreign aid of assistance on population control to nations requesting it. Commenting on the ensuing debate, Dwight Eisenhower[6] said, "I can not imagine anything more emphatically a subject that is not a proper political or Governmental activity. . . ."

The Kennedy Administration held different views. Beginning in 1961, a series of public statements by high government officials, among them the late Adlai Stevenson,[30] Under Secretary of State Ball,[2] Deputy Secretary of State Gardner,[11] and Secretary of Labor Wirtz,[33] indicated increasing concern with the explosive growth of population. The National Institutes of Health assumed increasing financial responsibility for basic research in human reproduction from which fundamental discoveries in conception control might be expected to emerge. The National Academy of Sciences issued its first population report calling for active governmental participation to curb population growth in 1963, and President Kennedy[19] formally endorsed reproductive research so that knowledge can "be made available to all the world so everyone can make his own decision."

The National Academy of Sciences in its second population report[23] suggested the appointment of an official "at a high national level" to facilitate action and urged that family planning be made an integral part of domestic medical programs. A group of distinguished senators and representatives lead by Senator Gruening helped implement this suggestion by the creation of the post of Deputy Assistant Secretary for Population and Family Planning in the Department of Health, Education and Welfare.

President Johnson[17] referred to the problems of population growth on at least forty occasions. Addressing the United Nations Twentieth Anniversary Meeting in San Francisco, he said, "Let us in all our lands —including this land—face forthrightly the multiplying problems of our multiplying populations and seek the answers to this most profound challenge to the future of the world. . . ."

The President singled out family planning in his Special Message to Congress on Health and Education as one of the four critical health problems requiring special attention, declaring "We have a growing concern to foster the integrity of the family and the opportunity for each child. It is essential that all families have access to information and services that will allow freedom to choose the number and spacing of their children within the dictates of individual conscience."[18]

In 1967, Congress authorized earmarked funds for family planning services within both maternal and child health, and foreign aid programs.

The importance of the population problem was emphasized by thirty of the world's leaders in the United Nations on Human Rights Day in 1967.[33] They stated that:

We believe that the population problem must be recognized as a principal element in long-range national planning if governments are to achieve their economic goals and fulfill the aspirations of their people.

We believe that the great majority of parents desire to have the knowledge and the means to plan their families; that the opportunity to decide the number and spacing of children is a basic human right.

We believe that lasting and meaningful peace will depend to a considerable measure upon how the challenge of population growth is met.

We believe that the objective of family planning is the enrichment of human life, not its restriction; that family planning, by assuring greater opportunity to each person, frees man to attain his individual dignity and reach his full potential.

President Nixon outlined the urgency and magnitude of the population problem in a special message to the Congress on July 18, 1969.[24] In addition to suggesting a Commission on Population, he indicated expanded activities in family planning in the Department of Health, Education and Welfare as well as in several other departments of the government. "It is clear," he said, "that domestic family planning services supported by the Federal Government should be expanded and better integrated." In particular, he stated, "Most of an estimated five million low income women of childbearing age in this country do not now have adequate access to family planning assistance even though their wishes concerning family size are usually the same as those of parents of higher income groups. It is my view," he said, "that no American woman should be denied access to family planning assistance because of her economic condition. I believe, therefore, that we should establish as a national goal, the provision of adequate family planning services within the next five years to all those who want them, but cannot afford them. This, we have the capacity to do." He went on to indicate that a separate unit for these services would be established within the Health Services and Mental Health Administration. He spoke further of the need for coordinating the efforts, both at the Federal level and the state level, and finally he concluded with the statement, "One of the most serious challenges to human destiny in the last third of this century will be the growth of the population. Whether man's response to that challenge will be a cause for pride or for despair in the year 2000 will depend very much on what we do today. If we now begin our work in an appropriate manner, and if we continue to

devote a considerable amount of attention and energy to this problem, then mankind will be able to surmount this challenge as it has surmounted so many during the long march of civilization. When future generations evaluate the record of our time, one of the most important factors in their judgment will be the way in which we respond to population growth. Let us act in such a way that those who come after us—even as they lift their eyes beyond earth's bounds—can do so with pride in the planet on which they live, with gratitude to those who lived on it in the past, and with continuing confidence in its future."

The shift in official thinking was accompanied by a spate of policy statements from professional organizations in the health and welfare fields (Table I).

In retrospect some of these organizations were slow to react to an increasingly important health problem. In many instances it was the people and not the professional societies that took the lead.

In all but two states, Connecticut and Massachusetts, no real statutory impediments to the administration of tax-supported

Table I. Policy statements on family planning*†

Organization	Date
American Public Health Association	1959 and 1964
American Public Welfare Association	1964
American Medical Association	1964
National Association of Social Workers	1962 and 1967
National Urban League	1964
Family Service Association	1964
American College of Obstetricians and Gynecologists	1963
Young Women's Christian Association	1964
American Assembly	1963
American Society of Zoologists	1960

*From F. S. Jaffe.[16]

†ED. NOTE: Several of these and other associations, notably the American Nurses Association, have issued more recent statements. Some are presented in Reading 5; others may be obtained from the executive officer of each association.

birth control existed. Since 1965, however, there have been a series of legislative actions that have encouraged the spread of family planning services in many states. In 1965 the Supreme Court of the United States, in a history-making decision, struck down Connecticut's archaic prohibition as a violation of the Bill of Rights.[12] Of particular interest was the Court's stress on the right of privacy under the Ninth Amendment of the Constitution.

The changing public attitude toward family planning and the deepening concern about population coincided with the introduction of two new and extremely effective contraceptives. Before 1960 the available contraceptives had a failure rate between 10 and 50 per cent. Some, such as the diaphragm, had a better record among highly motivated women, but in general because their use was connected with the sexual act, and privacy was required, they alone provided little hope as widespread techniques for population control.

The plastic intrauterine devices and the oral contraceptives possess a success rate in preventing pregnancy of a higher order of magnitude than previous contraceptives. Their use is not directly associated with coitus nor does it require privacy. Motivation remains an important factor although much less so in the case of the intrauterine devices and conceptually different with the hormonal compounds.

These new contraceptives were immediately and widely accepted. Their use and their adverse reactions have been subjected to extensive lay and scientific scrutiny. Perhaps the best review and most carefully documented assessment of these contraceptives appear in the three reports of the Advisory Committee on Obstetrics and Gynecology to the Food and Drug Administration.[8-10]

The oral contraceptives are the more popular of the two and the most controversial. Attemtping to analyze the source of controversy, the Advisory Committee indicated that the hormonal contraceptives have presented society with problems that are unique in the history of human therapeutics. They said, "Never have so many people taken such potent drugs over a protracted period of time for an objective other than the control of disease." This often quoted statement may not be entirely correct. Currently, an estimated 3.3 billion oral contraceptives are used each year (8.5 M women $\times$ 21 $\times$ 13). Both the amphetamines and tranquilizers are consumed in approximately 3 to 4 times this amount annually. In many instances the indications for their use are neither more or less medical than those for the hormonal contraceptives. The pill, however, has been exposed to a spate of publicity, committee investigations, and Congressional hearings that confound belief. Many of these have been conducted by sincere individuals earnestly seeking to establish scientific evidence. Unfortunately, some of the publicity, both lay and scientific, has been shabby, ill-advised, and careless of the truth.

There are both minor and major adverse reactions to both the intrauterine devices and the hormonal contraceptives. These have been detailed in many publications and are well summarized in the publications of the Food and Drug Administration. Perforation of the uterus with peritonitis and death has been estimated to occur at the rate of about 2 per 100,000 users of the intraterine devices. Pelvic inflammatory disease occurs in 2 or 3 per cent of "users" during the first year and falls off rapidly thereafter. Less serious are the minor complications of uterine bleeding, cramps, and pelvic pain. These too tend to diminish with use of the devices.

There are three possible serious complications of the hormonal contraceptives: thromboembolic disease, carcinoma of the breast and uterus, and metabolic disturbances. A cause-and-effect relation, imposing a serious health hazard, has been proved only in the case of thromboembolic disease. British and American investigators have shown that the risk of thrombophlebitis is increased about 4 to 7 times in users of the oral contraceptives. The risk of hospitalization is about 1 in 2,000, and excess deaths occur at the rate of about 3 per 100,000 users.

More recent data have correlated the occurrence of thromboembolic disease directly with the dose of estrogen. The smallest effective dose of the estrogenic component should therefore be employed.

Data derived from five species of experimental animals indicate that estrogen administered in the proper amount for the proper time is carcinogenic. Synthetic estrogens chemically similar to those used in the hormonal contraceptives have caused breast tumors in beagles. Lacking conclusive information about the applicability of existing animal data to women and sufficient observations of human disease, the Advisory Committee concluded that the potential carcinogenicity of the oral contraceptives could neither be affirmed or excluded at this time.

Hormonal contraceptives produce numerous effects on many organs, for example, the liver, the thyroid, and the adrenal. They also affect some of the body's homeostatic mechanisms; for example, they produce changes in salt and water metabolism and occasionally induce hypertension. There is no evidence, however, at this time that any of these drug-induced metabolic alterations pose serious health hazards.

After a very careful review of all the available data, the Advisory Committee to the Food and Drug Administration indicated that when potential hazards and values of the oral contraceptives were balanced they found the ratio of benefit to risk sufficiently high to justify the designation "safe" within the usual meaning of that word when applied to therapeutic compounds.

The public concern about the oral contraceptives led the Commissioner of the Food and Drug Administration to order a small insert placed in each package of oral contraceptives advising the user that the pills should be taken only on the advice of,

and under the supervision of, a physician. The insert also contains a warning about blood clotting disorders. It further informs the patient that a more detailed description of the effectiveness and the hazards of the hormonal contraceptives can be obtained from her physician. Never before in the United States have similar inserts been placed in prescription drugs.

The insert is worded to encourage the patient-physician relation. It, however, forecasts a trend and indicates a growing public demand for enforcement of the rights of the consumer. These were clearly delineated by the late President Kennedy in a special message to Congress in 1962—"The right to safety, to know, to choose, and to protest."

No discussion of modern contraceptives can fail to note the rapidly changing attitudes toward abortion and sterilization. These together with the modern contraceptives constitute the technical base upon which hope for voluntary control of fertility rests.

Therapeutic abortion, unlike any other surgical operation, is governed by statute or common law in all states, but the wording of the regulations differs widely. In the strictest sense, the law in most states does not permit the procedure for reasons such as illegitimacy, poverty, or rape, or on the basis that the infant is likely to be gravely malformed. Despite its apparent simplicity the law remains vague because the definitions of "life," "save," and "preserve," are subject to widely varying interpretation. Thus, many hospitals have set up abortion committees to decide the permissibility of abortion. Because the intent of these committees is to protect the reputation of the hospital, they have, in general, tended to be restrictive. Inadvertently, they discriminate against the poor.

Contrary to popular belief, today's stringent abortion laws are of fairly recent origin. Abortion was either lawful or widely tolerated before quickening in both the United States and Great Britain until 1803. In that year, amid a general overhaul of British criminal law, a basic criminal abortion law was enacted that made abortion prior to quickening illegal. Canon law, creating the dogma that in no circumstance is abortion justifiable, was established in 1869 by Pope Pius IX.[26]

The British law of 1803 became the model for similar laws in the United States, but it was not until 1821 that Connecticut enacted the nation's first abortion law. Throughout the nation abortion became illegal except to save the life of the mother. In a few states, the word "health" was added. Until very recently, therapeutic abortion in most states was legally permissible only if it was necessary to save the life of the mother. Two states extended the exception to "to prevent serious or permanent bodily injury"; and in another two, the exception read "to preserve the life or health of the woman." If the "health of the woman" be construed to include her mental health, still in only two states was therapeutic abortion legally permissible on psychiatric indications or to prevent the birth of a malformed child (as in rubella), which might affect the mother's mental health. Since therapeutic abortion to save the life of the woman is rarely necessary, it follows that the great majority of such operations performed in this country went and still go beyond the letter of the law. Nevertheless, experience has shown that if a reputable physician, with the written approval of two other reputable physicians, carries out the operation openly in an accredited hospital, the propriety of the operation is rarely questioned by officers of the law.

There is a growing body of both professional and lay opinion in favor of liberalization of the abortion laws. In 1943, the prestigious New York Academy of Medicine was among the first medical organizations to recognize the need for reform. Since that time the Academy has issued three statements on the subject; the last in 1969 favors repeal of existing abortion laws.

In 1959, the American Law Institute suggested a Model Penal Code governing abortion. This code would authorize therapeutic abortion when a licensed physician believes there is substantial risk that continuance of the pregnancy would gravely impair the physical or mental health of the mother, that the child would be born with grave physical or mental defects, or that the pregnancy resulted from rape by force or incest. Two physicians must certify their belief in writing in the justifying circumstance.

In 1967 the House of Delegates of the American Medical Association went on record as supporting reform of the abortion laws conforming to the general guidelines set forth in the Model Penal Code. In 1965 the American College of Obstetricians and Gynecologists recommended, in addition to the provision of the Model Penal Code, that social and total economic environment, actual or reasonably foreseeable, be considered as having a bearing on the health of the mother.

Between 1967 and 1969, eleven states have amended their abortion laws by extending the indications for therapeutic termination of pregnancy. The new abortion act in Great Britain (1967) is potentially the most permissive of all recently enacted statutes. It contains two significant clauses in respect to the ascertainment of health of the mother: (1) "Account be taken of the pregnant woman's actual or reasonably foreseeable environment." (2) "Account be taken not only of the effect of pregnancy of the mother but on any existing children of her family."

If liberally construed, the current British abortion law is tantamount to virtually unrestricted abortion.

The report of Governor Rockefeller's special commission to review the New York State Abortion Law was published in March, 1968.[27] The recommendations followed the Model Penal Code, but two additional indications for abortion were added as follows: (1) "The pregnancy commenced while the female was unmarried and under 16 years of age, and is still unmarried." (2) "When the female already has four living children."

The principal arguments in favor of a more permissive abortion statute were summarized by the Governor's special commission as follows:

1. The deaths, sterility and harmed physical and mental health, resulting from the large number of illegal abortions each year could largely be prevented if such abortions were performed by competent physicians in proper hospital surroundings, within the framework of reasonable legislation.

2. The wide disparity between the statutory law and actual practice encourages disrespect for the law and places upon the conscientious physician an intolerable conflict between his medical duty to his patients and his duty as a citizen to uphold the law.

3. The present law places an unfair discrimination on the poor. Persons with money may obtain safe abortions either by traveling to other jurisdictions, by going to high-priced competent though illegal abortionists, or by obtaining legal abortion here based on "sophisticated" psychiatric indications.

The divergence between the literal interpretation of the law and current medical practice has led today's physician into an area of grave legal risk. There are indications that the courts may take action when reputable medical practice in accredited hospitals does not conform to strict interpretation of rigid abortion laws.

In 1969 there were two court decisions of major importance in this field. On September 5, the California Supreme Court in the case of People vs. Belous declared the pre-1967 California abortion law unconstitutional on the following grounds: (1) The phrase "necessary to preserve life" is unconstitutionally vague; (2) "the fundamental rights of the woman to choose whether to bear children" is a right of privacy which the statute unconstitutionally abridges; (3) The statue violates the Fourteenth Amendment because of the "delegation of decision-making power to a directly involved individual" (i.e., the doctor might be penalized

for approving a request for abortion but not for denying a request).

In November, a decision in the United States District Court for the District of Columbia declared unconstitutional that part of the statute outlawing abortions other than those done "for the preservation of the mother's life or health." The reasoning was similar to and in part relied upon that in the Belous decision.

Currently the abortion laws are being challenged in several states. The complaints allege that these laws are unconstitutional on grounds similar to those cited in California.

Minority reports accompanying many of these reports and resolutions are best summarized by the conclusion to the Minority Report of the Governor's Commission Appointed to Review New York State's Abortion Law, as follows: "Because we consider the proposals of the majority of our Committee to be violative of the fundamental rights of the human child in utero and detrimental to our traditional and still viable ideas of the sanctity of human life and the integrity of the family unit, we dissent. . . ."

The reform of abortion laws along the guidelines drawn by the American Law Institute has not worked well. Although the number of abortions has increased slightly, the poor still find it difficult to obtain abortions even in situations of obvious merit. Illegal abortions have probably not decreased. The laws are vague and in many instances capriciously interpreted.[5,21,25,28]

Although some states, notably Alaska, Hawaii, and New York, have repealed their abortion laws, in most instances the solution to this complex problem may stem not from legislative reform of existing statutes but from action of the courts on the constitutionality of abortion laws.[20]

In 1970, the National Council of Obstetrics-Gynecology made two important statements regarding abortion.

1. The National Council of Obstetrics-Gynecology recognizes that the initiation, continu-

ation or interruption of pregnancy are the personal responsibility of each woman and should not be regulated by any law. Any health problems arising out of pregnancy are a concern of the pregnant woman and her chosen physician.

2. The National Council of Obstetrics-Gynecology recognizes voluntary abortion as one of the methods of population stabilization and control.

There is no federal policy concerning abortion. Recently, however, the Secretary of Health, Education and Welfare stated: "The Department has no policy regarding the means of bringing about repeal of existing abortion laws, whether through action of the courts, or state or national legislation. The Department is concerned, however, that whatever changes in the laws are effected they must ensure two principles: (1) safety for the patient, and (2) elimination of social and economic discrimination."[31]

The concern for safety and social justice should be overriding in the formulation of guidelines for the expanding use of abortion.

Many of the medical and surgical conditions that justify therapeutic abortion make permanent prevention of pregnancy also desirable. In a strict sense multiparity alone cannot be regarded as an indisputable medical indication for sterilization. It has, however, become an increasingly frequent justification for the procedure particularly in the presence of a variety of social and economic factors.

Many American couples now complete their desired families at an early age. The long-term use of contraception is uncertain and perhaps undesirable. Many women are now requesting sterilization after they have their desired number of children. In short, the proportion of sterilizations performed primarily for social reasons appears to be increasing.

A questionnaire study sent to a large number of obstetricians and gynecologists selected at random from various part of the United States revealed an overall incidence of 3.2 per cent in association with 177,433 live births. The incidence varied from 1.4

to 4.5 per cent according to the geographic area.[29] Moore and Russell[22] found a ratio of 1.6 deliveries in a survey of California hospitals. The data from the armed forces hospitals and other governmental institutions are fragmentary but indicate that female sterilization is rarely performed. Recent nationwide data are not available, but there is every evidence that both male and female sterilizations are being performed with increasing frequency, and that the public demand for these procedures exceeds the willingness of the hospitals and the doctors to carry them out.

The 1965 National Fertility Survey states that 8 per cent of the wives between 18 and 39 years of age, reported that either they or their husbands had been sterilized for contraceptive purposes. Female operations comprised 5 per cent and vasectomies 3 per cent of this total.[32]

There is a divergence of opinion whether voluntary control of conception will succeed in limiting the population. This divergence is justifiable because almost all population programs throughout the world are based on the concept that there is a fundamental family right to choose the number of their children. This concept presumes that if contraceptives were made easily available and if they were effective and acceptable the people would of their own accord so limit their offspring that the growth of the population would be reduced to supportable levels. Data proving these assumptions are not available although in a few countries, i.e., Japan, they appear valid.

The alternatives to voluntary contraception such as positive and negative incentives or outright governmental control do not appear feasible or desirable at the present time. In 1970 the United States spent about 80 million dollars on contraceptives services and research. Private agencies spent additional millions. These monies are directed toward making current and improved methods of temporary contraception available to all the people who wish to use them. Implied is the hope that easy availability of contraception will reduce the growth of population in this country toward zero. Whereas one cannot disagree with the concept that contraceptive information and services should be available to all, one ought to examine critically whether it is reasonable to assume that current contraceptive techniques can effect a marked reduction in population growth.

Women in the United States are reproducing at a level well below their physiologic potential and have been doing so for a great many years. Without fertility limitation women would average about 10 births per individual during their reproductive lives. Today this average is about 3 and would have to be reduced to 2.1 per woman to reach zero population growth. This objective may take as long as 50 to 70 years. Even without modern contraceptive methods the birth rate dropped to 18 per 1,000 population at the bottom of the depression. In other words without methods of a very high order of effectiveness and acceptability our population could reduce its fertility provided that the people were sufficiently motivated. Motivation provided by the unusual circumstances of the Great Depression is not likely to be a permanent feature of American life.

We do not know precisely all the factors that caused the low birth rate of the late 20's and early 30's. Contraception, late marriage, nonmarriage, and illegal abortion all played a role.

Some of these factors have continued to be operative. There are an estimated one million illegal abortions in this country annually. If these were eliminated, our population would probably exceed by 50 million the expected 300 million at the turn of the century. On one hand the intrauterine devices and the oral contraceptives offer vastly improved effectiveness and acceptability compared to the traditional contraceptives available in the depression. On the other hand, marriage has become more common than in the 1930's, and women marry ear-

lier. The proportion of women marrying by the age of 20 has nearly doubled since that time.

Our population growth has not been brought about by women having large families, but by an increase in the proportion of women having at least 2 children—an increase in moderate-sized families.

The recent survey by Bumpass and Westoff[3] indicated that a moderate proportion of "last children" are unwanted. There must be many other children who might be classified as relatively unwanted or at least unexpected. These children are often conceived because of carelessness in the use of contraception or because of contraceptive failure.

The factors of human frailty and method failures will always be with us. They probably cannot be eliminated even by improvement of methods nor do we know how effectively to stimulate perfect motivation. There is, furthermore, little indication that the improved modern contraceptives have performed better than their predecessors in reducing the birth rate. If voluntarism is to have a significant effect on population growth, temporary contraceptive methods will have to be supported by an increased use of sterilization and legalization of abortion. It is unrealistic to expect a woman who has completed her family by the age of 30 or 32 to employ present-day contraceptives successfully until the menopause. It is far more reasonable and psychologically more acceptable to employ either vasectomy for the male or tubal ligation for the female. Both of these operations are simple and without adverse reactions. There are no legal barriers to their performance provided that they are done with informed consent. In good hands they are reversible in a high percentage of cases.

The liberalization and repeal of abortion laws in the United States is proceeding at an unprecedented rate. Provided that the facilities and methods can be found to perform these operations safely and cheaply enough so that they will be available without economic discrimination, they along with sterilization may provide a contraceptive mix that will enable voluntarism to keep the population within controllable limits.

Women born in 1933, employing the commonly used contraceptives, have already an average of over three children per woman. If 50 per cent of these women had accepted sterilization after their third child the average number of children would be reduced to 2.7 per woman.

If one accepts the magnitude of unplanned births estimated by Bumpass and and Westoff[3] and assumes almost all of this excess could be eliminated with the acceptance of sterilizations and abortions, the average number of children born to the 1933 cohort would be reduced to 2.5 per woman. With a fertility of around 2.6 the projected population by year 2000 would be about 280 million.

There is hope that, in the United States, a continuing desire for small families and the changes in mores regarding abortions and sterilizations have arrived just at the opportune time. When they are combined with the usually available methods of contraception, an acceptable population growth rate may be achieved without negating the rights of families to choose the number of their children.

REFERENCES

1. Panel Discussion on a Public Controversy: Anatomy of a Victory, New York, 1959, Planned Parenthood Federation of America.
2. Ball, G., World Bank Meeting, September 18 to 23, 1961, Vienna.
3. Bumpass, L., and Westoff, C. F.: The extent of unwanted fertility in the United States: 1960-65. Annual Meeting of Planned Parenthood World Population, New York, October 28, 1969.
4. Draper, W. H.: Report of President's Committee to Study the United States Military Assistance Program, Washington, D. C., 1959, Superintendent of Documents, United States Government Printing Office.
5. Droegemueller, W., Taylor, E. S., and Drose, V. E.: Amer. J. Obstet. Gynec. 103:694, 1969.
6. Eisenhower, D. O.: Press Conference Statement, Washington, D. C., December 2, 1959.
7. Finn, J.: Commonweal, September 12, 1958.
8. Advisory Committee on Obstetrics and Gynecology of the Food and Drug Administration: Report on the Oral Contraceptives, Washington, D. C., 1966, Superintendent of Documents, United States Government Printing Office.
9. Advisory Committee on Obstetrics and Gynecology of the Food and Drug Administration, Report on Intrauterine Contraceptive Devices, Washington, D. C., 1967, Superintendent of Documents, United States Government Printing Office.
10. Advisory Committee on Obstetrics and Gynecology of the Food and Drug Administration: Second Report on Oral Contraceptives, Washington, D. C., 1969, Superintendent of Documents, United States Government Printing Office.
11. Gardner, R. N., Deputy Assistant Secretary of State for International Organization Affairs: United Nations Debate on Economic Development, December 10, 1962, and the American Assembly on May 4, 1963.
12. Griswald vs. Connecticut: 381 U. S. 479, June 7, 1965.
13. Guttmacher, A. F.: Birth Control Services in Tax Supported Hospitals, Health Departments and Welfare Agencies. May, 1963, New York Planned Parenthood Federation of America.
14. Harper, F.: Abortion Laws in the United States. Appendix A, *in* Calderone, M. S., editor: Abortion in the United States, New York, 1958, Paul B. Hoeber, Inc.
15. Hellman, L. M.: Eugen. Rev. 57:161, 1965.
16. Jaffe, F. S.: J. Soc. Iss. 23:145, 1967.
17. Johnson, L. B.: Address to the United Nations, San Francisco, June 25, 1965.
18. Johnson, L. B.: Special Message to Congress on Health and Education, March 1, 1966.
19. Kennedy, J. F.: Press Conference Statement, Washington, D. C., April 24, 1963.
20. Lucas, R.: North Carolina Law Rev. 46:730, 1968.
21. Monroe, K.: New York Times Magazine, December 29, 1968, and ASA Reprints (from the Association for the Study of Abortion, Inc.), New York, 1969.
22. Moore, J. G., and Russell, K. P.: Clin. Obstet. Gynec. 7:54, 1964.
23. National Academy of Sciences: The Growth of United States Population, Washington National Academy of Sciences–National Research Council Pub. 1279, 1965.

24. Nixon, R. M.: Special Message to Congress relative to Population Growth, July 18, 1969.
25. Overstreet, E. W.: Experience with the new California law, *in* Hall, R. E., editor: Abortion in a Changing World. New York, 1970, Columbia University Press.
26. Pilpel, H. F., and Norwick, K. P.: When Should Abortion be Legal? Public Affairs Pamphlet No. 429, 1969, New York, Public Affairs Committee.
27. Report of the Governor's Commission Appointed to Review New York State's Abortion Law. Hon. Charles W. Froessel, Chairman, State of New York, 1968.
28. Russell, K. P., and Jackson, E. W.: Amer. J. Obstet. Gynec. **105:**757, 1969.

29. Starr, S. H., and Kosasky, H. J.: Amer. J. Obstet. Gynec. **88:**944, 1964.
30. Stevenson, A.: Annual Dinner of Planned Parenthood World Population, October 15, 1963.
31. Veneman, J.: Letter to Senator Robert Packwood (D.-Oregon), May 18, 1970.
32. Westoff, C. F., and Ryder, N. B.: Contraceptive Practice and Fertility Control in the U.S.A., 1965. Presented at AMA Seventh Congress on Environmental Health, Washington, D.C., May 4-5, 1970.
33. Wirtz, W.: Organization for Economic Cooperation and Development, December 7, 1964.
34. World Leaders Declaration on Population: New York, 1967, Population Council.

4 Techniques of conception control

Dennis Smith*

The image of a man and woman living in harmony with their desired number of children, or with no children if that be their choice, is brought to mind by the term "family planning." Family planning, conception control, contraception, and birth control are sometimes treated as synonymous terms, but what they mean to the patient and her physician is the important fact to be discussed here. A vital task of the medical practitioner, and one too easily neglected in the crush of clinical practice, is to determine the precise intent of the patient when he or she uses these terms.

The physician or family planning practitioner may be confronted by a male or female patient who states plainly, "I want to use birth control." All too often the reply is to prescribe a method or at best to quickly list the methods available at that moment and place and then say, "Now which one do you want to use?" What is lost in this exchange is the meaning of "birth control" that the patient has in mind in relation to his own needs and abilities. Contraception and family planning must be tailored to the needs of the individual.

There is *no* universally applicable method. There is no *perfect* contraceptive. It is doubtful that there is even a definition of a perfect contraceptive, if by that we mean a single method for all people. Attempts at such a description include most of the following attributes: a high degree of acceptability, ease of use, convenience, economy,

a high degree of efficacy but with complete reversibility, and no side effects (medically or otherwise). The problem lies in the fact that we are dealing with individuals each of whom may have a particular concept of the attributes of the "perfect contraceptive."

Determining what the patient needs and wants in contraception is the real job of the practitioner. Discussion between the user and the prescriber must be complete. Each method should be outlined. The advantages and disadvantages should be presented. Hopefully the sexual practices, short- and long-term goals, and general health of the patient will be reviewed and understood by both. One cannot overstress that the method must be suited to the patient.

In discussing family planning one must bear in mind that this means limiting the number of children one has in order to safeguard the mother's health, to preserve the integrity of the family unit, and to help create a climate in which sexual love can be freely expressed without fear of pregnancy. There is a further responsibility to counsel those who are having a difficult time in conceiving. Infertility services are not the subject of our concern in this chapter, but must be included in any medical setting that claims to offer complete family planning services.

EFFECTIVENESS OF METHODS

To present individual methods to the patient, one must have a knowledge of each method and a way to compare the effectiveness of one method to another. Methods can be classified as to their *theoretical effectiveness* or to their *use effectiveness* (Table 1). The former implies that the method is used without error under ideal

---

*M.D., Assistant Professor of Obstetrics and Gynecology, Case Western Reserve University School of Medicine, Cleveland, Ohio.

Original article.

circumstances. Use effectiveness is a measurement under realistic conditions. The following formula is used to evaluate use effectiveness by failure rates per 100 woman-years of exposure:

Pregnancy rate =

$$\frac{\text{Number of pregnancies} \times 1200 \text{ months (100 years)}}{\text{Patients observed} \times \text{Months of exposure}}$$

Thus, if 100 couples used a method for an average of 3 years and if 30 pregnancies occurred despite its use, the equation would be:

$$\text{Pregnancy rate} = \frac{30 \times 1200 = 36{,}000}{100 \times 36 \ = 3{,}600} = 10$$

Failure rate levels depend on the behavior of particular populations, and on what the researcher decides to include or discard when considering irregularities in usuage. Thus the figures presented in Table 1 vary somewhat from source to source, but in general the order of use effectiveness is the same. One should bear in mind that at the end of 1 year of unprotected coitus 80% to 90% of women will have conceived.

METHODS
Oral contraceptives

Oral contraceptives, or the "pill," offer greater effectiveness than any of the other methods. They are also the most widely used medically prescribed method. The Food and Drug Administration reported in 1969 that more than 8 million women were taking oral contraceptives.[2] Those currently in use contain an estrogen and a progestin.

Estrogen and progestin are synthetic compounds used either in combined or sequential form. In the *combined* form the progestin and estrogen are present in every tablet. It is prescribed to begin on the fifth day of a menstrual period. A tablet is then taken daily at the same time for 20 or 21 days. Within 2 or 3 days after stopping the tablet, the patient will begin withdrawal bleeding. Again on the fifth day of bleeding

Table 1. Use effectiveness[1]

Contraceptive method	Average pregnancy rate per 100 women per year
Oral contraceptive (combined regimen)	0.2
Oral contraceptive (sequential)	1.4
Intrauterine devices	3.9
Diaphragm	12.0
Rhythm	14.4
Condom	14.9
Coitus interruptus (withdrawal)	16
Spermicides (foams, tablets, jellies, creams)	20.0 (jelly alone) 22.0 (foam tablets)
Douche	37.8
Prolonged lactation	Mostly ineffective

or on the eighth day after stopping the tablets, the patient resumes taking them. A variation with the combined form is one in which an inert tablet is substituted for the days off in the fourth week so that the patient simply takes a pill everyday.

The sequential form involves the administration of a tablet containing only estrogen for the first 15 or 16 days and then a tablet containing estrogen and progestin for the next 5 days, followed by no medication for a period of time as with the combined form.

The use effectiveness rates for the pill average from 0.2 to 0.7 pregnancies per 100 women per year.[1] The rates with sequential tablets are not quite as good. The major reason for failure in general is the omission of tablets from the cycle.

The mechanism of action of oral contraceptive tablets is primarily suppression of ovulation. There is a suppression of pituitary gonadotropins at the central nervous system level. Occasional ovulation does occur especially with the pills with low hormone content, but other antifertility factors are operative. These are the creation of a cervical mucus hostile to sperm, an unfavorable endometrium, and possibly an unfavorable tubal environment.

Oral contraceptives are desirable because they are unrelated to the sex act, easy to use, almost certainly effective, and esthetically pleasing. However, there are undesirable side effects. The minor side effects are very similar to those of early pregnancy and are probably caused by the estrogen. They include breast fullness and tenderness, nausea, vomiting, edema, weight gain, occasional breakthrough bleeding, headache, and occasional chloasma (pigmentation of the face). Most of these symptoms will diminish or disappear with a few months of continued use; however they are sufficient to cause some women to discontinue the use of oral contraceptives. Some patients will notice fewer such symptoms if changed to the lower dose tablets, which contain less estrogen.

More serious side effects have been attributed to the oral contraceptives. Thrombophlebitis and pulmonary embolism have been chief among these. In 1968, British researchers reported a relationship between the use of oral contraceptives and death from pulmonary embolism or cerebral vascular thrombosis in women of childbearing age without previous evidence of disease.[3] The annual mortality was estimated at 1 to 2 per 100,000 users between the ages of 20 to 34 years. The figure was slightly higher for an older age group. There are, however, many objections to these studies and a recent paper by Drill disputes the presumed causal relationship.[4]

There is no convincing evidence that the estrogen in contraceptive tablets causes cancer in humans. Estrogen does induce epithelial change in breast tissue, but no cancers have been demonstrated. The final relationship is not yet known because there is often a long latent period between the introduction of carcinogen and the development of cancer.

Cancer of the cervix has *not* resulted from the use of oral contraceptives. There

have been several studies done that purported to show evidence of carcinoma in situ in users. Estrogens are carcinogenic in several species of laboratory animals. However, to date, no studies have been designed that demonstrate that estrogens can cause cancer in man. There is, of course, an absolute need to remain vigilant with the pill, as with any new drug. Breast examinations, cytological smear of the cervix, and blood pressure determinations must be carried out at least annually on women using oral contraceptives.

Occasionally a pill user may become hypertensive. If this happens, the contraceptive tablets should be discontinued and an investigation carried out. Reversal of the hypertension is the usual case. There is also evidence that the use of the pill aggravates migraine headaches. In such cases it should be discontinued.

There is no evidence that the use of oral contraceptives causes diabetes mellitus. Abnormal glucose tolerance tests have been demonstrated in women taking the pill who previously had normal tests. However the incidence of such change is much smaller than previously believed and appears unrelated to permanent diabetes.

A rare patient may have prolonged amenorrhea after cyclical use of contraceptive hormone tablets. Most such patients have eventually resumed ovulatory cycles. One must remember that if the patient was anovulatory before the pills, she will be so afterward. Use of oral contraceptives on a continuous basis for more than 2 years is believed by some investigators to contribute to the likelihood of amenorrhea after termination of the contraceptives. Patients with uterine fibroids may have some increase in the size of fibroids. This is not in itself a contraindication, but the fibroid uterus must be frequently observed and the tablets discontinued if indicated.

An increase in the incidence of spontaneous abortions has been reported in women who become pregnant immediately after discontinuing the pill. Therefore, it is advised that conception be delayed until they have been off the medication for 3 months. There is no evidence of any genetic abnormalities in pregnancies occurring after hormone contraceptive use.

Estrogens do tend to hasten epiphyseal closure and thus should not be used as contraceptives in the immature female. They likewise may cause some inhibition of lactation if administered in the immediate postpartum period.

Intrauterine devices

A patient who objects to using oral contraceptives or for whom there exist contraindications may ask, "What other methods can I use?" She will usually follow this question with "What will give me the best protection?" Probably the next best protection after the oral contraceptives is the use of an intrauterine device (IUD). The intrauterine device is inserted into the uterus, where it may remain for indefinite periods of time. Intrauterine devices are particularly useful with patients who have a poor history of taking the pills, who forget or lose the pills, or who live in situations in which children may ingest, play with, or otherwise damage the tablet content of the package. The patient may simply wish to have a method that is always present and that she does not have to think about at any time. The intrauterine device may be the answer for such a patient.

Intrauterine devices are not new. The Gräfenberg ring was used in Germany in the late 20's and early 30's. This device was made of metal and was discontinued, primarily because it was assumed to cause infection of the lining of the uterus and the uterine tubes. Today, the devices are primarily made of soft plastic. The revival of the IUD came in the late 50's.

The devices currently available are of several types. The devices constructed of an inert plastic are the Lippes loop, a coil, a bow device, Dalkon shield, and other multiplications of sizes and shapes. There are two metallic devices, the Majzlin spring and a new device that is a soft plastic T wrapped with metallic copper wire.

These devices come prepackaged and can be inserted into the uterus, preferably at the end of the menstrual cycle, with relatively little discomfort to the patient, even without the use of anesthesia. Use of these devices in a woman who has never had children has previously been rather restricted but with the development of the Dalkon shield this is now fairly common.

At the moment, the mode of action of the intrauterine device is not known, but several theories have been advanced. One explanation is that the IUD causes a more rapid transit of the egg through the tube, with the result that, even if fertilized, it arrives in the uterus at a time when the lining of the uterus is not ready for implantation to occur. Another theory is that the device causes a foreign-body tissue reaction. The device has a use effectiveness rate slightly below that of the oral contraceptives. The average pregnancy rate per 100 women per year is between 1.5 and 4, depending on the specific type of device.[1]

The advantage of the intrauterine device is that the woman who is using it does **not** have to undergo any preparation at the time she is desirous of having intercourse. There is no interruption of the lovemaking or of the sexual style of the partners. There is nothing to be removed after intercourse, as with the diaphragm, nor is there the messiness of spermicides, which is objectionable to some women and their partners. The device is present at all times and for the user who has infrequent intercourse or intercourse at unexpected times this may be the ideal solution.

Undesirable side effects that may bother the woman and her sexual partner include such troublesome things as bleeding between periods (sometimes accompanied by cramps) and more frequently heavier bleeding or prolonged bleeding at the time of the period with intensified menstrual cramping. If the woman is willing to put up with these effects for several periods, they usually diminish to an acceptable level or disappear altogether. More alarming perhaps is the possibility of natural expulsion of the IUD, since the uterus does not always tolerate the foreign body. If the patient does not check each tampon or perineal pad at the time of discarding it, or check with the finger to feel the suture to make sure the device is still in place, the device may be expelled without the patient knowing it. This certainly contributes to the pregnancy rate with the IUD, but pregnancy is avoidable with proper counseling of the patient and subsequent diligence on her part. The expulsion rate varies greatly with the type of device and with the skill of the operator placing the device. Probably it is not much greater than 10% at the time of first insertion and is probably decreased to about 5% with a second insertion.

The most serious and least common complication is perforation of the uterus by the IUD. Whether this occurs at the time it is inserted or whether the device can erode its way through the uterine wall is not certain. The closed-loop type of device such as the bow, which may be extruded into the peritoneal cavity, offers a particular danger in that intestinal loops may be caught in the closed loop of the device. A more recent modification of the bow of which there is no closed loop has decreased this risk, although this modification has not been widely tested. The mortality with perforation of the uterus and with peritonitis has been in the range of 1 to 2 per 100,000 users, which is about the same as that of fatal result from the oral contraceptive.[5] Another serious result sometimes reported by individual investigators is a partial perforation resulting in the device embedding itself in the wall of the uterus. Attempts to remove the IUD in this situation may involve such damage to the uterus that hysterectomy becomes necessary. This could be a tragedy for a young woman who has not yet had her fam-

ily and one should bear this in mind in view of the increasing use of such devices in women who have not yet become pregnant.

On rare occasions, the woman's sexual partner has complained of irritation or injury to the penis from the projecting thread or plastic stem from the IUD. This is usually quite easily rectified by simply shortening the thread; however, care must be taken to leave enough thread to allow the patient to determine the IUD's presence. In general, the sexual partner is quite unaware of the presence of the IUD unless informed of its presence by his mate. In those infrequent cases in which an unwanted pregnancy does occur with the IUD in place, the incidence of abortion is higher than in patients without the device. There may also be a higher incidence of pregnancy occurring outside the uterus when a device is present. Pregnancy may carry to term even with the device in place.

There is no doubt that the IUD is an effective contraceptive agent. It is particularly suited for the woman who cannot or does not wish to take oral contraceptives. Its side effects are relatively infrequent. The device must always be inserted under sterile conditions. As with all contraception, the client should have as a minimum a cytological smear of the cervix and a pelvic examination before insertion. The uterus should be sounded, the location should be determined, and insertion should then be done by a well-trained and competently supervised individual. In the past, this has been done only by a physician; however, recent studies reveal that paraprofessional personnel who have been specifically trained to do the insertions can do so quite capably.[6] As with any other method, the patient must be given a specific schedule for follow-up visits and examinations. She also must be impressed with the fact that she does carry a device inside the uterus that has to be periodically checked. Health agencies and physicians utilizing this method of contraception should keep records so that patients with the IUD do not become lost to medical follow-up and move on to new communities forgetting that they have such a device in place.

Diaphragm

The next most effective method, and one that has been used for many years, is the diaphragm used with spermicidal jellies. The diaphragm is a cuplike rubber device inserted into the vagina in such a way that the cervix fits into the jelly placed by the woman in the cup of the diaphragm. The spermicidal jelly will kill sperm that passes the barrier provided by the diaphragm. The obvious advantage of using the diaphragm is that it gives a high level of protection when used regularly and properly by the patient. The use effectiveness rate is variable, ranging from 2 to 12 per 100 women per year.[7,8]

The diaphragm must be put in place, generally not more than an hour before intercourse and left in place for approximately 8 hours after intercourse in order to achieve its maximum effectiveness. There are no medical side effects with the exception of an occasional reaction to the spermicidal jelly. The failure of the diaphragm is usually attributable to its not being used with every act of intercourse, that it is inserted after genital contact during foreplay, that it has been used without the jelly, or that it has not been left in place for a proper period of time after intercourse.

If the diaphragm is fitted properly, the patient is not aware of its presence and there should be little loss of sensation that may occur with other mechanical methods such as the condom. The esthetic drawback is that at a tender moment during spontaneous sex play, the woman must interrupt, excuse herself, and insert the diaphragm. This can represent a distinct problem, particularly for persons with borderline sexual adjustments. Also, the woman may object to having to remove the device 6 to 8 hours later or it may be inconvenient for her to do so. The timing of intercourse may be such that it is inconvenient or potentially embarrassing to carry the device about with her. However, the diaphragm remains an effective method of contraception for those women who cannot or do not wish to use oral contraceptives or the intrauterine devices.

Rhythm

The use of the above methods may not be acceptable to a given couple because of religious beliefs. The use of rhythm is, however, acceptable in many such cases, and it may be utilized with fair effectiveness when complete instruction has been given and adequately understood. The need, of course, is to avoid intercourse during the time when the woman is ovulating.

At the present time, there is no exact way to determine the time of ovulation before it occurs. A temperature chart may be used since there is often a slight fall in body temperature just before ovulation, followed by a rise that is then maintained through the remaining period of time before the menstrual period. The ovum is released 14 days before the patient begins to bleed. This, of course, may bear little relationship to the last menstrual period.

If the patient has kept an accurate record of her cycle for a period of a year, she will have a very good idea of the period of time from the first day of one menstrual period to the first day of the next. This may vary between 25 and 30 days or even a shorter or a longer time. She should avoid having intercourse approximately 5 days before and after the day of ovulation. If the patient has a 28-day cycle, she would be expected to ovulate on the 14th day and should avoid coitus from the 9th to the 19th day of each cycle. For many patients, this may be too long a period of abstinence. Furthermore, if the couple does not like to have intercourse during the menstrual period (though it is not medically contraindicated), there may be very few days left in each month in which the couple can have intercourse.

Even following the formula given, pregnancies may occur. Sperm is certainly capable of living in the tube for several days, perhaps as long as a week, thus causing fertilization as much as 1 week after intercourse actually occurs. The average pregnancy rate reported for the rhythm method is 14.4 pregnancies per 100 women per year.[9]

Condom

An older method of mechanical contraception is the use of the condom. Some sort of sheath to cover the penis has been used since at least the 1500's. Vulcanization of rubber enabled mass manufacture at reduced cost and added greatly to the increased usage of the condom. Some condoms have been prelubricated and the best ones have a small area for pooling the semen and decreasing the possibility of rupture of the condom at the time of ejaculation. It has an added advantage of being a partial deterrent to the spread of venereal disease. The couple should not depend on the condom to prevent venereal disease, but it is the only contraceptive method which gives *any* protection or barrier to infection.

The use effectiveness of the condom varies greatly with the willingness of the male to use it properly and consistently. Reports of the average pregnancy rate vary from study to study, ranging from 7 to 15 per 100 women per year.[10]

There are several objections to the condom. An objection voiced mostly by males but also by some females is that it decreases the physical sensation during intercourse. The condom occasionally ruptures or occasionally the male may not remove it from the vagina simultaneously with the penis and there is spilling of seminal fluid. Sex play has to be interrupted in order to put the condom in place. Also, occasional vaginal-penile contact may take place during sex play before the condom is in place. If there has been partial emission of sperm, pregnancy may result.

The male should be instructed by capable personnel in the use of the condom. To most males this may seem ridiculous. They know from the time they are little boys how condoms are used. However, instruction does need to be given about the necessity for putting the condom on early during the preparation for the sex act. The male needs to be instructed that if the penis remains in the vagina after ejaculation when the erection is subsiding, there may be leakage of semen around the now loosely fitting condom. In this case, the male should be instructed to hold the condom to the base of the penis as withdrawal takes place so as not to leave it behind. Very often only the woman is seen for family planning counsel. If the condom is the method to be used, she should be instructed so that she, in turn, may instruct her partner.

Coitus interruptus

Another, and perhaps the most ancient, method of contraception is coitus interruptus. This is the withdrawal of the penis prior to the man's ejaculation. There are several objections to this method, not the least of which is that it may be very emotionally disturbing to both partners. It requires a great deal of sexual experience for the man to accurately perceive impending ejaculation and to exercise the willpower to withdraw from the vagina before it occurs. There are also some sperm contained in the lubricating fluids that are secreted during sexual excitement by the male. These may cause a pregnancy. Ejaculation may occur on the labia and enough sperm may gain entrance to the vagina and uterus to result in a pregnancy. Thus, even if withdrawal is accomplished, protection from pregnancy is not guaranteed.

Spermicidal agents

Other vaginal contraceptive methods involve the use of foam, tablets, jellies, and creams that are spermicidal. The jellies and foams are now the most commonly used and must be put in place *before* intercourse and the patient is instructed not to douche for a period of 8 hours *after* intercourse.

The effectiveness rates of these agents are less than for any of the previous methods. Depending on how these agents are used, use effectiveness rates may vary from 8 to 22 pregnancies per 100 women per year.[1] The combined use of foam by the female and a condom by the male obviously increases the effectiveness rate for both methods. It also increases the nuisance rate, but some couples do elect to use this procedure.

Douche

Finally, the use of douches after intercourse for the purpose of preventing pregnancy is probably of little value. Sperm begin entering the cervical opening immediately after being deposited. Once the sperm has gained access to the uterine cavity, no douche material can reach it. Moreover, the sperm gain entrance to the Fallopian tubes within approximately 30 minutes after ejaculation into the vagina.

Breast feeding

Another method sometimes practiced is prolonged breast feeding after the delivery of a child. There is relative infertility in the first 3 months of breast feeding, but occasional ovulation may occur. Regular ovulation will eventually occur, and there is no way of predicting when. The result is often an unexpected and unwanted pregnancy.

Sterilization

Thus far the discussion has been confined to reversible methods of preventing conception. There are irreversible methods available that may be spoken of as permanent contraception or, more commonly, as sterilization. Either male or female may undergo surgical procedures to prevent further conception. This is a major operation in the woman. It may be done at the time of childbirth, in which case an abdominal incision is necessary and a portion of each tube is removed with the remaining stumps tied. Several types of operations have been devised to accomplish this end. This is known as abdominal bilateral partial salpingectomy and it may also be performed when the patient is not pregnant. In the nonpregnant state, a bilateral partial salpingectomy may be performed through an incision made in the vagina. In a more recent procedure, laparoscopy, a laparoscope is inserted through the abdominal wall. Operating instruments inserted through the scope are used to cauterize and cut each tube on both sides. The effectiveness of this new method is not as yet widely evaluated. On occasion, there is an abnormality of the uterus present and hysterectomy may be the procedure of choice.

Sterilization in the male by means of vasectomy is a minor operation that can be performed on an outpatient basis. An incision is made in the back wall of the scrotum. The vas deferens, which conducts the sperm from the testes, is tied in two places and a small piece between the two ties is removed. It takes only a short time and the discomfort is mild.[11]

In the case of surgical sterilization procedures for either male or female, one must make clear to the patient all of the implications of not being able to reproduce and that the procedures cannot be reversed. One must listen to the patient and hear his or her understanding of the operation and listen to any fear he or she has about its altering sexual performance or sensation. What would it mean to the patient to be permanently sterilized and have a marriage dissolve either by divorce or by death of a partner? What kind of reaction would the patient have if some of her present children should die? If the patient is satisfied that he or she would not want the continued ability to reproduce under such circumstances, then one may rest fairly assured that psychological problems are unlikely.[12]

PROSPECTIVE METHODS

A number of newer methods of contraception are under investigation. Among the more promising are intrauterine devices with copper, injectable hormones, a male pill, and possibly the prostaglandins.

Among the copper intrauterine devices, the copper T appears to be the most promising. This is a T-shaped polyethylene device with wire wrapped around the vertical bar of the T. The metallic copper seems to protect against conception and to decrease the irritability of the uterus, and the T-shaped design is ideally suited for matching the shape of the uterine cavity. Findings from extensive field trials indicate that the device seems to offer very high rates of protection against pregnancy and very low rates of expulsion and side effects. It may soon be distributed for regular usage.[13]

Injectable progestins have been used and are successful in preventing conception, although those that are of short duration have certain drawbacks. One must return to the physician for an injection on a monthly basis. In the longer acting ones, a patient deciding to become pregnant sooner than originally desired must wait until the medication has been metabolized. There is also some problem in determining the precise duration of action of hormones injected in this way.

The use of medicinal substances by the male to inhibit spermatogenesis is possible; however, at this time, none is successful enough for practical usage. Reversible methods of vas ligation and tubal ligation have been and are under investigation. The use of a removable metal clip on the vasa of the male has demonstrated some promise, and other such mechanically reversible devices are under investigation.

SUMMARY

All of the methods that are currently available for contraception and family planning are relatively simple in their use. When used properly, several have a high rate of use effectiveness. Their acceptability to the patient and the patient's life style remains foremost in importance in determining their success.

Family planning physicians and paraprofessionals must bear in mind the difference in needs in their patients, ranging from the unmarried teenager who has not yet achieved her full gynecological and linear growth to the woman who desires to prevent pregnancy in her twilight menstrual years before the menopause brings her biological contraception.

The patients must be listened to regardless of what is in the physician's mind regarding her sexual practices, how big the family "ought to be," or how many more people the country can stand. These are not at this time a part of family planning on the individual basis. One has to develop sensitivity for what the patient is saying. Sometimes a young woman, while asking for contraception, may really be asking for information about sexuality, how she functions, her emotional problems or those of her mate, the conflicts she has with herself, her family, and her emergence into this heterosexual world. Describing methods and writing prescriptions, important as they are, can never replace listening to the patient and, if possible, to her sexual partner, and so helping them to decide what the best method for *them* will be.

REFERENCES

1. Garcia, C. R.: Medical and metabolic effects of oral contraceptives and their implications, Clin. Obstet. Gynec. 11:669, 1968.
2. Advisory Committee on Obstetrics and Gynecology, Food and Drug Administration, Second report on the oral contraceptives, Washington, D. C., 1969, U. S. Government Printing Office.
3. Vessey, M. P., and Doll, R.: Investigation of the relation between the use of oral contraceptives and thromboembolic disease, Brit. Med. J. 2:199, 1968.
4. Drill, V. A.: Oral contraceptives and thromboembolic disease, J.A.M.A. 219:583, 1972.
5. Advisory Committee on Obstetrics and Gynecology, Food and Drug Administration, Report on intrauterine contraceptive devices, Washington, D. C., 1968, U. S. Government Printing Office.
6. Ostergard, D. R., Broen, E. M., and Marshall, J. R.: Family planning and cancer screening

services as provided by paramedical personnel: A training program. In Advances in planned parenthood, Amsterdam, 1972, Excerpta Medica Foundation, vol. VII, p. 59.

7. Sagi, P. C., Potter, R. G., and Westoff, C. F.: Contraceptive effectiveness as a function of desired family size, Population Studies 15:291, 1962.

8. Tietze, C., and Lewit, S.: Comparison of three contraceptive methods: Diaphragm with jelly or cream, vaginal foam, and jelly/cream alone, J. Sex Res. 3:295, 1967.

9. Tietze, C.: The condom as a contraceptive, New York, 1960, National Committee on Maternal Health, Inc., No. 5.

10. Tietze, C., Poliakoff, S. R., and Rock, J.: The clinical effectiveness of the rhythm method of contraception, Fertil. Steril. 2:444, 1951.

11. Leader, A. J.: The structuring of a large scale vasectomy clinic, Advances in planned parenthood, Amsterdam, 1972, Excerpta Medica Foundation, vol. VII, p. 203.

12. Ziegler, F.: Psychosocial response to vasectomy, Obstet. Gynec. Survey 25:69, 1970.

13. Tatum, H. J.: Contraception with the endouterine copper T: A preliminary report. In Advances in planned parenthood, Amsterdam, 1972, Excerpta Medica Foundation, vol. VII, p. 29.

5 Professional association policy statements

The following association policy statements on family planning were issued by a number of the many professional associations to which health practitioners belong. Such statements usually evolve from concerns expressed about an issue of professional practice that affects both the practitioner and the public he serves. The statements may affirm a position that gives direction solely to the membership of a single profession or they may spell out relationships with other groups and institutions whose societal functions are similar or complementary. Statements of associations seek to exert an influence on society and are in turn developed in response to pressures from society. The statements are not binding in a legal sense, but they may exert considerable force when supported by the membership of an organization.

Most of the associations whose family planning statements are included here restrict membership to a single profession; one, the American Public Health Associa-

tion is a multidisciplinary group with representation from all of the health disciplines. These associations serve a variety of purposes at three different levels: the individual practitioner, the profession as a group with common occupational interests and goals, and the general public who are the consumers of professional services. Although membership in such organizations is voluntary, a large proportion of practitioners choose to belong because membership in a group merits them to exert a greater influence through concerted actions.

The statements are included in this section because they have a potential influence on the practice of any professional group in the area of family planning. One should note that in some cases the current statement represents the latest in a series of positions endorsed by a group, whereas for other associations this is the first such statement. The reader may obtain copies of similar policy statements by writing to the executive officer of the association in which he has an interest.

Original article.

AMERICAN MEDICAL ASSOCIATION
COMMITTEE ON HUMAN REPRODUCTION

The American Medical Association Committee on Human Reproduction was established by the Board of Trustees in 1963 to "review the earlier statements of the AMA on contraceptive practices and to prepare for review by the Board statements on this and other subjects related to human reproduction." On recommendation of the Committee and with the concurrence of the Board, the following actions and new policies were adopted by the House of Delegates in December 1964*:

AMA policy on human reproduction, including population control

1. An intelligent recognition of the problems that relate to human reproduction, including the need for population control, is more than a matter of responsible medical practice.
2. The medical profession should accept a major responsibility in matters related to human reproduction as they affect the total population and the individual family.
3. In discharging this responsibility physicians must be prepared to provide counsel and guidance when the needs of their patients require it or refer the patients to appropriate persons.
4. The AMA shall take the responsibility for disseminating information to physicians on all phases of human reproduction, including sexual behavior, by whatever means are appropriate.

AMA publication on reproductive control: A new AMA publication for physicians, dealing with all aspects and methods of population control (drugs, chemicals, devices, rhythm), was authorized and [has been available since] 1965.

AMA policy on dissemination of birth control information by lay bodies: Reversing an older policy statement that "disapproved propaganda" on conception control directed to the public by lay bodies, the House directed that the AMA "cooperate with the appropriate organizations in the field of human reproduction which have adequate medical direction."

AMA policy on dissemination of birth control information at tax-supported institutions: The prescription of child-spacing measures should be made available to all patients who require them, consistent with their creed and mores, whether they obtain their medical care through private physicians or tax- or community-supported health services.

Teaching of human reproduction in medical schools: In the belief that coordinated teaching programs on the many aspects of human reproduction are not included in the medical school curricula, the House stated that "emphasis be given to teaching in medical schools the total subject of reproduction, including sexual behavior. This teaching can be included in many present curricula and need not involve adding new courses."

To implement this action, the Committee prepared a suggested teaching guide indicating how many facets of this subject could be integrated into the present four-year medical school curriculum. This document was approved by the Council on Medical Education and was forwarded by the Council to the deans and department chairmen of all medical schools.

*Policy adopted by the House of Delegates at the Clinical Convention, American Medical Association, in Miami Beach, Florida, December 1964, and reprinted here with their permission.

AMERICAN PUBLIC HEALTH ASSOCIATION

Replacement reproduction and zero population growth*

The nation now faces critical questions concerning the implications of continued population growth. The vital arithmetic is relentless—population growth cannot be sustained indefinitely.

Reducing population growth per se is not the panacea for all the nation's problems, but it is one important and achievable means to help attain many desirable goals. Specific proposals to achieve population stabilization must be designed to maximize individual freedom and diversity of opportunity, as well as to avoid social and economic inequities. Concerns of minority groups not only must be an integral part of population policy, but also of high priority. The United States should continue to open its doors to immigrants, even though immigration produces one fourth of our population growth.

APHA calls for the establishment of a national goal of replacement reproduction at an average of 2.11 children per woman—within this decade. To help achieve this goal, APHA supports full provision of family planning services, including sterilization for men and women, safe legal abortions, expanded population research, and universal public education on the causes and effects of population growth.

*Resolution adopted by the Governing Council of the American Public Health Association, October 11-15, 1971, and reprinted here with their permission from Amer. J. Public Health 61:2540, 1971.

AMERICAN NURSES' ASSOCIATION

STATEMENT ON FAMILY PLANNING*

During the past years, there has been noticeable public concern over implications of the expanding world population and the human and natural resources available to maintain this population. It is evident that even the minimum in health care, food, and the other necessities of life are not now available to all individuals at a subsistence level. If the world population continues to expand at the present rate, these necessities will continue to diminish for even greater segments of the population.

The American Nurses' Association, the professional organization of nurses concerned with the health and welfare of individuals and families, feels that it is the responsibility of all registered nurses:

1. To recognize the right of individuals and families to select and use such methods for family planning as are consistent with their own creed and mores
2. To recognize the right of individuals and families to receive information about family planning if they wish
3. To be responsive to the need for family planning
4. To be knowledgeable about state laws regarding family planning and the resources available
5. To assist in informing individuals and families of the existence of approved family planning resources
6. To assist in directing individuals and families to sources of such aid

*Approved, September 1966, Board of Directors, American Nurses' Association, and reprinted here with their permission.

AMERICAN MEDICAL WOMEN'S ASSOCIATION, INC.

Incorporation of family planning and counseling into basic health services and universal quality medical care*

RESOLUTION

WHEREAS,	infant and maternal mortality and morbidity rates among the U.S. disadvantaged population has been disproportionately high;
WHEREAS,	poverty and attendant poor health care and lack of education has affected these rates;
WHEREAS,	a population explosion has compounded the social and economic problems of our society leading to a deterioration in our family structure and causing social upheaval;
WHEREAS,	women physicians have historically pioneered in the fields of health, birth control and planned parenthood; therefore, be it
RESOLVED,	That the American Medical Women's Association urge the American Medical Association and the National Medical Association and other medical groups to involve themselves more seriously and become more aware of the importance of incorporating family planning and counseling into the framework of basic health services and universal quality medical care in order to promote proper maternal and child health and welfare; family health and stability, and responsible parenthood.

*Resolution adopted by the House of Delegates at the Annual Meeting of the American Medical Women's Association, Inc., held in Cincinnati, Ohio, 1969, and reprinted here with their permission.

NATIONAL ASSOCIATION OF SOCIAL WORKERS

Goals of public social policy*

XVII. FAMILY PLANNING
The problem

The unique importance of the family in the development and maintenance of the physical, mental, and emotional health of its members underpins the determination of social workers to support social institutions and welfare programs that enhance and buttress effective family functioning. Our respect for the dignity and worth of each individual human being commits us to work toward the fulfillment of the highest potential in every person. While society has a responsibility to facilitate the well-being of each person, the individual must in turn assume some responsibility for the welfare of the community.

Within this philosophical framework, we direct attention to the individual and social consequences of unplanned and unwanted pregnancies. We believe that potential parents should be free to decide for themselves, without duress and according to their personal belief and convictions, whether they want to become parents, how many children they are willing and able to nurture, and the opportune time for them to have children. These decisions are crucial not only for the parents but also for the unborn child, the community, the nation, and the world. For the parents, the problem of unwanted children may be economic, social, physical, or emotional. If the birth occurs out of wedlock, the problems are compounded for everyone. The tragedy of the unwanted child both in or out of wedlock is often dramatized by cases of abuse and abandonment.

Continued.

*Reprinted with permission of the National Association of Social Workers, from *Goals of Public Social Policy revised*, New York, 1967, National Association of Social Workers, pp. 55-59.

NATIONAL ASSOCIATION OF SOCIAL WORKERS—cont'd

Advances in the United States in the standard of living, urbanization, medical technology, and understanding of both family and individual needs have produced a corresponding demand for family planning services. Many married persons and engaged couples using private physicians have had fairly ready access to medically approved methods of contraception. Until recently many medically indigent persons have been able to obtain similar help in family planning only from limited voluntary programs. This discrimination was the result of their low socioeconomic status.

Growing public pressure for government support of family planning services as a public health measure comes from several sources: young married couples who want financial and emotional security before venturing into parenthood, parents of large families who are overburdened and unable to break out of the poverty cycle, parents who want to give the children they already have brought into the world every advantage within their limited resources, and those concerned about the quality of family life. Along with the other professions responsible for enhancing family life, social work has to a large extent neglected to include birth control services as part of its overall task.

Problems that may occur in marital, extramarital, and premarital sexual relations require other types of professional intervention and counseling. Family planning services in themselves cannot be expected to solve these problems but can serve both the individuals and society by helping to prevent the frequent result of these relationships in the birth of unwanted children. Although society is ultimately responsible for the welfare of the child, much can be done through individual services to encourage and make possible responsible parenthood.

In many countries the dual problem of excess fertility and an inadequate supply of food and other essentials has reached disaster proportions, particularly in the underdeveloped countries. Especially in such areas, local or central government support of family planning is frequently sporadic or nonexistent, leaving people without access to family planning information and services. Governments in these countries lack funds and trained personnel to gather adequate demographic data, to develop family planning programs, and to raise their citizens' educational and employment level to the point at which family size would normally begin to level off. The disparity between world population and world food supply is increasing, and famine, with all its terrible consequences, may ensue unless effective programs of family planning can be developed.

The objective

Every child is born with the right to a family that has reasonable prospects for nurturing him successfully to adulthood. All individuals, regardless of income, should have access to knowledge of what constitutes good family life, and the means to achieve it. The ability to obtain information and services for planning conception is an important prerequisite to good family life.

A continuing partnership between the voluntary and the public sectors is necessary to assist families to plan for children. Adequate financing is necessary to make family planning programs and professional services available to all, regardless of ability to pay. Government policies and medical programs as well as medical programs under voluntary auspices should assure potential parents full access to the technical knowledge and resources that will enable them to exercise their right of choice about whether and when to have children. As part of the professional team operating these programs, social work, with its underlying emphasis and particular methods for enhancing self-determination, has a special responsibility.

The unprecedented rate of population growth, especially in the crowded urban centers, makes it vital that family planning should be accompanied by social, economic, and physical planning at the various levels of government. Freedom of choice in family planning in underdeveloped areas, within or outside our country, is especially difficult without raising socioeconomic and educational levels. A total approach to population policy should therefore include not only family planning but also the improvement of socioeconomic conditions, including the provision of food and essential goods and services basic to the satisfaction of family needs. Without such

NATIONAL ASSOCIATION OF SOCIAL WORKERS—cont'd

planning and development the democratic goals of optimum opportunity for individual achievement cannot be realized and the benefits resulting from family planning services may be nullified.

Recommendations

1. Comprehensive services. Family planning should include a range of services relative to child bearing and child spacing in order to offer means compatible with the individual's personal preference. Problems of both infertility and fertility control should be given adequate attention within the context of family planning. It is especially important that individuals and families having problems related to family planning should have access to, among others, social work, medical, psychological, and religious services.

2. Availability and accessibility of services. As a public health measure family planning services should be available as part of the community's public and voluntary health and welfare services. Public services must be available to all without the application of a means test. No action by government agencies or their personnel should be permitted to limit the ready availability of these services nor should any prohibition be placed against the giving of these services to individuals who want them.

3. Importance of freedom of choice. No coercion in the use of selection of a method of family planning should be permitted. The individual should be protected both in the exercise of self-determination of whether to engage in a program of family planning and in the choice of the method and type of family planning most compatible with personal beliefs and convictions. Clients of public and voluntary agencies should be clearly advised that their use or nonuse of family planning services will in no way affect any other benefits they are receiving through the agency.

4. Government support for services, education of personnel, and research. There should be active support for the development of community and statewide public voluntary health services for all methods of family planning. Government at all levels should take a vigorous and full-partnership role with other institutions of society in the broad study, planning, and programming needed to assure that the right of every child to a family and a world that can care for him adequately will be realized. Through its various channels, government should provide the financial incentive and official support to public and voluntary facilities for the wide dissemination of family planning services. Such government support should include the financing of research to evaluate the effectiveness of these family planning services and to develop improved methods of preventing, postponing, or promoting conception. Government aid is also needed to recruit and train essential professional personnel, to staff facilities, and to provide a high quality of service.

5. Community action and education programs. The family itself, schools, churches, and voluntary organizations, along with governmental health, education, and welfare agencies should fully educate all individuals on the rewards and responsibilities of family life. This should include programs on the purpose and availability of family planning services.

6. International responsibilities. The United States government and voluntary American social welfare organizations should, upon request, provide assistance to other countries for research, education, and training of personnel and operation of family planning programs. As far as possible the United States government should channel its family planning assistance through agencies of the United Nations and other multigovernment auspices. Because countries are at different stages of experimentation in the development of family planning and population policy, it is important to foster wide communication in regard to programs, methods, and results.

7. Responsibility of social workers. Social workers should take professional responsibility to assist clients in obtaining whatever help and information they need for effective family planning. Because in their day-to-day work social workers are knowledgeable about family and community resources, they have many opportunities to help clients obtain desired services. Individual social workers also have a professional obligation to work with a variety of groups on the domestic and international fronts for the establishment of family planning programs on a level adequate to ensure the availability and accessibility of family planning services to all who want them.

PART II
WHO NEEDS FAMILY PLANNING?

Many different positions have been argued by persons concerned with the question "Who needs family planning?" Some would reduce the question to the more basic form "Does *anyone* need family planning?" and reply no, since they view family planning as synonymous with contraception, which they consider morally wrong. At the other extreme are those, including many health professionals, who would say that nearly everyone needs some form of family planning.

Given this wide range of existing opinion, it would be tedious and perhaps useless to try to discuss all of the different points of view. On the other hand, to simply express a point of view that the editors consider most reasonable without discussing the processes involved in making that determination or without trying to place it in the context of other positions, would be likely only to perpetuate the present controversies. Also, students of the health professions need an awareness of alternative views for both personal and professional development. Hence, it is our aim here to provide general underlying considerations involved in all determinations of need, then to suggest how health considerations provide one criterion for determining who needs family planning, and finally to point out the need to take the client's own life circumstances—his values, fears, and knowledge—into account in assessing need.

There are three general considerations in determining need. The first consideration in examining the question of who needs family planning is that all answers to this question are ultimately derived from value judgments; the answers depend essentially on what an individual (whether health professional, client, or lobbyist) values or believes is right or wrong. In other words, an answer is right only in relation to a given value; there is no absolute answer for all. A deplorable example (in the value judgment of the editors) would be the hypothetical, but not implausible, physician who denies contraception to teenagers because of his personal belief that premarital sex is immoral. Further, that those engaging in it "deserve the punishment of pregnancy." His personal belief is valid for him but not necessarily for the patient.

The second general consideration is that family planning per se is not the thing that is valued. Rarely will someone be heard to advocate family planning because he thinks it is a desirable thing in and of itself. Rather, the specific act of contraception or the more general process of family planning is believed to facilitate or impede certain other goals that are desired or feared. Stated simply, family planning is virtually unanimously considered a *means* to some *end*. There is difference of opinion concerning the merit of the ends—more consumable family income, professional or occupational roles for the wife, more parental attention for each child, no children, and so forth, yet it is those personal, religious, or moral values associated with the means (contraceptive behavior) that is the cause of the most heated disagreement. The implications of this disagreement are serious for the health professional if he or she attempts to determine need solely on the basis of professional values, since those values involving either means or ends may not coincide with the patient's.

The third general consideration in assessing need is that an individual, whether professional or client, always values or cherishes many ends and attaches different relative importance to them. The relative importance of these values is revealed on the occasions when the individual is faced with a situation in which he must choose between two courses of action that will allow him to achieve one or the other of two ends, but not both at the same time. It is entirely possible and in fact frequently occurs that family planning can enhance the attainment of one value while simultaneously jeopardizing another. For example, a wife may forgo desired childbearing in order to maintain a marriage in which the husband insists upon having no children.

With these considerations in mind, we will attempt to answer the question of who needs family planning by identifying those values of health professionals to which family planning has been presumed to be related.

The most critical claim of interest to health professionals is that family planning is directly related to general physical health. The argument for this point of view is that family planning, or rather the lack of it, poses a health hazard to certain individuals. If the health professional's commitment to improving the health of all is assumed, then providing family planning services can be viewed as an integral aspect of preventive medicine.

In addition, the notion of what constitutes health has broadened considerably during recent years in recognition of the interplay between physical health and emotional well-being, with the health professional's role broadening in response to this recognition. In this broader context, it has been assumed that family planning also enhances emotional well-being.

A third claim relating family planning to the values of health professionals is that family planning promotes social well-being. Some may not consider it the professional concern or duty of the health professional to provide for any aspect of the individual's social well-being; however, increasingly frequent demands are heard from within and outside the health professions for greater social awareness and responsiveness to societal concerns. Indeed, much of the impetus for liberalization of state and federal policies on family planning came from within the health professions as indicated in Reading 3 by Hellman and by the professional association policy statements. The assumption is that increased ability on the part of individuals to consciously plan their families makes it more possible for other life goals (educational, economic, and so on) to be met while enhancing the marriage relationship. These social ends fit comfortably into the broadening role of the health practitioner.

These three values—physical, emotional, and social well-being—appear to be the most critical ones in determining who needs family planning from the point of view of the health professions. However, not all persons are equally in "need" of the three values discussed above, and of those in need, family planning is not equally promising for all as a means of achieving these ends. Some individuals or groups stand in greater danger than others of jeopardizing their physical health or emotional or social well-being if they are not provided with family planning services. These groups are identified in the articles contained in this section.

Finally, how do all these considerations affect the health professionals' involvement in family planning? First, the health professional should be certain of the relation of his personal views to his professional obligations and act on the basis of the latter. Second, given that there are no absolute criteria for who needs contraception and that different individuals cherish different things, the health professional therefore should focus on providing contraceptive services to those who desire it. That is, an individual's expressed desire for contraception must be taken as the prime indicator of need. It must, in other words, be assumed that for such individuals conception is congruent with their own values subject to the cautions raised by Smith in Reading 4. Third, the health professionals should not assume that individuals are aware of the health risks of unregulated intercourse. Hence, health professionals should make clear to their clients the possible consequences of unprotected intercourse and volunteer contraceptive counseling if necessary.

The first article in this part (Beasley, "Benefits of Family Planning to Family Health") has its primary emphasis on the physical health benefits of family planning. A review of medical evidence demonstrates higher risks of perinatal mortality, infant and maternal morbidity and prematurity with the young and the old, the recently pregnant, those of high parity, those with complications in their reproductive histories, and the poor generally. As the author states, although more evidence is required, the existing findings generally support the medical claims. A strong case is made for including family planning as an integral aspect of medical practice.

In the second article, Schwartz reviews the evidence linking unwanted pregnancy with departures from emotional well-being. Methodologically sound research in this area is sparse, but what evidence exists strongly suggests that the mother, the child, and the family unit of an unwanted pregnancy incur emotional and psychological handicaps. In light of this, the author argues that family planning should be an important health component for the primary prevention of mental illness.

Landmann, in "United States, Underdeveloped Land in Family Planning," focuses on the physical, emotional, and social health consequences of inadequate family planning services to the poorer segments of the population. Her article makes several important points. First, it documents the interrelationships among physical, emotional, and social health among the poor and the role of family planning as preventive medicine. Second, it shows that the family planning service and support provided by hospitals, physicians, and government bodies was inadequate at the time of her writing. This continues to be the case. Third, it provides evidence that many of the poor, who are most in need of family planning, actually desire smaller families than they are now having and would practice family planning if the means were made available to them.

The relationship of family planning to patient management in the case of genetic risk (such as congenital defects) is discussed by Macintyre. He provides sensitive and instructive discussion of the effects of the presence of a malformed or retarded child upon siblings and parents, and such discussion is the product of much experience in genetic counseling and diagnosis. A pioneer researcher in prenatal diagnosis, Macintyre details the procedures and limitations of amniocentesis and subsequent diagnostic procedures for saving the lives of normal babies who otherwise would be lost through therapeutic abortion in cases of possible genetic risk.

Sprey ("Family Design and Family Planning") approaches the question of need for family planning in a conjectural, futuristic, sociological vein. His point is that "family" is frequently omitted from considerations of family planning. This represents intellectually healthy behavioral contrast to the heavy medical emphasis found in the other selections in Part II. From this point, he proceeds to consider what may be emerging alternatives to the family design consisting of husband, wife, and their offspring. Thus, "family designs" are seen as alternative ways of living in which reproduction and planning take on new meanings.

Finally, Moore considers the question of need within the problematic context of induced abortion versus contraception as alternative means of family planning. Her primary concern lies with assessing the empirical evidence bearing upon the relation between these two approaches. Particular attention is given to sociological dimensions, that is, to the characteristics of women relying upon abortion in contrast to the characteristics of contraceptors. On the basis of an excellent review of findings in several countries, he concludes that reliance upon abortion is negatively related to contraceptive use and that abortion is a backup and emergency measure in the absence of adequate or effective contraceptives.

6 Benefits of family planning to family health

Joseph D. Beasley*

INTRODUCTION AND ASSUMPTIONS

This discussion reviews the benefits of family planning to individuals and their family units. Since the literature in this field is controversial and the data sketchy, it is important to establish the assumptions upon which this discussion is based.

The majority of married males and females in the United States are currently using some scientific, acceptable method of family planning.[1] They do so for a variety of reasons and will continue to make this their pattern of living regardless of the type of contraceptives available at any given time. However, for many complex reasons, an estimated 5 million poor families in the United States are *not* using scientifically acceptable methods of family planning.[2] Considerable recent data indicate that they do not follow such a plan because, first, there is marked national ignorance concerning human reproduction and contraceptive technology, a problem compounded for the poor by their low level of education,[3] and second, the lack of adequate medical services for this group and their inability to utilize what existing services there are make obtaining and applying sound principles of family planning extremely difficult.

However, availability of proper education and adequate health services plus respect for the patient's dignity and privacy

will bring about a continuing, effective response to family planning programs.[4] In other words, it is evident that the principal reason family planning is not practiced among the poor is lack of knowledge and lack of adequate services. If such education and services were within their reach, the lower socioeconomic group would follow patterns similar to those currently observed in the middle and upper socioeconomic group. In general, then, ours would soon be a nation in which lack of family planning practice among married couples would be highly unusual.

I am aware of the worldwide increase in the rate of population growth and of the staggering challenges it has for mankind. The human race must bring its growth and death rates into balance. Although the following idea not accepted and still debated, I believe it is manifest that with the continued neglect of this challenge, man's death rates, morbidity, and levels of social disintegration will, in themselves, exert eventual control over his rate of population growth.

Without entering into the controversy about whether family planning alone can be an adequate control or if government must initiate vast social and economic policy changes to bring about mandatory control of population growth, I believe that much of that controversy is irrelevant, because it is apparent that family planning must be an integral part of any population policy, be it formulated to control or expand the rate of growth. Any population policy must consider such variables as age at marriage, economic reward for family size, the gen-

*M.D., Professor and Chairman of the Department of Applied Health Sciences, School of Public Health and Tropical Medicine, Tulane University of Louisiana, New Orleans, Louisiana.

Original article.

eral level of education, health care, and economic survival of its children, as well as many other factors discussed in considerable detail by other authors.[5]

Therefore, whatever the population policy may be for any given unit of government, that policy will, of necessity, involve the utilization of some family planning methodology and its evaluation.

The fact is not widely recognized that the United States itself has an immense population problem. Indeed, the United States faces many problems, including the increasing amount of environmental pollution, the increasing changes in population characteristics, the increasing technological impact, and increasing social instability. For instance, conservative estimates expect America's childhood population (14 years and under) to leap from 53 million in 1960 to around 100 million in the year 2000.[6] Certainly such an increase in our childhood population will only aggravate existing inadequacies in developing each child's potential, particularly in the lower socioeconomic segment of society. With so many more children to be educated, given medical care, and eventually employed, this country may find itself totally unprepared to meet these needs.

The current disproportionate birth rate among the poor presents a serious problem. The first step toward resolving this problem is to make it possible for the poor to adopt and practice the methodology of family planning. The major task now is to make effective family planning services widely available, and simultaneously to direct our attention toward decreasing the norms for family size.

Many observers maintain that family planning is a weapon for decreasing the members of one segment or ethnic group of a population. Such a claim has been a matter of serious concern for United Nations' leaders and health administrators in various countries, especially the nations of Africa and Latin America. Unfortunately, such is-

sues have also been raised by certain militant racial groups of both the extreme left and the extreme right of our society. Evidence indicates, however, that resistance to family planning is usually caused by insufficient education, and prior experience with inadequate or unacceptable medical care. I believe that ultimately the women of low-income groups will be motivated toward family planning by sheer concern for their own welfare and that of their families. Hence, we can expect very little change in the increasing acceptance of family planning by black and white indigent families in the United States.

My final assumption is that inadequate knowledge of family planning and its practice among the poor is a symptom of a graver problem: the long-standing absence of adequate medical care for the poor. If overall health care were available, particularly for mother and child, family planning would easily be incorporated as an integral component. This could have taken place decades ago, and some of the current problems might have been eliminated. Indeed, it is assumed that comprehensive care is the goal in the delivery of health services to the poor, as well as other segments of the population. Perhaps family planning programs that incorporate new medical care concepts can serve as a catalyst to this endeavor.[7]

EVIDENCE OF THE HEALTH BENEFITS OF FAMILY PLANNING

Granted these assumptions, let us now address the question "In what way can family planning programs improve the physical and emotional health of individuals and family units?"

In general, most of the studies in this field have measured the effect of only one variable, such as the age at which pregnancy occurred or the number of pregnancies experienced, against such rates as stillbirths, infant mortality, or prematurity. This is less than adequate to further our knowledge. For example, major problems arise when one attempts to look at only one or two variables because of the possible unknown effects of other variables.

If we accept the assumption that our goal is to eliminate pregnancy-associated mortality and morbidity, we must examine those characteristics associated with reproduction that influence the outcome of the pregnancy. As an illustration, if an interval of 12 months or less increases the probability of prematurity or infant mortality, our society must be so alerted and individual families advised to increase the spacing period. If pregnant women of a specific age group are more prone to complications or death, again our society must be alerted and individuals encouraged to have their children during the mother's optimum age-span. These factors become even more important because of their broader implications since they may definitely influence the age at marriage or other social variables that may in turn affect rates of population growth.

Indeed, the results of these past studies have been incomplete. Different investigators with inadequate data, and often inadequate methodology, have described only part of the problem. Certainly one cannot say that the age at which pregnancy occurs completes the picture, nor does the spacing interval between the birth of one child and the birth of a subsequent child, nor, for that matter, does the spacing interval between all children dictate the total picture without including the woman's health at the time of pregnancy, her past medical and reproductive history, her marital status, and the complex emotional attitudes of the woman, as well as those of the persons within her environment. Obviously, there are many factors involved and many remain to be recognized.

In summary, the total picture certainly is not yet available and, as we travel at our relatively pedestrian rate of investigation, the problems in this area outpace us. Therefore, although the approach in the balance of this discussion is to review and examine

our available, though limited, knowledge, one is cautioned to be aware of the need for much more intensive research.

AGE

Clinicians can cite repeated examples of 45-year-old women or 13-year-old girls who have delivered healthy children without complications. Certainly, we acknowledge a remarkable difference between individual human beings and their reproductive performance under varied conditions. In contrast, the studies described below represent samples of experiences with large numbers of women. For instance, the British Perinatal Mortality Survey[8] represents women of an entire nation whereas other studies represent much smaller populations; yet each study speaks of averages and of characteristics applicable to the question "Is there increased probability of death or illness associated with the age of mother at reproduction?"

Generally, the lowest incidence of maternal mortality, perinatal mortality, and prematurity exists among pregnant women between the ages of 20 and 30, whereas considerably higher rates of reproductive wastage and perinatal death are associated with women reproducing at or below 16 years of age or at 35 years of age and older. As an illustration, data from the British Perinatal Mortality Survey indicate that perinatal mortality in mothers over 40 years of age is 104% greater than the national average of Great Britain and Wales, and pregnant women under 20 have a 23% higher chance of perinatal mortality than pregnant women aged 20 to 24 years. As another example, the Obstetrical Statistical Cooperative Study,[9] reviewing approximately 350,000 births occurring between 1951 and 1961, revealed that maternal mortality for mothers aged 30 to 39 was twice as high as those for mothers aged 20 to 29, or 13.8 as opposed to 6.6 per 10,000.

Heady and Morris[10] indicated that neonatal death rates, prematurity, and other complications are considerably higher in pregnant women below the age of 20. These rates prevailed regardless of the socioeconomic level of the patient and regardless of the medical care given. Hence, these three large, major studies support our contention that age alone can affect the prognosis or outcome of pregnancy to a considerable extent.

Other age-related factors, though less clearly understood, appear to be quite important. For example, Newcomb and Travendale[11] indicate that the risk of infant death or congenital defect is significantly greater in an expectant mother over 34 years of age. These older mothers demonstrated a 1.84 greater probability of delivering a child with cerebral palsy. This is one example of the need for additional research in this area. Our currently available data indicate that a child born of an older mother has a considerably higher probability of developing spasticity. Other reports deal with this problem in more detail.[12]

SPACING

For the purpose of this paper, "child spacing" refers to the interval between the termination of one pregnancy and the termination of a subsequent pregnancy. This definition is important because, as Nicholas J. Eastman[13] has pointed out, patients delivering with a short space interval will contribute a disproportionate number of premature births. Accepting this definition, I should like to look briefly at previous discourses concerning spacing of children.

The first work to obtain wide-scale recognition was published in 1925 by Robert W. Woodbury.[14] This work appears to have had considerable effect upon both medical practice and lay attitudes for about two decades. Woodbury's detailed study of causal agents in infant mortality gave special attention to the relative importance of the interval of time between births. His general conclusion was that "infants born at short intervals have markedly higher rates

Table 1. Four-year infant mortality

Interval, in years, between births	Infant mortality
1	146.7
2	98.6
3	86.5
4	84.9

of mortality from all causes. Evidently some factor which is intimately connected with the short interval, perhaps through the influence of frequent births upon the mother's health, affected the chance of life in the infants who closely followed preceding births."

His specific infant mortality figures for the first year of life (number of infant deaths per 1,000 live births) are shown in Table 1.

In summary, infants whose birth follows a preceding birth by only 1 year apparently face a chance of mortality 1½ times that of infants after intervals of 2 years or more. The lowest mortality for the entire first year of life is observed in infants born 4 or more years apart.

As Nicholas J. Eastman pointed out, these data were very quickly seized upon to justify birth control movements. In 1944, Eastman[13] published his study of case histories of 5,158 obstetrical patients, in which his findings differed somewhat from those reached by Woodbury and previous authors. With each of his 5,158 patients, the interval between the previous viable delivery and the termination of the present pregnancy was accurately known. In addition to this "direct" study, he also studied 33,087 cases in which the interval between births was not specifically recorded, but in which the age and parity of the patients were recorded. Therefore, by correlating the two factors, particularly greater parity in the younger age group, he was able to draw indirect conclusions about the effect of rapid childbearing and, hence, short intervals on maternal and fetal prognosis.

Some of his conclusions are the following:

1. Infants born from twelve to twenty-four months after a previous viable delivery (that is, during the second year) have at least as low a stillbirth and neonatal mortality rate as do infants born after longer intervals.
2. The longer the interval between births, the more likely the mother is to suffer from some form of hypertensive toxemia of pregnancy. The incidence of this complication is lowest with an interval of twelve to twenty-four months, significantly higher with twenty-four to forty-eight months, and much higher with an excess of four years. In the present study, these rates were equally true of white and colored ward and private patients.
3. In patients who have had a previous hypertensive toxemia pregnancy, the likelihood of repetition becomes progressively greater as the interval becomes longer.
4. The incidence of the following conditions is no greater when the interval is twelve to twenty-four months than when it is longer: premature labor, anemia, post-partum hemorrhage, and puerperal infection; nor are mothers in this brief interval group less able to nurse their babies. The weight of the mature babies was approximately the same regardless of the interval.*

Eastman drew almost no inferences concerning, in his words, the "very brief interval group," namely, the group delivering less than 1 year after a previous birth. He indicated much higher morbidity in the group experiencing a short spacing interval; however, he did not have a large number of cases and therefore drew no conclusions concerning this group.

Eastman concluded, "For the best maternal and fetal outlook we are inclined to believe that youth is a better ally than child spacing."[13] His comments were significant because they introduced the concept that other factors could definitely be involved. For example, he pointed to age as a com-

plicating factor and examined other clinical conditions that were not evident in certain large statistical studies.

I should like to emphasize that the studies of Eastman and Woodbury were reported some 20 years apart and the events recorded occurred, in some instances, as far apart as 25 years. I think that it is important to point out, however, that Eastman's study did not refute Woodbury's conclusion that reproduction occurring with short spacing intervals was associated for undetermined reasons with higher rates of reproductive wastage. Rather, it refined and extended Woodbury's pioneering work.

An indirect method of study also was employed by J. Yerushalmy[15] in an attempt to determine the effect of intervals between births upon the stillbirth rate. His study was based on more than 7,000,000 births between 1937 and 1941 and emphasized variables of parity and age of mother. Its basic thrust was to determine an "expected rate" for each parity and each age group under the testable assumption that the interval between births did not affect the stillbirth rate.

A comparison between the observed rates and the expected rates demonstrates the effect of an interval between births. This study indicated that relatively short as well as very long intervals were associated with higher stillbirth rates, whereas moderate intervals led to the lowest rates. This method does not lend itself to quantitative expression of the exact optimal interval for each parity and age grouping; therefore, Yerushalmy recommended that further study should be carried out to determine actual optimum intervals in the various parity and age groupings. Unfortunately, his recommendations have not been followed, and a definitive study has yet to be presented. However, Bishop[16] has shed some additional light in his report on 16,000 consecutive deliveries that occurred between 1956 and 1961. The relationship between prematurity and the interval since a previous pregnancy is reported in Table 2.

*Eastman, N. J.: The effect of the interval between births on maternal and fetal outlook, Amer. J. Obstet. Gynec. 47:462, 1944.

Table 2. Relationship of prematurity to interval since previous pregnancy

Interval	Percent of premature births
No previous pregnancy	11.4
More than 23 months	7.8
12 to 23 months	10.3
Less than 12 months	18.0

Table 3. Percent perinatal mortality by birth order according to socioeconomic status

Birth order	Middle and upper socio-economic group	Lowest socio-economic group*
First through fourth birth	2.6%	5.5%
Fifth birth	3.8%	6.0%
Sixth birth	4.7%	9.5%
Seventh birth	5.6%	12.1%

*Figures in this column are estimates.

Although there were no controls for age, parity, medical complications, or other factors reported, this study illustrated that a spacing interval of more than 23 months showed an incidence of prematurity of 7.8% and an interval of less than 12 months showed 18%.

The relationship of spacing to prematurity, perinatal mortality, or maternal mortality, is very complicated. Bishop's work was suggestive of a definite relationship, but it is also possible that women who have babies less than 12 months apart and who are, therefore, at a much higher risk, possess other characteristics that cause prematurity. In other words, prematurity may be caused by characteristics within the reproductive woman or her environment rather than by spacing interval. The importance of spacing as such on the outcome of pregnancy raises questions, but the evidence suggests that the combination of factors leading to sequential reproduction within a year is fraught with a high incidence of prematurity, perinatal mortality, stillbirth, and other complications. In reiteration, additional studies of the effects of pregnancy spacing that consider such variables as age, parity, and the medical condition of the mother are necessary.

PARITY

Parity refers to the number of pregnancies a woman has experienced that resulted in a viable infant or a product of conception weighing over 500 grams. The British Perinatal Mortality Survey[8] reviewed 16,994

single births that occurred during the week of March 3 to 9, 1958, and 7,117 single stillbirths that occurred during March, April, and May 1958, in England, Wales, and Scotland. Perinatal mortality figures were high for the first pregnancy, low for the second, average for the third, but rose steadily after the third. Indeed, the figures for the fifth and subsequent deliveries were 54% higher than for earlier deliveries.

The Obstetrical Statistical Cooperative Study reported in 1961[9] was based on 65,865 discharges at 16 hospitals. The hospitals were not chosen at random but generally represented a cross section of United States' experience during the stated year. Perinatal mortality in relationship to birth order is depicted in Table 3.

In both these studies, then, the perinatal mortality and other rates were higher for the first pregnancy, lowest for the second pregnancy, average for the third and fourth, and rose steadily after the fourth pregnancy. The rate increased markedly for the sixth and subsequent pregnancies. It is apparent that high parity is also associated with increased fetal risk.

PAST CLINICAL HISTORY

Specific clinical syndromes and conditions that tend to be aggravated by pregnancy are usually indications for family planning. Of course, with optimum care, successful completion of a pregnancy may occur despite serious conditions that may exist in the mother at the onset of pregnancy or that may develop during the course of pregnancy. In general, deferment or avoidance of pregnancy is advised in a variety of clinical conditions. Some of the more serious conditions that are usually further aggravated by pregnancy are the following:

1. Cancer
2. Cardiovascular renal disease
3. Severe anemia from any source, but especially sickle cell anemia
4. Endocrine diseases
   a. Diabetes mellitus
   b. Thyrotoxicosis
   c. Adrenal insufficiency
5. Chronic neurological diseases, such as multiple sclerosis and Parkinson's disease
6. Collagen diseases
7. Psychoses
8. Infectious diseases, for example:
   a. Tuberculosis
   b. Gonorrhea
   c. Syphilis
9. Malnutrition secondary to either protein and caloric depletion or both or specific vitamin deficiency.

Although these examples are specific, family planning may be indicated for many other reasons. For instance, after an operation, accident, or debilitating illness, or during a period in which either parent was experiencing severe mental illness, family planning should be a necessary and integral part of adequate maternal care.

Too often, insufficient emphasis is given to the preventative aspects of family planning. Indeed, a woman affected by any of these medical conditions might find her health further jeopardized when complicated by pregnancy. Family planning should be stressed not as a social movement, but as an important component of medical competence and complete patient management. It is too often discouraging that this viewpoint is omitted from most of the health profession training programs. Admittedly, the

clinician points with pride to the patient with severe complicating factors who comes through pregnancy alive and develops a viable fetus; but one must raise the question "Was it proper management to allow the patient with severe complicating factors to become pregnant?"

ABORTION

Abortion is currently believed to be a major maternal health problem in the United States. It is highly probable that family planning prescribed by the physician would reduce the number of conceptions resulting in abortion. This rationale assumes that abortion would decrease if family planning were more widespread. Present data supports this assumption. In 1966, the Population Council organized and supported a large-scale postpartum program in 25 hospitals. The following statement is taken from a report on that program:

> The total number of abortion admissions during the operational months of the program decreased by 26% in the United States hospitals and by 12% in the non-US hospitals as compared with the twelve months period preceding this program. This substantial decrease was completely disproportionate to the obstetrical admission decrease.[17]

Although these are preliminary findings, they suggest very strongly that the incidence of abortion will decrease as the prevalence of family planning increases. As indicated by Guttmacher's studies,[18] abortion was the cause of approximately 45% of maternal deaths in one large metropolitan area. Abortion rates alone present a strong medical indication for the use of family planning.

ILLEGITIMACY

Pakter et al.[19] have analyzed the relationship of maternal death, infant death, fetal death, and prematurity to marital status of the mother in New York City for the period 1955 to 1959. Their findings indicate that unmarried mothers have the most unfavorable outcomes. For the unmarried, maternal deaths were four times higher than for married women; infant mortality, late fetal deaths, and prematurity were each twice as high, and complications of pregnancy were 25% more frequent.

In general, other studies confirm these findings for large populations. Certainly many variables must be considered, but for whatever reasons involved, the infant mortality, maternal mortality, and perinatal rates are much higher among women who become pregnant out of wedlock than among married women. In consideration of the proportion of births in the United States reported as illegitimate, rates in New Orleans—as in most other large metropolitan areas—are in the area of 124 per 1,000 live births.[20] Any measure that would decrease the number of babies born out of wedlock could have a considerable impact upon existing maternal reproductive wastage. Roughly one half of the out-of-wedlock pregnancies that occur in the United States are among females under 19 years of age. The high rates of reproductive wastage observed in this group make it imperative that society develop acceptable means to prevent the occurrence of the illegitimate teen-age pregnancy.

HIGH-RISK MOTHERS

Many studies have documented the existence of a relationship between a previous pregnancy wastage or complication and the probability of similar events in any subsequent pregnancy. The results of the British Perinatal Mortality Survey,[8] cited here because it involved such a large population, are similar to various other studies. Previous findings regarding age and parity have already been cited. The implications of past obstetrical history upon future pregnancies from that major study are as follows:

1. A history of abortion increases the patient's overall mortality risk by 50%. The increase was only 9.6% in nulliparae with one previous abortion, but rose with each parity and with each additional abortion.

2. A previous premature, liveborn infant doubled the overall risk to subsequent siblings.
3. Any previous stillbirth or neonatal death multiplied the overall risk 2.6 times for a subsequent child.
4. Marked increases in overall risk accompanied histories of toxemia, antepartum hemorrhage, or cesarean section. Even toxemia in a first pregnancy increased the overall risk of a second pregnancy by 39%.
5. On a national basis, cases with no prenatal care had five times the amount of overall mortality.

It is important to approach the "high risk" problem from a very broad standpoint. For example, work done by McCalister and others[21] indicates that the prevention of conception among only patients who have experienced infant or perinatal mortality has negligible effects on the subsequent number of deaths occurring in the total population. My point is that one must change the characteristics of women who are reproducing in the total population if we expect to decrease reproductive wastage.

MATERNAL HEALTH MAINTENANCE

Maternal health maintenance was included to emphasize the great need to promote health and to prevent illness. Adding family planning to existing maternal health services constitutes a prerequisite to fulfilling this task. Other significant benefits of family planning services include screening for cervical carcinoma, immunization procedures, and nutritional programs. In other words, family planning is an integral and vital part of maternal and family health care and is only one of many services that would considerably enhance the health of the family.

Illustrating the devastating cycle that lack of family planning forces upon a family are the Candelaria Studies of Cali, Columbia,[22] which might well describe many of the ghetto and slum areas in the United States.

MATERNAL HEALTH

A family facing a fertility period of approximately 30 years is severely penalized emotionally and economically if it is unable to control its fertility in a rational manner. Thus, it seems essential to *incorporate rationality concerning procreation* if a family is to preserve and promote its mental well-being. Much more objective data on this general topic is necessary and such a literature is emerging.[23,24]

SUMMARY

Regardless of its population policy, a nation must be concerned with the health of its mothers, children, and family units, and family planning is an essential part of its health services. Specifically, enhancement of health may be achieved if reproduction occurs under optimum conditions, which afford the highest probability of a successful outcome. Indications for the use of family planning as a means of achieving these optimum conditions are the following:

Age. Reproduction in women 20 to 30 years of age is associated with the lowest incidence of maternal mortality, perinatal mortality, and prematurity. Reproduction occurring at ages 16 and younger, or 35 and older, is associated with the highest rates of reproductive wastage and perinatal death.

Spacing. A spacing interval of at least 1 and preferably 2 years seems to be associated with a lower incidence of maternal, infant, perinatal mortality and infant prematurity. The combination of a very young mother, reproduction at short intervals, and high parity is especially associated with high morbidity and mortality.

Parity. A high incidence of perinatal and maternal mortality is associated with the first birth; and the rate for the second birth is lower, after which the incidence increases with each birth. Reproduction in women of parity five or more is associated with much higher mortality and morbidity regardless of the age of the mother.

Reproductive history. Any patient with a history of either an infant death, stillbirth, premature infant, toxemia, child with a con-

genital defect transmitted through a dominant pattern, severe obstetrical complication, abortion, or any other medical condition that increases the risk of pregnancy to mother or child should be carefully appraised in relation to her need for both family planning and special care. In some instances, family planning offers a medical alternative of choice to the patient.

Optimum emotional conditions. Accumulated clinical experience indicates that the mental health of the mother, child, and family unit seem to be enhanced when pregnancy occurs under optimal emotional conditions, that is, when the pregnancy is desired by both parents and when the child is conceived after consideration of the welfare of both existing and potential children.

Abortion prevention. The successful practice of family planning reduces or eliminates the need to resort to induced abortion, which may be injurious to or cause the death of the mother. If induced abortion constitutes a major health problem, family planning is a necessary solution to that problem.

CONCLUSIONS

Family planning has been shown to be a scientific, important health measure, a necessity to the reduction of infant, perinatal, and maternal mortality, and an essential to the management of many family health problems. In addition, it offers subjective and emotional benefits supportive to family health and fulfillment. Because family planning is a sound medical practice, *any family health, maternal and child health, or national health program that fails to include family planning is medically inadequate* and cannot be expected to achieve the maximally possible reductions in the following:

Perinatal mortality
Infant mortality
Maternal mortality
Complications of induced abortion
Prematurity

Any physician who fails to consider family planning in his management of clinical situations exhibiting these specific medical needs is negligent. Any physician who, for any reason, is unable to include this aspect of medicine in his patient management should refer the patient to another physician for such management.

Regardless of the population policy of any given nation, family planning should be included in the medical services and in the national health plan. For instance, a nation wishing to increase its population could achieve an equivalent gain within an alloted time period and simultaneously improve greatly the quality of its national reproduction while improving and sustaining the health of its reproducing women.

REFERENCES

1. Westoff, C. F., and Ryder, N. B.: United States: Methods of fertility control, 1955, 1960, 1965, Studies in Family Planning 1(17):1-5, 1967.
2. Lindsay, G. N., Varky, G., Jaffe, F., Polgar, S., and Lincoln, R.: Five million women, New York, 1967, Planned Parenthood Publication No. 940, p. 10, 1967.
3. Beasley, J. D., and Harter, C. L.: Attitudes and knowledge relevant to family planning among New Orleans Negro women, Amer. J. Public Health 56:847-57, 1966.
4. Beasley, J. D., and Parrish, V. W., Jr.: A progress report on a Southern rural family planning research program conducted in Lincoln Parish, Louisiana, Advances in planned parenthood, Amsterdam, 1968, Excerpta Medica Foundation, vol. III, pp. 29-36.
5. Davis, K.: Population policy: Will current programs succeed? Science 158:730-739, 1967.
6. U. S. population growth 1960-2000, Washington, D. C., 1964, Population Reference Bureau, Inc.
7. Beasley, J. D.: The United States: The Orleans Parish Family Planning Demonstration Program, Studies in family planning 1(25): 5-9, 1967.
8. Butler, N. R., and Bonham, D. G., Perinatal mortality, London, 1963, E. S. Livingstone, Ltd.
9. Obstetrical Statistical Cooperative combined report, 1961, Brooklyn, 1961, Obstetrical Statistical Cooperative.
10. Heady, J. A., and Morris, J. N.: Variation of mortality with mother's age and parity, J. Obstet. Gynec. Brit. Empire 66:577-593, 1959.
11. Newcomb, H. B., and Travendale, O. G.: Maternal age and British order correlations, mutational from environmental components, Mutat. Res. 1:446-467, 1964.
12. Day, R. L.: The influence of number of children, interval between pregnancies, and age of parents upon survival of the offspring, Advances in planned parenthood, New York, 1967, Excerpta Medical Foundation, vol. II, pp. 23-31.
13. Eastman, N. J.: The effect of the interval between births on maternal and fetal outlook Amer. J. Obstet. Gynec. 47:445-466, 1944.
14. Woodbury, R. W.: Causal factors in infant mortality, a statistical study based on investigations in eight cities, Children's Bureau Publication No. 141, Washington, D. C., 1925, U. S. Government Publishing Office.
15. Yerushalmy, J.: On the interval between successive births and its effect on survival of infants, Hum. Biol. 17:65-106, 1945.
16. Bishop, E.: Prematurity, etiology and management, Postgrad. Med. 35:185-188, 1964.
17. Berelson, B.: National family planning programs: A guide, Studies in Family Planning 1(5s):1-12, 1964.
18. Guttmacher, A. F.: Induced abortion, N.Y. State J. Med. 63:2334, 1963.
19. Pakter, J., Rosner, H. J., Jacobziner, H., and Greenstein, F.: Out of wedlock births in New York City, Amer. J. Public Health 51:846-865, 1961.
20. Louisiana State vital statistical report for 1966, Baton Rouge, 1966, Louisiana State Health Department.
21. McCalister, D. V., Hawkins, C. M., and Beasley, J. D.: Projected effects of family planning on the incidence of perinatal mortality in a lower class non-white population, Amer. J. Obstet. Gynec. 106:573-580, 1971.
22. Aquirre, A.: Columbia: The family in Candelaria, Studies in Family Planning 1(11):1-5, 1966.
23. Pasamanick, B., and Lilienfield, A. M.: The association of maternal and fetal factors in the development of mental deficiency. II. Relationship to maternal age, birth order, previous reproductive loss, and degree of mental deficiency, Amer. J. Ment. Defic. 60:556, 1955-56.
24. Lieberman, J. J.: Preventive psychiatry and family planning, J. Marriage Family 26:471-477, 1964.

7 The role of family planning in the primary prevention of mental illness

Richard A. Schwartz, M.D.

It . . . would be one of the greatest triumphs of mankind, one of the most tangible liberations from the bondage of nature to which we are subject, were it possible to raise the responsible act of procreation to the level of a voluntary and intentional act, and to free it from its entanglement with an indispensable satisfaction of a natural desire(8).

—Sigmund Freud

Primary prevention of mental illness has been an elusive goal in modern psychiatric history. During the first half of this century, much effort was invested in developing child guidance clinics and programs of mental health education in the hope that these techniques would prevent mental illness. The Joint Commission on Mental Illness and Health, in reviewing this 50-year period in preventive psychiatry, was unable to find evidence that the incidence of mental illness has been significantly influenced by these measures. The report of the Joint Commission concluded: "Primary prevention of mental illness has remained largely an article of scientific faith, rather than an applicable scientific truth"(15).

Despite this pessimistic assessment by the Joint Commission, there has been in recent

Dr. Schwartz is clinical director, Fairhill Mental Health Center, 12200 Fairhill Rd., Cleveland, Ohio, 44120, and clinical instructor, Department of Psychiatry, Case Western Reserve University School of Medicine, Cleveland, Ohio.

Reprinted from *American Journal of Psychiatry* 125:1711-1718, 1969. Copyright 1969, the American Psychiatric Association.

years a growing interest in developing new methods of primary prevention of mental illness. Among these are imaginative programs of mental health consultation, efforts to impart mental health skills to community "caretakers" (e.g., teachers, clergy, public health nurses, and parole officers), and programs designed to help certain "high-risk" subgroups of the population cope better with life crises(2, 4, 35). Since these programs are of recent origin and have been tried only on a limited scale, it is too early to tell whether they will prove successful in achieving a reduction in the incidence of mental illness.

A potentially useful addition to the growing array of preventive psychiatry techniques, to be examined in this article, is the inclusion of family planning services in ongoing mental health programs. Although proponents of family planning have long emphasized mental health considerations as important aspects of the rationale for family planning programs, psychiatrists, with few exceptions(21, 23), have not shown a corresponding interest in family planning. The role of unregulated fertility in the etiology of mental illness and the possible application of family planning concepts in preventive psychiatry are subjects about which little has appeared in the psychiatric literature.

In this article I explore some of these interrelationships. The first section covers pertinent research from the fields of fertility and population dynamics and presents evidence that uncontrolled fertility is an important contributing cause of mental illness. In the second section I discuss the current status of family planning programs in the United States, pointing out the existence of a large unmet need for such services. Finally, I discuss ways that mental hospitals, clinics, and community mental health centers can incorporate family planning services into their programs without excessive expense or disruption of normal activities.

UNCONTROLLED FERTILITY AND THE ETIOLOGY OF MENTAL ILLNESS

Among the possible consequences of uncontrolled fertility are the following: the birth of unwanted and unloved children, illegitimacy, premarital pregnancy, intensification and perpetuation of poverty, postpartum psychosis, and excessive population growth. Each of these areas will be examined in further detail and its relationship to mental health discussed.

The unwanted child

The viewpoint that the unwanted child is less likely to receive adequate parental love and acceptance, thereby suffering increased vulnerability to mental illness, has been eloquently expressed by Karl Menninger:

> The reason that contraceptive knowledge and counsel seem to the psychiatrist to be essential is based not upon considerations of the welfare of the adult, but on the considerations of the welfare of the child. Nothing is more tragic, more fateful in its ultimate consequences, than the realization by a child that he was unwanted. . . . planned parenthood is an essential element in any program for increased mental health and for human peace and happiness. The unwanted child becomes the undesirable citizen, the willing cannon-fodder for wars of hate and prejudice(23).

I have encountered no writings that seriously dispute these sentiments, indicating that most people today are willing to accept them as self-evident truths requiring no scientific proof. The relationship between wanted versus unwanted status and life outcome has never been systematically investigated. In fact, as Pohlman has pointed out,

the difficulties of retrospective or prospective research into this problem are considerable; the mother may repress, deny, or conceal her true feelings about a given child either before or after childbirth; her feelings may be ambivalent, changing at different stages of the pregnancy or child-rearing process; and in certain subgroups, such as the poor, the very concepts of "planning" or "wanting" a child may lack meaning(28).

Recent studies of the relationship between birth order, family size, and mental illness provide perhaps the closest scientific documentation of the hypothesis that the unwanted child has a greater chance of developing mental illness. Studies by Schooler (39, 40), Gregory(9, 10), Barry and Barry (1), and Farina and associates(6), analyzing large groups of psychiatric patients with varying diagnoses, show that in families with four or more children the children in the last half of the birth order were significantly more likely to develop mental illness than children in the first half of the birth order. In one of Schooler's studies, it was further shown that compared to first-born *patients,* last-born patients were sicker, showed a lower degree of social competence, and a higher incidence of bizarre and self-destructive behavior(40).

None of these investigators was able, on the basis of evidence obtained, to explain fully the relationships observed. The most likely explanation to emerge was that the later born children in large families are more likely to have been unwanted and unplanned and are therefore less likely to be given adequate care and affection. In support of this hypothesis, a large-scale demographic survey has demonstrated that the larger the family, the greater the likelihood that the last-born child was unwanted. Whereas 11 percent of parents with two children said that their last-born child was unwanted, the rates went up to 28 percent for parents with three children, 41 percent for parents with four children, 45 percent for parents with five children, and 47 percent for parents with six children(41). This same study further revealed that 17 percent of *all* families in the United States reported that their last-born child was unwanted.

Illegitimacy

The psychological hazards of being an unwanted child are compounded if the child is also illegitimate, due to the social stigma attached to illegitimacy in our society. The rate of illegitimacy is on the increase. There were, in 1965, 291,000 illegitimate births in the United States as compared to 250,000 in 1962 and 150,000 in 1952(13). In 1950 one out of 25 children born in the United States was illegitimate. By 1960 the figure was one out of 19, and by 1965, one out of 15(36).

Adoption affords an opportunity for many illegitimate children to be reared in a stable two-parent family. The question of whether adopted children are more prone to develop psychiatric difficulties remains unsettled at the present time. Several reports in the literature indicate that adopted children may suffer from psychiatric difficulties at a rate up to 100 times higher than that of the general population(38). These studies, however, have been challenged as methodologically unsound in a recent paper by Kirk and associates(17).

Whatever the merits of adoption as a "solution" for illegitimacy, it should be recognized that only one-half of illegitimate children eventually are adopted. Of the remainder many are nonwhite and are not adopted because of a shortage of nonwhite adoptive parents and/or disinclination to give up children for adoption within the nonwhite subculture. Many illegitimate children are reared in foster homes because the natural mother, although unable to care for the child herself, is nevertheless unwilling to release the child for adoption. Between 33 and 60 percent of children reared in foster homes have been found to be suffering from severe emotional difficulties, according to one large survey(22).

Premarital pregnancy

It has been shown that illegitimate *births* represent only a small fraction of the total number of illegitimate or premarital *pregnancies*. By correlating data from marriage and birth certificates, Christensen found that between 20 and 25 percent of all couples were expecting a child at the time of marriage(5). In a Detroit study, Pratt found that 25 percent of white and 52 percent of nonwhite women were pregnant at the time of marriage(29). The younger the age at marriage, the more likely the chances of premarital pregnancy. When the husband was under 20 years of age and the wife under 18, 60 percent of white women and 82 percent of nonwhite women were premaritally pregnant. A retrospective study of birth and marriage certificates by Rele showed that there has been a gradual rise in the past 50 years in the rate of premarital pregnancy, from 74 per 1,000 married women in 1905, to 83 in 1920, 90 in 1930, 119 in 1950, and 160 in 1959(34).

From the mental health point of view these statistics show the existence of a serious and largely unrecognized problem. A great many young people, between one-fourth and one-fifth of our entire population, are being forced into early marriages with partners they may not have wished to marry. It does not seem unreasonable to assume that had many of these young people been able to wait until they felt ready for marriage, completed their education, and been able to choose their partners freely their chances for personal happiness and for becoming good parents might be greatly increased.

Not unexpectedly, the rates of divorce are higher than average among couples in which the wife is pregnant before marriage. In one survey, for example, 4.9 percent of all sample marriages ended in divorce, but 13 percent of couples who had their first child within the first *nine* months of marriage were later divorced, and 17.2 percent of the couples who had their first child within the first *six* months of marriage were later divorced(5).

Poverty

Since the "rediscovery" of poverty in the late 1950s by Harrington(11) and others, statistics on poverty in the United States have become well known. In 1962 there were 35 million people whose annual incomes were less than $3,000 for families and $1,500 for unattached individuals(16). These totals include 15 million children (26). Epidemiological studies(12) have documented a higher than average rate of mental illness, particularly psychosis, among poor people, which would suggest that poverty may be an important contributing cause of mental illness. Child-rearing practices among the very poor are frequently characterized by neglect, lack of affection, brutality, and inconsistency. Children raised under these conditions are often unable to learn in school, grow up without job skills, and thus perpetuate the poverty cycle(27, 33).

A small subgroup of the poor, the so-called multiproblem family, has been singled out for special scrutiny. In a St. Paul study (3) it was found that the multiproblem group, consisting of but six percent of the community's families, absorbed more than 77 percent of the relief load, 51 percent of health services, and 56 percent of adjustment services in mental health, casework, and corrections.

One of the conditions perpetuating poverty in this country is the lack of birth control services available to the poor, with the result that the poorest, least educated persons tend to have the most children. In 1962 one-half of all families with annual incomes of less than $3,000 had four or more children, whereas only one-fourth of the families with incomes in excess of $10,000 had four or more children(24). Poor families not only have larger families but more *unwanted* children: the last-born child was unwanted in 21 percent of families earning

less than $3,000 per year, as compared with only 15 percent of families earning in excess of $10,000 per year. For women with grade school educations, the figure was 32 percent, as compared with only 11 percent for college educated women(41).

Postpartum psychosis

According to Kummer, two percent of all females admitted to United States mental hospitals during the period 1916-1946 were suffering from antepartum and postpartum psychosis(19). That the higher than expected incidence of mental hospitalization associated with childbirth is more than a statistical artifact, reflecting delayed admissions of patients who had become ill *during* pregnancy, has been shown. By comparing rates of admission during the total childbearing period (pregnancy plus three months after childbirth) with expected admission rates for women in general, Pugh and associates (30) were able to show that admission rates for psychosis in the childbearing period ranged from one and one-half to two and one-half times higher than expected in the various age groups studied.

There has been no study undertaken yet to determine the frequency of unwanted conceptions among patients with postpartum psychosis. One would expect that a positive correlation would be found, in view of the tendency for most people to avoid situations they anticipate will be overwhelmingly stressful. Clinically evident postpartum psychosis can be regarded as similar to the exposed portion of an iceberg, the submerged part representing the extensive numbers of women who are overburdened by too many or poorly spaced children and whose health, efficiency, and maternal capacity is impaired to a significant, if subclinical, degree.

Excessive population growth

The term "population explosion" usually refers to conditions in the underdeveloped part of the world, where excessive population growth has negated all efforts to increase living standards. Here in the United States, the rate of population growth has also been high, but because the standard of living has continuously risen and because our resources are so abundant we have been able to absorb these increases in population relatively painlessly. In recent years, however, as air and water have become more polluted and as water shortages have developed in several parts of the country, it has become apparent that there are limits, even in the United States, to the capacity of the natural environment to support an expanding population.

The population of the United States has increased sixfold in the one hundred years 1860-1960, from 31 million to 179 million. The population increased by 19 million in the decade 1940-1950, by 28 million in 1950-1960, and by another 17.5 million from 1960-1966. This rate of population growth, coupled with inadequate community planning, is threatening our standard of living and national well-being.

Air and water pollution have been mentioned as problem areas. Others include overly congested urban areas without adequate transportation, housing, or schools, continuous traffic jams on the highways, suburban sprawl, overcrowded parks and recreational areas, and severe shortages in such vital public services as medical care and education. While no one can say what the ideal population size of the United States should be, the prospect of our population doubling by the year 2010 (the projected estimate if the current rate of growth continues) is one that most authorities agree poses a severe threat to the nation's physical and emotional health and well-being.

CURRENT STATUS OF FAMILY PLANNING PROGRAMS IN THE UNITED STATES

Much attention and publicity has been given recently to the "revolution" in contraception brought about by the introduction of the oral pill and the intrauterine device. As

of January 1966 an estimated 3,815,000 women were using oral contraception(37). This publicity has obscured the fact that large segments of the population, particularly the poor, continue to be without adequate family planning services. A recent survey by the Planned Parenthood Federation has shown that of five million medically indigent fertile women who are not pregnant or seeking pregnancy only one-half million, or ten percent, are currently being serviced by all government and private family planning services combined(14).

Another study showed that as many as 46 percent of women in some lower income groups have never had a discussion with any professional person about family planning (32). Lack of family planning services for the poor is part and parcel of the over-all pattern of substandard medical services in poverty areas. The existing system of publicly financed medical care is inadequately staffed and financed and tends to be concentrated in large, impersonal, and often inconveniently located hospitals. These hospitals are geared to handling acute illness and are poorly equipped to deliver prevention-oriented medical services of any kind.

Although there are some 700 state and local government-supported birth control clinics in 35 states, they serve only 200,000 women per year, a small fraction of the total medically indigent population(20). On the federal level, one million dollars has been made available for family planning programs through the Department of Health, Education, and Welfare and the Office of Economic Opportunity. It has been calculated that in order to provide services for the estimated five million medically indigent women a sum of *one hundred million* dollars per year is needed. Current federal programs come nowhere near that amount.

The problems of negative attitude and inadequate motivation for family planning among the poor have received considerable study. Rainwater(31) has noted that the poor tend to be pessimistic regarding their ability to control their destiny. They tend to regard themselves as being at the mercy of powerful forces beyond their influence. As a result, they tend to accept events as they happen and to show little faith that any sort of planning can appreciably affect their lives. Although they may wish for small families, they seem unable to make a sustained effort toward this goal. Rainwater has also observed that the poor tend to rely on magical thinking with respect to contraception. When they practice contraception they often feel that, as long as they are careful *most* of the time, they will be rewarded by fate for having good intentions.

Although these motivational problems are real, it has been amply demonstrated that lack of motivation can be successfully overcome in the great majority of women from even the poorest class by a well-conceived and well-administered birth control program. In a large Planned Parenthood study in Chicago, in which 14,000 women were given birth control pills, it was found that 75 percent continued to take the pill regularly for 30 months after they first came to the clinic (7). In this group 83 percent were nonwhite, one-half had not completed high school, and one out of six were welfare recipients. As a practical matter the problem of motivation has probably received undue attention and certainly should not be used as an argument to justify society's failure to provide adequate family planning services for the poor.

FAMILY PLANNING PROGRAMS IN PSYCHIATRIC TREATMENT CENTERS

In the long run, overcoming deficiencies in family planning services for the poor will ultimately depend upon increasing the supply of doctors and other trained medical personnel, locating clinics in poverty areas, increasing the purchasing power and educational level of the poor, and improving the technology of contraception. Meanwhile, there is a serious unmet need for family planning services which mental health agencies may be able to alleviate.

According to statistics collected by the Department of Health, Education, and Welfare, there are approximately 412,745 women patients of childbearing age treated in the psychiatric hospitals and clinics of this nation each year(18, 25). No attempt has yet been made to determine how many of these women are using contraception, desire to use contraception, or are well informed about contraception. However, it is known that 78 percent of all patients under psychiatric care (at least in New Haven, Conn.) are from social classes IV and V, the segment of the population with least likelihood of access to birth control(12). For many of these women, their psychiatric treatment may provide them with their only meaningful medical contact of any kind for long intervals of time and thus afford an opportunity for the initiation of birth control assistance. Even more affluent women psychiatric patients may be in need of guidance and information about birth control, especially if psychological handicaps have interfered with their learning about and obtaining contraceptive assistance.

There are many kinds of services and functions needed in a comprehensive family planning program. These include case-finding, education and information services, counseling and psychotherapy, referral to family planning centers, direct contraceptive service, and programs aimed at increasing community support for family planning. Certain of these functions, such as prescription of birth control pills and insertion of intrauterine devices, require the services of general practitioners or gynecological specialists and, as such, cannot be readily performed by psychiatric personnel. Other functions can be carried out by mental health facilities with minimal expenditure of time and effort and without significant disruption of normal routine.

Case-finding is perhaps the most useful function that mental health professionals can perform in family planning. It requires only that doctors, nurses, and social workers be alert to the possibility of unmet needs for birth control assistance in the patients they come in contact with every day and that they be willing to initiate discussion of this subject if it appears necessary. As long as the subject is broached in a tactful manner there is little likelihood of offending or upsetting the patient should she prove to be uninterested or resistant to the idea of birth control. Although patients are often too embarrassed by their lack of knowledge about birth control or too apathetic or depressed to be able to inquire about it on their own initiative, they are often grateful for a chance to discuss the subject once it has been raised. An aid to case-finding that can be employed is the use of posters and leaflets describing family planning services and facilities in waiting rooms, on hospital bulletin boards, etc. These materials can readily be obtained from local Planned Parenthood agencies.

Providing education and information about the existence and location of family planning clinics, the types of birth control techniques, and their relative effectiveness, limitations, and cost is another useful function that mental health personnel can perform. The degree of ignorance and misinformation about birth control, especially among the poor, is startling, Areas of ignorance and misinformation commonly encountered in patients are: highly exaggerated notions about the dangers of birth control pills, unawareness of the existence of the intrauterine device, the belief that foams and jellies are a highly effective form of contraception, unawareness of the existence of low-cost or free services in the community, and the belief that doctors are, on principle, unwilling to provide contraceptives without a definite health justification.

Needless to say, failure to become adequately informed about birth control methods or to follow through and implement a wish for family planning may be one expression of the illness for which the patient originally sought treatment. It requires initiative and sustained effort to successfully practice family planning(42). Regressed psychiatric patients have difficulties in performing adequately in this area, as in other areas of their lives. Many patients often require psychotherapy and other treatment before they can seek out and make effective use of family planning services.

Although most communities have some type of family planning clinic available to which psychiatric patients can be referred for direct services, some communities, especially in rural areas, may lack such facilities. Psychiatric institutions in these areas (such as state hospitals) may wish to set up programs for direct contraceptive services. This could be accomplished by setting aside one or two hours each week for a birth control clinic under the supervision of staff physicians or consultants from the outside community or by referral to outside private physicians. State departments of mental health may wish to consider assuming the cost of contraceptives for indigent patients, as is done in the case of tranquilizers. Such expenditures might conceivably save the state considerable sums in the long run.

On the level of community action, psychiatric organizations such as the American Psychiatric Association and its district branches can perform a useful role in helping to educate the public about the need for greatly expanded, publicly financed family planning services.

REFERENCES

1. Barry, H., III, and Barry, H., Jr.: Birth Order, Family Size and Schizophrenia, Arch. Gen. Psychiat. 17:435-440, 1967.
2. Bolman, W. M., and Westman, J. C.: Prevention of Mental Disorder: An Overview of Current Programs, Amer. J. Psychiat. 123:1058-1068, 1967.
3. Buell, B.: Preventing and Controlling Disordered Behavior, Ment. Hyg. 39:365-375, 1955.
4. Caplan, G.: Principles of Preventive Psychiatry. New York: Basic Books, 1964.
5. Christensen, H. T.: Child Spacing Analysis via Record Linkage: New Data Plus a Summing Up from Earlier Reports, Marriage and Family Living 25:272-280, 1963.
6. Farina, A., Barry, H., III, and Garmezy, N.:

Birth Order of Recovered and Nonrecovered Schizophrenics, Arch. Gen. Psychiat. 9:224-228, 1963.

7. Frank, R., and Tietze, C.: Acceptance of an Oral Contraceptive Program in a Large Metropolitan Area, Amer. J. Obstet. Gynec. 93:122-127, 1965.

8. Freud, S.: "Sexuality and the Aetiology of the Neuroses," in Collected Papers, vol. 1. New York: Basic Books, 1959, p. 238.

9. Gregory, I.: An Analysis of Familial Data on Psychiatric Patients: Parental Age, Family Size, Birth Order, and Ordinal Position, Brit. J. Prev. Soc. Med. 12:42-59, 1958.

10. Gregory, I.: Family Data Concerning the Hypothesis of Hereditary Predisposition Toward Alcoholism, J. Ment. Sci. 106:1068-1072, 1960.

11. Harrington, M.: The Other America. Baltimore: Penguin Books, 1963.

12. Hollingshead, A. B., and Redlich, F. C.: Social Class and Mental Illness. New York: John Wiley & Sons, 1958.

13. Isaac, R. J.: Adopting a Child Today. New York: Harper & Row, 1965.

14. Jaffe, F. S.: Financing Family Planning Services, Amer. J. Public Health 56:912-917, 1966.

15. Joint Commission on Mental Illness and Health: Action for Mental Health, New York: Science Editions, 1961, p. 70.

16. Keyserling, L. H.: "Key Questions on the Poverty Problem," in Dunne, G. H., ed.: Poverty in Plenty. New York: P. J. Kenedy & Sons, 1964.

17. Kirk, H. D., Jonassohn, K., and Fish, A. D.: Are Adopted Children Especially Vulnerable to Stress? Arch. Gen. Psychiat. 14:291-298, 1966.

18. Kramer, M.: Some Implications of Trends in the Usage of Psychiatric Facilities for Community Mental Health Programs and Related Research. Public Health Service publication no. 1434, 1966.

19. Kummer, J.: Post-Abortion Psychiatric Illness —A Myth? Amer. J. Psychiat. 119:980-983, 1963.

20. Langer, E.: Birth Control: U. S. Programs Off to Slow Start, Science 156:765-767, 1967.

21. Lieberman, E. J.: Preventive Psychiatry and Family Planning, J. Marriage and the Family 26:471-477, 1964.

22. Maas, H. S., and Engler, R. E.: Children in Need of Parents. New York: Columbia University Press, 1959.

23. Menninger, K.: "Psychiatric Aspects of Contraception," in Rosen, H., ed.: Therapeutic Abortion. New York: Julian Press, 1954.

24. Nortman, D. L.: The Population Problem. New York: National Educational Television, 1965.

25. Office of Biometry, National Institute of Mental Health: Outpatient psychiatric clinics, 1964, Annual Statistical Report, 1966.

26. Orshansky, M.: Counting the Poor: Another Look at the Poverty Profile, Social Security Bulletin 28:3-29, 1965.

27. Pavenstedt, E.: A Comparison of the Child-Rearing Environment of the Upper-Lower and Very-Low-Lower Class Families, Amer. J. Orthopsychiat. 35:89-98, 1965.

28. Pohlman, E.: "Wanted" and "Unwanted": Toward Less Ambiguous Definition. Eugen. Quart. 12:19-27, 1965.

29. Pratt, W. F.: Premarital Pregnancy in a Metropolitan Community, read at a meeting of the Population Association of America, Chicago, Ill., April 23-24, 1965.

30. Pugh, T. F., Jerath, B. K., Schmidt, W. M., and Reed, R. B.: Rates of Mental Disease Related to Childbearing, New Eng. J. Med. 268:1224-1228, 1963.

31. Rainwater, L.: And the Poor Get Children. Chicago: Quadrangle Books, 1960.

32. Rainwater, L.: Family Design. Chicago: Aldine Publishing Co., 1965.

33. Rainwater, L.: Crucible of Identity: The Negro Lower-Class Family, Daedalus 95:(1) 172-216, 1966.

34. Rele, J. R.: Some Correlates of the Age at Marriage, Eugen. Quart. 43:1-6, 1965.

35. Riessman, F., and Hallowitz, E.: The Neighborhood Service Center: An Innovation in Preventive Psychiatry, Amer. J. Psychiat. 123:1408-1413, 1967.

36. Rise Is Reported in Illegitimacy, New York Times, October 29, 1967, p. 36.

37. Ryder, N. B., and Westoff, C. F.: Use of Oral Contraception in the United States, 1965, Science 153:1199-1205, 1966.

38. Schechter, M. D.: Observations on Adopted Children, Arch. Gen. Psychiat. 3:21-32, 1960.

39. Schooler, C.: Birth Order and Schizophrenia, Arch. Gen. Psychiat. 4:91-97, 1961.

40. Schooler, C.: Birth Order and Hospitalization for Schizophrenia, J. Abnorm. Soc. Psychol. 69:574-579, 1964.

41. Whelpton, P. K., Campbell, A. A., and Petterson, J.: Fertility and Family Planning in the United States. Princeton, N. J.: Princeton University Press, 1966.

42. Ziegler, F. J., Rodgers, D. A., Kriegsman, S. A., and Martin, P. L.: Ovulation Suppressors, Psychological Functioning and Marital Adjustment, J.A.M.A. 204:849-853, 1968.

8 United States, underdeveloped land in family planning

Lynn Landman*

On the question of birth control, the United States is itself a backward country and ought to be labeled as such.[1]

That this harsh description is apt is all too easily demonstrated.

An estimated 5,300,000 American women aged 18 to 44—poor and medically indigent women—need subsidized family-planning services.[2] Seven out of eight of them, however, are now denied the fundamental human right, to say nothing of health right, to plan their families; to decide whether, when, and how many children to have.

The consequences of this denial are not unlike the consequences in developing countries: A shockingly high infant mortality rate, at least in part traceable to the milieu into which poor children are born;[3] a disproportionately high maternal mortality rate, ascribable in large measure to an unplanned and uncontrolled maternity cycle, that is, pregnancies begun when mothers are physiologically too young, pregnancies coming too close together, and pregnancies continuing to a point in time when the mothers are physiologically less efficient;[4] increasing resort to illegal abortion as a desperate means of controlling family size; perpetuation of poverty, with its disastrous social consequences in terms of overcrowded cities, inadequate schools, expanding slums, increasing crime rates, to name just a few.

Evidence is mounting that mental retardation, too, is a hazard encountered roughly twice as often among the children of the poor as among middle- and upper-class chil-

---

*Lynn Landman, B.A., is Editor of Women's Medical News Service, 3 West 57th Street, New York 10019. This news service provides daily and weekly newspapers with features and a regular column dealing with women's health and emphasizing family planning in all its aspects. It is a public service supported by G. D. Searle & Co., developers of the first oral contraceptive.

A journalist for 20 years, Mrs. Landman has lived in various parts of the Far East, including India on a Ford Foundation grant and China as a foreign correspondent. She is coauthor of *Profile of Red China,* New York: Simon and Schuster, 1951.

[1]Spurgeon F. Kenny, M.D., "Champion of Birth Control," *Life* (October 6, 1967), p. 48.

[2]*Five Million People,* study issued by Planned Parenthood-World Population, October 18, 1967, and based on a special tabulation by the U.S. Census Bureau of the characteristics of 35,000 women, aged 18-44, living in poverty in March, 1966; Arthur A. Campbell, "Family Planning and the Reduction of Poverty in the United States," using a different measure, estimates that some 4,600,000 women in this category need subsidized family-planning services. The paper is published as Attachment A in the report, *Implementing DHEW Policy on Family Planning and Population,* June 30, 1967, p. 20.

Reprinted from *Journal of Marriage and the Family* 30(2):191-201, May, 1968. Copyright National Council on Family Relations.

[3]Earl E. Huyck, Ph.D., "Highlights of White-Nonwhite Differentials," *Health, Welfare, and Education Indicators,* February-October, 1965, p. iv; Edwin M. Gold, M.D., "Views on Family Planning—Health," *Regional Conference on Family Planning (Region II),* U.S. Department of Health, Education, and Welfare, December, 1966, p. 14.

[4]Richard L. Day, M.D., "Factors Influencing Offspring," *American Journal of Disabled Children,* Vol. 113 (February, 1967), pp. 179-185; Alexander Kessler, M.D., Ph.D., "Maternal Health and Infant Mortality," paper delivered April 11, 1967, at Eighth Conference of the International Planned Parenthood Federation, Santiago, Chile.

dren. Experts maintain that adequate medical care, of which family planning is an important component, could reduce the incidence of mental retardation among the poor.[5]

Perhaps the most tragic consequence of denying equal opportunity for family-planning information and services to the poor is the entrapment of huge numbers of poor children in the web of poverty, thus denying them an opportunity to develop their full potential as human beings, as creative, contributing members of American society.

For an eloquent discussion of preventive psychiatry and family planning, and the crucial role the family life expert could play in helping develop both stable individuals and stable families, one need only refer to the essay, "Preventive Psychiatry and Family Planning," by E. James Lieberman, M.D., that appeared in the November, 1964 issue of [the Journal of Marriage and the Family].

PROFILE OF THE POOR

An impressive body of sociological data confirms that the poor do want to plan their families.[6] They want even fewer children than their middle-class compatriots. Indeed, research has established that when economic differences between poor and middle-class are equalized, the former poor, particularly the non-white poor, prefer to have and indeed do have smaller families than white middle-class persons.[7]

Nonetheless the poor continue to be plagued by excess fertility, that soulless

euphemism for having more children than one wants. Does the trouble lie with the poor? Are they indeed so "hard core" that they are unreachable by the techniques now known to family-planning experts and social scientists? Or does the problem lie elsewhere—in the indifference of those in a position to make services available; in a low priority (or no priority) afforded family planning among those in responsible positions?

Answers will emerge, this writer believes, out of an examination of precisely who the 5,300,000 poor women are who need subsidized family-planning assistance, where they live, how much education they have, to what extent they are trying to make their own way, and an examination of the extent of services now available to them.

According to a landmark study released in mid-October, 1967,[8] a study which does much to destroy the stereotype of those needing subsidized health services, two-thirds of the 5,300,000 not now being reached live in the nation's cities. Of these, more than half live in the country's 110 largest Standard Metropolitan Areas with population of 250,000 persons or more. Only 7.5 percent live on farms.

Further, nearly 70 percent of the target group lives in or near areas officially designated as "poverty areas."

What this means is that the majority of the target population lives in areas where hospitals and other health facilities are found and where there are concentrations of trained medical and paramedical personnel, to say nothing of social and behavioral scientists.

WHITE MAJORITY

Contrary to general assumptions, seven out of ten women in the target group, or 3,695,000, are white. Three out of ten, or 1,585,000 are nonwhite.

---

[5]Joseph T. English, M.D., speech at regional meeting in Huntington, West Virginia, of American Association on Mental Deficiency.

[6]Particularly P. K. Whelpton *et al., Fertility and Family Planning in the U.S.,* Princeton, New Jersey: Princeton University Press, 1966; R. Freedman *et al., Family Planning, Sterility and Population Growth,* New York: McGraw-Hill, 1959; C. Westoff *et al., Family Growth in Metropolitan America,* Princeton, New Jersey: Princeton University Press, 1961.

[7]Cf. footnote 6.

[8]*Five Million People, op. cit.*

In the Census Bureau's Northeast, North Central, and Western regions, there are approximately four whites in the target group to each nonwhite; even in the 16 states of the Bureau's Southern region there are three whites to every two nonwhites.

Because nonwhites in the general population are disproportionately poor, however, more than half of all fertile nonwhite women not seeking pregnancy need subsidized family-planning help compared to one out of six white women.

SELF-SUPPORTING

Another stereotype shattered by this study is that those needing subsidized family-planning services are likely to be welfare recipients. The facts, however, show something quite different.

More than 4,500,000, or 86 percent, of the women needing this assistance live in families which support themselves. Although self-supporting, such families often do not have the resources for medical care in general, or for family planning in particular. Two-thirds of those needing subsidized family planning have less than 70¢ a day for food for each member of the family; the near-poor have less than 90¢ a day. In many communities free or low-cost clinics, public or voluntary, are not readily available or do not exist. As will be shown further on, many of the hospitals in which poor women deliver their babies do not provide family-planning services. Other state and local health facilities also frequently fail to do so.

Only 14 percent, or 750,000, live in families whose major source of income is from public welfare.

Not only are the vast majority of the families self-supporting, but nearly half the women in the target group work at least part of the year. Almost one in five is employed full time.

Mobile though most Americans are known to be, this particular population has roots in its communities. Seven out of eight of the women lived in the same county over

at least the preceding 12-month period. Two out of three did not move at all.

These women are also, for the most part, married. Three out of five are married and currently living with their husbands. One out of four is separated, widowed, or divorced. One in six is single.

MOSTLY LITERATE

Poor though they are, the target group of women is by no means illiterate.

Three-fourths have been to high school, and four out of ten are high-school graduates. One of ten has had some college education. Just over one of four has had only an elementary-school education. These are women, then, quite able to read booklets and instructions concerning family planning.

Most of this group is young. Almost 50 percent of them is between 18 an 29 years of age; under 19 percent is between 30 and 34 years. Just over 32 percent is 35 to 44 years old.

As previous studies have pointed out, however, they tend to have more children and to have them earlier and at closer intervals than middle-class couples. Age for age, their fertility is already higher than their middle-class sisters. One out of five of the 570,000 women in the target group aged 18-19 already has at least one child compared to one out of 12 non-poor women of this age. Similarly, almost one-sixth of the 2,600,000 poor women under 30 has four or more children compared to one out of 28 middle-class women.

Analysis of age-specifics shows that these poor women will have much larger completed families than they say they want if subsidized family-planning services are not made available to them.

The study further shows that the risk of poverty of these women will increase from 10 percent if they have one child to 47 percent if they have six children.

Some of the effects of family size were explored recently in a report made to the

Senate Subcommittee on Employment, Manpower, and Poverty.[9]

Many adults who today are counted as non-poor were born into poor families. Contrary to expectation, however, they did not remain poor:

> One of the several characteristics that differentiate between these adults and poor adults also born into poor families [is] the number of siblings their poor parents had.
>
> For one thing, among poor families with the same family income, per child resources will be greater in the smaller families, with resultant returns from such greater "investment." Apart from monetary resources, children with fewer brothers and sisters are able to receive greater attention time from parents. Children from smaller families . . . can take better advantage of learning situations in and out of school. Dropout rates in turn are lower among such children: they have more years of formal schooling. And, needless to say, greater education is associated with higher occupational status, higher income, and lower unemployment.
>
> Education is a major stepping stone out of poverty. . . . We know that unemployment rates, for example, among persons without a high school degree are the highest; among persons with a high school degree are the next highest, and among persons with a college degree unemployment rates are the lowest. We know that the greater the number of years of schooling, the greater the chances for gaining a higher status, higher income occupation. We know that education and income are positively correlated.
>
> But it is not very widely known that one of the factors that affects the amount of education one receives is the number of brothers and sisters in one's family. That is, educational achievement is partly explained by size of family.

The report called attention to a recent analysis of the educational achievement of 45,000,000 men (ages 20-64). The analysis shows that the rate of completion of high school is related to the number of brothers and sisters they had: 73 percent of those with no siblings completed high school; 60 percent of those with one to three siblings; and 39 percent of those with four or more.

> Even among groups with low income, a higher proportion of adult men with 12 or more years of schooling come from families with small numbers of children than from families with large numbers of children.
>
> The conclusive incontrovertible point in the statistical analysis is that the amount of a child's education is affected by the number of children in the family—at every age and every socioeconomic level (even with birth order considered.)
>
> For the purpose of seeking effective solutions to the problem of poverty in this country, the crucial point is that poor families today can increase the chances for greater education for their children (and thus reduce the odds for poverty of those children by the time they become adults) in direct proportion to their efforts to practice family planning. . . . It does make a difference in "life chances" for a child born into a poor family if he has many or few siblings.

CONTRACEPTIVE ACCEPTORS

What evidence is there that the target population described would, if offered family-planning services, accept them and become long-term contraceptors?

In addition to the now-familiar studies of Bogue of a poor southern rural Negro population,[10] and of Tietze and Frank of a poor urban (Chicago) population,[11] and of Maddox of a poor 100-percent white population in the heart of Appalachia,[12] and of numerous other such reports with which socio-

[9]Harold L. Sheppard, Ph.D., "Effects of Family Planning on Poverty in the United States," report prepared for U.S. Senate Subcommittee on Employment, Manpower, and Poverty of the Committee on Labor and Public Welfare, September, 1967. Also available in pamphlet form from the W. E. Upjohn Institute for Employment Research, 300 South Westnedge Avenue, Kalamazoo, Michigan 49007.

[10]Donald J. Bogue, Ph.D., "The Rural South Fertility Experiments," Community and Family Study Center, University of Chicago, 1965.

[11]Richard Frank, M.D., and Christopher Tietze, M.D., "Acceptance of an Oral Contraceptive Program in a Large Metropolitan Area," *American Journal of Obstetrics and Gynecology*, 93:1 (September 1, 1965), pp. 122-127.

[12]Paul Maddox, M.D., report at annual meeting of Planned Parenthood-World Population, October, 1964, and interview with staff member, Information Center on Population Problems, 1965.

logists and family life experts are familiar, there is new evidence of responses of communities heretofore assumed to be thoroughly unresponsive.

At a recent meeting, Joseph D. Beasley, M.D., Director of the Center for Population and Family Studies of Tulane University Medical School, described a $2,000,000 project designed to bring birth control to 23,000 poor women in New Orleans.[13] He reported that in the first three months the program served 1,500 patients. Eighty-five percent of them kept their birth-control appointments, and 95 percent of them made follow-up visits.

He told this writer that the same kind of response was elicited from women living far from an urban center, in a swampy, remote backwater area. Dr. Beasley emphasized that the project's early success disproved "the myth that poor men and women are not really interested in family planning services and won't use them even when they are offered."

"As a matter of fact," he noted, "the program shows that they will utilize family planning services if they are made aware of the existence of such services."

No elaborate motivational apparatus seems necessary, he emphasized, except perhaps for professionals involved in such programs. It is often they, the pretrained, who need to be taught, Dr. Beasley said, that long-held stereotypes are invalid; that dignity and humane treatment in a clinic are the birthright of the poor as they are of those more privileged; that ignorance is not stupidity. Nor is it necessary, he explained, to give a course in human reproduction and physiology prior to giving family-planning information and services. Dr. Beasley noted that even middle-class women often have an inadequate knowledge of these subjects, but this does not keep them from practicing family planning effectively.

There were no organized family-planning services in Louisiana when Dr. Beasley and his colleagues at Tulane initiated two small pilot studies in 1964 under a Children's Bureau grant, and birth-control clinics were considered illegal there. (On August, 1965, the governor approved a reinterpretation of criminal code which legalized family-planning clinics.)[14] "From the standpoint of family planning," Dr. Beasley commented wryly, "Louisiana was an underdeveloped land."

Working as a team with physicians, sociologists and other social scientists at the Population Center were able to use available demographic and health statistics, birth records, and census data to estimate the potential case load, the six major neighborhoods where the poor live, and to assign priorities for service to the poor. The physician told this writer that the social scientists were a key element in conceptualizing the design, defining the need, and planning specific elements of the program.

NEW YORK EXPERIENCE

From a different milieu, New York's Negro ghetto, Harlem, comes additional evidence of the responsiveness of the poor. Here is an excerpt from a report by D. P. Swartz, M.D., M.Sc., F.R.C.S.(C), F.A.C.O.G., *et al.,* describing the rapid expansion of contraceptive services as part of maternal health care in a large department (3,800 deliveries and 1,000 abortions per year) of a municipal hospital serving a largely nonwhite medically indigent population:[15]

The provision of birth control services to a public population as an essential part of obstetric and gynecological care in general, and of maternity care in particular, is a service which is used eagerly by indigent patients. Cer-

[13]Joseph D. Beasley, M.D., "Louisiana Family Planning Demonstration Program," speech, New York, October 18, 1967.

[14]Information and Education Department, Planned Parenthood-World Population.
[15]D. P. Swartz, M.D., M.Sc., FRCS(C), FACOG, *et al.,* "The Introduction of Contraception in an Urban Public Hospital," *American Journal of Obstetrics and Gynecology,* 97:2 (January 15, 1967), pp. 189-196.

tainly in the initial phases of such a program no unusual or complex methods of stimulating motivation are necessary.

More important than some recent emphasis upon these aspects of the problem are the traditional problems associated with the clinic delivery of medical care of any kind; namely, clinic hours, clinic staffing in quality and quantity of personnel, suitable space for patient instruction in newer methods in language understandable to the patient, free access to the clinic without complex reappointment arrangements, simplicity of drug dispensing without lengthy waiting in pharmacy lines, availability of competent and sympathetic assistance if complications develop in the use of a given method, easy transfer from one method to another if either partner finds one method unsuitable after trial, sound medical counseling about initial choice of method.

This is to emphasize that, if a medically sound and organizationally efficient service is made available to public patients, it is apparent that they will use the service in numbers that will tax the ability of public clinics to keep pace with the growth in clinic volume.

In this department, the volume has grown from its very small beginning registration of 207 new patients in 1963 to 1,943 new registrations and 7,248 total visits in 1965.

There are important dividends for the medical community, as well

As teachers in our specialty it is apparent that, as our clinic patients have an opportunity to discuss matters of conception control with us and with our residents-in-training, they are revealing problems of marital and sexual adjustment not often heard previously in public clinics.

Thus, a new opportunity and an important challenge are developing to learn and teach healthy principles of sex counseling. This will add another large dimension to a program which must be understood as part of a broad health service—not just the provision of one more kind of device or medication.

For those who really believe that the stable family unit is important to our culture, meeting these challenges will provide an opportunity to contribute in a very direct way toward improving marital harmony and happiness among the disadvantaged, as well as to reduce the problems of unwanted pregnancies.

New York City is virtually a laboratory demonstration of how much can be accomplished in a relatively short period of

time given energetic leadership, resourcefulness, innovative courage, and funds.

Until 1958 there was a ban on contraceptive prescription in New York's municipal hospitals.[16] Since the ban was lifted in that year, mainly as a result of a vigorous attack launched by physicians and supported by various community groups as well as the local press, all 14 municipal hospitals with obstetric services have instituted family-planning clinics, with heartening results. A significant proportion of the 40,000 women delivered at these institutions now receives contraceptive services, with results of great importance not only to the individual families concerned but to the community as a whole.

The chief of obstetrics and gynecology at one municipal hospital told this writer that admissions for treatment of complications arising from illegal abortions have declined from 1,175 in 1960 to 800 in 1966; deliveries have declined over a three-year period from 4,500 to 3,000; postpartum visits are up substantially.[17]

In another hospital a professor of obstetrics explained that there have been 1,100 fewer births in the two years since broad family-planning services have been made available, a drop of 14 percent. He estimates that some 3,700 new patients a year come for family-planning services.[18]

The drop in one year (1965) saved the city some $300,000 in welfare expenditures

---

[16]Louis M. Hellman, M.D., "The Relationship of Contraceptive Programs to Maternal and Child Health," unpublished paper made available to author.

[17]Interview by this author with Dr. Martin L. Stone, Director of Obstetrics and Gynecology, New York Medical College-Metropolitan Hospital Center. "Hostility Overcome by Proper Hospital Care," story released by Women's Medical News Service, June 29, 1967.

[18]Interview by staff member of Women's Medical News Service with Drs. Louis M. Hellman and Schuyler Kohl, Chief and Professor, respectively, Downstate Medical Center College of Medicine. "Quality of Life Improved by Clinic," story released by Women's Medical News Service, March 10, 1966.

alone, since about a third of the clinic's patients receive welfare assistance.

And the hospital saved about $80,000 in one year because there were 800 fewer deliveries. Attendance at the postpartum clinic rose too. Approximately 46 of every 100 women returned for the six-week examination before the advent of the family-planning clinic; after its establishment the figure rose to 60 out of 100. In most hospitals, establishing a family-planning clinic doubles postpartum returns.

It must be emphasized that this success is being achieved among the most impoverished of the 5,300,000 women needing subsidized family-planning services. They are the ones with largely elementary-school education. They are the Negro and Puerto Rican poor, those of whom discriminatory practices have taken their largest toll in terms of poor education, poor housing, poor job opportunities, poor health.

This population has the highest newborn mortality rate in the city, the highest prematurity incidence, the second highest incidence of late or no prenatal care, and an infant mortality rate two to four times higher than that of the country as a whole.[19]

And yet this population is highly motivated enough to flock to the clinics from every part of the sprawling boroughs. They are able, willing, and eager users of the newest birth control methods—oral contraceptives and intra-uterine contraceptive devices —as well as the traditional ones, where indicated. "Our chief problem is lack of space and personnel," one physician told us, "not lack of interest on the part of the patients."

Within a relatively short period (the last five years) since the expansion of subsidized family-planning clinics in New York City occurred—there are now 72 such facilities— about half the target population of 200,000 has been reached.[20]

A recent analysis emphasized:[21]

It is significant that this growth has been accomplished with only minor attention to educational activities. Most of the hospitals confine their efforts to lectures and dissemination within the hospital about the availability of service. . . . The primary information mechanism is word-of-mouth communication.

The remarkable aspect of the New York City record, therefore, is that approximately half the indicated population has been enrolled by programs which have been fundamentally understaffed, underfinanced and uncoordinated.

This provides impressive confirmation that the single most strategic decision is to establish free or subsidized services which are geographically accessible to the population in need. . . .

Furthermore, the impressive results thus far, with resources which must be regarded as minimal, suggest a challenging question: What would be likely to happen if adequate resources were made available so that quality services could be delivered with respect, energy, and skill? If enough staff were assigned so that patients receive the personal attention they require and deserve? If clinics were not overcrowded? If budgets permitted more evening and weekend clinics? [author's note: As of this writing, only two municipal hospitals offer evening clinics], shorter waiting times in the waiting rooms, accelerated procedures to obtain supply refills, improved educational efforts, etc.?

From every part of the country the story is the same. In the District of Columbia, response from the target population was so great that the program was expanded from one begun with a one-thousand-dollar allocation in 1962 to one allocated $200,000 two years later, and $575,000 in 1967.[22]

During the first 21 months of the D.C. clinics' operations, almost 7,000 new patients were admitted. The District's Director of Public Health told a family-planning seminar in California in 1966:

[19]See footnote 17.
[20]Gordon W. Perkin, M.D., "A Family Planning Unit for Your Hospital?" *Hospital Practice,* 2:5 (May, 1967), pp. 64-72.

[21]Frederick S. Jaffe, "Programming for Community Needs," *Proceedings of Regional Conference on Family Planning,* Region II, Department of Health, Education, and Welfare, December, 1966, p. 33.
[22]Murray Grant, M.D., M.P.H., speech at Southern California Family Planning Seminar, February 18, 1966, made available to author.

A study of the first 993 cases reveals that whereas approximately 207 pregnancies would have been expected, in actual fact only 66 such pregnancies occurred after they began to participate in our birth control program.

SPONSORSHIP VARIED

Success in providing family-planning services to a target population depends not so much on sponsorship: In Louisiana the chief sponsor is a medical school. In New York City the municipal hospitals provide some of the leadership. In the District of Columbia, it is the local health department. In many communities across the land, Planned Parenthood-sponsored clinics provide the bulk of the services. In most areas, and especially for the large middle class that can pay for health care, private physicians are the source of family-planning information and service.

But while there are many resources in communities in every section of this land through which family-planning services might be brought to the 5,300,000 women needing them, virtually every one of these is doing a grossly inadequate job.

PUBLIC HEALTH SERVICES

Here is the way the picture looks nationwide, according to a Ford Foundation study:[23]

As of 1965, not more than 150,000 women in the United States received family-planning information and service through local health departments. (In 1967 the estimate rose to 200,000 for health department services.)

Of the 3,072 counties in the United States, public health services are available in 2,425 through 1,557 local health departments. About 650 counties (21 percent of the total) are not served by local health departments. Nearly 10,000,000 people, or

better than five percent of the United States population, live in these counties.

The best estimates indicate that some family-planning services are offered in about a third of all local health departments in 32 states and the District of Columbia.

There is more than slight evidence that even where provided the services are far from optimum, according to the study referred to above:

> In many areas, the local health department is geographically situated in a location considerably removed from the area of greatest health need.
>
> Many local health officers must supervise the public health programs of several counties, severely limiting their ability to focus the necessary time and attention on the development of a new program.
>
> The organizational structure of state and local health departments frequently does not permit the employment of non-professional workers as patient recruiters for family planning services; evening clinics and satellite clinics operating in poverty areas are also frequently difficult for official agencies to staff, fund, and operate.

HOSPITAL PROGRAMS

There is general agreement that hospital-based family-planning services are the most effective and economic way of reaching large numbers of women at the very time they are likely to be most receptive to family-planning information.

According to a U.S. Department of Health, Education, and Welfare (HEW) report,[24] "the great majority of all births in the United States (97.4 percent in 1963) takes place in hospitals with a physician present." (In 1940 only 56 percent of all births took place under these circumstances.)

As Dr. Howard C. Taylor, Jr., former Chief of Obstetrics and Gynecology at Columbia University's College of Physicians and Surgeons and now Director of the In-

[23]Gordon W. Perkin, M.D., and David Radel, *Current Status of Family Planning Programs in the United States,* pamphlet, Population Program, Ford Foundation, October, 1966.

[24]Anders S. Lunde, Ph.D., "White-Nonwhite Fertility Differentials in the United States," *Health, Education and Welfare Indicators,* February-October, 1965, p. 13.

ternational Institute for the Study of Human Reproduction has noted:[25]

> Only a little consideration is needed to show that the giving of contraceptive advice shortly after parturition will be more effective, in preventing conception, than if offered at some later date.

Data show, he explained, that assuming no contraception about half the women who have given birth will have conceived within three months of the first postpartum menstrual period, four-fifths within one year.

> The period of pregnancy and the puerperium offer unique opportunities to reach . . . women . . . in a systematic manner . . . when the subject of family planning is clearly relevant.
>
> A particular advantage of this approach is that the women will be introduced to the idea of family planning in the name of "child spacing" after her first delivery.

Dr. Taylor maintains that to work primarily in the hospital setting with women who have just completed a pregnancy and are most immediately concerned about the next pregnancy, is "to place the emphasis where maximum results could be obtained with a minimum of effort."

How many of our hospitals do, indeed, offer these services at the time when "maximum results could be obtained with a minimum of effort?"

The Ford Foundation report cited above estimates that "less than five percent of all United States short-term general hospitals reported the availability of family-planning services in 1965, according to data from the American Hospital Association."

Only 175 of 4,995 hospitals with under 500 beds, or 3.5 percent, reported the availability of family-planning services. It is in these hospitals that over 80 percent of all hospital births take place.

In 1966, according to a special communication to the author from Frederick Jaffe, Vice President of Program Planning, Planned Parenthood-World Population, less than one-fifth of hospitals with large maternity services (500-plus births) reported providing any family-planning services.

It is estimated that no more than 200,000 medically indigent women received family-planning services through U. S. hospitals.

PRIVATE PHYSICIAN

Another important resource through which medically indigent women might obtain family-planning services is through visits to private physicians. This is, after all, the way the vast majority of middle-class women in urban and rural communities obtains family-planning services.

At the present time, however, this resource is not available to the poor. Having no money with which to pay for private medical care, they do not often make their way to the offices of the private physician for any medical care. Nor do physicians, for obvious reasons, encourage such visits.

In any case, other factors intervene between the physician and the patient. The Ford study points out:

> While a majority of private physicians will prescribe contraception on request, relatively few will initiate discussion of the subject.

Since many of the poor either do not know that family planning exists or are too inhibited in this area to bring the matter up themselves, physician reluctance is a matter of some importance.

In addition, birth control has not yet become a routine part of medical practice, experts agree. An important reason for this has to do with the education of physicians. A recent study on family-planning content in the curriculum of 78 non-Catholic medical schools in the United States found the following:[26] While 71 of the schools do in-

[25]Howard C. Taylor, Jr., M.D., "A Family Planning Program Related to Maternity Service," *American Journal of Obstetrics and Gynecology,* 9:5 (July 1, 1966), pp. 726-731.

[26]Christopher Tietze, M.D. *et al.,* "Teaching of Fertility Regulation in Medical Schools," *Journal of American Medical Association,* 196:1 (April 4, 1966), pp. 20-24.

clude training in contraception in their curricula, half of the 71 schools devote two hours or less to training in family planning during the four-year curriculum. Scarcely enough time in which to develop expertise in so vital a health area!

FEDERAL PARTICIPATION

There is a consensus that, the dimensions of the problem being what they are, it is urgent that family-planning services be supported by funds from the federal government. But like medical education in birth control, the federal government's budget for the support of such programs has been grossly inadequate.

Informed observers estimate that approximately $10,000,000 to $12,000,000 was allocated for direct family-planning programs last year, against an estimated need of $100,000,000 a year to reach all of the fertile poor and medically indigent women in the land.[27] This minimal allocation was made despite a stream of statements emanating from the President on the importance of family planning and from his Secretary of Health, Education, and Welfare, to say nothing of innumerable statements from congressmen, Republican and Democratic alike. And it was made despite the fact that a study conducted by an agency of the federal government concluded that "Birth control is probably the most cost-effective antipoverty measure available."

A comparative study of various ways to reduce infant mortality by another federal agency, the Public Health Service, concluded that a major birth control program funded at $90,000,000 for five years was not only the most cost-effective way to deal with in-

fant mortality but would produce results at a rate of effectiveness seven times higher than the next most effective program.[28] The American Medical Association's Committee on Maternal and Child Care concurred in these findings.[29]

Funds thus far allocated are a long way from implementing this plea from President Johnson:

> Let us in all our lands—including this land —face forthrightly the multiplying problems of our multiplying populations and seek the answers to this most profound challenge to the future of the world. Let us act on the fact that less than five dollars invested in population control is worth $100 invested in economic growth.[30]

Policy statements have been more plentiful than funding and program implementation. The pace of both of these has been stately, to put it kindly.

As one expert reporting to a Senate subcommittee put it[31]:

> The agency which has been indulging in the most enunciations—the Department of Health, Education, and Welfare (HEW)—has apparently done the least to carry out programs.

He pointed out that the difficulty in estimating precisely how much HEW allocates for family-planning programs lies in the fact that the department prefers to include family planning in its comprehensive health programs.

While the idea of comprehensive funding is a valid one, the facts of American bureaucratic life intervene in execution. An ex-

---

[27]Population Council estimate, private communication; Planned Parenthood-World Population estimate, private communication.

According to the report, *Implementing DHEW Policy on Family Planning and Population,* September, 1967, p. 19, about $14,515,000 was spent by DHEW and O.E.O. in 1967 for information, counseling, and services.

[28]Elinor Langer, "Birth Control: U.S. Programs Off to Slow Start," *Science,* Vol. 156 (May 12, 1967), p. 766.

[29]Mrs. Katharine B. Oettinger, keynote address annual meeting of Planned Parenthood-World Population, October 18, 1967, p. 5.

[30]Lyndon B. Johnson, address in San Francisco, June 25, 1965, on the occasion of the twentieth anniversary of the founding of the United Nations.

[31]Sheppard, *op. cit.*

planation of why comprehensiveness does not work comes from Senator Joseph Tydings (Democrat, Maryland), one of the leading exponents of federal support for family planning in Congress. He said in a Senate speech last April[32]:

> In the competition for funds appropriated generally for health programs, family planning programs are at a considerable disadvantage. They are relatively new and involve only a few staff people.
>
> By contrast, the older, firmly established health programs have batteries of bureaucrats who are committed advocates. Family planning programs are ignored because they lack advocates within the bureaucracy.

TO THE MOON

An indication of priorities for family planning was made crystal clear in a recent speech by Mrs. Katharine B. Oettinger, Chief of the Children's Bureau and Deputy Assistant Secretary for Family Planning and Population in HEW.[33]

In discussing a bill before Congress concerned with the extension of family-planning services to the poor, she pointed out:

> Principal impetus will be provided by the increase in the authorization for the Maternal and Infant Care projects, which provides for grants to local and voluntary agencies for family planning clinics and related services.
>
> In addition, state health departments will be expected to emphasize family planning services in their maternal and child health programs, and to plan the extension of such services so they will be available in all parts of the state by 1975.

HEW's target date seems a little remote in the face of the needs, in the face of the enormous responsiveness of the poor when family-planning services are offered, and in the face of ample evidence that public policy on every level supports the extension of family planning to all Americans who wish it, provided only that there shall be no coercion.

One may be pardoned for wondering why the target for reaching the poor with birth control should take almost as long as the target for reaching the moon.

As Frank Notestein, Ph.D., noted demographer who heads the Population Council, pointed out in a recent article,[34]

> The main obstacles to the development of highly successful birth control programs everywhere lie in the organizational and administrative field.

VIGOR POSSIBLE

A more vigorous approach to family-planning services for the poor was described recently by Gary D. London, M.D., Associate Director for Family Planning, Office of Economic Opportunity (OEO).[35]

Two years ago, less than half a million dollars was spent for family planning by OEO. In 1966 the figure had risen to $2,500,000. In fiscal 1967 the amount allocated was more than $4,500,000. The 121 OEO-funded projects include small, storefront facilities offering counselling and services a few hours weekly and utilizing the help of part-time physicians and volunteers, as well as family-planning components in large hospital/university complexes.

If Congress authorizes the $10,000,000 proposed for these programs in fiscal 1968, Dr. London expects that approximately 300,000 women will be served in that year alone. He concluded:

> A more accelerated program, beginning in the present fiscal year, could be developed to serve 1,500,000 women by the end of fiscal year 1969.

---

[32]Senator Joseph Tydings (Democrat, Maryland), speech delivered on floor of the Senate, April 12, 1967, and made available to the author.

[33]Oettinger, *op. cit.*

[34]Frank Notestein, Ph.D., "The Population Crisis: Reason for Hope," *Foreign Affairs,* 46:1 (October, 1967), pp. 167-180.

[35]Gary D. London, M.D., address on Office of Economic Opportunity and Family Planning, New York, October 18, 1967.

In explaining why it is sometimes difficult to "deliver" family-planning programs even in cities where there are existing health facilities, Dr. London is particularly illuminating:

Cities have old, well-established medical resources and systems for delivery of health services. In many cases, these older established systems are not entirely responsive to, or often knowledgeable about, the needs of the poor in the community they serve.

Thus, while the task of identifying or even contacting the poor patient may not be as large in the city as in a rural area, the task of altering the attitudes of established community leadership may be much greater.

Further, the problems of drawing together a group of isolated medical services and well-established, independent systems of delivery of health care into a unit which functions cooperatively and innovatively can be difficult indeed.

We've learned that absence of available services or absence of the money with which to pay for available services are not the only barriers faced by the poor.

Despite mounting evidence that birth-control programs are, to use a phrase heard in medical circles, "medically desirable, economically feasible, and socially acceptable," they still receive woefully little financial support from the government.

NO REASONABLE DOUBT

The evidence is in.

The technology, imperfect though it is, works effectively enough to afford virtually all fertile women wanting it protection against unwanted births.

The poor, their life-style notwithstanding, have demonstrated over and over again that they want families as small or smaller than middle-class parents. They are not so fatalistic, not so without hope for their future— and that of their children—that they fail to respond when birth-control services are offered to them with dignity and understanding.

As Dr. Alonzo Yerby has written in reference to New York City,[36] but as reports from widely disparate communities in every section of the United States confirm[37]:

Experience has demonstrated conclusively that large numbers of impoverished parents in all ethnic groups are prepared to utilize modern family planning services if they are provided with even modest amounts of dignity, compassion, and skill. This should set to rest, once and for all, the spurious notion, held by far too many administrators and professionals, that there is little point in initiating family planning services for the poor because "they won't use them anyway." To be sure, they will not use it if the service is so organized as to be virtually inaccessible, if its policies and atmosphere are such as to challenge the patient's integrity and subject her to threatening and insulting inquiries, or if the patient must spend hours in a dingy waiting room before being seen for a couple of minutes by a harassed and often hostile physician. But the poor will respond in large numbers to services that are genuinely accessible, dignified, and properly organized.

This is so whether they live in urban centers or in rural areas, whether they are poor American Negro or poor American white.

This is so whatever their religious affiliation. Neither Protestant Christianity nor most forms of Judaism forbid contraception. And it is plain that many communicants of Roman Catholicism are going where their conscience leads them. Judging from incontrovertible evidence, one may say it is leading them to modern methods of family planning.

Science and social science have provided the armamentarium, the insights, the methodology. Now it is time that they work to-

---

[36]Alonzo S. Yerby, M.D., M.P.H., "Barriers to Utilization of Health Services," from pamphlet of same name, New York, March, 1967, p. 18.

[37]See "Public Health Programs in Family Planning," supplement to *American Journal of Public Health,* January, 1966. For a worldwide view of the response of the poor, see "International Postpartum Family Planning," *Studies in Family Planning,* August, 1967, publication of The Population Council.

gether to apply their findings to a population waiting to be served.

CONCLUSIONS

The two major stumbling blocks in the provision of subsidized family-planning services are money and motivation.

Virtually all experts agree that between $90,000,000 and $100,000,000 a year is required to provide these services to the 5,000,000 poor and near-poor women needing such assistance. This is "less than one percent of the amount currently expended for health by government agencies," according to a recent report by the President's National Advisory Commission on Rural Poverty.

Minimal though the total is, only about a quarter of that sum [became] available in fiscal 1969, which [began] in July, 1968.

In the face of the need, this sum is grossly inadequate. It must in fairness be pointed out that even this amount is 100 percent more than was appropriated when support of family planning was considered political suicide.

It is apparent that, until the federal government sets a more realistic budget, a great many poor and near-poor women are going to continue to produce more children than they themselves want or can care for, and will become more deeply mired in poverty. In one way or another, American society will pay the far greater cost in social disequilibrium for years to come.

As important perhaps as money, in this writer's opinion, is the question of motivation—motivation not of the poor, but of the various levels of officialdom concerned with the provision of services.

As we have shown, all but a fraction of American babies are born in hospitals. It is scandalous (and irresponsible) that institutions with obstetric services should not routinely provide this vital service to all who want it. Indeed, the question might be asked why all general hospitals that serve women should not have family-planning clinics.

Surely a woman attending a diabetic clinic or a heart clinic, or a woman suffering from other conditions in which pregnancy is either contraindicated or might best be postponed, should be able to obtain—and urged to obtain—contraceptive counselling on the same premises.

There can no longer be any reason for neglecting to make family-planning services an integral and priority part of the care given to women through the entire network of state and local health facilities.

Social service agencies serving families should make family-planning counselling a routine aspect of their guidance. Obviously, there must be no coercion, no hint that clients opting not to accept family planning will be punished in any way. But the greater punishment, it seems to this writer, is the denial of information on the basis of which the poor can make rational decisions, choices, in this area of their lives.

Family life education, by whatever name it is called, should routinely include family-planning education. It should do so not as a way of reducing the incidence of out-of-wedlock pregnancies (though it may indeed achieve this objective), not as a way of fighting venereal disease (though again it may do so successfully), but most simply because family planning is central to family health.

This point need not be elaborated for readers of this journal [Journal of Marriage and the Family]. Young people are entitled to know that the timing and spacing of children in a family, as well as the total number of children, can affect the whole future of the family as a unit and of each individual in it; that family planning is an important part of overall health care; that both maternal and child health are affected by family planning; that mental health, too, is related to family planning.

On the professional level, no medical, nursing, or social work student; no future health administrator; no future teacher should complete his education without a thorough grounding in family planning in all its aspects. This is not now the case. It is all too possible for physicians, to name but one example, to know almost as little about contraception as their patients and to be as inhibited in introducing the subject.

Finally, enthusiasm for family planning must have practical expression in the bureaucratic apparatus. Policy statements are not enough. Implementation must follow. Such statements must be enforced by explicit policy design; by definition of priorities and objectives; by assignment of personnel with responsibility for carrying out policy; by realistic budgeting; by reporting systems to enable program-effectiveness assessments to be made.

Study after study has shown the responsiveness of the poor to program input even when the program has been far from ideal. What has not thus far been demonstrated is the degree of responsiveness of the health and welfare establishment to the needs of the poor in this area.

9 Prenatal diagnosis, an essential to family planning in cases of genetic risk*

M. Neil Macintyre†

Among the most important concepts presented in support of family planning is that the family unit benefits most when the child is born at an appropriate time, when it is wanted, and when its presence in the family does not pose a serious emotional or financial threat. There is no such appropriate time for the birth of congenitally malformed and mentally retarded children, since probably they are the most unwanted of all children and since they always represent a serious threat to the emotional stability of all members of the family unit and a potential strain on the financial resources of either the family or society or both.

Regardless of how reasonable and laudable our societal demands with respect to parental attitudes and behavior toward children may seem under normal circumstances, these demands are unrealistic and may be even cruel and destructive, when applied to the parents and other relatives of a defective child.

Many articles have been written for the lay public, describing the moral strengthening and unifying of the family that the presence of a defective child engenders. The unrealistic and biased nature of such dissertations is obviated by the fact that they rarely mention and never describe adequately the destructive aspects of such a situation. It is not to be denied that some malformed and retarded children are loved and can make some positive contribution to the family; but to suggest that their positive value is such that it outweighs their negative impact is to imply that the birth of a defective child is a desirable event. To make such a suggestion is to deny the truth. No parents, given an opportunity to choose, would elect to produce an abnormal child.

During the past decade the increase in knowledge and diagnostic capabilities in human genetics has been so great that genetic counseling, together with prenatal genetic evaluation where applicable and selective abortion when indicated, now must be recognized as important aspects of the total concept of family planning.

This essay discusses the effects of a defective child on the family unit; the development, applicability, and limitations of prenatal diagnostic techniques; and some principles of genetic counseling. These subjects will be recognized as important not only to all professionals involved in the management of human reproduction but also to prospective parents, particularly when a genetic problem exists or is suspected.

THE DESTRUCTIVE EFFECT OF A DEFECTIVE CHILD ON THE FAMILY UNIT
Effect on the parents

One of the most ego-involved behavior patterns in our society is the decision and

*Adapted in part from references 3, 5, and 6.
†Ph.D., Professor of Anatomy, Departments of Anatomy and Pediatrics, Case Western Reserve University, Cleveland, Ohio.

Original article.

actions on the part of a married couple that lead to the production of a child. This behavior represents not only an expression of each person's love for the other, but also the fulfillment of a deep and basic individual need to provide continuance of oneself into posterity. It is no wonder, then, that such a couple looks forward to the birth of the child with pride and satisfaction and with the expectation that this baby will represent a combination of all that is best in each of its parents and will be one of the most beautiful children ever produced.

When the baby is born deformed and/or mentally retarded, the depth and the magnitude of the emotional shock to each of the parents is unrecognized by most people. Such a lack of appreciation of the problem is understandable in view of the fact that the average individual does not care to think about such distressing events and usually protects himself further by the reassuring belief that such a catastrophe will never happen to him. As the result of this general lack of understanding of the emotional destruction wrought by the birth of a defective child, our society tends to make pompous judgments with regard to the appropriate behavior to be exhibited by such parents.

For example, it is expected of parents that they love their offspring, but it is not unnatural for the parents of a malformed child to experience feelings of revulsion or even hate for that child because of the terrible blow to their egos that its birth has produced. Furthermore, it is not unnatural for such parents to harbor the secret wish that the child would die; whereas our society finds such a thought abhorrent and totally unacceptable. Consequently, deep feelings of personal guilt are generated in the minds of the distraught parents who, not infrequently, overcompensate by obvious and often repeated proclamations of deep devotion and appreciation for the child. Tragically, the more unrealistic and hypocritical the behavior of such unfortunate parents is,

the more acceptable and laudable it is in the eyes of society. There is a tremendous need for such parents to express their true feelings and emotions to someone who will understand and sympathize. Therefore the services of a competent counselor are not only desirable but virtually essential in such cases.

After parents have had a defective baby, particularly if it is their only child, it is natural for them to feel a great desire to initiate another pregnancy in an effort to demonstrate their true reproductive capabilities to society by producing a perfectly normal child. However, if the basis for the abnormal child's deformities is known to be genetic, signifying that a subsequent pregnancy will carry with it a recognized risk, the unfortunate couple feels trapped, frustrated, fearful, and embittered.

Regrettably, in our society, genetic diseases or conditions are looked upon as a distinct stigma. For this reason, when a defective child's condition is found to be genetic in origin, the parental feelings of guilt and fear, and of being somehow abnormal, may become intolerable. Under such circumstances each member of the couple is likely (either inwardly or openly) to accuse the other of being responsible, and such recriminations may well lead to the destruction of the marital relationship.

The existence of a genetic problem places a strain on another aspect of the marriage as well. Genetic risk is associated with a fear of pregnancy, and the resulting anxiety is an almost inevitable threat to the stability of a couple's sexual relationship. The deterioration of this important aspect of marital harmony leads to frustration and additional anxiety, which also can destroy the marriage.

Effect upon siblings

There is a widespread and totally unrealistic attitude among adults that the presence of the defective, mentally retarded child in the family is a beneficial and maturing experience for its siblings because it teaches them to be understanding, tolerant, self-sacrificing, and so on. In actual fact, such a situation is likely to cause serious and permanent damage to the sociopsychological development of a sibling.

Regardless of how well the parents may handle the job of bringing up a defective, retarded child in the family, it is impossible for them to prevent all of the destructive psychological effects that such a situation will have upon the siblings of the abnormal child. In the first place, parents have little control over the behavior of other children and adults outside of the family unit. As youngsters, the normal siblings are bound to be subjected to the candid and often cruel comments of their peers with respect to their abnormal sibling and their relationship to it and are likely to become hypersensitive to such remarks and also to the unnatural glances and other behavior on the part of adults in the presence of the abnormal child. For the normal sibling, such experiences are bound to result in the feeling of being stigmatized, particularly if a genetic problem is known to exist. Such a child is likely to develop the feeling that something is wrong with him, that he can never be normal, that he is less than fully acceptable to society, or even that he is somehow unclean. When playmates are invited to the home in which an abnormal child is present, situations that are painfully embarrassing to the normal sibling frequently will occur, resulting in the refusal to have friends in the home.

It is normal for a child to want to stand up for its own rights in competition with its siblings and to be able to express anger and frustration when these feelings are aroused by the behavior of brothers or sisters. An abnormal, retarded child is a source of strong feelings of antagonism, anger, and frustration to its normal siblings; but the expression of these natural feelings ordinarily is denied them because of parental protection of the defective child. Thus, the nor-

mal sibling is denied the opportunity to stand up for his own rights because it has been made abundantly clear to him by his parents that he is expected to understand, protect, and be self-sacrificing and tolerant toward his abnormal sibling. These admonitions usually are repeated sufficiently often that when natural aggressive feelings occur in the normal child he comes to feel very guilty about them.

Frequently, the presence of a defective child prevents a family unit from taking vacation trips together or participating in a variety of other social situations in a normal fashion. Furthermore, the financial burden imposed as the result of required medical care, special schooling, and other needs may deny the family many pleasurable activities that might otherwise be available to it. To the normal children, such restrictions and denial are bound to be a source of frustration, anger, and stigmatization.

The above are but a few of the more obvious situations that prevent or impede the normal sociopsychological development of normal siblings in the presence of an abnormal child. These deleterious effects are likely to occur even when the parents are behaving in the best possible fashion under the circumstances. Obviously, when the parents are so emotionally distressed by the situation that their behavior is disruptive, the effects upon the children are even more severe.

It might appear from the above statements that the best answer is found in institutionalizing the defective child. In some cases, such a decision certainly is warranted; however, it is almost invariably associated with a deep parental sense of sadness and of guilt for abandoning the child, and these effects do not go unobserved by the other children. In short, there is no really good answer to the problem.

This discussion has confined itself to the effects that the defective child has upon the parents and the normal siblings; but one should note that emotional distress, guilt, fear, and stigmatization will be felt by grand-parents and other blood relatives as well. Therefore, one must recognize that the birth of a defective and retarded child is ac-companied by serious emotional conse-quences to all family members and rela-tives, and when a genetic problem is rec-ognized as being the basis for the unfortu-nate child's defects, this knowledge can affect the family planning of a large number of individuals.

DEVELOPMENT OF CYTOGENETIC TECHNIQUES AND THEIR APPLICATION TO PRENATAL DIAGNOSIS
Chromosome abnormalities and cytogenetics

By the early 1960's, techniques had been developed for culturing and preparing hu-man cells in such a way that individual chromosomes could be visualized and stud-ied. Such studies showed that in some cases congenital malformations are associated with demonstrable chromosomal anomalies re-sulting in genetic imbalance. Chromosome analysis was soon recognized as an impor-tant diagnostic tool.

There are several types of chromosomal abnormalities that can cause congenital mal-formations and mental retardation in man. The most common are "trisomy," a condi-tion in which an extra chromosome is pres-ent in the cells of the individual; "mono-somy," in which a chromosome is missing; "deletion," in which a portion of a chromo-some is missing; and "translocation," in which two chromosomes have become fused together or have exchanged parts.

The most common major congenital mal-formation syndrome in man is Down's syn-drome, commonly known as "mongolism." Approximately one in every 600 live births is a mongoloid child. About 95% of the cases of Down's syndrome arise in a non-hereditary fashion because of a genetic ac-cident known as "nondisjunction" which oc-curs in the particular egg cell that becomes

involved in the fertilization leading to the formation of the defective child. In non-disjunction, the two members of a chromo-some pair (in this case, pair No. 21), which should separate during the formation of an egg or sperm cell, remain together, so that the resulting egg cell (ovum) contains two chromosomes No. 21. At the time of fer-tilization, the sperm contributes its normal one No. 21 chromosome, and the result is three No. 21's instead of the usual two. This is the condition known as trisomy. Down's syndrome is technically known as the trisomy-21 syndrome. The likelihood of a couple's producing a mongoloid child on the nondisjunctional, nonhereditary basis is related to the age of the mother. The older a woman is, the greater is the probability that she will produce such a child.

Approximately 5% of the children born with Down's syndrome are produced by an individual who is a "carrier" of a chro-mosome translocation in which chromosome No. 21 is fused to another chromosome. Such a carrier individual is perfectly nor-mal developmentally but, because of having the abnormal chromosome condition in all cells, runs a high risk of producing a mon-goloid child. The risk in the case of a mother with such a chromosome translocation is about one chance in four with every preg-nancy regardless of her age.

Down's syndrome is used as an example here because the condition is well known. However, most of the types of cases of con-genital malformations resulting from various kinds of chromosomal imbalance are even more seriously abnormal than is the child with Down's syndrome.

In addition to the fusion type of trans-location, described above, there are other chromosomal rearrangements known as "balanced reciprocal translocations." In such a translocation, two different chro-mosomes have exchanged parts, and an in-dividual who carries a reciprocal translo-cation runs a 50% risk of producing a child with serious defects.

When the chromosome analysis of a mal-formed child indicates the presence of a hereditary type of chromosomal imbalance, the child's parents customarily are tested to ascertain which may be a carrier of the problem. Then, ordinarily it is recommended that additional studies be performed on the blood relatives of the carrier, because any or all of them could themselves be carriers and have no knowledge of the greatly increased risk that they have of producing defective children.

Application of cytogenetics to prenatal diagnosis

Underlying reasons for the development of techniques. Once an individual learns that he or she is a carrier of a chromosome translocation and is informed about the great risk of producing congenitally malformed children, the information invariably has an important effect upon such a person's thinking and behavior. If a young unmarried individual is involved, knowledge of the high genetic risk and fear of its implications may preclude normal dating activities, courtship, and marriage. For married couples, the knowledge of such a risk denies them the emotional freedom to initiate a pregnancy, particularly if they already have produced a defective child. Unplanned pregnancies do occur in some such cases, however, and give rise to a tremendous amount of anxiety and fear. Under such circumstances, virtually without exception, such couples have elected therapeutic abortion rather than face the risk that their child will be born seriously deformed.

Interrupting a pregnancy in such circumstances is particularly distressing to the parents because of their recognition that, even with the known high risk, there is at least a 50% chance that the child will be perfectly normal.

My realization and that of certain other scientists of the tragic and terrifying dilemma posed by situations such as described above stimulated research in an effort to find a

safe and reliable way of predicting, early in pregnancy, whether the fetus was normal or genetically unbalanced. In 1965, working independently, I, at Case Western Reserve University in Cleveland, and Dr. Harold Klinger, at Albert Einstein University in New York, developed the tissue culture techniques that allowed us to produce the first chromosome preparations from cultured fetal cells derived from amniotic fluid withdrawn from pregnant women.

Amniocentesis and prenatal chromosome analysis. Amniotic fluid for use in prenatal diagnosis is obtained by a procedure known as "transabdominal amniocentesis," which involves passing a needle through the abdominal and uterine walls of the mother and into the amniotic cavity containing the fluid that surrounds the fetus. This procedure, drastic as it may sound to the layman, is neither painful nor hazardous. Before being used to obtain fluid for prenatal genetic evaluation, amniocentesis was performed thousands of times in connection with the monitoring of the progress of Rh disease in affected fetuses.

Cells in the amniotic fluid are all fetal in origin, and although the majority are not living, some are still viable and can be used to initiate tissue cultures in the laboratory. Once a sufficient number of such cultured cells have been grown, they may be subjected to the same techniques used for chromosome preparations from leukocyte cultures used in testing individuals who have already been born. Amniotic fluid to be used as a basis for prenatal evaluation ordinarily is obtained no earlier than the fifteenth week after the onset of the last menstrual period. Where chromosome analyses are involved, the results usually are available within 2 weeks after the initiation of the cell cultures; hence, the knowledge of whether the fetus is genetically normal or abnormal should be available by the end of the seventeenth week of gestation.

Applicability of prenatal chromosome analysis. In general, the following four types of situations are considered to be appropriate indications for prenatal chromosome analysis.

Translocation carrier parent. As noted above, when a parent is the carrier of a fusion type of translocation leading to an increased probability of producing a child with Down's syndrome, the risk is approximately 25% if the mother carries the translocation. It is somewhat lower if the father is the carrier. In the case of a reciprocal translocation, the risk is 50% regardless of which parent is the carrier. As mentioned earlier, whenever a translocation is found to exist in a parent, the knowledge of the high risk is associated with such a high level of anxiety and fear whenever a pregnancy occurs that, prior to the availability of prenatal diagnostic techniques, couples who found themselves in such a situation sought, and somehow obtained, therapeutic abortions on the basis of the risk. *Now that the diagnostic techniques are available, they should be used in high-risk cases in order to save the lives of the normal babies that would otherwise be destroyed through therapeutic abortion.*

Previous defective child with a nonhereditary chromosome abnormality. Whenever a couple has produced a defective child with a chromosome abnormality, even though the parents' chromosomes are normal and the problem is not hereditary, such as in the majority of cases of Down's syndrome, the anxiety level associated with any subsequent pregnancy is likely to be extremely high. The resulting emotional strain on both parents is so extremely unpleasant as to be a real threat to their psychological and physical health. Under such circumstances, proving that the unborn child does not carry a chromosomal abnormality serves a very useful purpose in making the remainder of the term of pregnancy relatively anxiety free. In rare cases, of course, the analysis will demonstrate that the fetus actually is genetically unbalanced.

Maternal age factor. As previously mentioned, there is a positive correlation between increasing maternal age and an increase in the probability of producing a child with defects, particularly Down's syndrome. The calculated probability of producing a mongoloid child, based on maternal age only, increases about a hundred fold from a woman's earliest to latest reproductive years. The risk is about one chance in 3,000 at age 15, and approximately one chance in 30 at age 45. Since it is generally known that the "older mother" has a greater risk, there is both an emotional and a practical reason for performing prenatal diagnoses in pregnancies occurring to women in this category.

Sex-linked disorders. Certain diseases are known to be "sex linked." This means that they are associated with a defective gene on one of the sex chromosomes. In human sex-linked conditions, virtually all those of any importance are carried on the X chromosome rather than on the Y chromosome. Since it is impossible to see a single defective gene under the microscope, the chromosomes of an individual affected by, or carrying, a sex-linked disorder appear to be entirely normal. Nevertheless, prenatal chromosome analysis is of some value in connection with a pregnancy where the risk of a sex-linked disorder is known to exist, since characteristically such disorders affect only one sex. For example, if a pregnant woman is known to be the carrier of an X-linked disorder such as hemophilia, none of her daughters will be hemophilic but the risk of a male child's being affected is 50 per cent. If a prenatal chromosome analysis indicates that the fetus is a female, it rules out the possibility of a hemophilic child. However, if the fetus proves to be a male, there would still be no way of determining whether or not it is suffering from the disease. Thus, in cases of X-linked problems, the prenatal chromosome analysis technique cannot give a complete answer in every instance, but it can improve the basis for judgment.

PRENATAL BIOCHEMICAL ANALYSIS
OF HERITABLE METABOLIC DISORDERS

The tissue culture techniques for growing fetal cells from amniotic fluid were developed originally to serve as a basis for performing prenatal chromosome analyses. Recently, however, researchers have shown that such cultures can serve also as the basis for biochemical tests to determine the presence of certain heritable metabolic disorders. These are genetic conditions related to defects at the gene level, that is, dominant or recessive genes, which cannot be detected under the microscope and consequently cannot be ascertained through a chromosome analysis. The majority of genetic problems are of this type.

Many of the heritable metabolic disorders are extremely serious and some of them lead to death of a child within the first few years of life. A good example of such a condition is Tay-Sachs disease, in which the child is apparently normal at birth but within a few months starts to demonstrate the effects of this tragic disease of the nervous system. Degeneration progresses irrevocably to death within three or four years, and the emotional strain on the parents is devastating. Tay-Sachs disease is inherited as an autosomal recessive condition and, if both parents carry the recessive gene, there is a 25% risk of producing a child with the condition and a 50% risk of producing a carrier. Tay-Sachs disease is one of the genetic metabolic disorders that can be detected prenatally by applying the appropriate biochemical tests to fetal cell cultures derived from amniotic fluid.

At the time of this writing, approximately a dozen heritable disorders can be diagnosed prenatally by using either amniotic fluid alone or uncultured or cultured amniotic fluid cells. In most cases it is necessary to culture the cells, and because the biochemical tests involved require a large number of cells, the delay between the time of obtaining the fluid and the time of completing the analysis is considerably longer than the interval required for a chromosome analysis. This increased delay not only adds to emotional strain but also may lead to legal problems if it appears that the pregnancy should be terminated. No general statement can be made with respect to the legal restrictions on therapeutic abortion, because the governing laws vary so much from state to state.

PITFALLS AND LIMITATIONS
IN THE USE OF PRENATAL
EVALUATIVE TECHNIQUES

For any laboratory technique to be consistently dependable and accurate, it is important for those performing and evaluating the procedure to recognize both the limitations of the technique and the possible pitfalls associated with it that might lead to erroneous interpretations. Whether you ever will be directly involved in using prenatal analytical techniques or in evaluating their results, it seems advisable to mention both the limitations of their applicability and the possible problems involved in their use. For any professional who may be recommending certain tests, or for any potential patient on whom the tests may be performed, a general understanding of the nature, availability, capabilities, and appropriate applications of the procedures is valuable.

Problems common to cytogenetic
and biochemical analyses

Risk of amniocentesis. Earlier in this chapter it was noted that the procedure of amniocentesis, whereby amniotic fluid is removed, is neither painful nor hazardous. The most painful part of the procedure is the injection of a small amount of local anesthetic under the skin at the point where the larger needle will be inserted. At this writing, amniocentesis for genetic evaluation has been performed approximately 1,000 times and there have been no reported cases of damage to the fetus or the mother as the result. Therefore, the risk of the procedure must be judged as being extremely low, although it would be wrong to suggest that any such technique is completely devoid of potential risk.

Culture failure. Of the sizable population of cells in amniotic fluid, only a relatively small number are viable and usable for the establishment of cell cultures. Such cultures are considerably more difficult to initiate than are standard fibroblast cultures, and there is always a possibility of a culture failure. Such a failure requires a second amniocentesis and, more importantly, delays the diagnosis and prolongs the period of anxiety associated with waiting for the results.

Maternal cell contamination. All the cells within the amniotic fluid are fetal in origin and therefore any that grow are usable as a basis for a fetal genetic evaluation. However, when the needle used in amniocentesis is passed through the mother's tissues and into the amniotic cavity, it may carry with it a few maternal cells, which, if they are included in the sample of amniotic fluid withdrawn, can grow in the laboratory and become a source of confusion or error in evaluation. Recognizing this potential hazard, experienced professionals will withdraw and discard a small amount of fluid before obtaining the main sample in a fresh syringe. Furthermore, the amniotic fluid should be divided into several culture flasks, and if the final chromosome analysis indicates a chromosome complement identical to that of the mother, the analysis should be repeated at least twice, using cultures from other flasks.

Multiple pregnancies. The term "multiple pregnancy" refers to the presence of more than one fetus in the womb, such as twins or triplets. Almost without exception in such cases, each fetus has its own amniotic sac. Thus, a single amniocentesis will lead to a diagnosis of one fetus only. For this reason, multiple pregnancies are associated with incomplete prenatal diagnoses.

Problems specific to cytogenetic analysis

Deceptive karyotypes. The normal human chromosome complement is made up of a total of 46 chromosomes, consisting of 22 pairs of so-called autosomes and one set of two sex chromosome (XX in the female, and XY in the male). One member of each chromosome pair was contributed originally by the mother's ovum, and the other member was contributed by the father's sperm cell.

In cytogenetic analysis, the chromosomes from individual cells are photographed under the microscope, and prints are made from these photographs. The individual chromosomes are cut out of each print and rearranged in pairs in a prescribed arrangement known as a "karyotype." Under ordinary conditions, the karyotype of a single cell is representative of the chromosome complement of the individual as a whole.

In the majority of cases of congenital malformations resulting from chromosomal imbalance, the chromosome abnormality is obvious. For example, in the condition of trisomy an entire extra chromosome is present in the karyotype, and in cases of translocation or deletion, chromosomes of abnormal size are evident. However, there is always the possibility that deletions or translocations may involve such a small amount of chromosomal material that they go undetected. In such cases, the chromosome karyotype would appear normal even though an abnormality exists. Furthermore, a child may be born with defects and still have an entirely normal karyotype. Congenital malformations arise for a number of reasons, some of which have no genetic basis. Consequently, one should make clear to parents whose unborn child is being diagnosed either cytogenetically or biochemically, that no one can guarantee them a perfect baby.

Mosaicism. The term "mosaicism" as used in cytogenetics refers to a situation in which more than one cell line exists in the same individual. This indicates that the genetic accident underlying the production of the abnormal cell type occurred at some time soon after the fertilization of the ovum, so that the original normal cell line persists but is accompanied by the abnormal cells.

Mosaicism leads to an overall genetic imbalance and congenital malformations, so that in performing a cytogenetic evaluation it is important that a sufficient number of cells be analyzed to rule out the presence of an abnormal cell line.

Problems specific to biochemical analysis

Erroneous diagnosis of original genetic problem. For each of the heritable metabolic disorders capable of being diagnosed prenatally, the biochemical test or tests involved are specific to the particular disorder. Certainly, then, in order for the tests to be correct and accurate, the nature of the suspected disorder must be known.

Prenatal diagnoses for such disorders are undertaken only when it is known that a genetic risk is present. For example, in the case of a metabolic disorder transmitted as an autosomal recessive condition, both parents are assumed to be carriers of the recessive gene involved if they have already produced a child with the disorder. Under such circumstances it would be reasonable to undertake a prenatal evaluation of any subsequent pregnancy. However, if the disorder has been incorrectly diagnosed in the original case of the defective child, the biochemical tests used for the prenatal diagnosis will not be correct since the wrong condition will be tested for.

Variability and possible unreliability of certain biochemical tests. Some of the biochemical tests used in prenatal evaluations are highly complex, and results may vary from laboratory to laboratory. It is particularly important that such tests be used for prenatal evaluation only by highly experienced laboratories where consistency of results has been established.

Another problem affecting the reliability of biochemical analyses is the fact that in the case of several of the metabolic diseases that are potentially capable of being diagnosed prenatally, adequate normal values for the factors (enzymes or whatever other factor is specific to the diagnosis) to be tested for are not yet established for various fetal ages.

In short, although reliable biochemical tests exist for the postnatal evaluation of numerous metabolic diseases, relatively few have been sufficiently tested in prenatal diagnoses to be considered reliable at this stage in the development of the art. However, there seems little doubt that as research in this area progresses, an increasing number of genetically controlled metabolic disorders will join the list of those that can be accurately evaluated prenatally.

PRINCIPLES OF GENETIC COUNSELING

Expert and effective genetic counseling is partly a science but also an art. It requires in the health professional a combination of specific scientific knowledge, experience in handling patients with genetic problems, and the type of personality that makes it possible to establish in his patients feelings of trust, confidence, and easy communication. Effective counseling techniques cannot be learned from a book, but there are some principles that should be kept in mind by all individuals associated in any way with the management of cases involving a genetic problem.

Of course, the counselor must have up-to-date knowledge of those genetic fundamentals that have applicability to the types of cases with which he deals. Obvious and basic as this statement may appear to be, it is worthy of being stressed, because the body of knowledge in genetics is expanding so rapidly that even those professionals dealing with genetic problems on a day-to-day basis find it difficult to keep up with the field. Many of the old concepts of genetics are now recognized as incomplete and some have been proved to be erroneous.

As the result, an earnest and honest professional who has learned some genetics in the past may fall into the trap of undertaking genetic counseling without realizing the potentially disastrous results of his own lack of complete competence. Genetic counseling should be recognized as being potentially the basis for life-or-death decisions. This is particularly true in the case of prenatal evaluations, but any genetic counseling is likely to have an effect upon a couple's decision of whether to have more children. Erroneous or incomplete information from the counselor may result in unnecessarily frightening a couple and thereby wiping out the entire future lineage that might have arisen from them. Conversely, failure on the part of a would-be counselor to understand all potential hazards of a particular situation may result in the production of a badly defective child by a couple who were unaware of their risk.

Any professional who undertakes to inform his patients with respect to genetic problems should be acutely aware of his limitations and be prepared both philosophically and emotionally to seek the assistance of a more competent individual when necessary.

The importance of making a proper diagnosis has been mentioned previously. In this regard there is a definite difference between cases associated with a heritable metabolic condition and those involving a chromosome abnormality. In the former, since attention is on the disease entity or syndrome, the requirements are that it be accurately diagnosed, that it be recognized as having a genetic basis, that the mode of transmission and the recurrence risk be understood, and that the availability and reliability of laboratory tests for its prenatal diagnosis be known. When a cytogenetic anomaly is involved, the basis for diagnosis is the karyotype rather than the abnormalities of the affected individual. Therefore, the important considerations are the determination of whether the condition is familial

and whether it can be accurately diagnosed prenatally.

Early in the counseling relationship it is important for the counselor to determine what preconceived ideas his patients may have with respect to the genetic condition in question. He should also evaluate their desire for additional children, learn what their religious background is, and try to determine how much of an emotional shock the knowledge of their genetic problem has produced. In other words, he should learn as much as possible about his patients as people and about their reactions to the situation, so that he can best serve not only as an effective informant but also as a trusted confidant who is capable of providing understanding and emotional support.

The problems that a couple with a genetic problem face may be varied in nature and relate to various aspects of family life, such as financial burden, concern over what information to give to their children and how to give it, and the potential deterioration of the sexual relationship. If a counselor does not feel competent to deal with all of these varied problems, he should at least be aware of their existence and be prepared to refer the patients to other individuals from whom they may obtain the necessary guidance.

One of the most difficult tasks that a counselor faces is that of keeping his own biases under control. The counselor's job is to provide his patients with accurate data, interpret those data if necessary, point out alternative decisions, allow the patients to come to a free choice, and continue to provide support for them whether he personally agrees with the choice that they have made. It is not the job of a counselor to tell a couple what to do.

Hopefully, from these brief remarks, one will have gained the impression that genetic counseling is a complex and demanding undertaking that should not be entered into by unqualified persons. However, it is hoped that all professionals involved in any aspect of family planning will recognize the important part that genetics plays in their field of interest and endeavor. If a genetic problem is recognized or suspected in connection with the family planning management of a couple, every effort should be made to place them in the hands of a competent genetic counselor so that they may receive accurate and appropriate advice. If no such individual is readily available, it is suggested that contact be made through the nearest medical center or the local office of The National Foundation—March of Dimes.

SUGGESTED READINGS

1. Abortion and the law, ed. 2, Cleveland, 1972, The Press of Case Western Reserve University.
2. Levine, H.: Clinical cytogenetics, Boston, 1971, Little, Brown & Co.
3. Macintyre, M. N.: Counseling in cases involving antenatal diagnosis. In Dorfman, A., editor: Antenatal diagnosis, Chicago, 1972, University of Chicago Press.
4. Macintyre, M. N.: "Chromosomal problems of intrauterine diagnosis." In Intrauterine diagnosis. In Birth defects: Original article series, VII(5):10-14, April 1971. The National Foundation—March of Dimes.
5. Macintyre, M. N.: Problems and limitations of prenatal genetic evaluation. In Aladjem, S., editor: Risks in the practice of modern obstetrics, St. Louis, 1972, The C. V. Mosby Co.
6. Macintyre, M. N.: Genetic risk, prenatal diagnosis, and selective abortion. In: Abortion and the law, ed. 2, Cleveland, 1972, The Press of Case Western Reserve University.
7. Milunsky, A., Littlefield, J. W., Kanfer, J. N., Kolodny, E. H., Shih, V. E., and Atkins, L.: Prenatal genetic diagnosis, New Eng. J. Med. 283:1370-1381, 1441-1447, 1498-1504, 1970.

10 Family design and family planning

Jetse Sprey*

The expression "family planning" consists of two parts "family" and "planning." Since it is planning—or lack of it—that forms the subject matter of this book, its linkage to the family indicates that the reproductive behavior that occurs within the institutional boundaries of the family is under scrutiny. This means that the "planning" discussed here operates in a value system that is part and parcel of the normative arrangements defining marriage and the family in our society.

This latter point is relevant for two reasons. First, many professionals who offer guidance and help in the area of conception control are better trained to deal with it as a "health" phenomenon than a familial one. Basic as health considerations may be, their application to the family planning process loses much of its meaning outside the interlocking contexts of marriage and the family. Illustrative of this is the fact that reproductive planning outside marriage can only be aimed toward the avoidance of birth and has no meaning beyond that narrow scope.

Second, if we posit the social primacy of the element of "family" over that of "planning," the exploration of changes in our contemporary family design becomes of great interest to students of fertility and family planning. As an initial premise, many observers note that our present-day, monolithic, family design is in a state of transition. This change is, in my view, directed toward the establishment of legitimate, so-cially sanctioned, alternate designs for living, in addition to our traditional family form. This trend—which presently still contains many elements of temporary faddism—may be expected to lead to the establishment of a plurality of viable life careers for adults. Some of the latter may remain temporary stages in the individual life cycle. Others may develop into more or less permanent patterns of living. Each successful alternative to marriage and the family will, however, manifest its own complex interdependence with the process of human reproduction. It is to the tentative exploration of such linkages that this paper is devoted.

Family planning—the activities associated with the wanting and having of children—affects, and is influenced by, the functioning and structuring of families. The structure of a given family unit, that is, the more or less stable way in which its members relate to each other through the vehicles of their culturally prescribed roles, depends for its stability on the effectiveness and outcomes of the family planning process. On the other hand, Rainwater,[12] in 1965, and also Hill, Stycos, and Back,[10] in 1959, have demonstrated that the specific type of familial structure effectively conditions the quality of procreative planning. This particular interdependence is not the focus of this paper. It is taken for granted. As stated earlier, my concern is with the interrelationship between our family system as it manifests itself socially, legally, and culturally in its totality and the management of reproduction, childrearing, and sexuality. In this context the term "family design" describes the family as a design for living, or a way of life.

---

*Ph.D., Associate Professor of Sociology, Case Western Reserve University, Cleveland, Ohio.

Original article.

CONTEMPORARY FAMILY DESIGN

Our present-day family is solidly embedded in law and custom. As two lawyers, Goldstein and Katz (1965),[7] stated it in the introduction to a tome on family law:

The law, without explicitly defining family, assumes that "family" is essential to the evolution and growth of a viable society. This assumption rests on another assumption: that family like law itself, is one of the basic processes for the control of human behavior.

and further:

Family law . . . is defined as the process for deciding what relationships should be labelled "family," under what circumstances such relationships may be established, administered, and recognized, and what consequences should accompany these determinations.

What then are those relationships that are labeled "family"? The answer seems so self-evident that its validity, and the premise that our current family design is "essential to the evolution and growth of a viable society," are rarely questioned. Families, we all know, should consist of two parents, one of each sex, and their children. In the past, and presently in certain segments of our population, grandparents and other close relatives could be included in households. But the trend is away from this, with our current ideal being the so-called neolocal conjugal family unit: a group consisting only of parents and their offspring and living on its own. A couple without children, regardless of the duration of their marriage, is somehow not considered to constitute a family.

Our contemporary family is seen to be a very private group. The relationships between its members are defined as close and exclusive of most outsiders. The only bond considered more exclusive than the family is the marital dyad. Illustrative of such specialness is the fact that husbands and wives cannot be forced to testify against each other in a court of law. The law respects the view that they are "one" in their relationship to the outside world. This conception of privacy is, historically speaking, fairly new. Until the seventeenth century the family "ensured the transmission of life, property, and names, but did not penetrate very far into human sensibility."[1] In contrast the current family is expected to satisfy a desire for privacy and a need for identity. Only in modern times do we see, what many sociologists consider a major function of the family, that is, its provision of an antidote against the stresses and strains of our impersonal, organized, urban way of life. What is less well understood is the fact that this vital function tends to be monopolized by the family and that this same prescription toward familial intimacy, in the absence of viable alternatives, may become one of the most destructive and emotionally stifling aspects of the modern family.[4]

The relevance of the foregoing to our discussion lies in the fact that, regardless of the merits or demerits of the contemporary family, there exists, at this writing, no real viable alternative design for living. Some sociologists tend to see the increasingly open choice of marriage partner as evidence of our "liberation" from the institution of marriage, but this assumption is invalid. Being single, or a return to that status, is, in our contemporary society, no viable life career. On the contrary, remaining unmarried is frequently an involuntary event. Our contemporary family has thus, to a very large extent, a control over the access of adults to other adults in our society. The ability to derive companionship and sexual fulfillment from a relationship with others, on a more or less permanent and voluntary basis, is quite limited outside the marital context. Furthermore, the access that adults have to the lives of children is, with few exceptions, almost totally monopolized by the family. This last point is taken up in the next section.

THE VALUE OF CHILDREN

Children have been traditionally considered an asset to a family. Their presence, in numbers, was needed to overcome the effects of high infant and child mortality and had distinct economic and social advantages. The latter is no longer the case in highly industrialized societies. One or two children suffice to transmit the family line. As far as their economic advantage is concerned, it may be pointed out that the estimated cost for a typical American family to raise and educate a child is approximately $40,000.

Why then, in the face of this, do married couples still plan families, and frequently larger ones than they really need? In answer, two interrelated social factors must be considered. First, there is the still remarkably pronatalist nature of our familial subculture. It requires little effort to recognize the many ways—some subtle, others not—in which procreation in quantity is still positively sanctioned in our present-day culture. For example, a planned childless marriage still is seen as deviant, that is, something that requires a special reason. Accumulated folk "wisdom" reflected in sayings like "cheaper by the dozen" is not counterbalanced by statements presenting a reverse point of view. On the contrary, we find that many people, professionals and laymen alike, still tend to distrust and pity the only child. Where pity *is* due, as in the case of the birth of quintuplets, we find instead congratulations and national jubilation. In summary, the kind of cultural stereotype about our family design that was so aptly labeled by Goode as the "classical family of Western nostalgia"[8] is still resonant with the "patter of little feet."

The second factor to be focused on may, on the surface, seem less evident but is, in my view, even more relevant in its consequences for family planning and fertility control. It reflects the earlier mentioned familial monopoly within the realms of *both* procreative and nonprocreative sexuality and that of child care. Interdependent with this condition is what Judith Blake[3] refers to as the "non-economic utilities" of children. In other words, to many contemporary

adults the possibility of contact with children, not necessarily on a long-time basis, is very important. Some like all children, others have preferences for certain sex or age categories. Children provide adults with access to major social roles: those of parents and, equally relevant perhaps, those of grandparents. Most of such access is, however, with very few exceptions, only available by having children of one's "own," thus, through participation in the institution of the family. And even within the family context the options are limited. The steady reduction in family size, especially among the middle class, limits the exposure to small children to a few years, while also reducing the probability of access to both sexes. Each of these considerations is at least partially responsible for the fact that even within the planned contemporary family, parents have more children than one would "rationally" expect.

It is considerations like the foregoing that leads Judith Blake[3] to conclude:

> The family complex may bow to depression, stoop to war, and shrink into an urban apartment, but until non-familial roles begin to offer significant competition to familial ones as avenues for adult satisfaction, the family will probably continue to amaze us with its procreative powers.

It is argued below that such "avenues for adult satisfaction" indeed are part of some, currently still experimental, alternate family designs. A number of these designs provide access to adults; others make a continuing, wide-ranging contact with children possible. Furthermore, and most important, many lack the prerequisite of lifelong commitment, so that the option to participate in more than one during the adult life-cycle remains open.

PROSPECTS FOR CHANGE

Changes in our contemporary family design may come about in two, not necessarily independent, ways. Both are relevant to our topic. In the first instance we find the social acceptance and legitimation of those family forms that currently still are considered deviant, or marginal. The second category goes beyond this and presumes the institutionalization of a number of contemporary "experimental" forms—no more than fads and fancies at this writing—at some future time. To conceive of this latter category, we must consider each of the present-day "givens" within the social realms of marriage and the family as open to challenge.

A recent discussion of traditional family forms by Sussman[13] may serve as a starting point. He distinguishes between a wide variety of family units, of which the following are pertinent to our discussion:*

1. Nuclear family—husband, wife, and offspring living in a common household.
2. Nuclear dyad—husband and wife alone: childless.
3. Single-parent family—one head, as a consequence of divorce, abandonment, or separation, and usually including minor children.

This very brief array covers what little variation that currently exists within the realm of institutionalized reproduction in our society. Childless marriages, that is, childless by intent or infertility rather than default, still tend to be considered, by many, a violation of the family norms.

As for the single-parent family, its status is, at best, marginal. This is illustrated by the fact that much of the efforts designed to help such families are not really aimed at making this type of unit a truly self-sustaining and functioning entity, but rather at its elimination and prevention. Single parents are urged to remarry; single women are counseled against unwed motherhood. The social position of single parents still is a stigmatized one, with the amount of stigma

---

*Sussman's exhaustive, but descriptive, treatment is not duplicated here. Some of his types are paraphrased and included in our scheme.

being associated with the nature of the originating event. Unwed mothers are stigmatized most, widows and widowers least. In the latter case the situation is obviously not his or her fault. Instead, we frequently find anger and blame aimed at the unfortunate departed.[11] Most relevant is that in all circumstances someone has to be blamed for the inception of a socially undesirable situation.

It is not surprising and is typical that in all these single-parent forms the role of family planning is seen as strictly preventive. Indicative of this role is the fact that unwed mothers are blamed by some for not being "good" and by others for not being "careful." Single women, whether formerly married or not, who *plan* their families obviously have no place in our current procreative scheme of things.

NEW DESIGNS FOR LIVING

To provide for a somewhat comprehensive and realistic appraisal of potential alternatives to our present-day, monolithic, family design, we must specify those areas of interpersonal activity that are controlled within its context. It will then be possible to raise, for each of these areas, the question "Is its inclusion still socially realistic and warranted?"

Control of sexual intimacy. There is a growing evidence that some individuals, especially among the ranks of the young and the formerly married, are seeing the marital contract no longer as a necessary part of a close, nonprocreative, sexual relationship. On the other hand, however, there is another nonprocreative category—the homosexual—that is beginning to demand the right to legal marriage. Contradictory as these two trends may seem, they reflect, in my view, a similar underlying value change. In the first instance, it is not so much marriage as a public commitment that is rejected, but rather its one-sided procreative and life-long implications. Marriage, as a social and legal sanction of an interpersonal bond—whether this be a homosexual or heterosexual one—has certain legal, economic, and social advantages and seems to serve, on the emotional level, as a reinforcement of mutual trust and commitment. To be viable, this type of marriage would, of course, require a simple, civil, divorce procedure, and, in its heterosexual manifestation, free access to all aspects of modern contraceptive technology. It would also need a value system in which the rationality and foresight that is essential to successful reproductive control would not conflict with the emotional, possibly romantic, definition of the relationships in question. In other words, relationships of this nature are only viable if the participants are capable of the rational and planned elimination of all its procreative consequences.

The establishment of the above-mentioned type of social outlets would, in my opinion, result in an increase in the average age at first pregnancy and reduce the rate of family-oriented marriage. It would, furthermore, alleviate the burdens of being single.

Prescription of monogamy. One of the basic aspects of our contemporary family system is its monogamous structure. This premise is challenged on two counts. There are people who feel that, given the trend toward smaller families, both children and parents will be better off in some form of communal family.* This would be a unit in which all adults are considered "parents" to all children. A second emphasis (the two are not exclusive) stresses the fact that, given our current preoccupation with interpersonal intimacy, the strain associated with the marital dyad would be alleviated when the size of the spousal group was enlarged. The empirical truth of either of these claims

is as yet unknown and lies beyond the scope of this paper. Relevant, however, is the fact that individuals are at this time experimenting with communal designs for living[2,5,6] and that some form of legal acceptance of this kind of family design, at a future time, cannot be ruled out.

Prescription of two-parenthood. In a previous section the "involuntary" and temporary connotations associated with our contemporary single-parent family design were stressed. The notion that families must have two parents, one of each sex, to be "normal" is being challenged. Single women, occasionally supported by groups in the Women's Liberation Movement, are beginning to demand the right to either bear, or adopt, children legitimately. Furthermore, representatives of homosexual groups, especially female ones, have raised the issue of a family consisting of parents of the same sex. In a number of such cases divorcees with children have established Lesbian relationships and demand to have their relationships legalized. The validity or societal merits of these demands is not at issue here; it suffices to observe that requests like these are being voiced. In a number of states single individuals are already allowed to adopt children; the extension of this privilege to single-parent procreation seems quite possible.

Assumption of permanence. Marriage still is considered to create a lifelong bond in our society. Our high divorce rate has not shaken this value, but is generally seen as an indication that many individuals are prone to make mistakes in the selection of their lifelong companions. Indicative of this is the ongoing effort by professionals and laymen alike to improve our mate selection procedures. The possibility that the married state, as traditionally prescribed in our culture, would not agree with a sizable proportion of our adult population tends to be ignored. It is not possible to predict whether our marriage-is-for-keeps type of value orientation will ever disappear. There is little evidence, even among the young and the

---

*I realize that the term "commune" means all things to all people. For the sake of brevity our discussion is limited to those types that would challenge some structural aspects of our current family design.

formerly married, that this is about to happen.

There are indications, however, that intimate relationships of a noncontractual and nonpermanent nature are becoming more common before marriage. Many of such bonds still derive their rationale from marriage, in the sense that they are seen as either a trial, or a marital learning experience, rather than being just ends in themselves. To us their relevance, regardless of their rationale, is twofold. The possibility to cohabit with others, including members of the opposite sex, under a variety of conditions, on a basis of involvement rather than contractual, lifelong commitment alleviates the social deprivations of the unmarried status in life. It would also, as is the case in planned childless marriages, require contraceptive skills, and a value system designed to protect and culturally justify the social realm of nonprocreative sexuality.

The question remains: "What does the foregoing add up to?" Empirically speaking, it is very little, but it does provide a perspective within which the future existence of nonfamilial adult roles can be dealt with. And that seems worthwhile, even within the fairly narrow scope of this paper. Each of the alternate designs identified above is currently being experimented with in a wide array of forms and by a variety of people. None has been legally and socially accepted as yet, and it is impossible to say which one or ones will be or in what form. One thing is certain, however, each alternative has its own many-faceted connection with human reproduction, sexual expression, and childrearing and thus deserves the scrutiny of those who are concerned with issues of fertility control and family planning.

ALTERNATE FAMILY DESIGNS AND REPRODUCTIVE PLANNING

Family planning, as it is rapidly becoming part of our culture, is associated with legitimate procreation, that is, the birth of children in conjugal, two-parent families. The establishment of alternate designs for legitimate reproduction will not eliminate this relationship, but merely extend it into additional settings. Some of the latter, and their possible connection with fertility and family planning, are sketched below.

The single-parent family. It is possible to conceive of the single-parent family as a legitimate design for procreation, rather than just a residual unit. If this happens families of this type may be expected primarily to be female headed. Those women who opted for this design would, statistically speaking, form a small and selective minority. The fertility of this family type would be totally female controlled and would require access to those contraceptive means best suited for this purpose. I feel that two of the main sources of recruitment would be (1) single women who under traditional circumstances would have been part of a two-parent family and (2) divorcees and young widows, who would prefer this kind of design over remarriage. In view of this, one may hypothesize that the existence of the single-parent family, as a legitimate procreative option, will tend to reduce both the total marriage and remarriage rates. Families of this nature must, of necessity, be planned and may be expected to be small in size, since they reflect, in my view, a conception of children that is oriented toward quality rather than toward quantity.

The communal family. Legitimate communal family designs may come about in two forms, depending on the goals and values of their membership. One type would leave the legal form of conjugal *marriage* intact, but pool the childrearing resources of its contributing conjugal units. This would result in a kind of "extended" family unit made up of nonrelatives. Central to the inception and functioning of this kind of family would be the shared meaning of having children among the adult members. One may expect, for example, that the need to be with children would take preference over that of "owning" them, that is, having one's own biological offspring. Adoptive parenthood would have to rank equally with its biological counterpart. The fact that under these conditions children have access to peers, while adults have the option to be involved with children of both sexes other than their own, will therefore serve as an important motivational factor in the familial planning of each participating couple.

The second communal type goes well beyond the above arrangement and would actually represent a form of group marriage, or polygamy. Here all adults would be parents to all children, while all would be somehow married to each other. Again, there is reason to believe that the average fertility of this kind of family would be low. The Constantines[5] comment on this fact in their report on contemporary group marriage in this country. Alan Guttmacher, in a recent communication from East Africa, mentions that on that continent, where polygamy is legal, "the number of births per wife in a polygamous marriage are fewer than in a monogamous one."[9] These data are, of course, far from conclusive but do provide some plausibility to my contention that if communal type of family designs were to be legitimized their average fertility would lie below that of a comparable number of conjugal units. Be this as it may, there seems little doubt that family planning, in all its ramifications, will be an integral part of the constitutive process of effectively functioning communal families.

NONPROCREATIVE DESIGNS FOR LIVING

Earlier I argued that one of the most important potential nonprocreative factors in our future pluralistic family design is the establishment of such alternate life styles that allow for the fulfillment of nonprocreative sexuality. The option to remain single, or to return to that position, without suffering emotional and sexual deprivation is one major alternative. Secondly, there would be the acceptance of childless marriage as

an end in itself rather than a contractual prelude to reproduction. And finally, there would be the legal possibility to establish socially recognized homosexual relationships. A prerequisite to the effective management of the first two options is, of course, the easy access to an advanced contraceptive technology and a value system within which procreative control is positively sanctioned.

CONCLUSION

The aim of this paper was to place family planning within the framework of our changing family system. It was posited that our current monolithic family design will gradually expand into a more pluralistic one. As a result of such a development, the current monopolies the family holds in the realms of intimate adult relationships and that of child care will either disappear or be greatly limited. I do not believe that this will mean the end of our contemporary family design, but will lead to a reduction in the proportion of those adults who opt for this way of life. The availability of meaningful relationships outside the context of traditional marriage and the increased access to the company of the children of others will, in all likelihood, affect the traditional family. It may well shorten the duration of many marriages and can also be expected to decrease the average family size.

In view of the complexity of the association between family planning as a reflection of a changing reproductive *ethic* and the basic changes in our thinking about the family, a final comment seems in order. There seems to be agreement on the assumption that if our society is to survive in a livable form a general reduction in fertility must somehow be brought about. This means that at some future time there will be proportionally fewer children in our social world. It is this simple demographic fact that adds great relevance to our discussion of alternate family designs, especially those that provide increased access to children, because we may predict that in a society in which children are scarce their "value" will increase. An increase in value has, in our type of society, traditionally led to an increase in "production." It is ironic to note that one of the main values that seems to underlie our present movement toward fertility control, that is, the desire to establish a value system in which procreation would mean the begetting of children as unique individuals rather than mere components of a given family size, may well contain the seeds of its own destruction. It would lead to two contradictory results: fewer children, but a concomitant greater worth of children. Such a destruction, therefore, will take place, in my opinion, unless a family design is established through which adults who need to hear the voices of children will indeed be allowed to listen.

REFERENCES

1. Aries, P.: Centuries of childhood, New York, 1965, Vintage Books.
2. Berger, B., et al.: Child-rearing practices of the communal family. In Skolnick, A. S., and Skolnick, J. H., editors: Family in transition, Boston, 1971, Little, Brown & Co., pp. 509-523.
3. Blake, J.: Demographic science and the redirection of population policy. In Sheps M. C., and Ridley, J. C., editors: Public health and population change, Pittsburgh, 1965, University of Pittsburgh Press, pp. 41-69.
4. Cooper, D.: The death of the family, New York, 1971, Vintage Books.
5. Constantine, L. L., and Constantine, J. M.: The group marriage. In Gordon, M., editor: The nuclear family in crisis: The search for an alternative, New York, 1972, Harper & Row, Publishers, pp. 204-222.
6. Fonzi, G.: The new arrangement. In Gordon, M., editor: The nuclear family in crisis: The search for an alternative, New York, 1972, Harper & Row, Publishers, pp. 180-196.
7. Goldstein, J. and Katz, J.: The family and the law, New York; 1965, Free Press of Glencoe, Inc.
8. Goode, W. J.: World revolution and family patterns, New York, 1970, Free Press of Glencoe, Inc.
9. Guttmacher, A.: Benefits of polygamy. In Planned Parenthood-World Population newsletter, New York, January 12, 1972, p. 3.
10. Hill, R., Stycos, J. M., and Back, K. W.: The family and population control, Chapel Hill, N. C., 1959, University of North Carolina Press.
11. Marris, P.: Widows and their families, London, 1958, Routledge & Kegan Paul, Ltd.
12. Rainwater, L.: Family design, Chicago, 1965, Aldine Publishing Co.
13. Sussman, M. B.: Family systems in the 1970's: Analysis, policies, and programs; Ann. Amer. Acad. Polit. Soc. Science 396: 40-56, July 1971.

11 Induced abortion and contraception: Sociological aspects

Emily C. Moore, M.A., M.S.*

Although induced abortion and contraception are often viewed as alternatives, total fertility control includes both pregnancy prevention and pregnancy termination—the "fireproofing" and the "fire extinguisher."

There are several possible life patterns which the individual woman may follow: no contraception, no abortion; regular contraceptive practice, and accidental pregnancies carried to term; regular contraceptive practice, abortion used to terminate accidental pregnancies; initial use of contraception, then a change to reliance on abortion; one or more abortions, then a change to reliance on contraception; continuous reliance on abortion alone; sporadic reliance on either or both methods combined.

The following sections bring together available evidence on the relationship between abortion and contraception.

RELATIVE MERITS OF INDUCED ABORTION AND CONTRACEPTION
Medical aspects

From a medical point of view, which is the preferred means of fertility control? If mortality is the sole criterion for judging a method's medical merits, we may conclude from the model proposed by Tietze

---

*Staff Associate, Demographic Division, The Population Council, New York, New York.

Reprinted from Newman, Sidney H., Mildred B. Beck, and Sarah Lewit, editors: *Abortion Obtained and Denied: Research Approaches,* New York, 1971, The Population Council, pp. 131-155. Copyright The Population Council.

that a combination of perfectly safe but not entirely effective contraception and in-hospital abortion to terminate contraceptive failures entails the lowest risk.[1]

Personal aspects

Why is abortion used so widely, even when contraceptive techniques are known and available; i.e., why is it often preferable from the woman's point of view? Some suggested answers are the following:

1. Except for sterilization and the IUD, no other birth-prevention technique is a one-event procedure. (Injections and implants are once-every-three-to-four-months, possibly one-a-year actions.)

2. Abortion does not require the knowledge or consent of the husband.

3. It is coitus-independent, as are IUD's and orals.

4. Unlike nearly all contraceptives (except for injections, implants, and continuous conscientious use of the pill), once begun it is 100 percent effective, although attempts may be unsuccessful. Perhaps it should be stated instead that there is continuous uncertainty associated with the use of most contraceptives, whereas the woman knows almost immediately whether or not an abortion attempt has been successful. Unsuccessful abortion attempts are certainly difficult to enumerate and have a wide range in terms of seriousness of intent and degree of effort.

5. Abortion is not based on the probabilities of conception, but on the certainty of a recognized pregnancy; i.e., it requires

hindsight, not foresight; is curative, not preventive. The small proportion of coital acts which result in pregnancy may encourage many women to "take a chance" and be unprotected.

6. Abortion is the only method to avert a birth which may have been desired at the time of conception but which, due to changed circumstances, may no longer be wanted.

7. Compared with mechanical and chemical means, abortion is technically simple. For the unmarried, separated, widowed, or divorced, with infrequent or unanticipated intercourse, abortion is possibly cheaper and/or more appropriate than other methods.

Economic aspects

Three considerations must be included here: cost to the woman and to society of (1) abortion, (2) various means of contraception, and (3) combinations of the two.

Where abortion is either illicitly performed or legally obtained only with great difficulty and expense, contraception is less costly to the woman. Where abortion is provided by the state free or with minimal cost, and there is a charge for contraceptive services, the reverse is true. Where both are free, the woman will not be influenced in her choice by cost factors.

Abortions legally performed are usually said to be more costly to society than the provision of contraceptive services or the provision of neither; however, providing contraceptive services alone or neither contraception nor abortion may result in the necessity for hospital emergency care of illegally induced abortions. The comparative costs to society of hospital bed-days, transfusions, antibiotics, laboratory use, and time of medical and paramedical personnel, for abortion only, for contraception only, or for both or neither have not been determined.

The medical profession's willingness or reluctance to provide contraceptive services or to perform abortions or deliveries, and the payment they receive for each of these tasks may be important determinants of relative use. There appear, however, to have been few attempts to document this.

RELATIONSHIP BETWEEN ABORTION AND CONTRACEPTION— MUTUAL EFFECTS
Attitudes

Westoff, Moore, and Ryder found a direct relationship between positive attitudes toward contraception and more liberal views on abortion; the relationship held true regardless of race or religion.[2]

Girard and Zucker obtained similar results in France; opposition to abortion was positively related to opposition to contraception.[3]

Knowledge

While a number of attitude surveys on the subject of abortion have been conducted in the United States, Japan, Great Britain, and elsewhere, almost no attempt has been made to determine the level of knowledge about abortion. Thus, it is not yet possible to compare abortion knowledge with contraceptive knowledge in the same community, nor to see how attitudes vary with level of knowledge.

In a pilot survey conducted in Washington Heights, New York City, in 1968—1969 in response to the question "Would you please tell me how abortions are done," 38 percent of 169 women expressed no knowledge whatsoever of any medically acceptable method of inducing abortion.[4] Even "see a doctor" was considered knowledge of acceptable method; i.e., 38 percent described only folk methods or no method at all. Among a number of variables with which "some knowledge" was positively associated was the respondent's approval of contraception and knowledge of modern contraceptive methods. She was not asked if she knew how or where to obtain an abortion.

Either/or

It is sometimes suggested for the individual seeking abortion that "she should have used contraceptives," when she is clearly already pregnant. It has been proposed that sterilization should follow every legal abortion, or that a mass sterilization program would obviate the need for abortions. These proposals ignore the variety of circumstances, such as rape, rubella, an unmarried woman, an unstable marriage, or a woman suffering from a temporary illness in which a particular pregnancy may be unwanted but a future one welcomed.

A clear distinction needs to be made between the individual family's requirements for satisfactory fertility control and society's requirements: a society may decide that funds are better invested in contraceptive programs rather than in legal abortions, or vice versa, although concentration on one to the exclusion of the other may be unsatisfactory to individuals and their families who might prefer to have access to both.

Availability and motivation

To what extent either abortion or contraception is used may be determined less by individual preference than by availability. Access to abortion and contraception may vary widely according to region, income, local climate of opinion, age, range of permissible indications, and even the time at which a request is submitted relative to the filling of monthly quotas; thus, the "choice" between abortion, contraception, and delivery may not be based at all on reasons noted.

Romania and immediately postwar Japan are especially conspicuous for high rates of abortion and nonavailability of modern contraceptives.[5] High rates of legal abortion among the unmarried in Great Britain may be partially due to their difficulty in obtaining contraception.[6] Nonavailability is a determining factor varying not only by marital status but by region as well: of 200 local

health authorities, only 34 provide "full family planning service."[7]

Sometimes access to both abortion and contraception is limited: U. S. hospitals with the most restrictive abortion policies tend also to provide the least contraceptive services.[8] The consequences are higher rates of delivery, illegal abortion, and/or contraceptive services from private physicians or clinics in the areas served by such hospitals.

Hubinont has noted the inverse relationship between active family planning programs and estimated abortion rates in European countries.[9] He concludes that such programs apparently have more effect than the provisions of abortion laws on the frequency of abortion.

It has been suggested that abortion and contraception merely provide the means for fertility control when motivation already exists. "The use of abortion on a mass scale as a means of birth prevention is not the result of government policy; on the contrary, it was public pressure on the government which made legally available, on a very wide basis, a form of control which had been embedded in the social customs of Tokugawa, Japan."[10] However, ease of access may also enhance desire. Some who argue that liberalization of abortion laws would have an insignificant effect in India, for example, note that motivation for small families already existed in Japan and eastern Europe prior to liberalization of abortion laws but does not yet exist in India. Others contend that surveys in India, demonstrating a "desired family size" notably smaller than "actual family size," indicate a reservoir of ready motivation for use of abortion should it become legally available. Motivation for control of family size, while already substantial before liberalization in Japan and eastern Europe, must have been greatly stimulated when abortions became more easily obtainable, since birth rates, already declining, decreased even more sharply thereafter.

Use of abortion; use of contraception

Let us now examine the evidence for various contentions regarding the effects of abortion and contraception on each other. The case is sometimes based on small non-representative samples and insufficient evidence, but the accumulation of data and analysis from a variety of situations makes it possible for us to draw some tentative conclusions. Where abortion remains an illicit act, or at least a private matter, data remains sketchy and analysis restricted by necessary estimates and conjectures.

Possible combinations are the following:

Static situations (either unchanging conditions, or a situation which is investigated at only one point in time):

1. Low contraceptive use — High abortion incidence
2. High contraceptive use — Low abortion incidence
3. Low contraceptive use — Low abortion incidence
4. High contraceptive use — High abortion incidence

Dynamic situations (investigated in before-after situations):

5. Liberalization of abortion law raises contraceptive use.
6. Liberalization of abortion law lowers contraceptive use.
7. Restriction of liberal abortion law raises contraceptive use.
8. Restriction of liberal abortion law lowers contraceptive use.
9. Introduction of family planning program raises abortion incidence.
10. Introduction of family planning program lowers abortion incidence, either immediately or after some delay.

A clear distinction should be made between abortion *rates* per population, or per woman, and abortion *ratios* per pregnancies, or per live births. A population using contraception successfully may have a very low abortion rate, but a very high abortion ratio; i.e., there may be a major reliance on contraception, but once an unplanned pregnancy occurs, it is very likely to be aborted.

1. In the absence of availability of contraception, is abortion incidence (rates and ratios) likely to be high, particularly in a culture with a small family norm?

It is not surprising that among eastern European countries, the highest abortion rates and ratios have been recorded in Romania (before the 1967 change in its law) and in Hungary, the two eastern European countries with reportedly very poor use of contraceptives and extremely low birth rates (14.3 in Romania, 1966, and 14.5 in Hungary, 1967). Examples from developing countries could also be cited.

2. Where there has long been access to and widespread use of contraception, is abortion incidence correspondingly lower? That is, can low abortion rates (per population) be expected, even if abortion ratios (per pregnancies or live births) are high?

According to Hubinont, "The existence of family planning services and the absence of legal restrictions on the access to contraception [in western Europe] does indeed correspond with a lower estimate of the incidence of illegal abortion."[11]

The United States is considered a highly "contracepting" population with a relatively low estimated abortion rate. Declaring abortion rates either "high" or "low" in countries where only a small proportion are legally performed, is however, a precarious undertaking.

3. Illustrating low contraceptive use and low abortion rates and ratios are societies with unusually high fertility; e.g., Hutterites in the United States.

4. High contraceptive use coupled with high abortion ratios can best be illustrated by the studies which find that individuals who abort tend also to contracept, and vice versa, more than their counterparts in the same society.

a. Are aborters more likely to be contraceptors than are nonaborters? Evidence from Israel, Brazil, Taiwan, Japan, South Korea suggest this is so.[12] The last example, the Seoul survey, reports that while current users of contraceptives constituted only 9 percent of the total sample, 48 percent of the women who had aborted were practicing contraception.

b. Are contraceptors more likely to resort to abortion than noncontraceptors? Evidence from studies in Taiwan, India, Greece, Chile, and Japan supports this contention.[13]

Women who use contraceptives, of course, are selected strongly for a higher motivation toward fertility control. They are likely to resort to abortion when their contraceptive efforts fail. The greater the expectation of avoiding pregnancy, the greater is the likelihood of an induced abortion once a pregnancy has occurred.

5. Liberalization of abortion laws raises contraceptive use.

This is an unlikely occurrence in the absence of a deliberate effort to cause it to occur, although increased use of both methods of fertility control may logically occur simultaneously. Most proponents of liberalized abortion laws stress the desirability of extending contraceptive use and discouraging use of abortion wherever possible.

On an individual level, an unpleasant experience with abortion may inspire a woman to begin or improve contraceptive use.

6. Liberalization of abortion laws lowers contraceptive use.

It is sometimes suggested that the consequence of liberalization of abortion laws in eastern Europe has been to weaken reliance on contraception. However, the evidence is scanty,* and there is contrary evidence to suggest that concerted efforts to encourage contraceptive use can prevent

such undesirable effects. Moreover, the contraceptives in use were primarily traditional methods; evidence from societies in which more modern methods are in widespread use and in which abortion laws are then liberalized (Great Britain, and some states of the United States) has not yet been obtained.

7. Restriction of legal abortion laws raises contraceptive use.

Romania and Bulgaria are the only recent examples of a situation in which a permissive abortion law has become less so. Bulgaria's change was not so drastic, and data on contraceptive use are lacking. Following an initial rise in birth rates after deliberalization in Romania, apparent control over fertility in that country indicates some increased reliance on contraception as well as on illegal abortion.

8. Restriction of liberal abortion laws lowers contraceptive use.

This is unlikely and unknown to date. It is conceivable that lowered contraceptive use and more restrictive abortion laws might simultaneously occur in a situation of strongly coercive pronatalist policy—restriction of abortion law plus restriction on importation, manufacture, and distribution of contraceptives.

9. Introduction of a family planning program raises abortion incidence.

There is evidence from Korea, Taiwan, and Chile to suggest this unanticipated and undesirable event.[14]

The discovery that abortions may increase after the introduction of measures designed to cause abortions to decrease must be a disappointment to program administrators. There are indications, however, that this may be a transitional state of affairs. "A Family Planning program carries with it an awakening to the necessity for limiting the family in many marginal sectors, beyond the possibilities of local services, and this, added to the failures of contraceptives in use, will lead to the interruption of pregnancies already undesired."[15]

---

*Szabady and Klinger state that ten years after liberalization, roughly the same proportions are using some method of contraception, but there was an apparent shift to less reliable methods, which may, however, have been due to the survey method. The same may not occur in a population using better methods to begin with. Szabady, E., and Klinger, A., "The 1965-66 Hungarian study on fertility, family planning, and birth control," *Demográfia*, 9:135-161, 1966.

10. Have we any evidence that a family planning program can lower abortion incidence either immediately or eventually?

a. Reduced abortion *without* an intervening period of increased abortion seems to have been the case in Denmark, where a decline in abortions started at the same time as the "enlightenment" campaign of the Danish Family Planning Association;[16] in Poland, Czechoslovakia, and Yugoslavia, where the adoption of active family planning policies in recent years has been accompanied by a plateau or slight dropping off in abortions;[17] and in Yugoslavia, where an experiment was conducted in Belgrade, Subotica, and Sarajevo, utilizing randomly selected alternate postabortal patients for experimental and control groups.[18] The control group had the same access to family planning as the general population, while the experimental group was given intensive exposure to family planning education. After three years, the results were that 99.2 percent of the experimental and 37.7 percent of the control group were using contraception; the former had significantly lower repeat abortion experience; 124 legal abortions were performed during the study period on experimental women and 508 on control women.

Faundes reports that abortion rates in Chile have fallen significantly between 1964 (before the institution of an intensive family planning education-and-services project in 1965) and 1968.[19]

Accounting for the differences between the findings in San Gregorio and those of Monreal and Armijo, Faundes, et al. suggest:[20]

There are some differences between both programs that may explain why the rates of abortion decreased in San Gregorio and not in the rest of the Southern Area [of Santiago]. One of these differences refers to the capacity of the clinics, that in many sectors of the Southern Area—with the exception of San Gregorio —is insufficient to satisfy the demand for a quick and timely assistance. Delays and rejections are therefore frequent. . . . Another difference is related with the location of the clinics. In the Southern Area there are extensive zones with large population that do not have contraceptive services. This implies that many women have to travel relatively long distances for attention, which makes it difficult not only to begin the use of a contraceptive but also to obtain an adequate follow-up and opportune advice or treatment of inter-current conditions.

b. Reduced abortion incidence *with* an intervening period of increased abortion may have occurred in Taiwan, where "the annual incidence of induced abortion among the respondents of the 1967 island-wide KAP survey significantly increased between 1964 and 1965. The increase after 1965 was rather small. The island-wide family planning program was started in January 1964 . . . the program might have caused an increase in the incidence of induced abortion, particularly at the initial stage."[21] Although actual reduction is not yet observed, the rise appears to have slowed down or halted. In Japan, the annual number of live births remains steady and reported abortion rates are steadily declining; either contraceptive practice *is* improving and reducing the need for abortion, or the reporting of abortion is deteriorating.

In 1952, concerned by the rapid rise in induced abortion, the Japanese Minister of Health urged all local areas to increase contraceptive education and services. Several experiments at introducing family planning intensively in villages were initiated, and accumulated evidence indicates that following an initial rise in abortions, the rates of abortions eventually dropped off*—more rapidly than the overall decrease for Japan as a whole.[22]

The small-scale intensive efforts to promote contraceptive success demonstrated in

---

Ratios—abortions per live births—generally increased reflecting a stronger motivation to eliminate unwanted births.

Japan, Chile, and Yugoslavia would be difficult to extend to an entire nation. A changeover from reliance on abortion to contraception does seem to be feasible, but concerted efforts appear to be needed and large-scale illustrations are still lacking.

We have noted that the presence of a family planning program may initially stimulate the abortion rate; it may do so by motivating acceptors whose contraceptives fail to persist in their initial intention to prevent births, and by motivating persons for whom contraceptive services are not immediately available. Two crucial considerations for those initiating a family planning program would seem to be whether or not widespread services can be set up rapidly enough to service the newly motivated, and whether or not the program should assume responsibility for the increased number of abortions which result from program-stimulated motivation which is followed by method failure.

Monreal and Armijo express their view on this matter:[23]

> Leaving cultural prejudices aside, it may be asked if it would be more suitable, at least in those cases of the failure of contraceptives recommended by the health services, to use the same services for induced abortion. Without doubt, this would diminish the risks and acknowledge a necessity strongly felt by Chilean women at this time.

> This means that the fight against induced abortion should be carried on with a new mentality which will consider its incorporation in the prevention programs.

And later, quite explicitly, they state:

> It is suggested that induced abortion ought to be considered in the programs of prevention of abortion and family planning and should be carried out by the Health Services especially in those cases where contraceptives have failed.

It should be noted that such a policy is already in practice, in a limited fashion, in the Tunisian family planning program where women with five or more living children are aborted on request as part of the pro-

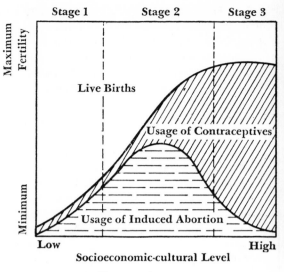

FIGURE 1

gram's activities. The Tunisian law on abortion was changed in order to permit the incorporation of abortion in the family planning program.

Requeña has suggested a diagram (Figure 1) which illustrates the three stages through which a society may pass, from no birth prevention, to primary reliance on abortion, and to major reliance on contraception with some residual abortions to "mop up" when contraceptives fail. The diagram presents stages over time through which a society passes, as well as concurrent patterns observed in three strata of society at one point in time.

If Requeña's diagram accurately illustrates the necessary stages through which a society must pass, it would seem unlikely that the interim (abortion) stage could be easily or quickly bypassed.[24]

DEMOGRAPHIC EFFECTS OF ABORTION AND/OR CONTRACEPTION

Abortion can clearly be a powerful agent in averting births, even though it must occur with great frequency, when used exclusively. In fact, it is in situations in which abortion has been the primary factor (such as Japan and Romania) that the most dramatic changes in births over short periods of time have been observed.

Used in combination with contraception, it can theoretically be even more effective, as shown by Potter, i.e., it need be resorted to less frequently in order to have important impact.[25] Potter reasons that in a noncontracepting population, the average time involved in induced abortion is 9 months, including 5 months of ovulatory exposure; for a live birth it is 21 months (30 months if lactation is prolonged). Under these conditions, 100 induced abortions account for 900 months of marriage duration, during which 43 (900/21 months) or 30 (900/30 months) live births might have occurred. Thus 100 abortions are needed to avert 43 or 30 live births (roughly 2 or 3 to 1).

When combined with effective contraception, an induced abortion becomes more nearly equivalent to averting a live birth. Assuming 90 percent effectiveness of contraception, the mean length of ovulatory exposure is increased from 5 months to 50 months. One hundred induced abortions now require 5,400 months of marriage duration, equivalent to 81.8 live births with no lactation (5,400/66 months) and 72 births if lactation is prolonged (5,400/75 months).

Only rarely is an attempt made to attribute proportionate amounts of total fertility decline in real populations to abortion and contraception. Muramatsu suggests 70—75 percent abortion and 30—25 percent sterilization responsible for the fertility decline in Japan between 1947 and 1957.[26] Monreal and Armijo estimate births averted 50 percent by abortion and 50 percent by contraception in Chile.[27] The reasoning behind these estimates is, however, not supplied.

To my knowledge, no one has attempted to estimate the relative effects of abortion and contraception on birth rates in the United States. A more accurate abortion figure than the current estimate of one-

million-per-year, combined with more up-to-date contraceptive use figures (anticipated from the 1970 National Fertility Survey) would make this possible.

Reports of fertility declines have several shortcomings in common. Some fail to note the degree of declining fertility prior to widespread access to legal abortion or to the introduction of a family planning program. Most suffer from lack of appropriate controls; i.e., it is difficult to determine to what extent fertility would have been reduced anyway, in the absence of either liberalized abortion laws or the introduction of a family planning program.

Conclusions

While more research is needed on the complex interrelationship of abortion and contraception, some tentative conclusions can be drawn:

1. Poor use of contraception, or use of poor contraception, promotes abortion use.

2. Good use of contraception, or use of good contraception, reduces abortion use.

3. Abortion is probably an essential, if undesirable, interim measure between no fertility control at all and preventing births by contraception; abortion should not be seen as the preferred method; it can be used initially as an emergency measure in the absence of contraceptives, and eventually as a back-up measure when contraceptives are in general use.

4. While abortion is only one means by which a population already wishing to limit family size can do so, its ready availability (legally, or with little fear of prosecution) probably serves as a stimulant to its use.

SUGGESTIONS FOR FUTURE RESEARCH

1. Bumpass and Westoff report that "of the women who originally desired only two children but have borne three or more children, four-fifths report their last pregnancy as unplanned. Women who desire only two children achieve their desired number very

early in the childbearing years, and consequently face a longer period of exposure to the risk of unwanted births than do women desiring larger families. One-third of these women experienced at least one accidental pregnancy, but this is consistent with a reasonably high contraceptive efficacy of over .995 per fertile period over the average of seven years since the birth of their second child."[28]

What could the reduction in unwelcome births be if women had access to *total* fertility control; i.e., including legal abortion? As abortion laws in the United States are repealed or declared unconstitutional, the opportunity for such measurement will present itself. Since it would be desirable to be able to predict what the reduction could be before the laws are actually changed, we may make two assumptions:

a. In countries where abortions are widely available, most "unwanted" births do not occur. It may be that not only definitely "unwanted" births may then be eliminated, but also the gray zone of strong ambivalence as well; i.e., legal abortion could mean the difference between an "acceptable" three-child family and a "preferred" two-child family.

b. A substantial proportion of women who find themselves unwillingly pregnant would avail themselves of legal abortion were it available.

2. Comparative effects of abortion and contraception availability on illegitimacy rates should also be examined; when it becomes possible to terminate unplanned pregnancies legally, is there a greater reduction in illegitimacy than when a family planning program is introduced?

3. In the case of WEUP (willful exposure to unwanted pregnancy[29]), would access to after-the-fact termination result in preventing the birth, or would the woman reject the use of abortion as well; i.e., should the phenomenon be labeled WEUP or WEUC (willful exposure to unwanted childbirth)?

4. The question of availability of contraception or abortion is not merely one of comparing the former with the latter; it is also a matter of comparative availability of either to certain subgroups in the population. In research on utilization, we must ask abortion/contraception for whom, where, under what circumstances.

Requeña's model for class/time variations in reliance on abortion and contraception suggests research for others to determine the extent to which his model is applicable. Further analysis of abortion and contraceptive use by certain characteristics is indicated; e.g., Negro-white differentials in the United States, ethnic variations in eastern Europe, class, residence, and age differentials, etc.

5. It is often not clear whether use of contraception precedes abortion or whether abortion promotes the use of contraception. It is most important that further research be done on individual reproductive histories.

6. The relationship between abortion and contraception might be entirely different were knowledge of one or the other to be increased. We now know something of contraceptive knowledge but almost nothing about abortion knowledge; the latter should be included in KAP surveys.

Knowledge questions in future studies should probe the woman's familiarity with methods employed and her knowledge of where to look if she wanted an abortion.

7. To our knowledge, there exists no attitude surveys comparing women's feelings toward both contraception and abortion per se. Women should be asked which they would prefer under what circumstances; their preferences would then have to be examined in relation to their levels of knowledge regarding both procedures.

8. Physicians' attitudes are vital to the implementation of either a contraceptive program or a permissive abortion law. In addition to examining relative fees to the physician for delivery, abortion, and contraceptive care, physicians should be asked their attitudes toward all three. Most opin-

ion surveys determine only the physicians' position on abortion law reform or repeal.

9. Fees to the physician are just one aspect of the relative "cost" of abortion and contraception to determine why one, rather than the other, is utilized; we should also examine the cost to the woman (economic and psychological) and the cost to society (economic and social).

10. While some studies have been conducted to examine the psychological and social cost of abortion and nonabortion, and some of the psychological aspects, such as libido changes and willful exposure to unwanted pregnancy, and social aspects, such as illegitimacy and decreased fertility and its effects on changing life styles, of the use or nonuse of contraception, these have not so far been conducted on a comparative basis. A suggested "starter set" for some comparisons of outcomes might be the following:

POSSIBLE CONSEQUENCES

Alternatives	Psychological	Social
Use contraceptives	freedom from fear of pregnancy guilt, remorse, regret	lower birth rate aging population fewer abortions health care required
Don't use contraceptives	fear of pregnancy guilt from abortion pressures from delivery and child bearing	higher birth rate higher abortion rate welfare services for excess fertility
Use abortion	guilt, remorse, regret free from unwanted child	cost of services and facilities lower birth rate
Don't use abortion	unwanted child	welfare services for excess fertility infanticide

11. Psychological studies particularly suffer from considerable social context bias, and the difficult problem of adequate controls. Many examine only the *post*abortal state of dissatisfaction, guilt, or remorse. Those which do include the preabortion or prepregnancy state of the aborting woman are not designed to compare the short- or long-term consequences of abortion vs. delivery and child-rearing.

12. A further cost to the woman and to society is medical sequelae. Tietze has provided a model comparing mortality costs.[30] We must also examine nonfatal sequelae and compare risks entailed in the use of orals, IUDs, abortion, and pregnancy. Women will make choices based on their limited knowledge of other women's side-effects from taking pills, or pelvic infections and uterine perforations with IUDs, and will compare them to what they know of abortion risks.

13. In assessing the medical capacity to handle abortions, the number of practicing obstetricians and gynecologists, number of deliveries, and number of present hospital admissions and bed-days for abortions and deliveries should be a noted and anticipated load in the event of a liberalization of the law.

14. The physician and psychiatrist offer us one perspective by reports on small series of patients, examined in depth; demographers and statisticians provide us another perspective—birth rates up or down, abortions up or down. But there are more social aspects of the abortion/contraception question which deserve the attention of social scientists.

For example, the economist can tell us

not only what the trade-offs are of education costs and agricultural development vs. costs of family planning programs, but can also tell us something of the cost to society of providing full contraceptive care, and of providing delivery services and a variety of services for welfare, illegitimate, and other unplanned and/or unwanted births.

15. What can the anthropologist tell us? Apart from additions to the list of gruesome methods of accomplishing abortion, he can tell us that certain pregnancies not only can be but must be terminated in certain societies; this information throws the problem in a different light and gives us comparative societal norms by which to view our own attitudes and practices.

For instance, what do we know about American Indian attitudes and behavior? If abortions were to be made available in Indian hospitals, would they respond with charges of genocide or would such a service be seen as a normal part of health care? Or would the response vary by tribe? We ought to know.

16. It's a pity to report that the sociologist's concern with abortion has been almost exclusively an interest in attitude surveys. The sociologist has found out a great deal about fertility behavior and about contraceptive knowledge, attitudes, and practice, but abortion has been almost entirely ignored. Kantner and Zelnick found that among a group of Negro women assembled to discuss fertility behavior, the topic of abortion was not volunteered, and when suggested by the moderator, was greeted with a strongly negative reaction; later the same women spoke approvingly of "bringing on a late period."[31] This tells us something about attitudes and behavior and helps us to formulate our questions.

17. We might also take a look at infant mortality figures and explore the problem of unconscious infanticide, as Viel has done in Chile.

18. We need better analysis of abortion data than merely x percent were under 20,

y percent were 20 to 24, and so on. It is interesting to note, for instance, whether the investigator classifies women as ever married vs. never married, or currently married vs. currently not married. That is, what to do with the widowed, single or divorced (and consensual unions, concubines, etc.) might tell us something about the investigator's *own* attitude toward the subject's sexual activities.

19. The political scientist—or the political sociologist—can also contribute. There has been a gradual change in social/ political climate regarding contraception, but we are witnessing a sudden change with respect to abortion. At the least we need a historian to chart the events. All of us can make informed guesses about the dynamics of social change, but I would prefer better analysis than my own informed guesses. The dynamics of the change, the pressure groups, the individuals, the lines of influence, should be examined. We used to hear that a large Catholic population meant death to a family planning program; was that the political reality? Is the noninvolvement of the black community due to noninterest? Are efforts concentrated elsewhere? Or is there a strong antiabortion feeling (Westoff, Moore, and Ryder found Negro views less liberal than white views).[32] What about the genocide issue—how deeply has it penetrated the black community? Is there a single antiabortion, anticontraception feeling, or are they separate and distinct?

20. Although it is of academic interest to know the optimum balance of abortion and contraception, it is of little use unless there is a realistic possibility for the allocation of funds, allowing so much for abortion and so much for contraception. That is, it would not seem worthwhile to designate as top priority a research undertaking to determine how many abortions would be needed to have x effect, and what their cost would be compared to that of providing contraception, if there is not even a remote

possibility of the findings' being implemented in the country under study.

21. It should also be noted that when oral abortifacients become available, many of the comparisons between abortion and contraception which we now propose to study will be altered.

22. Funds should be made available for the translation of entire reports in foreign languages (not just tables), wherein a wealth of valuable data lie, inaccessible to most English-speaking researchers.

23. Every piece of research is a pilot study. Researchers should consider the opportunities for replicating others' case studies, in addition to contributing original approaches.

24. A systematic index of research findings, which would go beyond current abstracting services, should be designed in order to prevent duplication and to provide baseline information for new research. Legal indices provide guides to precedents, confirmations, and reversals; an abortion index might classify research findings in a similar manner.

NOTES

1. Tietze, C., "Mortality with contraception and abortion," *Studies in Family Planning*, **45**:6-8 (September 1969).

2. Westoff, C.; Moore, E. C.; and Ryder, N., "The structure of attitudes toward abortion," *Milbank Memorial Fund Quarterly*, **47**(pt. 1):11-37 (January 1969).

3. Girard, A., and Zucker, E., "Une enquête auprès du public sur la structure familiale et la prévention des naissances," *Population*, **22**:439-454 (May-June 1967).

4. Moore, E. C., and Dobson, L., Based on data collected in survey sponsored by The Population Council.

5. Taeuber, I., *The Population of Japan* (Princeton: Princeton University Press, 1958).

6. Potts, M., Talk at Planned Parenthood—World Population (New York: October 1969) (unpublished).

7. "News and notes," *British Medical Journal*, **3**:245 (July 26, 1969).

8. Eliot, J.; Hall, R.; Willson, R.; and Houser, C. "The medical aspects of abortion: the obstetrician's view," *Abortion in a Changing World* (ed. R. E. Hall), **1**:85-95 (New York: Columbia University Press, 1970).

9. Hubinont, P.; Brat, T.; Polderman, J.; and Ramdoyal, R., "The global aspects of abortion: abortion in western Europe," *Abortion in a Changing World* (ed. R. E. Hall), **1**:325-337 (New York: Columbia University Press, 1970).

10. Glass, D. V., "Fertility and birth control in developed societies, and some questions of policy for less developed societies," *Proceedings of the Seventh Conference* (International Planned Parenthood Federation) (Amsterdam: Excerpta Medica International Congress Series No. 72, 1963), pp. 38-46.

11. Hubinont *et al.*, "Abortion in western Europe."

12. Bachi, R., "The global aspects of abortion: abortion in Israel," *Abortion in a Changing World* (R. E. Hall, ed.), **1**:274-283 (New York: Columbia University Press, 1970); Hutchinson, B., "Induced abortion in Brazilian married women," *America Latina*, **7**:21-33 (October-December 1964); Chow, L. P.; Freedman, R.; Potter, R. G.; and Jain, A. K., "Correlates of IUD termination in a mass family planning program: the first Taiwan IUD follow-up survey," *Milbank Memorial Fund Quarterly*, **46**:(pt. 1):215-235 (April 1968); The Population Problems Research Council, *Fifth Opinion Survey on Birth Control in Japan*, Population Problems Series No. 16 (Tokyo: Mainichi Newspapers, 1959), pp. 1-44; Hong, S., *Induced Abortion in Seoul, Korea* (Seoul: Dong-A Publishing Co., 1966), pp. 1-99.

13. Chow *et al.*, "First Taiwan IUD follow-up," pp. 215-235; Jain, A., "Fetal wastage in a sample of Taiwanese women," *Milbank Memorial Fund Quarterly*, **47**(pt. 1):297-306 (July 1969); Chow, L. P.; Huang, T. T.; and Chang, M. C., "Induced abortion in Taiwan, Republic of China: a preliminary report" (Taichung: Taiwan Population Studies Center, May 1968), pp. 1-27 (mimeographed); Janmejai, K., "Socio-economic aspects of abortion," *Family Planning News*, **4**:55-57 (March 1963); Agarwala, S. N., "Abortion rate among a section of Delhi's population," *Medical Digest*, **30**:1-7 (January 1962); Mohanty, S. P., "A review of some selected studies on abortion in India," *Demographic, Social and Medical Aspects of Abortion* (Bombay: Demographic Training and Research Center, 1968), pp. 57-73; Valaoras V., "Greece: postwar abortion experience," *Studies in Family Planning*, **46**:10-

16 (October 1969); Requeña, M., "Social and economic correlates of induced abortion in Santiago, Chile," *Demography,* **2**:33-49 (1965); Populations Problems Research Council, *Birth Control in Japan,* pp. 1-44.

14. Hong, *Induced Abortion in Seoul, Korea,* pp. 1-99; Chow *et al.,* "Induced Abortion in Taiwan," pp. 1-27; Requeña, M., "Chilean programme of abortion control and fertility planning, present situation and forecast for the next decade" (United Nations: CELADE, 1969) (mimeographed).

15. Monreal, T., and Armijo, R., "Evaluation of the program for the prevention of induced abortion and for family planning in the city of Santiago" (Santiago: Universidad de Chile, 1968) (mimeographed).

16. Foreningen for Familieplanlaegning, "National report of Denmark," *Sex and Human Relations: Proceedings of the Fourth Conference of the Region for Europe, Near East and Africa* (International Planned Parenthood Federation, 1965), pp. 209-211.

17. Potts, M., "Legal abortion in eastern Europe," *Eugenics Review,* **59**:232-250 (December 1967).

18. Gold, E., Personal communication.

19. Faundes, A., unpublished data.

20. Monreal and Armijo, "Prevention of induced abortion and family planning in Santiago" (see note 15); Faundes, A.; Rodriguez-Galant, G.; and Avendaño, O., "The San Gregorio experimental family planning program: changes observed in fertility and abortion rates," *Demography,* **5**:836-845(1969).

21. Chow *et al.,* "First Taiwan IUD follow-up," pp. 215-235.

22. Koya, Y., *Pioneering in Family Planning: A Collection of Papers on the Family Planning Programs and Research Conducted in Japan* (Tokyo: Japan Medical Publishers, Inc., 1963), see especially Chapters 2, 3, and 6.

23. Monreal and Armijo, "Prevention of induced abortion and family planning in Santiago."

24. Requeña, "Chilean programme of abortion control and fertility planning" (mimeographed), p. 11.

25. Potter, R. G., "Birth intervals: structure and change," *Population Studies,* **17**:155-166, (November 1963).

26. Muramatsu, M., "Changing Japan, rapid decline in the birth rate: abortions outnumber births," *Family Planning,* **7**:3-8 (October 1958).

27. Monreal and Armijo, "Prevention of induced abortion. . ." (see note 15).

28. Bumpass, L., and Westoff, C., "The prediction of completed fertility," *Demography,* **6**:445-454 (November 1969).

29. Lehfeldt, H., and Guze, H., "Psychological factors in contraceptive failure," *Fertility and Sterility,* **17**:110-116 (January-February 1966).

30. Tietze, "Mortality with contraception and abortion," pp. 6-8.

31. Kantner, J., and Zelnick, M., "Exploratory studies of Negro family formation: common conceptions about birth control," *Studies in Family Planning,* **47**:10-13 (November 1969).

32. Westoff *et al.,* "Structure of attitudes toward abortion," pp. 11-37.

PART III
WHO USES FAMILY PLANNING?

The introduction to Part II presented some basic considerations for determining who needs family planning and identified certain groups that are the most in need from the viewpoint of the health professions. The articles contained in Section II extend the consideration of need by encompassing economic, genetic, and sociological approaches to the determination of need. In this section we will explore the issues of who actually practices family planning and what particular methods are used.

The general factors involved in an individual's decision to practice family planning are (1) knowledge, (2) availability of means, (3) values, motivation and need, and (4) social support. We will discuss each one of these in turn, as well as their relationships to each other. This provides an orientation that will facilitate appreciation of the articles included in this section.

KNOWLEDGE

Three types of knowledge are involved in an individual's practice of family planning: his knowledge about family planning, his knowledge of methods and how to use them effectively, and his knowledge of reproduction. For all three types, both the amount of knowledge and the accuracy of it are important. The KAP (knowledge, attitudes, and practices) studies by behavioral scientists show that the American public have much "information" about reproduction and contraception, but that their information is often woefully inaccurate. Thus many know that on certain days of the menstrual cycle conception is hightly unlikely, but many also "know" the wrong dates, believing that it is safe in the middle of the menstrual cycle.

How many family planning methods are individuals aware of? The evidence shows that virtually all adults and near-adults know of one or more family planning methods. This is true regardless of whether one is talking about teen-agers or Catholics or any other group. In fact, at the present time most sexually active females have used at least one method of family planning at some time. Specifically, the publicity surrounding the contraceptive pill has been so great that most people know of its existence, with increasing proportions of married females 19 to 44 years of age having used this method.

The picture is less clear-cut with regard to knowledge of the effective use of family planning. There is a fair amount of misinformation regarding the relative effectiveness of various forms of family planning. Although there is little hard data, what evidence there is indicates that the effectiveness of such methods as foams, creams, sprays, rhythm, and withdrawal is overrated by many individuals and particularly by those who rely on them. This seems to be especially true among those with less formal education. In consequence, such individuals are more likely to have unwanted children.

Finally, knowledge about reproduction: It is not necessary to have much knowledge in this area in order to use certain family planning methods effectively. However, most methods do require some knowledge about reproduction as it is related to the method's effectiveness. Several examples should make this clear. Particularly among the young, one finds individuals who feel that occasional unprotected intercourse is not dangerous. This belief often has dire consequences. Another belief is that if you miss taking the pill, it is all right as long as you do not have intercourse during those days. Thus the pill may not be taken until intercourse is resumed. It is not known how widespread these and similar misperceptions are, but it would be a wise policy to overestimate rather than underestimate their extent.

AVAILABILITY

It is obvious that even if a person knows a great deal about family planning, he cannot practice it well unless the means are available. However, the question of what is available to a particular individual is more complex than it would first appear. Here it is important to distinguish between *objective* and *subjective* availability.

Objectively, some forms of contraception are available to everyone. These would include abstinence, withdrawal, and rhythm. In addition, nonmedically prescribed contraceptives such as foam and condom are objectively available to most segments of our society. Finally, the medically prescribed (and most effective) family planning methods (the pill and intrauterine devices) are available objectively to most married couples, to a lesser extent to single females, and to a still lesser extent to teen-age females.

From an individual's subjective point of view, however, the situation is somewhat different. In order for family planning to be subjectively available, the individual must have the resources to obtain it. Although the cost of family planning is relatively low, it can pose a hardship for poor generally, as well as some of the young and some of the nonwhite.

In addition, to be subjectively available, the individual must have access to distribution points. For medically prescribed services this means that the individual must know of, and understand that he has access to, medical persons who are willing to prescribe for him. As we will see, this again may be particularly difficult for teen-agers, the poor, and the nonwhite. And these groups were among those whom we defined as being most in need.

In short, subjective availability appears to be greatest, by and large, for methods that are among the least effective (foam, sprays, withdrawal), or the least esthetically desirable from an individual's point of view (abstinence, condom).

VALUES, MOTIVATION, AND NEED

An individual's decision to practice family planning can be viewed as his own determination of whether he needs family planning. Each individual has a set of values or goals that he cherishes. Some of these are of utmost importance to him, others are relatively less important, and still other things are essentially irrelevant. These values are of course subject to change. They emerge out of a person's own life experiences and out of his contact with other individuals and groups who help define a "good life" for him. The importance of this statement lies in the fact that individuals who share much the same life experiences and are exposed to similar viewpoints tend to develop similar values. For the majority of Americans, values such as economic security, time for leisure, family life, and sexual activity can be presumed to rank quite high, although obviously there will be differences between individuals and groups. For the majority of married couples, having between two and four children is also one of their values.

One must keep in mind that family planning is often viewed as a means to other ends. Hence the question emerges: "What connection is there between family planning and an individual's values?" Here of course we are dealing with an individual's subjective perceptions. He may value health and see that family planning enhances well-being. But he also may not make such a connection. The individual, in other words, may believe that certain family planning methods facilitate his achieving his own goals, or he may see certain methods as interfering with his values, or he may not see any connection at all between family planning and his values. In this context, the same considerations apply as those discussed in connection with the question of who needs family planning; family planning may facilitate some of the goals of an individual at the expense of others, and different individuals may not consider the same things (such as physical health) as most important.

What evidence is there to indicate what role family planning plays in the life style of Americans? Several different kinds of data can be drawn upon. First, most Americans approve of the general notion of family planning. From this we can infer that for most people family planning is consistent with at least some of their own values and they perceive it as being consistent with the values of others. This holds true even for groups whose life experiences are quite different. Thus the poor are in general favorable toward family planning, as are the young and the nonwhite. Even among Catholics there is a steadily increasing proportion who view family planning favorably despite its potential conflict with religious values.

A second kind of evidence concerns desired family size. For many individuals, their completed family size is larger than that initially desired, and a fair proportion of individuals report that their last child was not really desired. This proportion increases with the number of children a mother has, and it is greater among the poor and the non-white. Although family planning would thus seem to be logically consistent with the values of such persons, the possibility of conflicting values creates room for differences in family planning practices.

SOCIAL SUPPORT

A final major component in determining who practices family planning is the social support an individual receives regarding family planning. Although it is self-evident, it is nevertheless worth drawing attention to the fact that individuals do not act, think, believe, or make decisions in a vacuum. From birth on they live in a network of other people who help shape their thoughts, beliefs, and values and who encourage some actions while disapproving others.

Much has been written in sociology regarding how groups influence individuals, but it cannot be dealt with here. Suffice it to say that the social environment, from relations between mates to the general society, does indeed exert a powerful influence on the whole life style of individuals. In the specific case of family planning these influences can be both positive and negative.

The first article in Section III (Westoff and Ryder) provides an overview of who uses family planning on a national level among married couples. It also reveals what trends there are in the use of family planning over the years 1955, 1960, and 1965. It shows that there was a continuing increase during this time period in the use of family planning by married couples. Second, with the advent of the "pill" there has been a shift in favor of this method. The pill is widely accepted by whites and nonwhites and by Protestant, Catholic, and Jewish couples. Finally, it shows that conformity of Catholics to the traditional Church doctrine regarding family planning is on the decline, especially among those who are infrequent church attenders.

Rothenberg and McCalister's article extends from that of Westoff and Ryder to describe who used family planning methods obtained from the hospital and nonhospital clinics of a major metropolitan area in 1971. Within this population of the poor and near-poor, the pill was chosen by the majority, followed by the IUD, diaphragm, and other methods. The two types of clinics, hospital and nonhospital, are shown to attract clients from somewhat different segments of the population, the former drawing more heavily from the postpartum, the young, the less educated, the black, and recipients of welfare. The nonhospital clinics drew more never-pregnant clients and, of those who have been pregnant, those with fewer children.

Most family planning programs have been geared to females, and especially married females over 18 years of age. The article by Arnold reports the experience of "A Condom Distribution Program for Adolescent Males." This innovative program suggests that among unmarried teenagers it is expected that the male will take the initiative in using contraception if it is to be used at all. Hence female-oriented programs may be largely unsuccessful among teen-agers. The evidence is too fragmentary to be conclusive, but it suggests also that informal, community-based programs are a better way of reaching teen-agers than are formally established family planning clinics.

The article by Fujita et al. "Contraceptive Use Among Single College Students" examines the family planning practices of a sample of a somewhat older and more educated group. In this group they found, as expected, that family planning knowledge was quite extensive. Yet among the sexually active, there was a substantial proportion who did not regularly use contraception.

A large number of the factors often assumed to be related to the adoption and continued use of family planning is examined in the article by McCalister and Thiessen. The evidence presented is bleak from a medical point of view. It suggests that those most in need of family planning, on the basis of the criteria established in Section II, are not more likely than are others to attend family planning clinics, or to adopt and continue in the short run to use medically prescribed family planning methods. If anything, they are somewhat less likely to do these things. Each of these three stages of commitment to family planning—clinic attendance, method adoption, and continued use—is properly viewed as a distinct point of decision making for the individual. Events related to each part of the process, including intervening life experiences, affect subsequent stages of family planning practice. The generally low associations found at each stage in this medically indigent, nonwhite sample shows again that family planning is a complex process involving more than simply availability or knowledge.

12 United States: Methods of fertility control, 1955, 1960, & 1965

Charles F. Westoff
Norman B. Ryder*

The 1965 National Fertility Study provides the opportunity to examine changes over a decade in the methods of fertility control employed by married couples in the United States, because its design is comparable with those of the surveys conducted in 1955 and again in 1960.[1] Three circumstances make such an examination especially interesting at this time. First, the birth rate has been declining since 1957; this change cannot be explained without analysis of fertility regulation. In the second place, the oral contraceptive has recently emerged as a leading method of birth control.[2] Thirdly, the Catholic Church is currently reviewing its position on the subject of birth control.

COMPARABILITY OF THE SURVEYS

All three of the national sample surveys collected data for white married women, ages 18-39, husband present. The coverage of the 1960 study also included Negro women, and the upper age limit was extended to 44. The 1965 study provided a double sample of Negro women, and enlarged the age span further to include all married women, husband present, born since July 1, 1910. The data presented in this paper, however, cover only women, 18-39, from all three surveys.

In some respects the data included here are not completely comparable over time. In both 1955 and 1960, the methods of contraception ever used were determined by responses to a single general question on use; in 1965, the question was asked specifically for each separate inter-pregnancy interval and methods *ever* used were estimated by summing over all intervals. This change was introduced with the intention of increasing the accuracy of report; the consequence may have been to increase the incidence of methods used, at the expense of comparability. Another particular differ-

*This report is by Charles F. Westoff, Princeton University, and Norman B. Ryder, University of Wisconsin, directors of the 1965 National Fertility Survey. This is a revised version of a paper presented at "The Fifth Notre Dame Conference on Population," December 2, 1966. The paper is based upon data collected in the 1965 National Fertility Study under a contract with the National Institute of Child Health and Human Development. The authors would like to acknowledge the able assistance of Susan Hyland of the Office of Population Research, Princeton University, who was responsible for the data processing.
[1] The principal reports of these studies are: Ronald Freedman, Pascal K. Whelpton and Arthur A. Campbell, *Family Planning, Sterility and Population Growth,* New York: McGraw-Hill, 1959; Pascal K. Whelpton, Arthur A. Campbell and John E. Patterson, *Fertility and Family Planning in the United States,* Princeton, N. J.: Princeton University Press, 1966.

[2] Norman B. Ryder and Charles F. Westoff, "Use of oral contraception in the United States, 1965," *Science,* 153(3741):1199-1205, September 9, 1966.

ence was a modification of the way in which information was obtained concerning the practice of douching for contraceptive purposes. A third difference was the ordering of options on the card to which the respondent was referred in replying to the question about methods used; it is suspected that a changed order is responsible for the substantial report of abstinence as a method in 1960 but not in 1955 or 1965. A fourth small difference is that age was defined in 1955 and 1960 as age at time of interview, but in 1965 as age at midyear, 1965; in consequence, the women in 1965 are some four or five months older, on the average, than the women in the previous two surveys. Finally, the surveys of 1955 and 1960 were conducted by the Survey Research Center, University of Michigan while the survey for 1965 was conducted by National Analysts, Inc., Philadelphia. Differences between these organizations in procedures for obtaining a national sample do not appear to have affected comparability. With these exceptions then, the estimates for comparisons through time would appear to be reliable within the limits of sampling variability.

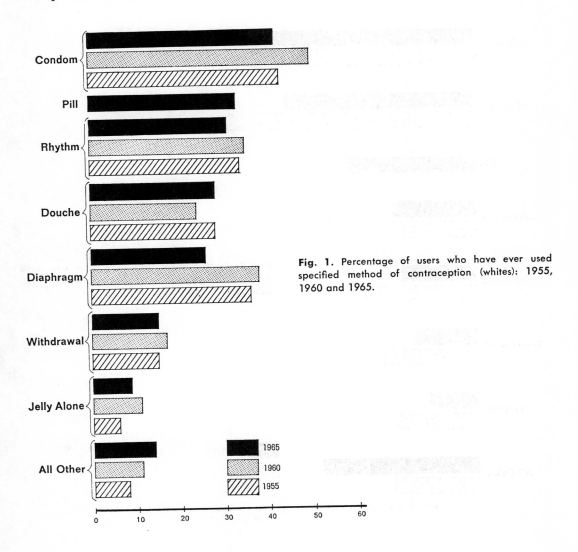

Fig. 1. Percentage of users who have ever used specified method of contraception (whites): 1955, 1960 and 1965.

METHODS EVER USED

It is of some importance for interpretation of the results of this paper, which refer to using couples, that the proportion of couples reporting that they had ever used contraception[3] rose between 1960 and 1965, continuing a trend observed between 1955 and 1960. The increase is most evident among those who had the lowest rates of reported use—the nonwhites, the Catholics and the younger women. The general trend of fertility regulation will be the subject of another report; the focus here is on the different methods of fertility control reported by users.

Between 1955 and 1960, the number of

[3]Couples are classified as using contraception on a motive basis rather than on an action basis. This procedure excludes behavior which is contraceptive in effect but not in stated intent, such as use of the pill for medical reasons only. The extent of the latter activity is not insignificant, particularly for Catholics. (See Ryder and Westoff, *op. cit.*, p. 1200.) To the extent that there is dissimulation about reasons for using the pill, the estimates of use of oral contraception reported in the present paper are understated.

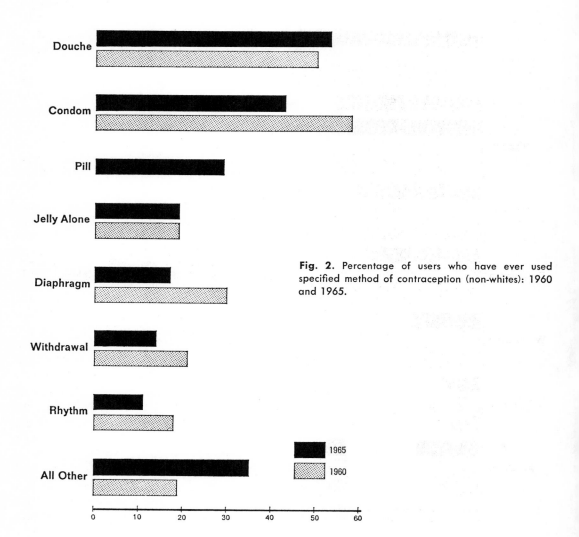

Fig. 2. Percentage of users who have ever used specified method of contraception (non-whites): 1960 and 1965.

methods per using couple increased by ten per cent (from 1.70 to 1.86); two methods showed statistically significant increases— condom, and jelly (alone). By 1965, the number of methods per using couple had increased to 1.98, perhaps in part because of the procedural change noted, but almost certainly also because of the availability of a new method, the oral contraceptive.

It is apparent from Table 1 that there has been a major change in the use of various methods between 1960 and 1965. For whites and nonwhites alike, the use of rhythm, diaphragm and condom decreased sharply in favor of the oral contraceptive. First licensed for contraceptive prescription in June, 1960, use of the pill has increased at an increasing rate; by the time of our interviews in late 1965, 33 per cent of white women and 29 per cent of nonwhite women ever using any method reported having used the pill. It seems that the pill has been adopted primarily by couples who would otherwise have used, or were formerly using, the diaphragm, the condom, or the rhythm method. Although the douche shows an apparent increase in use, the change is probably artifactual.[4]

The residual category of "all other" methods is comprised principally of suppositories, foam, and the intra-uterine contraceptive device. The last of these, which did not become generally available until 1964, is reported as a method used by 1.3 per cent of white users and by 2.8 per cent of nonwhite users. These proportions may be expected to increase considerably in the years ahead. Suppositories were employed by 6 per cent of white users and by 16 per cent of nonwhite users in 1960; the proportions

were approximately the same (5 per cent and 17 per cent respectively) in 1965. Use of the vaginal foam method was insignificant in 1960, but by 1965 the method had been employed by 7 per cent of white users and by 15 per cent of nonwhite users.

There are some important differences in the patterns of change in use of different methods among the major religious groupings of the white population. The methods most used by Protestant couples in 1955 and in 1960 had been the condom and the diaphragm; both declined substantially by 1965. Reliance on the condom and the diaphragm was even more pronounced among Jewish couples; by 1965, use of both had declined, but less so than for Protestants, and use of the pill is less frequent than for Protestants.

Among Catholic women the picture of change is dominated by the appearance of the pill between 1960 and 1965. The number of methods used per couple has increased from 1.57 to 1.69 and there has been a decrease in the proportion reporting that they have ever used the rhythm method. "Abstinence" as a method was reported by 9 per cent of women using any method in 1960, and by less than 1 per cent in 1965; the difference is probably attributable to the change in salience of the method in the questionnaire format.

CHANGES IN METHODS MOST RECENTLY USED

In Table 1, the methods described are those which the respondents have *ever* used. In consequence, the experience reported may extend for some of the women back over 25 years prior to the date of interview. In order to examine the most recent behavior of the samples, Table 2 has been prepared. It differs from Table 1 in that the methods are those used most recently; in temporal terms the appropriate comparison is between the techniques of fertility control employed by American couples during the first half of the 1950's and those of a decade

---

[4]Douching may be used for personal hygiene as well as for contraception. The reported figure refers only to women who asserted contraceptive intent. Furthermore, douching is frequently a supplementary technique to other methods of contraception. Much of the use reported in this paper involves techniques employed in combination.

Table 1. Percentage of users who have ever used specified method of contraception by color and by religion of white wives, 18-39: 1955, 1960, and 1965

Method	Total white 1955	1960	1965	Protestant 1955	1960	1965	Catholic 1955	1960	1965	Jewish 1955	1960	1965	Nonwhite[1] 1960	1965
Number of users	1,901	1,948	2,445	1,362	1,347	1,648	453	466	655	64	101	55	160	651
Percentage reporting:														
Condom	43	50	42	48	56	45	25	28	28	72	74	67	58	43
Rhythm	34	35	31	25	27	21	65	67	59	8	9	13	18	11
Pill	—	—	33	—	—	36	—	—	25	—	—	25	—	29
Douche	28	24	28	32	28	32	18	17	20	11	8	14	50	53
Diaphragm	36	38	26	41	46	31	17	12	11	56	51	45	30	17
Withdrawal	15	17	15	17	18	15	13	17	15	6	4	9	21	14
Jelly alone	6	11	9	8	14	11	2	4	4	2	8	2	19	19
All other	8	11	14	12	12	17	4	12	8	3	2	2	19	35
Total[2]	170	186	198	183	201	209	144	157	169	158	156	177	215	219

[1]The 1955 sample was confined to the white population.
[2]The total exceeds 100 because many couples reported two or more methods ever used.
Source: Percentages for 1955 and 1960 adapted from Whelpton, Campbell and Patterson, op. cit., Table 156, p. 278 and Table 196, p. 360.

Table 2. Methods of contraception used most recently, by religion of white wives, 18-39: 1955 and 1965

Method	Total white[1] 1955	1965	Protestant 1955	1965	Catholic 1955	1965	Jewish 1955	1965
Number of users:[2]	1,901	2,445	1,362	1,648	453	655	64	55
Per cent total:	100	100	100	100	100	100	100	100
Condom	27	18	30	19	15	15	56	44
Rhythm	22	13	12	4	54	36	2	—
Pill	—	24	—	27	—	18	—	22
Douche	8	6	9	7	4	4	—	—
Diaphragm	25	10	29	12	12	4	37	27
Withdrawal	7	5	7	5	8	7	3	—
Jelly alone	4	2	5	3	—	1	2	—
Other single methods	2	6	2	7	1	4	—	—
Condom and douche	1	3	1	3	1	2	—	—
Pill and any other	—	3	—	3	—	2	—	—
Rhythm and douche	2	2	2	1	3	2	2	2
Other multiple methods	2	8	3	9	2	5	2	4

[1]Totals include white women of other religions.
[2]Includes a small number of women who reported using contraception but for whom specific method is unknown.
Source: The 1955 data were tabulated in a slightly different form in Christopher Tietze, "The Current Status of Contraceptive Practice in The United States," Proceedings of the

later. A further difference between Tables 1 and 2 is that whereas methods *ever* used are described in Table 1—and thus many couples are included more than once—each couple is represented only once in the distributions of Table 2. The data for 1960 are omitted because the procedures followed in 1960 do not permit comparability.[5] While the bases for the 1955 and 1965 estimates are not exactly the same,[6] they are more alike than either is with the 1960 study.

The impact of the pill on the distribution of methods used is revealed more clearly in the data on methods most recently used than in the comparison of methods ever used. Reliance on the condom, the diaphragm and rhythm—which amounted in terms of separate use to 74 per cent in 1955—had declined to 41 per cent by 1965. The pill which is responsible for this change has now become the most popular method of contraception used by American couples, a fact that would be even more pronounced if the comparisons were restricted to the younger women in the sample. The method showing the greatest concomitant decline is the diaphragm followed by the rhythm method and the condom.

The patterns of change are not the same for couples of different religions. Among couples with Protestant wives, use of the diaphragm and condom have declined appreciably and use of the rhythm method has virtually disappeared. The pill now clearly dominates the picture as the most popular method.

The patterns of change for Jewish cou-

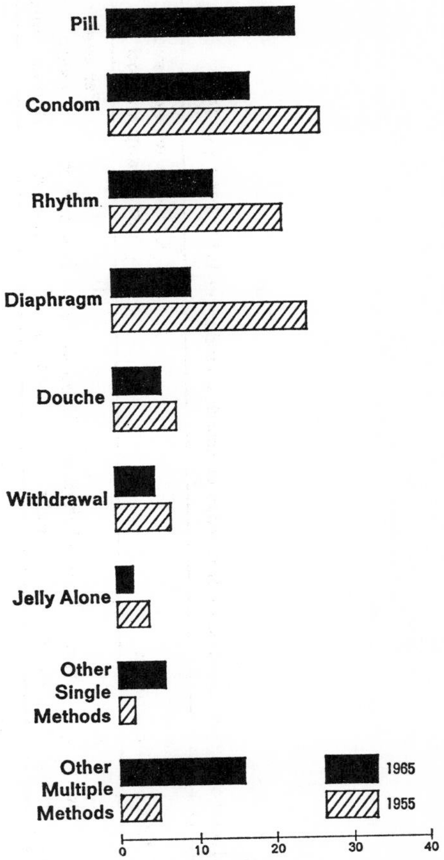

Fig. 3. Method of contraception used most recently by white women: 1955 and 1965.

ples seem reasonable, although the numbers in the two studies are quite small. As with Protestants, both the condom and diaphragm have declined in popularity with the adoption of the pill, but both methods continue to be used by Jewish couples much more extensively than by others. Thus 71 per cent of Jewish couples still depend on these two mechanical methods compared with only 31 per cent of Protestants and 19 per cent of Catholics.

Among couples with Catholic wives, the major change has been a decline in reliance on the rhythm method—from 54 to 36 per cent. The extent of use of the condom has not changed, but the diaphragm

[5]In 1960 the respondents were not queried about which method they used last if they were alternating use among two or more methods.
[6]In the 1965 study, unlike the 1955 investigation, the respondent who last used a method in an interval prior to the last pregnancy was not asked which method was used last if the couple used methods alternately. As a result, a higher proportion of couples interviewed in 1965 are classified in the category "Other Multiple Methods."

Table 3. Percentage of Catholic women conforming to Catholic doctrine on contraception by frequency of church attendance: 1955, 1960 and 1965

Year and frequency[1] of church attendance	All Catholic women						Catholic women ever using any method	
	Number of women	Per cent total	Total conformed	Non-users	Used rhythm only	Used other methods	Number of women	Per cent using rhythm only
Total								
1955	787	100	70	43	27	30	453	47
1960	668	100	62	30	31	38	466	45
1965	843	100	47	22	25	53	655	32
Regular								
1955	533	100	78	45	33	22	293	60
1960	525	100	69	32	37	31	357	54
1965	607	100	56	23	33	44	468	43
Less Frequent								
1955	254	100	53	40	13	47	152	22
1960	143	100	35	25	10	65	107	13
1965	236	100	26	21	5	74	186	6

[1]"Regular" means "regularly" in the 1955 and "once a week" in the 1960 survey to questions on the frequency of attendance at religious services. In the 1965 survey the category means "once a week or more" to a question on attendance at Mass.

Source: Percentages for 1955 and 1960 adapted from Whelpton, Campbell and Patterson, *op. cit.*, Table 160, p. 285.

has declined in use from 12 to 4 per cent. The pill appears to have become the second most popular method of fertility control among Catholic couples.

CATHOLIC CONFORMITY

Although reliance on the formally approved rhythm method is still the most common contraceptive practice by 1965, nearly two-thirds of the Catholic women who report having used some method of fertility control have at some time employed practices inconsistent with traditional Church doctrine, a position which although under review by ecclesiastical authorities, has at this writing not been changed.

Since the data presented thus far are restricted to those who report use of some method of fertility regulation, and since Catholics who use no method are also conforming to doctrine, an assertion about conformity requires consideration of the behavior of all Catholic women. Table 3 therefore includes all Catholic women as well as those who reported ever having used a method. It should be emphasized that this analysis reverts to the concept "ever used"; although it includes recent behavior it is not confined to the immediate past.

The proportion of all Catholic women who have attempted to regulate their fertility by use of the rhythm method exclusively has changed only a little between 1955 and 1965 (from 27 per cent to 31 per cent to 25 per cent); meanwhile the proportion using no method has declined from 43 per cent to 30 per cent to 22 per cent. In consequence, the proportion not conforming (in this sense) has increased from 30 per cent to 38 per cent to 53 per cent. In 1965 a majority of married Catholic women aged 18-39 reported having used methods inconsistent with the traditional Church doctrine on birth control.

Individuals differ widely of course in their adherence to religious values and church requirements, and among Catholics at least such variation is associated with contraceptive behavior. To assess the significance of this dimension for the change over the years we include in Table 3 a simple breakdown of Catholic respondents by whether they attend church regularly or not.[7] As expected the proportion conforming varies directly with the frequency of attendance. The more interesting observation, however, is that for both categories of attendance the trend over time is toward non-conformity. And this generalization holds regardless of whether the comparisons are based on all Catholic women or only on those who reported ever having used some method of family limitation.

There is an understandable temptation to infer that the trend toward non-conformity among Catholic women is a response to the deliberations of Church officials about fertility regulation, reflecting confusion in the public mind about the possibility of change in the official position. Although this may be part of the explanation of the acceleration in the decline of conforming behavior between 1960 and 1965, it does not seem satisfactory as a complete explanation of the change because it represented a continuation of a trend already observed between 1955 and 1960. Furthermore, the acceptance of oral contraception, which is principally responsible for the increase in non-conforming behavior among Catholics between 1960 and 1965, is paralleled by an even greater adoption of the pill by non-Catholics. The most significant finding of the 1965 National Fertility Study, to date, has been the increase in the use by married couples of fertility regulation in general and oral contraception in particular, a proposition that holds for Catholics and non-Catholics alike.

[7] Additional more refined measures of religiousness are available in the 1965 study and will be included in subsequent reports.

13 Family planning in hospital and nonhospital settings

Leslie Rothenberg*
Donald McCalister

The preceding article by Westoff and Ryder presents information on the methods of fertility control in use by married couples throughout the United States at three points in time: 1955, 1960, and 1965. It provides evidence of the widespread use of contraceptive agents of varying types in the population; also, the findings indicate that an increasing proportion of the total population is using medically effective contraceptives. Data from the 1970 National Fertility Study reveal that this trend has continued with 22.3% of wives under 45 years of age in the total population currently using the pill, and a total of 27.1% using either the pill or the intrauterine device in 1970.[1] The respective percentages for 1965 were 15.3% and 16%. This evidence of increasingly widespread use of medically effective contraceptive methods in samples of the general population of the United States is encouraging, whether one's concern lies with the physical, mental, and social well-being of individual families or with population growth in general.

Our purpose in this paper is to examine further the question of current contraceptive practices but to restrict our attention to the practices of clients of hospital and nonhospital clinics. This limits our consideration to the two different types of medical sources of family planning services that are used primarily by the poor and near poor.

Although family planning is important for all persons, the needs of the low-income segment of the population of the United States are most pressing at the moment.

The general question of *how* to best provide services to meet those needs is unresolved. Limitations of funds, personnel, facilities, and so forth have often led to consideration of how to use scarce resources most effectively. This, in turn, has led to the more general question of the effectiveness of particular strategies and institutional settings in the delivery of services.[2]

Effectiveness is measured in a variety of ways (such as client satisfaction, pregnancies averted, cost/benefit analysis, number of persons served, and fertility rate declines). Our discussion touches upon an additional element of effectiveness: Do family planning clinics located in different institutional settings draw clients from different segments of the population? If so, what are the apparent differences? Are the differences understandable in terms of client characteristics? Are there differences in the types of contraceptive methods chosen? That is, some persons may be more inclined to use one sort of facility and method than another; if so, why and what are the medical and social characteristics of these persons in relation to that facility?

The distinction between hospital-based family planning services and those provided in nonhospital clinics is therefore an important one and one that is in keeping with the theme of this book: medical and behavioral considerations in the delivery of health care. The multipurpose health-care

*Leslie Rothenberg, the senior author, is a doctoral candidate in sociology at Case Western Reserve University, Cleveland, Ohio.

Original article.

milieu of the hospital often contrasts sharply with the more focused activities of either a neighborhood health center or a single purpose, free-standing family planning clinic. The latter are not as tradition bound; their staffs frequently include more paraprofessional personnel. As organizations, they tend to be more in tune with, and responsive to, the characteristics and use patterns of their clientele. This is often represented by operating on a walk-in basis, rather than scheduling patients on a group or individual appointment basis, by being open in the evening or on weekends, and, in sum, by adapting the provision of service to the convenience of the client population rather than to white collar personnel. Not surprisingly, the characteristics of patients in nonhospital clinics frequently differ from those in hospital clinics. We have used the term "client" rather than "patient" to this point because of this defining a further distinction between the manner in which clinic personnel may respond toward a person. For example, a medical management approach to illness typifies hospital activities; but, is the person wanting family planning service ill? We will return to this distinction later in the discussion.

Although there are numerous published reports of the characteristics of patients in clinics of one type or another,[3-5] there are few that deal with more than one type of clinic or that describe all clinics in a geographic area as does this report. As one will note, this is an unfortunate omission since the characteristics and needs of patients may differ from one type of clinic setting to another, and it would be of value to know whether these findings might be generalized across the nation. This discussion provides a summary description of approximately 19,000 women using family planning clinics in the Cleveland (Ohio) Metropolitan Area during 1971. These clinics are available to the poor and near poor of the entire area. Although the data are not characteristic of the total indigent population of the Cleveland area, they do provide an accurate description of all family planning clinic patients. The clinic population is further described according to the type of clinic attended, that is, whether it is located in a hospital facility or a nonhospital facility (such as neighborhood health centers and free-standing clinics).

The main value of these data to health professionals interested in family planning lies in their accurate description of the current choices and characteristics of *all* clinic patients in one of the nation's 10 largest metropolitan areas.

BACKGROUND

Nominal family planning clinic services were begun in Cleveland in 1927 under the auspices of the Maternal Health Association. However, it was not until the mid-1960's, when MHA had become a Planned Parenthood affiliate, that significant expansion occurred in the number of clinic facilities, in the annual number of patients served and in the number of additional agencies offering services.

By 1970, approximately 14,000 patients per year were receiving services from 23 clinics operated by seven different public and private agencies. These agencies included one public and three private hospitals, the City of Cleveland Department of Health and Welfare, the Cleveland Maternity and Infant Care Program, and Planned Parenthood of Cleveland, Inc. The last one has consistently accounted for roughly 45% of the annual patient load; the hospitals accounted for approximately 42%, and the remainder were served by the City Health Department and the Maternity and Infant Care Program clinics.

The 23 clinics constitute a loose-knit consortium with a functioning interagency patient referral system, a centralized patient outreach and follow-up service, and, as of April 1969, a centralized patient record system. Since December 1969, federal funds have been received by this consortium of clinics first from the Office of Economic Opportunity and, as of 1971, from the National Center for Family Planning. The federal funds have provided impetus to the expansion of services so that patient loads have increased from a constant level of about 14,000 per year in 1969 and 1970 to 18,720 in 1971. Major changes in the manner of offering services between 1969 and 1971 and their implications are discussed below in relation to this increased patient load and to changes in its composition.

The 23 clinics have been combined into two categories for this report; hospital and nonhospital. The rationale is simply that the hospital clinics are more similar to each other than they are to the nonhospital clinics in mode of providing service, in having a large proportion of postpartum patients, and in being located in multipurpose health care settings. One should bear in mind the fact that many of the hospital clinic patients

are postpartum since it indicates a group of patients coming to family planning via pregnancy in contrast to another group (such as nonhospital users) for whom more independent decision making is perhaps required.

All data reported here are drawn from the standard clinic interview conducted with all patients each year.

CLINIC POPULATION
Demographic characteristics

Key demographic characteristics of all Cleveland family planning clinic users are summarized in Table 1. The distribution of clients over each characteristic is shown in percentages for the total clinic population, for hospital clinic users and for nonhospital clinic users.

Of the nearly 19,000 women in the clinic-using population, 42% attended hospital clinics. These women tend to differ in certain respects from those using nonhospital clinics. Hospital clinic users tended to be a

Table 1. Clinic population: Percentage of demographic characteristics of all patients by clinic type, 1971

	Hospital clinics	Nonhospital clinics	Total clinic population
Age			
16 or less	7.3	2.2	4.2
17-20	32.3	25.7	28.6
21-35	55.5	59.7	58
36-45	4.8	10.5	8.1
46 or more	0.1	1.9	1.1
Education			
8th grade or less	8.5	4.3	6
9-12	87.4	73.9	79.6
Beyond high school	4	21.8	14.4
Marital status			
Never married	42.9	37.6	39.8
Now married	34.2	43.8	39.8
Other	22.9	18.5	20.4
Ethnicity			
Black	77.4	57.4	65.9
White	21.7	41.3	33
Other	0.8	1.3	1.1
Welfare recipient			
Yes	62	29	43
No	38	71	57
Total number	7,946	10,774	18,720

somewhat younger and less educated group. Of the hospital clinic patients, 88% were between 17 and 35 years of age whereas 85% of the users of nonhospital clinics fell into this age category. Twice as many of the latter group were in the 36- to 45-years-of-age bracket as was the case in the former group.

Likewise, differences existed between the two groups in educational achievement. Although 22% of the nonhospital population reported attending school after graduating from high school (such as college, vocational training), only 4% of women attending hospital clinics had had a similar educational experience.

Certain other differences are apparent between the two groups. The hospital clinic population contained a larger percentage of women reporting that they had never been married (43%) than did the nonhospital population (37%). Similarly, the former contained a higher proportion of divorced, separated, and widowed women (23%) than did the latter (19%).

Differences in racial composition also characterized the two groups. During 1971, the hospital clinic population was 22% white and 77% black; the nonhospital clinic group was 41% white and 57% black. The two populations also were characterized by different proportions of welfare recipients. Although 43% of the total population of 19,000 women reported that they received public assistance, 62% of the hospital population were in this category compared to 29% of the nonhospital clinic patients.

The 1971 population of clinic users was compared with the characteristics of the 1970 population. (Tables for the latter are not presented because of space limitations.) The 1970 data were collected in the same manner by the same questionnaire as were the 1971 data. By comparing these two sets of records, we may add a limited time dimension to this descriptive report. This is useful in view of the rapid growth of the total patient load since 1969 and in view

of changes in clinic procedures discussed below.

The total clinic population grew by nearly 31% from 1970 to 1971. This is perhaps the most striking difference between the 2 years. The age distribution of the hospital clinic patients remained almost constant over the 2-year period; however the 1971 nonhospital population included a larger proportion of younger women than it did in 1970. The proportion of nonhospital clients in the 17- to 20-years-of-age bracket increased by 8% from 1970 to 1971.

The educational characteristics of the two groups of clinic users remained stable over the 2-year period; the only noticeable change was a 5% increase in the number of nonhospital clinic users who reported education beyond the high school level.

A comparison of the marital status of patients from 1970 to 1971 shows an increase in the proportion of never married women using these facilities. The proportion of women currently married declined in both clinic populations, whereas the percentage of women separated, divorced, or widowed remained fairly stable. The increase in never married women in hospital clinics from 1970 to 1971 was approximately 5%; in nonhospital clinics this increase was just over 12%.

The proportion of white clients increased between 1970 and 1971, especially in the nonhospital clinics. The proportion of welfare recipients attending family planning clinics increased from 37% in 1970 to 43% in 1971; most of this growth occurred in the hospital clinics.

Our perspective concerning the clinic patients is broadened somewhat by making a brief comparison of the characteristics of the 1971 clinic population to the total female population of Cuyahoga County, which includes Cleveland, drawing upon statistics from the U. S. Census Bureau 1970 summary statistics for Cuyahoga County. Considering women 17 to 44 years of age only in the county's population, it was found that the clinic population contains a greater proportion of young women than does the general population. For example, 50% of the women in the county's population between the ages of 17 and 44 years are in the 21- to 34-years-of-age bracket. This range, however, accounts for 59% of the hospital clinic users and 61% of the nonhospital clinic users.

The clinic populations are also characterized by a higher proportion of women who have never been married than is the case in the general population. Almost 24% of the county's female population over 14 years of age have never been married, whereas 43% of the 1971 hospital population and 24% of the nonhospital population were never married. Blacks are also more heavily represented in the clinic population than in the general female population of the county; correspondingly, whites are underrepresented. Thus, although 20% of the general female population is black, 77% of the hospital and 57% of the nonhospital populations are black. This reflects in part the fact that all clinics are located in the City of Cleveland and that they draw heavily from the inner-city population, which is largely black in contrast to the mainly white suburbs. However, since the socioeconomic status of the county population is similarly distributed, the picture is not distorted as regards the users of clinics relative to the total population.

Fertility histories

During 1971, 47% of the hospital clinic clients and 45% of the nonhospital clients were new to the family planning system. The following comments focus primarily on their fertility histories.

The number of previous pregnancies reported by new clients during 1971 varied considerably for hospital and nonhospital clinics. Almost 40% of the women appearing as new clients at the hospital clinics reported one pregnancy, whereas only 24% of the new nonhospital clients had experienced one pregnancy (Table 2). Likewise,

the proportion of new clients at hospital clinics who reported two, three, four, and five or more pregnancies exceeded the respective proportions of nonhospital clients in each group. For example, 21% of the new hospital clients had had two pregnancies compared to 14% of the new nonhospital clients; 12% of the hospital group had had three pregnancies compared to 8% of the nonhospital group, and so on. In contrast, the nonhospital group included a larger proportion of women indicating that they had never been pregnant. Forty-four percent of the nonhospital group had never been pregnant, compared to only 5% of the hospital clinic users.

Thus, new patients using hospital clinics in 1971 tended to have been pregnant more often than those using nonhospital clinics; a large proportion of the women using nonhospital clinics tended to have never been pregnant. The pregnancy history of women new to the clinic system in 1971 tends to be similar to the pregnancy histories of their 1970 counterparts, with the major exception of a large increase in never pregnant patients in nonhospital clinics.

As would be expected by the nature of the two different types of clinics, women using hospital-based clinics tended to have terminated a pregnancy more recently than those using non–hospital based clinics. Thus 42% of women using hospital clinics during 1971 had terminated a pregnancy during the preceding 12 months, whereas only 8% of those attending nonhospital clinics had terminated a pregnancy in the same length of time.

In summarizing the fertility characteristics of women new to the clinic system during 1971, one may note that hospital clients reported a greater frequency of pregnancies than did nonhospital clients. In fact, 44% of the new clients in nonhospital clinics had never been pregnant. Finally, 42% of the hospital clinic users had terminated a pregnancy during the last 12 months compared to only 8% of nonhospital clinic users.

Table 2. Clinic population: Percentage of fertility characteristics by clinic type, new patients only, 1971

Number of pregnancies	Hospital clinics	Nonhospital clinics	Total clinic population
Never pregnant	4.6	43.5	26.2
1	45.8	24.1	33.6
2 to 4	39.6	26	31.9
5 or more	10.1	6.4	8
Total number	3,836	4,841	8,677

Table 3. Clinic population: Percentage of contraceptive methods selected by clinic type, 1970 and 1971

Contraceptive methods selected	Hospital clinics	Nonhospital clinics	Total clinic population
1971			
Pill	63.3	71.5	68.0
IUD	27.7	12.4	20.0
Diaphragm	1.7	7.6	5.1
All others	5.0	8.5	6.9
Total number	(7,946)	(10,774)	(18,720)
1970			
Pill	63.5	66.5	65.2
IUD	27.2	14.2	19.8
Diaphragm	2.6	12.3	8.0
All others	6.5	6.8	6.7
Total number	(6,195)	(8,118)	(14,313)

Contraceptive methods dispensed

The oral contraceptive pill was most often chosen by the 18,720 women attending family planning clinics during 1971. Sixty-eight percent of these women accepted the pill as their contraceptive method (Table 3). The intrauterine device (IUD) was the next most often selected method (20%), whereas the diaphragm was chosen by only 5% of the clinic users. The 1970 and 1971 patterns of contraceptive preference are very similar. (During 1970, 65% of the 14,000 clinic users selected the pill.) The percentage of women selecting the IUD and the diaphragm as contraceptive methods remained nearly constant between years as did the small percentage of those selecting the condom, spermicidal agents, rhythm, and so forth.

Only two factors appear clearly to influence the choice of contraceptive method: (1) whether the clinic was located in a hospital setting and (2) the age of the client.

In regard to the first factor (Table 3), clients of hospital clinics were less likely to select the pill as their contraceptive method than were clients of nonhospital clinics. This finding is somewhat surprising since the hospital client tends to be somewhat younger than her nonhospital counterpart and generally younger women tend to select the pill more often than do older women. Regardless of clinic type, however, pill use is high: 63% among hospital clients and 72% among nonhospital clients.

The incidence of IUD and diaphragm selection also appears to be related to clinic type. The IUD was the most popular alter-

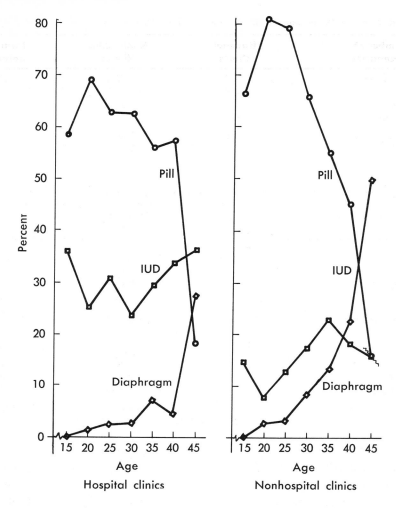

Fig. 1. Contraceptive use by age for users of Cleveland Family Planning Clinics, 1971.

native to the pill in both types of clinics. Almost 28% of the hospital clients selected the IUD as their contraceptive method with only 2% preferring the diaphragm. In nonhospital clinics, only 12% of the clients selected the IUD; thus it is only slightly more popular than the diaphragm (7.6%).

In summary, within this population of 19,000 women, the pill is by far the most popular contraceptive method. Users of nonhospital clinics are somewhat more likely to select the pill as their contracep-

tive method than are users of hospital clinics. The use of the IUD and diaphragm also appears to be affected by clinic type: the IUD is a much more popular method in hospital clinics than in nonhospital clinics, whereas the diaphragm is more popular in nonhospital than hospital clinics.

The second factor appearing to influence choice of contraceptive method is client's age (Fig. 1). For example, 70% of all 19 year olds attending hospital clinics and 81% of those attending nonhospital clinics selected the pill. Only 55% of all 35-year-old clients at these clinics selected the pill, however. This finding is not at all surprising since age is a frequent contraindication for the pill. Use of the diaphragm also appears to be affected by age. As Fig. 1-1 indicates, the percentage of clients selecting the diaphragm as their contraceptive method increased for older groups. Use of the IUD does not appear to be affected by age.

There is some evidence that the contraceptive preferences of women new to the clinic system in 1971 tended to be somewhat different from the contraceptive preferences of women who have previously used the system as their source of service. Although the pill ranks as the most popular choice for new clients and IUD as the second most popular choice, the diaphragm is in fourth place for new clients but it is in third place for continuing clients.

It is of interest to note two factors that do not seem to have had a noticeable affect on client choice of method. The first is a desire for more children. The pill is the method of first choice among women desiring more children as well as among those not desiring more children. Likewise, the IUD is the second choice among both groups of women, with the diaphragm being the third choice. The second factor not appearing to noticeably influence a woman's choice of method is the number of months since termination of her last pregnancy. The ranked use of the pill, IUD, and diaphragm was the same regardless of the length of time since a woman's last delivery.

Thus the type of clinic used and the client's age tend to affect the choice of contraceptive method, whereas expressed desire for more children and length of time since last pregnancy do not seem to be related to choice of method. In all cases, however, the pill was the method of first choice followed by IUD and then the diaphragm. These characteristics did not change between 1970 and 1971.

Summary of findings

We shall first summarize the major differences between the populations of hospital and nonhospital clinics and the changes in population characteristics between 1970 and 1971. After this, the findings are discussed briefly in relation to changes in clinic procedures that were implemented in early 1971. Finally, some of the more important implications of these data for health professionals in family planning will be addressed.

The main differences in demographic characteristics between the 1971 hospital and nonhospital clinic populations are that the hospital clinics had a greater proportion of never married, separated, widowed, and divorced clients, a greater proportion of blacks, and more clients who were welfare recipients. In contrast, the nonhospital clients were somewhat older and had more years of schooling.

Fertility characteristics of patients differed sharply between the two types of clinics, as would be expected. In regard only to new patients in 1971, 44% of the nonhospital clinic population had never been pregnant compared to only 5% of the hospital patients. Of those who have been pregnant, 24% of the nonhospital and 46% of the hospital patients had been pregnant only once. A greater proportion of the hospital clinic patients also had experienced two or more pregnancies. In regard to all patients, 42% of those in hospital clinics had terminated a pregnancy within 1 year whereas only 8% of those in nonhospital clinics had done so.

Ninety-three percent of all patients selected a prescription method of contraception (pill, 68%; IUD, 20%; diaphragm, 5%). The pill was the most frequent choice in both types of clinics but more so in nonhospital clinics (72% versus 63%). The IUD was inserted in a greater percentage of the hospital patients 28% versus 12%), whereas the diaphragm was chosen by nearly 8% of the nonhospital patients and by only 2% of those seen in hospital clinics.

Comparison of the total clinic population to the 1970 population of females aged 17 to 44 residing in the county, which includes Cleveland, reveals that the clinic population contains a higher proportion of young women, of black women, and of women who have never been married.

The major change in the clinic populations between 1970 and 1971 was a 31% increase in the total number of patients. This increase resulted in a larger proportion of never married patients in both types of clinics, especially in the nonhospital clinics (12% versus 5% in hospital clinics). The 1971 nonhospital clients also included an increased proportion of younger women and of whites.

DISCUSSION

What is the significance of these differences and changes? As we noted earlier, a much greater proportion of the hospital clients come to family planning because of pregnancy, as evidenced by the shorter period of time since their last delivery. Also, each of the hospital obstetrical services offers family planning information and clinic appointments to staff patients prior to their release from the hospital after delivery. This is a time at which the postponing or avoiding of future pregnancies is of greatest conscious concern to many patients.[6] In turn, they are in a medical milieu and may tend as a group to be more responsive to what they might perceive as a recommended medical regimen. Clients of nonhospital clinics whose pregnancy experiences are not so recent are likely to attend for a more diverse set of reasons.

The differences in demographic characteristics between the two types of clinic populations are explained in part by recency of pregnancy. That is, the age range of 20 to 24 years is the peak period of reproduction among the staff patient population of Cleveland. The hospital clinic population, being largely those post partum, is younger

than is the nonhospital clinic population. Also since these are staff patients, the greater proportion of unmarrieds, of blacks, and of welfare recipients is understandable on the grounds of less economic self-sufficiency.

Indeed, the hospital clinics draw largely from the staff obstetrical population of the area, whereas the nonhospital clinics draw from a broader population in terms of age, reproductive experiences, and to some extent socioeconomic status. This is an important consideration in interpreting the changes in population composition of the nonhospital clinics between 1970 and 1971.

In early 1971, several changes were made in patient eligibility criteria and in administrative operating procedures for the nonhospital clinics. Briefly, these changes involved a lowering of the minimum patient age, the acceptance by some clinics of unmarried women for the first time, a switch from an appointment system to a walk-in policy, and the addition of evening and weekend clinics. These changes are in the direction of adapting the clinic criteria and schedules closer to the facts of life for the sexually active poor and near poor, the working female, and those for whom the time-scheduling of activities (such as appointments) is unfamiliar in relation to their life styles. The result is that the total clinic population size increased substantially and especially in the proportions of young, of unmarried, and of white patients attending nonhospital clinics.

Thus, these changes, which contrast sharply with the more traditional routine of hospital facilities, can be seen as serving to fill a previously unmet need within the community. This point is most dramatically illustrated by the increase during 1971 in never pregnant women attending nonhospital clinics. These persons are controlling conception *before* the fact and so, hopefully, enhancing their future prospects for genuine planning of their families.

We may only speculate concerning reasons for the differences between the two types of clinics in the proportions of patients selecting the IUD and the diaphragm. The greater relative popularity of the IUD in hospital clinics may be attributable in part to the accentuated concern of some postpartum patients with avoiding pregnancy in the near future. That is, the IUD as an always present method that is not coitus related may appear to the patient to involve less risk of accidental pregnancy in contrast to the daily taking of the pill or to coitus-related methods such as the diaphragm, condom, and so forth.

A further possible reason for the difference in IUD use is that medical personnel in the hospital setting may view the patient somewhat differently than is the case in the nonhospital setting. Indeed, the woman using a hospital family planning clinic, especially if she is recently postpartal, is likely to be viewed as a *patient*. In contrast, the woman using a nonhospital clinic is often more likely to be viewed as a *client*. This is a potentially important distinction as the former is one who is *treated* whereas the latter, unless there are medical complications, is more likely to be given *service*. The difference is one of emphasis in the extent to which a medical treatment perspective premised upon illness is relied upon by medical personnel in viewing the individual. In this light, the IUD may be seen as not being as subject to patient error or misuse and, therefore, control or management of the patient rests more firmly in the hands of the practitioner.

The difference in use of the diaphragm between the two types of clinics is subject to less speculative interpretation. The diaphragm tends to be more frequently used by older women of whom the nonhospital clinics have the greater proportion. This is borne out clearly in Fig. 1, which indicates the use of the diaphragm to increase with age of the patient whereas the pill use declines with age.

CONCLUSION

The data that we have presented provide a clear and accurate picture of the characteristics of almost 19,000 clinic clients and their preference for contraceptive methods during 1971 in Cleveland. The differences in characteristics displayed by type of clinic facility are indicative of uniqueness within each of the two populations in what has drawn the client to family planning and in how she may be regarded by the clinic personnel.

The changes during 1971 in the mode of operating the nonhospital clinics, with the resulting changes in composition of the clientele, provide a telling example of the limitations of more traditional agency policies. More importantly, however, this also provides instructive examples of how to better meet the needs for family planning services by a broader segment of the population. The advantages of adapting the provision of medical care, at least contraceptive care, to the convenience of the target population seem to be clear.

REFERENCES

1. Preliminary unpublished estimates from the 1970 National Fertility Study.
2. McCalister, D. V., Hawkins, C. M., and Beasley, J. D.: Projected effects of family planning on the incidence of perinatal mortality in a lower class non-white population, Amer. J. Obstet. Gynec. 106:573-580, 1970.
3. Reynolds, J.: Delivering family planning services: Autonomous vs. integrated clinics, Family Planning Perspect. 2(1):15-22, 1970.
4. Forrest, J. E.: Postpartum services in family planning: Findings to date, Reports on Population/Family Planning No. 8, pp. 1-15, July 1971.
5. Siegel, E., Thomas, D., Coulter, E., Tuthill, R., and Chipman, S.: Continuation of contraception by low income women: A one year follow-up, Amer. J. Public Health 61:1876-1898, 1971.
6. McCalister, D. V., McGee, C. T., Forti, T., and Hawkins, M.: Family planning and the reduction of pregnancy loss rates, J. Marriage Family 31:668-673, 1969. (See Table 1.)

14 A condom distribution program for adolescent males

Charles B. Arnold*

Family planning services directed toward adolescents are not new. For the past 5 years, several projects in the United States have published findings about pilot programs serving adolescent women. Some programs are directed toward never pregnant women; some directed toward those who are or have been pregnant.[1] Except for four reported projects, adolescent males have been virtually ignored by American family planning programs.[2-5]

The burgeoning general interest in family planning services for teen-agers has been commented upon in the preliminary report of the Federal Commission on Population Growth and the American Future.[6]

As a society, we have been reluctant to acknowledge that there is a considerable amount of sexual activity among unmarried young people. The national study (a public opinion survey made for the Commission) which disclosed that 27% of unmarried girls 15-19 years old had had sexual relations further revealed that girls have a considerable acquaintance with contraceptive methods; over 95% of all girls 15-19, for example, know about the Pill.

Contraceptive practice, however, contrasts sharply with this picture. Although many young women who have had intercourse have used a contraceptive at some time; this group is characterized by a great deal of "chance taking." The majority of these young women have either never used, or at best, have sometimes used birth control methods. We deplore the various consequences of teenage preg-

nancy, including the recent report from New York that teenagers account for about one-quarter of the abortions performed under their new statute during its first year.

Adolescent pregnancy offers a generally bleak picture of serious physical, psychological and social implications for the teenager and child. Once a teenager becomes pregnant, her chances of enjoying a rewarding, satisfying life are diminished. Pregnancy is the number one cause of school drop-out among females in the United States.

The psychological effects of adolescent pregnancy are indicated by a recent study which estimates that teenage mothers have a suicide attempt rate ten times that of the general population.

The Commission is not addressing the moral questions involved in teenage sexual behavior. However, we are concerned with the complex issue of teenage pregnancy. Therefore, the Commission believes that young people must be given access to contraceptive information and services.

Toward the goal of reducing unwanted pregnancies and child bearing among the young, the Commission recommends that birth control information and services be made available to teenagers in appropriate facilities sensitive to their needs and concerns.

BACKGROUND

Implicit in the Commission's statement is the concept that family planning services for teenagers should be female oriented. Services for adolescent males have been far fewer than for females. It is likely that some generally held beliefs are the basis for this neglect. Inner-city adolescent males are believed to be hard to reach, reluctant to use condoms for hedonistic reasons, and, in some cases, militantly opposed to birth control in any form. In contrast to any previously published reports, the findings from

*M.D., Professor of Public Administration, Graduate School of Public Administration, New York University, New York.

Original article.

138

the evaluation of a program that we conducted in a North Carolina city suggested that these beliefs were myths; our data indicated that inner-city adolescent males from low-income families were willing to use condoms and to assume a major share of the responsibility for preventing unwanted births if they were given the chance to do so. The means by which that opportunity was extended and the adolescent males' subsequent response are described in this chapter.

This project originated in a county with a large and quite successful family planning program,[7] a part of the County Health Department Maternal and Child Health Services. It became apparent to program directors, however, that despite the increasing program effectiveness for enrolling adult women, adolescents were scarcely seen at clinic services. This absence was particularly noted because the health department had an explicit policy to offer contraceptive services to teen-agers regardless of their previous fertility history. That is, a never pregnant teenage girl could get services were she to request them.

Various fertility indicators in the county suggested that adolescent fertility was a problem. The drop-out rate for pregnant high school girls had increased in the county, particularly among students attending schools located in the lower socioeconomic areas. The fertility rate for black women 10 to 19 years old was about 60 per 1,000 women. In a countywide fertility survey in 1967, it was discovered that 56% of the black women in the county had their first pregnancy before their twentieth birthday.[8] In contrast, only 36% of white women had their first pregnancy by that age.

COMMUNITY ORGANIZATION AND SOCIAL SUPPORT

Informal conversations were held with a variety of influential members of the black community in the county. The purpose of the conversations was to learn of their perceptions of the teenage fertility problem. It soon became apparent to us that these community members were greatly concerned about the problem, which touched virtually every level of the community's socioeconomic strata. In effect, we were given a mandate by these leaders to attempt to develop a program. In turn, they assured us of their cooperation and efforts to inform others in the community of the proposed project's purposes.

At this point, a hiatus occurred in our attempts to build social support in the community while we sought and obtained federal support for a local community project. Once having secured that support, we hired a young woman who had worked in a local antipoverty program for several years and who was adept at working with inner-city youth. She continued to build our rapport with the community by meeting with a variety of community agency personnel in recreation, housing, and health. Uniformly, her experience was the same as ours had been previously: Virtually everyone was enthusiastic about a program to provide contraceptive services and sex education to adolescents.

Subsequently, a group of three adolescent female outreach workers were hired and trained to work in the project. They made home visits throughout the intended target area discussing with parents and teen-agers the purposes of the project and providing an opportunity for discussion in question-answer sessions. We attempted to characterize the project at the outset as having a major interest in the psychosexual development of young people and only secondarily was the project concerned about the provision of contraceptives. This approach was well-accepted by the community.

Subsequently, a series of sex information sessions were held in local recreation centers throughout the target area. The principal purpose was to alert us to the kinds of problems for which adolescents sought information. This, in turn, enhanced our capacity to communicate with them. Further, the sex information sessions enabled us to project an image to the community's youth of a nonjudgmental, open-minded approach to the subject of sex. These sessions ran continuously, one or two sessions a week for about 6 months.

The initial orientation of the project was toward recruiting adolescent women into the family planning services provided by the County Health Department. Despite vigorous efforts made by the young women outreach workers and the sensitive cooperation of the County Health Department, the recruiting results were very disappointing. After 4 months of intensive effort, only 12 adolescent girls made a visit to the family planning clinic. Believing that the atmosphere of a public clinic was partly responsible for this low level of participation, we made arrangements with local general practitioners to provide the same services at minimum cost (paid by the project grant). This effort, too, was unsuccessful.

THE CONDOM PROJECT

In May 1969, based on the experience of Kangas and Gobble et al., condoms were purchased by the project and made available at no cost through our office and, as well, through an antipoverty, summer youth program located in the building next door. During the subsequent 6 months, approximately 1200 condoms were distributed. Each young man receiving a condom was also asked to give his name, address, and the number of condoms taken. During this period, the adolescent outreach workers were female. There was no apparent hesitation by the young men to come into our office, request, and receive condoms from these young women. This was comparable to the experience reported by Gobble and his coworkers. In December 1969, a male outreach worker joined our staff and began to develop new sites for condom distribution. The female outreach workers were comfortable dispensing condoms from the project office, but deemed it inappropriate to dis-

tribute them elsewhere, such as in a pool hall, barber shops, stores, and the like.

THE CONDOM AS A CONTRACEPTION FOR ADOLESCENTS

There are several reasons that commend the condom as an important contraceptive for adolescents: (1) Its antifertility potential is very high when used properly: approximately 95% effective.[9] (2) There are virtually no health or medical risks associated with its use. (3) It is easily carried, is relatively inconspicuous, and can be kept in a wallet, a purse, or a pocket. (4) It is quite acceptable by adolescents, particularly males. In our experience we found that males were expected by teen-age females to take the initiative in preventing pregnancies. In our community they were believed by women to be more generally knowledgeable about sex matters, including contraception. (5) Once used, most adolescents found them to interfere only minimally with the physical satisfaction of sexual intercourse. (6) Storage, distribution, and handling of condoms pose no special problems (such as shelf life), as do the pill, IUD, foams, and jellies. (7) It is inexpensive. And (8) it does not require medical examination or prescription.

In Durham, North Carolina, during 1968, Kangas[3] used commercial outlets, such as barber shops and grocery stores to distribute condoms to teen-agers. Because of his experience, we approached two small grocery stores and a barber shop in January 1970 to ask their proprietors if they would distribute condoms free of charge to young men when they entered their establishment. The proprietors agreed, but seem mildly dubious. We then observed the distribution pattern in these places over a 3-month period. During that time, the shops made the condoms available as requested. Virtually no difficulties were encountered in the distribution. The number of condoms that were distributed increased weekly. The owners became increasingly comfortable with their role and the use of their shops as distribution points.

One member of the project staff, a 20-year-old young man was primarily responsible for condom distribution. He located the shops, explained the details of participation to the shopkeepers, maintained the distribution network, much as any salesman or detail man might do for a pharmaceutical house. He learned the idiosyncracies of the various sites; for example, one place invariably exhausted its condom supply on the weekends, necessitating a call on Friday afternoon and a stockpiling for the up-and-coming weekend. He observed a variety of different patterns of condom distribution practices. For example, one shopkeeper put up a large sign with the word "free" above a visible box of condoms; others would be less demonstrative; one or two would keep them under the counter and not visible to the casual observer. One grocer, when a young man would come in and buy a six-pack of beer, would inevitably put a package of condoms in the shopping bag with the pack of beer saying, "Here, you might need these." In all, the effectiveness of this program could be primarily attributed to the energy and resourcefulness of this young man and to the high degree of cooperation obtained from the participating shopkeepers.

An expansion of use of commercial sites for the distribution of free condoms was made in March 1970, approximately 3 months after the trial began. Six additional sites were located within the inner-city area. The nine original sites then included five barber shops, two grocery stores, a pool hall, and a restaurant. Later, the proprietors of the new sites also agreed to distribute the condoms free of charge to those young men who appeared to be under the age of 20, to attempt to determine the seriousness of their requests for condoms (attempting to omit trivial uses of them), and to restrict the maximum number of condoms given to any individual at one time to 12. An evaluation protocol was developed in order to determine the feasibility of the commercial sites for free condom distribution.

RESULTS OF THE PROGRAM EVALUATION

Because this family planning program functioned as a small system, it became necessary to use a broad-gauged approach to assess it. The following several evaluation areas will be referred to:

1. Program operations and feasibility
2. Social characteristics of condom users
3. Reported condom use and related sexual behavior
4. Observations on program organization
5. Demographic effect of the project

The data describing the adolescent males and their participation were derived from three separate studies. The first was a probability sample of clusters of adolescent males who received condoms at various stores and shops during the initial 13-week period of the project. This consumer survey was repeated 1 year later and the data compared. The third component of this part of the evaluation consisted of a cluster sample of condom recipients studied midway between the other two surveys. In the two surveys with consumers done a year apart, the data gathered were confined to factors directly related to the distribution network. In the other study, 134 condom recipients were interviewed for about 30 minutes regarding their condom use and associated sexual behavior.

Program operations and feasibility

From the two consumer surveys we learned that there was very little difference in the distribution of condoms by the day of the week or by the time of the day except for Friday and Saturday when the number of condoms distributed seemed fewer.

In general, the condom recipients lived rather near to the distribution sites. Two thirds of the young men lived within four city blocks of the respective shops and stores.

In the 3-month feasibility study of condom distribution prior to the development of the full-scale program, we believed that shopkeepers would not be overburdened by requests for condoms. That is, the practical question existed: "Would the time required for distribution activities by shopkeepers be such that regular business activities would be interfered with?" Our data indicated that on the average, 7.5 young men per day came into the shops requesting condoms, a number confirming our earlier impression that condom distribution was not a burden.

Interestingly, the type of shop or store was not important in the distribution network. It appeared that the pattern of distribution was random. For further program development plans, this information was important because it did not seem to rule out any particular kind of shop or business as a potential outlet.

Social characteristics of condom users

The participants in the condom distribution program were remarkably similar in their general social characteristics to all those adolescent males residing in the target area. Their average age was 18 years. Their mean educational level was 11.5 years of schooling. Ninety-two percent were single. The average number of siblings in their families was 3.9.

Reported condom use and related sexual behavior

We queried the samples each time about the duration of time that had passed since they had last used a condom. After 13 weeks of the project 60% of respondents indicated they had used a condom within the past week. A year later a different group of respondents yielded practically the identical proportion.

We also inquired whether they had ever used a condom before. By the end of the thirteenth week of the project every condom recipient interviewed indicated that he had used a condom before. A year later the same result was obtained. We inferred from this observation that we had in effect "saturated" the target area with our distribution network; young men who would use condoms knew of the distribution sites and were receiving condoms.

As a test of the contraceptive intent of the project, we asked the sample of condom recipients this question: "The last time you had sexual intercourse did you use a rubber?" We assumed the aggregate response to this question would provide us with an estimate of the fertility control possibilities in this program. Over the course of the first year the positive response to that question ranged between 69% and 81%. Such a variation was within the limits of the sampling error for the data. This level of reproducibility of results suggested that the condom had considerable contraceptive potential within the teenage population in this project's target area.

We also asked the condom recipients whether their sexual partners were using any kind of contraception. In each of the three surveys during the project's first year only 15% of the respondents indicated that their sexual partners were independently using contraception. We inferred from this that at least among the condom users the burden of contraception was assumed largely by the males. It is not known whether a different set of proportions exists among the sexually active adolescent males who do not use the condom. We suspect, however, that adolescent males are generally expected by their sexual partners to assume the major responsibility for contraception.

Observations on program organization

In a complex and innovative social program of this kind it is virtually impossible to summarize briefly the organizational arrangements that took place. These have been partially described elsewhere.[10]

To understand some of the organizational

issues, put yourself in the position of organizing this project in the summer of 1968. Imagine for a moment the task of developing a project for which there were no previous program models, one that planned to have no formal or direct organizational ties to other family planning or other programs in the community. Further, staff it with three teenage outreach workers and hire a director who had community organizational experience with young people, but no prior experience in family planning programs. In addition, recognize that it would be necessary to experiment rather self-consciously with the patterns of organization and community relations necessary in order to make such a program work. Further, complicate things somewhat by making the project's originators white upper-middle-class professionals and the project personnel black lower-middle-class nonprofessionals. Basically this picture is the one that characterized the program's organization.

Often, day-to-day situational problems in the lives of the program staff constituted major barriers to effective day-to-day program continuity. The loss of an outreach worker's spouse's job, a serious illness in the family, an automobile accident, a superficial gunshot wound of the arm of an outreach worker, and a threatened jail sentence for one member of the staff were but a few of the problems that periodically brought operations to a standstill. These general problems of organizing projects among the poor have been described recently by Kegeles.[11]

The administrative and financial instability of the sponsoring institution (a local university) introduced a set of sporadic external crises (money matters, purchasing condoms, policy issues) that in addition to those described above were a source of concern to all members of the project. Additionally, our federal funding agency precipitated annual crises in the project when they failed to provide adequate assurance to the adolescent staff of their sincerity to re-fund the project for the forthcoming year. The staff,

concerned about job security, would virtually be incapable of work until the renewal notice had been received.

Another interesting and somewhat unexpected development occurred when the condom project began to become very successful and widely reported in journals and the press. The young women outreach workers became jealous of the young man who was the condom distributor. This largely took the form of petty gossiping and attempts by them to undermine the confidence of the project director in his work. His "success" sharply contrasted with their "failure" to get girls to use family planning methods.

No discussion of organizational problems is complete without mentioning the fears by some of the local staff about the evaluation and the evaluators. This was sufficiently great at times to cause periodic breakdowns in communication and considerable secretive behavior on the staff's part.

It is important for one to remember, after reading the problems cited above, that this was a "successful" project. That is, it was widely reported by the press, in magazines, at professional meetings, and in professional journals. The project was frequently regarded as innovative, productive, and programmatically effective. The recitation of these problems is not intended to undermine the project's accomplishments, but rather to underscore their commonplace nature in a community action effort. To attempt to promote such programs means one must face these issues. Generally speaking, crises were spaced out over time, encountered by everyone in a reasonable manner, and usually resolved as expeditiously as possible. It is only when attempting to chronicle them retrospectively that one begins to sense the difficulties of effective maintenance of continuity in neighborhood family planning or community action projects.

The evaluation data indicated the appropriateness of the choice of commercial outlets for distribution purposes in this project. That is, in our project, adolescents were comfortable in going to stores and shops they ordinarily frequented. Additionally, the commercial outlets were appropriate because frequently the shopkeepers recognized or knew personally the adolescent and often had good relationships with them. The shops and their managers were selected by our staff because we felt they had this quality.

In addition, this kind of distribution scheme was sensitive to the special needs of adolescents. The kind of brief encounter between the shopkeeper and the adolescent permitted privacy to be maintained. The growth of the project and its acceptability seemed to underscore the sense of trust the adolescents had for the shopkeepers. Also, the adults respected the privileged nature of the communication implicit in condom distribution. It is probable that in many cases adolescents sought shops in which they were not known or recognized. In those cases, anonymity was guaranteed them when they made their request. In no case were records kept so that the adolescents could be identified or so that any socially damaging evidence existed about their sexual behavior.

A word about the men and women who maintained the shops and distributed the condoms is essential. In effect, they represented the community in this project. Their sensitivity to factors that affected their sales indicated that condom distribution was accepted by adults in the community. This seemed to substantiate our earlier impression that the adult members of this community were concerned about adolescent sexual behavior. The project capitalized on the shopkeepers' intuitive understanding of the community acceptability of its goals. In an era in which much is written and discussed about community control of neighborhood social service projects, this project represented a highly decentralized, nonbureaucratic approach to such control.

Demographic effect of the project

In September 1971, age-specific fertility rates were computed for black women (10 to 19 years) residing in the target area and elsewhere in the county. These rates were compared for a 3-year period prior to the project and for a 1-year period after it was fully operational.

The non–target area fertility rate was virtually the same before and after the project began. The target area, however, showed a 19% decline. This difference was statistically significant using a one-tailed chi square test.

We are unaware of any new social forces that might have accounted for the decline other than the condom project. Our community surveillance was reasonably broad and sensitive. We believe that the decline in the target area was real and might be attributed to the condom distribution program. This finding suggests the need for further exploration of innovative teen-age family planning project designs.

REFERENCES
1. Furstenburg, E., Jr., Markowitz, M., and Gordis, L.: Birth control knowledge and attitudes among unmarried pregnant adolescents: A preliminary report, J. Marriage Family 31:34-42, 1969; and a later report on that project by Gordis, L., Finkelstein, R., Fassett, J. D., and Wright, B.: Evaluation of a program for preventing adolescent pregnancy, New Eng. J. Med. 282:1078-1081, May 7, 1970.
2. Gobble, F. L., Vincent, C. E., Cochrane, C. M., and Lock, F. R.: A nonmedical approach to fertility reduction, Obstet. Gynec. 34:888-891, December 1969.
3. Kangas, L. W.: A condom distribution program to reduce unwanted teenage pregnancies. Unpublished manuscript, Carolina Population Center, Chapel Hill, N. C., 1969. For an updated report on this program, see Schonfeld, W. H.: Evaluation of the condom distribution program in Durham County, North Carolina. Unpublished manuscript. Carolina Population Center, Chapel Hill, N. C., 1970.
4. Goldsmith, S.: San Francisco's Teen Clinic, Family Planning Perspect. 1:23-26, October 1969.
5. Arnold, C. B., and Cogswell, B. E.: A condom distribution program for adolescents: The findings of a feasibility study, Amer. J. Public Health 61:739-750, April 1971; see

also Arnold, C. B.: Use patterns and reported sexual behavior of urban, adolescent condom users, J. Sex Res. (In press.)

6. *New York Times,* Population report excerpt, March 17, 1972, p. 18.
7. Arnold, C. B., Sauls, A. R., Fribourg, S., and Bethel, M. B.: Interorganizational cooperation for family planning referral in Wake County, North Carolina, Family Planning Perspect. 2:42-46, March 1970.
8. Arnold, C. B., Slagle, S. J., and Omran, A. R.: An epidemiological study of timing failure-type pregnancies, Amer. J. Public Health. (In press.)
9. Tietze, C., and Hagaman, J. B.: The acceptability and effectiveness of the condom as a contraceptive method, Amer. J. Med. Sciences 210:189-95, August 1945.
10. Cogswell, B. E., and Arnold, C. B.: Organizational efforts to link adolescents to a sex information program. Paper presented at American Sociological Association, 64th Annual Meeting, San Francisco, Calif. September 1, 1969.
11. Kegeles, S. S.: Problems of experimental research in the urban ghetto, Med. Care 7:395-405, September-October 1969.

15 Contraceptive use among single college students

A preliminary report

Byron N. Fujita, B.A.
Nathaniel N. Wagner, Ph.D.
Ronald J. Pion, M.D.

Little data on contraceptive use among unmarried adolescents or college students has been gathered. In a 1940 study, Riley and White[22] state that among the 447 single women interviewed, the figures on actual use of fertility control "were not numerous enough to be presented." In a recent British study of single adolescents, Schofield[23] found contraception was an infrequent occurrence despite the fear of pregnancy. Kirkendall[14] in America observes that college men who had more lasting and permanent friendships with their sexual partners were more likely to practice contraception.

In the social sciences, there are two major reasons for this absence of data. First, the recent direction of studies about premarital sexuality has been attitudinal[1,5,9,10,20,21,24] rather than behavioral.[12,13] This emphasis has precluded the accumulation of data on contraceptive use. Any assertion regarding rates of premarital or nonmarital intercourse and contraception or, for example, the extent of the "sexual revolution" in America, must of course appreciate the difference as well as the relationship between attitudes and behavior.

Second, in existing behavioral studies on college students,[2-4,6-8,11,15,16] the most frequently sampled premarital population, there is a noted lack of contraceptive inquiry. It appears that this exclusion is not accidental. The hesitancy in recent years to examine behavior rather than attitudes may be indicative of attitudinal sensitivities. Despite the apparent frankness about sex and the freedom to discuss it, investigators have anticipated problems with the college students or their parents. Perhaps admitting to intercourse for females is demanding enough. Contraceptive use raises the question of premeditation—an additionally sensitive area. The present investigators did not anticipate such problems and did not find them.

THE STUDY

The present study was conducted in the summer, fall, and winter of 1968. Initially, students were randomly selected at a large, coeducational Northwest university. More females were randomly selected than males. A letter explaining the study was sent to each individual. This was followed by a telephone conversation in which the purpose of the study was reaffirmed, questions the subjects had were answered and an appointment was made. For each sex, approximately 80 per cent of our selection agreed to participate. The 446 respondents (163 male and 283 female) were then interviewed.

The survey consisted of two parts. First, a written questionnaire asking about basic sexual physiology and contraception was ad-

From the Department of Obstetrics and Gynecology, University of Washington School of Medicine, Seattle, Washington.

ministered. A face-to-face interview immediately followed. Well-trained graduate and
medical students were used as interviewers.
Males interviewed male respondents and females interviewed females. The focus of the
interview was sexual behavior including contraception. Of particular interest was the
sexual activity which had occurred in the
year preceding the interview.

In our sample, males were generally older
but had completed less years of college than
females. The mean age for males was 20.3
and for females 19.9. While 47.6 per cent
of the males were 20 years old or more, 31.2
per cent of the females were in this age
range. While 50.2 per cent of the males had
completed their sophomore year of college,
69.8 per cent of the females had done so.

RESULTS

In our sample, 74 (45.5 per cent) males
and 86 (30.5 per cent) females had engaged
in intercourse at least once in their life. Compared with other college studies, these rates
are lower for males and higher for females.

The consistency of contraceptive use in
every relationship was assessed for 50 per
cent of the males and 60 per cent of the
females.* Our definition for "sufficient" protection was relatively strict; the participant
must have been using (to his or her knowledge) some form of contraception (including
withdrawal or rhythm) on every occasion
in the relationship. It was determined that
54 per cent of the males and 46 per cent of
the females in this subsample did not meet
these criteria.

The focus of the study was the activity
in the year preceding the interview. In this
period, 57 males (35 per cent) and 82 females (29 per cent) had engaged in intercourse. These involvements occurred in four
types of relationships. Behaviorally defined,
these were the "steady," "steadily," "casual,"

*This assessment was the result of a later refine-
ment in the research design. Earlier participants
were not asked this question.

Table I. Distribution of intercourse in past year
according to dating types*

Dating type	Male (No. = 163)		Female (No. = 283)	
	No.	%	No.	%
Steady	26	15.9	77	27.2
Steadily	28	17.2	21	7.4
Casual	7	4.3	3	1.1
Pickup	4	2.4	1	1

*Note: 57 males (35 per cent) and 82 females (29 per cent)
reported these figures.

and "pickup" dating types.* Table I presents
the incidence of intercourse in each of these
categories. It may be observed that both
sexes exhibit a strong affinity to the steady
and steadily for intercourse. Females in particular favor the steady relationship.

Tables II and III report the use of withdrawal in these subsamples. Eight males (14
per cent of those who had had intercourse
in the past year) and 33 females (40 per
cent) reported its use. Tables IV and V present the use of rhythm in the past year. Seven
males (13 per cent) and 25 females (31 per
cent) used this method.

Although there is a substantial percentage
of "no answers"† for females, a comparison
of use is interesting. In terms of the participant using withdrawal and rhythm at least
once in any relationship, females demonstrated a more frequent use of both these
methods. Since the incidence of intercourse
in the casual and pickup categories is so low,
it is difficult to determine trends between

*The definitions were as follows: (1) steady—a
person who was dated four or more times and had
been dated exclusively; (2) steadily—a person
who was dated four or more times without ex-
clusiveness; (3) casual—a person dated three or
less times (excluding the pickup situation); (4)
pickup—a "date" in which no prior commitment
had been made to the "dating" situation.
†Again, this was the result of a later refinement
in the research design. Early female participants
were not asked specifically about their use of withdrawal or rhythm.

Table II. Dating type and use of withdrawal among males*

	Dating type									
	Steady		Steadily		Casual		Pickup		Total	
Use	No.	%	No.	%	No.	%	No.	%	No.	%
Yes	5	20	3	11	—		—		8	12
No	21	80	25	89	7	100	4	100	57	88
Total	26	100	28	100	7	100	4	100	65	100

*Note: 8 (14 per cent) of these males used withdrawal in the past year.

Table III. Dating type and use of withdrawal among females*

	Dating type									
	Steady		Steadily		Casual		Pickup		Total	
Use	No.	%	No.	%	No.	%	No.	%	No.	%
Yes	27	35	9	43	—		—		36	35
No	17	22	4	19	1	33	1	100	23	23
No answer	33	43	8	38	2	67	—		43	42
Total	77	100	21	100	3	100	1	100	102	100

*Note: 33 (40 per cent) of the females relied on withdrawal in the past year.

Table IV. Dating types and use of rhythm among males*

	Dating type									
	Steady		Steadily		Casual		Pickup		Total	
Use	No.	%	No.	%	No.	%	No.	%	No.	%
Yes	5	20	2	7	—		—		7	11
No	21	80	25	89	7	100	3	75	56	86
No answer	—		1	4	—		1	25	2	3
Total	26	100	28	100	7	100	4	100	65	100

*Note: 7 (13 per cent) of these males relied on rhythm in the past year.

Table V. Dating types and use of rhythm among females*

	Dating type									
	Steady		Steadily		Casual		Pickup		Total	
Use	No.	%	No.	%	No.	%	No.	%	No.	%
Yes	22	29	5	24	1	33	—		28	27
No	21	28	7	33	1	33	1	100	30	30
No answer	34	43	9	43	1	33	—		44	43
Total	77	100	21	100	3	100	1	100	102	100

*Note: 25 (31 per cent) of these females employed rhythm at least once in the past year.

Table VI. Contraceptive use among males according to dating type*

Contraceptive type	Steady		Steadily		Casual		Pickup		Total	
	No.	%	No.	%	No.	%	No.	%	No.	%
Oral only	9	35	10	36	—		—		19	29
Condom and oral	1	4	—		—		—		1	2
Condom only	9	35	10	36	2	28	2	50	23	35
Condom and foam	1	4	1	4	—		—		2	3
Foam, cream, jelly only	—		—		1	14	—		1	2
Diaphragm and foam	1	4	—		—		—		1	2
IUD	—		—		—		—		—	
No answer	—		—		—		—		—	
None	5	19	7	25	4	57	2	50	18	28
Total	26	100	28	100	7	100	4	100	65	100

*Note: 57 males (35 per cent) reported this distribution. Of these males, 16 (30 per cent) reported no contraceptive use. Like the "diaphragm and foam" category, the "condom and foam" category means the two were used in conjunction. "Condom and oral" means the condom was used and then oral contraceptive.

Table VII. Contraceptive use among females according to dating type*

Contraceptive type	Steady		Steadily		Casual		Pickup		Total	
	No.	%	No.	%	No.	%	No.	%	No.	%
Oral only	26	34	3	14	1	33	—		30	30
Condom and oral	9	12	1	5	—		—		10	10
Condom only	17	22	3	14	1	33	—		21	21
Condom and foam	3	4	2	10	—		—		5	5
Foam, cream, jelly only	4	5	1	5	—		1	100	6	6
Diaphragm and foam	—		—		—		—		—	
IUD	—		—		—		—		—	
No answer	—		6	29	1	33	—		7	7
None	18	23	5	24	—		—		23	23
Total	77	100	21	100	3	100	1	100	102	100

*Note: 82 females (29 per cent) reported this distribution. Of these females, 18 (22 per cent) reported no contraceptive use. Like the "diaphragm and foam" category, the "condom and foam" category means the two were used in conjunction. "Condom and oral" means the condom was used and then oral contraceptive.

dating types. However, in contrast to no use, there is some evidence suggesting that males are less apt to use withdrawal and rhythm with casual and pickup dating types than with the steady or the steadily. Compared with females, there is some evidence that males are more apt to use withdrawal with the steadily than with the steady.

Excluding withdrawal and rhythm, the forms of contraceptive use are reported in Table VI for males and Table VII for females. For males, the condom alone and the oral contraceptives are the most frequently employed methods. The other methods (and combination of methods) yield low percentages with no use of the IUD reported.

A critical variable is the absence of any contraceptive use. This is reported in the category "none." A total of 16 males (30 per cent) reported the 18 cases in which no contraception (excluding withdrawal and rhythm) was used. The 18 cases constituted 28 per cent of all encounters cited by males.

It should be noted that Kirkendall's impression of male contraceptive use in differing relationships is supported in these data. The steady and steadily relationships yield a lower percentage of no contraceptive use.

For females, the profile is somewhat different. While females also favor the condom alone and oral contraception, this latter method is used more than the condom alone —the reverse of the males' priority. In addition, female use of the condom and oral contraception,* foams, creams, and jellies alone, and condom and foam in combination is greater than for males. For females, there was no use of the diaphragm as well as the IUD.

A total of 18 (22 per cent) females reported the 23 cases of no contraceptives. With a substantial number of cases in the steady category, the none response constituted 23 per cent of the total cases (102) reported for the past year.

COMMENT

Two related issues regarding contraceptives and young people are of particular importance to the physician. They are illegitimacy and unwanted pregnancy. At present one of every 11 children in this country is born out of wedlock.[25] In addition, one of every 6 women gives birth within 8 months after her first marriage.[17] The negative effects of unwantedness on the child and of the unwanted child on the marital relationship are well documented.[18] Pregnancies which force

---

*This category was created for those relationships in which the condom was used before the female secured oral contraception. This does not mean they were used in conjunction.

marriage may be a source of continuing regret and sometimes subsequent divorce.

Recently single college students have been the focus of much concern. This concern is appropriate as in 1966, the median age of first marriages for females was 20.5 and for males 22.8.[26] Since approximately 46 per cent of young adults go to college, one would expect many of these individuals to have attended college. For these individuals, an out of wedlock conception or a forced marriage presents severe problems.

In this study, the rates of withdrawal, rhythm, and other contraceptive use may be surprising to some and confirming to others. Whether or not the present study presents relatively high or low rates, the critical issue is why an individual who is active would not be using contraception. Essentially, the dynamics of contraceptive acquisition may be described in three parts. They are knowledge of contraception, motivation, and accessibility of contraception.

It may be stated with a high degree of confidence that most college students today know of contraception. The present openness and frankness about sexuality among college students in general attests to this. In addition, the wide and intensive publicity about oral contraceptives in the mass media have made at least cursory knowledge unescapable. A further consideration is the relative knowledge level of college students. In the factual measure administered to our sample, participants demonstrated an overall understanding of the facts. The persistent use of rhythm and withdrawal in particular represents the notable rift between knowledge and behavior. In addition, some participants were under the illusion that infrequent intercourse was only a partial risk for pregnancy. Strictly speaking, this may be true, but statements such as, "I didn't do it very often—how could I get pregnant" reflects ignorance of pregnancy risk. In short, it may be tentatively concluded that knowledge in itself was not the major inhibiting agent of contraceptive use in this sample.*

A more complex problem is the motivational aspect of contraceptive use. For the single college student there are cogent inhibitory factors. Among the more important are: (a) the problem of storing or carrying contraceptives, especially for those living at home; (b) the fear of "incriminating" evidence of premarital activity if contraception is discovered by or revealed to parents or peers; (c) the existence of a mythology which sanctions spontaneity as the appropriate circumstances for premarital intercourse.[18] To plan to have intercourse is often perceived as a double evil—sex outside marrage and in cold blood. The "nuisance" factor is also present, although this seems more a rationalization for not using contraception. In our interviews, all of these motivational problems were found, each with its own variation. Our clinical impression was that often these participants were stuck at a platitude, a posititon in which the sexual relationship was fully embraced, but the sexual responsibility of contraceptive use was neglected.

Several comments by participants noted the inaccessibility of actual contraceptives. For the single college student the major sources are physician in a private setting, pharmacies, and health services. The need for better service from the first two sources has been cited elsewhere.[27,28] Regarding the third source, that of student health services, the need for comprehensive service is equally important. Since fear of pregnancy alone does not seem to be an effective deterrant to premarital intercourse, many couples are using no or inadequate contraception. When presented with an already active college student or a student planning sexual activity (who wants to be responsible by using contraception), health services have the responsibility to at least refer if not service contraceptive needs. The rate of out-of-wedlock pregnancies is alarming. The evidence of forced marriages is compelling. Physicians and health facilities of which they may be a part can do much to prevent the human suffering and misery arising out of unplanned and unwanted pregnancies.

---

*In addition, it should be noted that "no experimental evidence has been supplied to support the thesis that contraceptive information and supplies made available to the unmarried will increase the number of premarital sexual unions."[19]

REFERENCES
1. Bell, R.: J. Social Issues **22**:43, 1966.
2. Bromley, D. D., and Britten, F. H.: Youth and Sex, New York, 1938, Harper & Brothers, p. 36.
3. Burgess, E. W., and Wallin, P.: Engagement and Marriage, Chicago, 1953, J. B. Lippincott Company, p. 350.
4. Ehrmann, W.: Premarital Dating Behavior, New York, 1959, Henry Holt, p. 33-34, 46.
5. Foote, N. N.: Social Problems **1**:161, 1964.
6. Freedman, M. B.: Merrill-Palmer Quart. **2**:47, 1965.
7. Gilbert Youth Research: Pageant **7**:10, 1951.
8. Grinder, R. E., and Schmidt, S. S.: J. Marriage Family **28**:471, 1966.
9. Halleck, S. L.: J. A. M. A. **200**:108, 1967.
10. Halleck, S. L.: Med. Aspects Hum. Sexuality. **2**:14, 1968.
11. Hamilton, G. V.: A Research in Marriage, New York, 1929, Albert & Charles Boni, p. 343.
12. Kinsey, A. C., Pomeroy, W. B., and Martin, C. E.: Sexual Behavior in the Human Male, Philadelphia, 1948, W. B. Saunders Company.
13. Kinsey, A. C., Pomeroy, W. B., Martin, C. E., and Gebhart, P. H.: Sexual Behavior in the Human Female, Philadelphia, 1953, W. B. Saunders Company.
14. Kirkendall, L. A.: Premarital Intercourse and Interpersonal Relationships, New York, 1961, Julian Press, pp. 284-286.
15. Landis, J. T., and Landis, M.: Building a Successful Marriage, Englewood Cliffs, New Jersey, 1957, Prentice-Hall, Inc., p. 216.
16. Luckey, E. B., and Nass, G. D.: J. Marriage Family **31**:374, 1969.
17. National Center for Health Statistics: Trend of Illegitimacy in the United States; 1940-1965, Washington, D. C., 1968, United States Government Printing Office, Series 21, No. 15.
18. Pohlman, E. H.: Psychology of Birth Planning, Cambridge, Massachusetts, 1969 Schenk-

man Publishing Company, pp. 300-304, 306-325, 352-355.

19. Reiss, I. L.: J. Social Issues **22**:126, 1966.
20. Reiss, I. L.: Premarital Sexual Standards in America, New York, 1960, Free Press of Glencoe, pp. 219-221.
21. Reiss, I. L.: The Social Context of Premarital Sexual Permissiveness, New York, 1967, Holt, Rinehart, & Winston, pp. 16-18, 25-27.
22. Riley, J. W., and White, M.: Amer. Sociology Rev. **5**:890, 1940.
23. Schofield, M.: The Sexual Behavior of Young People, Boston, 1965, Little, Brown & Company, p. 108.
24. Smigel, E. O., and Seiden, R.: In Sex and the Contemporary American Scene, Philadelphia,

1969, American Academy of Political and Social Science, p. 17.
25. U. S. Bureau of the Census: Statistical Abstracts of the United States, Washington, D. C., 1969, United States Government Printing Office, p. 500.
26. U. S. Bureau of the Census: Statistical Abstracts of the United States, ed. 88, Washington, D. C., 1967, United States Government Printing Office, Table 75: "Median Age of First Marriages, by Sex: 1920-1966."
27. Wagner, N. N., Millard, R. P., and Pion, R. J.: J. Amer. Pharm. Ass. **10**:258, 1970.
28. Wagner, N. N., Perthou, N., Fujita, B., and Pion, R. J.: Postgrad. Med. **46**:68, 1969.

16 Prediction in family planning

Prediction of the adoption and continued use of contraception

Donald McCalister, Ph.D., F.A.P.H.A.
Victor Thiessen, Ph.D.

INTRODUCTION

This report presents a summary of the findings of a prospective, exploratory investigation of factors which may influence the adoption and continued use of the oral contraceptive and of the intrauterine contraceptive device (IUCD) by medically indigent women. The investigation explores the extent to which selected reproductive, social, and social psychological factors may be predictive of attendance at a family planning clinic and of the adoption and subsequent use of the pill or IUCD.

The factors selected are among those which have been assumed in other reports to be important, either (1) in defining the need by women for family planning or (2) as indicators of patient readiness to accept

Dr. McCalister is Associate Professor of Sociology, and Dr. Thiessen is Assistant Professor of Sociology, Case Western Reserve University Department of Sociology (11027 Magnolia), Cleveland, Ohio 44106.
Support of this investigation was provided by Research Division, Children's Bureau, HEW Grants PH-900 and H-40.
This paper was presented before the Maternal and Child Health and Health Officers Sections of the American Public Health Association at the Ninety-Seventh Annual Meeting in Philadelphia, Pa., November 12, 1969.

Reprinted from *American Journal of Public Health* **60**(8): 1372-1381, August 1970. Copyright American Public Health Association.

family planning services. However, the possible importance of these factors in predicting who *will accept* family planning with *what results* is problematic since the designs of earlier studies have not permitted adequate analysis of this problem.

Adequate analysis requires that all members of the study population have access to family planning services and that data which bear upon all sources of service be available to the investigator. It also requires that prospective observations be obtained on those women who do *not* make use of the services, as well as on those who do. With the exception of the design of the research reported by Siegel, et al.,[1] these conditions do not appear to have been met in other reported studies. On the basis of the findings reported in this paper, some directions for further and more focused research will be suggested.

Study design

The investigation employed a panel study design involving a series of five home interview waves between October, 1965, and January, 1968.

Reproductive histories, social background data, and social psychological data were obtained in the first three interviews. Family planning clinic appointments were offered at the end of the third interview. Appointments were for free instruction, examination, and service in a special family planning clinic located in the Department of Obstetrics and Gynecology of Tulane University. It is im-

153

portant to note that there were no other family planning clinics in southern Louisiana at the time and that this was a recently established and unpublicized clinic. Private physicians were the only alternative sources of prescription contraceptives until June 27, 1967, when a public family planning clinic opened.[2]

Fecund women who refused to make a clinic appointment were home-contacted for a fourth interview concerning their reasons for refusal. In the same wave, those who failed to meet scheduled appointments were contacted and both groups were offered new appointments. Subsequent clinic attendance and adoption of contraceptive methods were monitored through clinic records for all respondents. All women not surgically sterile at the time of clinic appointment offers were eligible for contact in the fifth interview wave one year later to obtain postclinic pregnancy data and to determine current contraceptive method use.

The sample

Two main samples were involved in the investigation, the nature of these being dictated by the purpose of the total study of which this analysis is only a part. One was a simple probability sample of 100 of the 364 medically indigent black women who were registered as experiencing stillbirth or infant death in the New Orleans metropolitan area in 1964. The second sample was a matched control sample of indigent New Orleans women delivering a surviving infant in 1964, with no detectable prior pregnancy loss experience. The samples were matched on the basis of maternal age, race, gravidity, and legitimacy of the 1964 product of conception.

A third sample was drawn only for methodological reasons and has not been included in this analysis. This was a simple probability sample of 62 of the remaining 264 cases from the 1964 indigent loss population. These women were contacted only for clinic appointment offers and subsequent

observation of clinic attendance, method adoption, and method use one year later. This provided a partial check on the extent to which exposure to the first three interviews might have influenced response to clinic appointment offers in the main study samples. Since no significant differences were found, it may be assumed that the two main samples are free of bias from this source.

In the main samples, 93 of the women with loss experience were contacted and interviewed, of whom 92 could be matched with a control. Contact was maintained with 172 of the combined total of 185 women through the fifth interview two and one-half years later. Women who were surgically sterile by the time of the fifth interview, as well as those who had used the pill or IUCD prior to the initial offer of clinic appointments, have been excluded from this report leaving a total of 104 cases. Since prior analysis failed to reveal any significant differences between the original samples with respect to pregnancy spacing,[3] clinic attendance, postclinic pregnancies, and method use,[4] or reliability of attitudinal fertility data,[5] the samples have been pooled for the purpose of this report.

Social characteristics of the 104 women at the time clinic appointments were offered were as follows. The average age was 27.4 years and the median age 26 years. There was an average of 5.5 pregnancies per woman with 46 per cent having been pregnant six or more times. Fifty-six per cent of the respondents were in a legal or common-law marital union; 13 per cent had never been married. Seventy-six per cent had not completed four years of high school. Thirty per cent were Catholic. The first marriage or pregnancy (which ever came first) had occurred within five years prior to the offer of clinic appointments for 33 per cent of the women and within ten years for 64 per cent. Forty-four per cent of the total had terminated a pregnancy within one year, while 56 per cent had experienced fetal or

Table 1. Correlations of predictor variables with criterion variables

Predictor variables	Clinic attendance (N = 104)[a]	Clinic adoption of pill or IUCD (N = 61)[b]	Pill or IUCD in use at one year (N = 61)[b]
A. Reproductive history variables			
Gravidity	−.03	.10	.14
Ever experienced fetal or infant death	.04	−.21	−.16
Last delivery ended in fetal or infant death	−.09	−.24	−.22
Months between last delivery and clinic appointment offer	−.20	−.18	−.31
Ever delivered an illegitimate child	−.02	−.16	−.22
Number of currently living children	−.07	.17	.18
Number of children living with respondent	−.06	.20	.23
Time to termination of next desired pregnancy	.12[c] (n = 31)	.03[d] (n = 22)	.12[d] (n = 22)
B. Social, familial and situational variables			
Age	−.24	−.12	−.05
Marital status (currently married)	.12	−.02	.09
Highest grade completed	−.09	−.02	.03
Religion (Catholic)	−.18	−.12	−.08
Duration of family of procreation	−.18	−.06	.05
Number of children in family of origin	.12	.18	.19
Number of transitions in family of origin	.01	−.09	−.18
Number of father substitutes	.11	−.34	−.26
Number of mother substitutes	.10	−.02	−.14
Miles from home to clinic	.02	.12	.22
Home offer of reimbursement for clinic attendance costs	.31[e] (n = 54)	.01[f] (n = 18)	−.19[f] (n = 18)
C. Fertility knowledge and attitude variables			
Knowledge of ovulatory cycle	−.02	−.08	−.03
Knowledge of reproductive physiology	.06	−.03	−.04
Desire for family planning information	.19	.04	−.01
Would accept clinic appointment if offered	.11	−.07	−.02
Desired family size	.10	−.18	−.08
Ideal family size	.07	−.07	−.05
Number of additional pregnancies expected	−.03	−.24	−.17
D. Communication variables			
M.D., R.N., or pharmacist as most frequent source of information	.10	−.01	.11
Mate objections to family planning	.10	−.32	−.32
Frequency of visiting with neighbors	−.18	−.07	.12
E. Attitudes toward medical personnel and medicine			
Negative perceptions of public clinics	.04	.07	.02
Acceptance of physician judgment	.10	.11	.19
Acceptance of folk medicine	.12	.09	.01
Perceived rejection by medical personnel	−.03	−.03	.05

Continued.

a. For a sample size of 104, r ≥ .19 is significant at the .05 level.
b. For a sample size of 61, r ≥ .25 is significant at the .05 level.
c. For a sample size of 31, r ≥ .36 is significant at the .05 level.
d. For a sample size of 22, r ≥ .42 is significant at the .05 level.
e. For a sample size of 54, r ≥ .26 is significant at the .05 level.
f. For a sample size of 18, r ≥ .47 is significant at the .05 level.

Table 1. Correlations of predictor variables with criterion variables—cont'd

Predictor variables	Criterion variables		
	Clinic attendance (N = 104)[a]	Clinic adoption of pill or IUCD (N = 61)[b]	Pill or IUCD in use at one year (N = 61)[b]
F. Social psychological dimension of decision-making			
General anxiety	.14	−.13	−.16
General risk-taking	.05	.02	.05
Alienation	.00	−.10	−.04
Traditional family orientation	.18	.11	.15
Vertical mobility aspirations	−.14	.01	−.01
Time orientation:			
Past	.00	.01	−.09
Future	.06	−.04	−.05
Present	.22	.01	−.08
Acceptance of children	−.13	−.30	−.15
Risk-taking in fertility	−.04	−.23	−.26

infant death on at least one occasion. All had terminated at least one pregnancy.

In summary, the research site permitted control of patient access to the only available clinic source of prescription contraceptives in an area in which no family planning clinic had existed previously. The sample includes only women of demonstrated fecundity who had not used the pill or IUCD prior to the study and who were homogeneous in terms of race and socioeconomic level (i.e., all were black and eligible for tax-supported medical services). This is regarded as a near-ideal experimental situation in which to investigate the antecedents of adoption and subsequent use of the pill or IUCD.

THE CRITERION VARIABLES

Three criterion variables are employed in this report: (1) family planning clinic *attendance,* (2) in-clinic *adoption* of the oral pill or of an IUCD, and (3) *use* of the pill or IUCD one year after the initial offer of clinic appointments. Although all three variables pertain to family planning, each defines a distinctive type of behavior. Thus, clinic attendance does not necessarily imply

method adoption. Nor does in-clinic method adoption necessarily imply the subsequent use of that method. Further, the continued use of the pill or IUCD one year later may reflect use of a method initially adopted in the clinic with subsequent service being obtained from a source other than the original clinic. Therefore, each of the criterion variables is treated as a separate dimension in the adoption and use of contraception.

Data from the total of 104 women are analyzed in relation to clinic attendance while the analyses of adoption and continued use are based upon the 61 women who attended the clinic.

THE PREDICTOR VARIABLES

Six sets of characteristics of the respondents are analyzed in relation to each of the criterion measures. These sets of characteristics are referred to as "predictor" variables, and are presented as the six subsections of Table 1. The sheer number of predictor variables, together with the need to limit the length of this report, made it necessary to omit detailed presentation of the data and measurements in order to communicate the scope of the most relevant findings. Description of the measures may be obtained from the authors.

Pearsonian correlation coefficients are presented in Table 1 as summary measures of association. Since these coefficients place restrictions on the data that may not always be met, percentage comparisons were also computed. Whenever such comparisons add further information or differ substantially from the coefficients, they are discussed in the text.

Two general methods have been used in assessing the relationships which are reported. First, the data have been examined for those relationships which are statistically significant. Although it is technically inappropriate to compute significance tests on data that are not randomly selected from a well-defined or meaningful population, they are reported here since our purpose is the essentially descriptive one of cautiously assessing which predictors appear to be related to the criterion variables.

Secondly, certain additional variables were selected for discussion because their correlation coefficients, though not statistically significant, were of a magnitude which suggests a relationship. The two different sample sizes for the criterion variables make this additional reporting desirable, since correlations which would be significant with one sample size may only approach significance for a smaller sample.

RESULTS
A. Reproductive history variables

In this first section, the relationship of eight reproductive history variables with the criterion measures will be discussed (Table 1). The reproductive history variables chosen are those which make family planning "desirable" from a medical point of view. Yet only one of the measures is significantly related to one or more criterion variables. Women who have recently terminated a pregnancy are more likely to have attended the clinic, as well as to continue to use the pill or IUCD at one year. This

finding, which is also reported by Siegel, et al., for clinic attendance,[6] suggests the possibility of increased spacing of *future* pregnancies and stresses the desirability of postpartum programs. Further evidence for the possibility of increased spacing is the fact that those who adopted the pill or IUCD and those using these methods at one year were less likely to have had any additional pregnancies during the year following clinic appointment offers. In this connection it is important to note that 49 per cent of the sample had a mean nonpregnant interval of six months or less over their entire reproductive histories. Eighty-nine per cent had an average interval of twelve months or less.

None of the other reproductive history variables are significantly related to the criterion variables; however, a few of them are worthy of comment.

Ever having delivered an illegitimate child appears to be related to use at one year of the pill or IUCD but, from a medical viewpoint, in an *adverse* direction: continuing users of the pill or IUCD are less likely to have delivered an illegitimate child. Those who adopted these methods are also less likely to have delivered an illegitimate child but this relationship is not as strong. Although it is generally considered medically and socially desirable that women likely to deliver out of wedlock adopt effective contraceptive methods, these data suggest that the opposite may be more likely to occur.

Having experienced an infant or fetal death on the *last* delivery appears to be related to adoption and continued use of the pill or IUCD but again in the *wrong direction;* those who experienced such loss were substantially less likely to adopt or to continue the use of these methods. Having *ever* experienced such loss is related to adoption and use in the same direction.

The number of currently living children and the number of children living with the respondent are positively associated with method adoption and with continued use.

While not strongly related, this does suggest that the use of prescription methods increases with the number of surviving children.

In terms of both future fertility and obstetrical risk in future pregnancies, these findings offer a mixed outlook. On the positive side, they suggest increased pregnancy spacing. On the negative side, however, gravidity, risk (defined as infant or fetal death), and illegitimacy appear to be either unrelated or adversely related to the adoption and continued use of contraception.

B. Social, familial and situational variables

Five social background characteristics of the respondents—age, duration of family of procreation, marital status, education, and religion—were analyzed in relation to the criterion variables. Again, the results are mixed regarding the implications for risk and future fertility. Women between the ages of 20 and 24 are significantly overrepresented among clinic attenders but not among adopters and users of the pill or IUCD at one year. While this is the age range characterized by the highest fertility and shortest spacing among the indigent in New Orleans,[7] the finding is more suggestive of interest in acquiring information than of immediate desire to control conceptions within this age group.

A measure of the duration of the family of procreation was devised by subtracting age at marriage (or age at first pregnancy if out of wedlock) from age at time of the clinic offer. This measure is related to the criterion variables in the same manner as age, but not as strongly.

The remaining background variables (marital status, education, and religion) are not significantly related to the criterion measures. This is not too surprising in the case of education, due to the rather uniformly low educational level of the sample. Although of little predictive value, the religious variable would seem to be of some importance. Catholics appear to be less likely to attend a clinic or to continue use of the pill or IUCD.

Sociologists have generally found that an individual's family of origin exerts prevasive influence on the family of procreation. Two specific characteristics of the family of origin were examined. First, is the size of the respondent's sibship related to the criterion measures, regardless of her completed fertility? The direction of the relation indicates that women from large families of origin are somewhat more likely to adopt and continue to use the pill or IUCD, but these relationships are not statistically significant.

The second characteristic is family instability. Is experience with family instability during a woman's youth subsequently related to differential adoption and use of contraception? Our data do not indicate this to be the case. Women whose real father remained in the family of origin were significantly more likely to adopt and continue use of the pill or IUCD. The same direction of relationship appears in the case of presence of the respondent's real mother and of few or no transitions in the family of origin during the respondent's childhood and adolescence. (Transitions in the family of origin simply refer to the number of persons entering or leaving the respondent's household.) Thus, to the extent that there is any relationship, it is the offspring from the larger and more stable families who adopted and continued the use of prescription methods.

Two situational variables were tested for their relation to clinic performance. The first was the distance between the home of the respondent and the clinic, since distance was regarded as a possible barrier to clinic utilization. It was not a barrier; women living farther from the clinic actually appeared more likely to have continued use of the pill or IUCD up to one year. However, this may be unique to New Orleans and in part attributable to the quality and economy of public transportation there.

The second situational variable concerned

place of reimbusement for expense incurred in attending the clinic. Women who failed to meet the initial clinic appointment but who did accept a new appointment during the fourth interview were randomly assigned to one of two groups. In one, the women were offered $2 in cash at their home to defray travel or child care costs incurred in attending the clinic. In the other, the women were told that $2 in cash would be waiting for them at the clinic. All were told that no obligation was attached to acceptance of the money and no mention was made of money unless an appointment had been accepted. Offer of reimbursement at the home was significantly related to clinic atendance, but *not* to method adoption or to use. The weak correlations involving the latter two variables suggest that attendance may have been prompted by a feeling of obligation due to receipt of the money, but an obligation which did not extend to method adoption and use. The implications from these two situational factors are that increased convenience of access to family planning services does not act as a powerful inducement.

C. Fertility knowledge and attitude variables

Eight measures of fertility knowledge and attitudes frequently assumed to be meaningful in relation to the adoption and use of contraception are included in this analysis. Only one of these measures is significantly related to any of the criterion measures. There is a statistically significant relationship between stated desire for family planning information and clinic attendance; however, this relationship has no practical significance since only 9 of the 104 respondents expressed no desire for information.

The number of additional pregnancies expected was unrelated to clinic attendance. Of the women who did attend, there is a strong indication that the fewer the number of additional pregnancies a woman ex-

pected, the more likely it was that she would adopt and perhaps continue to use the pill or IUCD.

Overall, then, the findings in this section are negative. On the basis of the data, it appears that fertility knowledge is unrelated to adoption and use of contraception; those who are aware of the ovulatory cycle and of the rudiments of reproductive physiology are not more likely to engage in effective contraception. Nor is a woman's desired family size or her image of the ideal family size related to position on the criterion variables. These findings are surprising in view of the frequency with which patient readiness to accept family planning has been inferred from such measures. Although precise comparison is difficult, these findings appear to parallel those reported by Siegel, et al.[8]

D. Communication variables

Three communication variables were also examined in relation to the criterion variables. The first deals with the most frequently used source of family planning information. Women who reported using physicians, nurses or druggists as their primary source appear to be no more likely to attend the clinic or to adopt and continue to use a prescription method than are women whose primary source of information is from printed matter or from family and friends.

A second communication dimension, mate objection to family planning, was found to be significantly related to adoption and also to continued use of the pill or IUCD; women whose mates objected to family planning were less likely to adopt the pill or IUCD or to continue use at one year.

The third communication measure concerns frequency of visiting with neighbors. Although not significant, it appears that those who attended the clinic are least likely to visit neighbors frequently. The inconclusive nature of these relationships merits further investigation, focusing on the content of communications about fertility control, the credibility of sources of information, and the permeability of lay communication networks.

E. Attitudes toward medical personnel and medicine

Four multi-item attitude scales involving medical personnel and folk medicine were developed. The question posed is whether negative attitudes toward medical personnel, public clinics, and scientific medicine act as deterrents to clinic attendance, method adoption, and use. None of these scales was significantly related to any of the criterion measures although acceptance of physician judgment may be related to continuation of method use. It is especially interesting to note that negative perception of public clinics is unrelated to the criterion measures. This may reflect the overriding influence of the importance to the respondents of receipt of family planning services. This line of reasoning is consistent with the findings presented on the situational variables, where neither distance from home to clinic nor place of reimbursement for expenses was related to adoption or use. The same explanation is plausible in relation to the other health attitude dimensions. An alternative interpretation is that family planning is not perceived as a health dimension. These two explanations appear equally plausible in light of the findings and merit further research to resolve the ambiguity. In either case, attitudes concerning medicine and medical personnel, as measured here, are generally unrelated to the adoption and use of contraception.

F. Social psychological dimensions of decision-making

The final set of predictor variables involves (1) general attitudinal dimensions presumed to influence decision-making, and (2) specific attitudes more directly relevant to fertility. Each of these attitudinal measures are multi-item scales, with the exception of time orientation.

Of the six general attitudinal variables, only time orientation was significantly re-

lated to any criterion variable; women with a present time orientation, as opposed to past or future, were more likely to attend the clinic. Traditional family orientation ("closeness" of family) bordered upon significance in relation to attendance but not to adoption and use. The fact that none of the other general attitudinal scales was related to any of the criterion measures suggests strongly that such attitudes lack predictive utility.

The two scales which were more specifically relevant to fertility involved acceptance of children and risk-taking in fertility. Acceptance of children was negatively related to all of the criterion measures, with the negative relationship to clinic adoption of the pill or IUCD being statistically significant. Risk-taking in fertility proved somewhat negatively related to adoption and significantly so to use at one year. That is, those with a quite specific desire to minimize the risk of pregnancy appear to be more likely to adopt and use contraception. These variables may represent two different dimensions of desire to limit or space pregnancies. Viewed as such, these findings combine with the negative relations between additional pregnancies expected and method adoption and use to stress that women not wishing to have additional children or desiring to space pregnancies are more likely to adopt and use effective contraceptives.

While this conclusion seems a statement of the obvious, it will be recalled that the measures of desire for family planning information, desired family size, and ideal family size had no predictive utility. As a comment on measurement this suggests that greater direct predictive utility may be found in quite specific fertility attitude measures, and perhaps in indexes combining them.

CONCLUSION AND SUMMARY

The design of this exploratory study has permitted a conveniently controlled examination of the predictive utility of a wide array of variables in relation to attendance at a family planning clinic and to the adoption and use of the pill or the IUCD. Pains were taken to maintain methodological rigor throughout the investigation, and these mitigate in part the limitations regarding generalizability of the findings which are imposed by the sample design. The parallels in findings between this and Siegel's research, given the wide differences in samples and study designs, lend further confidence to the findings.

The findings can be summarized by the simple statement that most of the variables examined here were not significantly related to the criterion measures. In addition, few of those that were related to the criterion measures were associated in a direction favorable to either reduced fertility or to reduced biomedical and social pathology involving future fertility. Finally, the predictive utility of all variables examined is low. In statistical language, the proportion of "explained" differences in the criterion variables is assessed by the square of the correlation coefficients. Our highest correlation proved to be $-.32$ which means that the strongest "predictor" accounts for only 10 per cent of the differences.

The fact of such low associations poses problems. We must attempt to assess why, by and large, there are such weak relations. Looking beyond the scope of the present study, we must ask what our criterion variables are measuring. That is, what is the meaning of attending a clinic or of adopting the pill or IUCD or of continuing to use such contraceptives one year later. It is assumed that each is a behavioral expression of desire for fertility control. Logically, however, attendance does not necessarily imply method adoption. Nor does adoption necessarily imply use at a later time. Therefore, the three may define somewhat different types or degrees of desire for fertility control along a time dimension which permits change to occur in response to intervening stimuli. If so, predictability might be strengthed by combining the three criterion variables into a single measure.

Further analysis of these data which follows this suggestion is under way. It also goes a step further in employing a composite criterion variable involving type and consistency of contraceptive practice over time. These measures have greater theoretical meaning than do individual behavioral variables and may yield findings of clearer practical import concerning fertility control and the use of family planning clinics. Preliminary results are promising.[9]

In summary, the findings reported suggest the need for a reassessment of the conceptualization and measurement of the criterion variables. This is seen as a necessary step in the attempt to comprehend factors which underlie the use of family planning clinics and, more broadly, factors leading to fertility control. A considerable amount of further research involving more sophisticated measures and more generally representative samples is needed before much light will have been cast on the dynamics of the adoption and use of contraception.

REFERENCES

1. Siegel, Earl; Thomas, Donald; Tuthill, Robert; Coulter, Elizabeth; and Chipman, Sidney. Factors Associated With Involvement of Low-Income Women in a Public Family Planning Program. A.J.P.H. **60**:1382 (Aug.), 1970.
2. Beasley, Joseph D., and Harter, Carl L. Introducing Family Planning Clinics to Louisiana. Children **14**,5:188-192 (Sept.-Oct.), 1967.
3. McGee, Charles, and McCalister, Donald. Relationship of Maternal Age and Pregnancy Spacing to Perinatal Mortality and Low Birthweight Delivery. Mimeographed, Case Western Reserve University, 1969.
4. McCalister, Donald; McGee, Charles; Forti, Theresa; and Hawkins, Morton. Family Planning and the Reduction of Pregnancy Loss Rates. J. Marriage & the Family **31**,4:668-673 (Nov.), 1969.
5. McCalister, Donald, and Frankowski, Ralph. Time Series Reliability of Qualitative Family Size Data. Mimeographed, Case Western Reserve University, 1969.
6. Siegel, et al., op. cit.
7. McGee and McCalister, op. cit.
8. Siegel, et al., op. cit.
9. Thiessen, Victor, and McCalister, Donald. Predictions in Family Planning. Mimeographed, Case Western Reserve University, 1970.

PART IV
THE DISPARITY BETWEEN WHO NEEDS AND WHO USES FAMILY PLANNING

The contents of Part II presented justifications for family planning from somewhat different points of view. These included the physical, emotional, and social well-being of individuals and of families. On these grounds, a number of overlapping groups were singled out as being most in need of family planning. They included teen-agers, persons over 35 years of age, the grand multiparae, the ones who are recently post-partal, those with genetic risk, the poor, and the nonwhite. These groups encompass much of the fertile female population. In Part III, four general factors involved in individual's decisions regarding family planning were presented. These were (1) knowledge about family planning, (2) subjective and objective availability of family planning methods, (3) values concerning the use of family planning methods, and (4) social support for family planning.

The question addressed in this section is: "To what extent are the groups already identified as being most in need of family planning also the ones most likely to utilize it?" The contents of Parts II and III hint at many of the possible reasons for a disparity between those whom we would consider to be in need and those who actually practice family planning. In this section those reasons are addressed more directly.

The disparity between who needs and who uses family planning is approached in three different ways. First, it is described from a preventive health viewpoint, then from the viewpoint of the behavioral dynamics of prospective clients, and, finally, from the viewpoint of the relationships between society and the health practitioner.

PREVENTIVE MEDICINE VIEWPOINT

It is quite appropriate to regard family planning as a component of preventive health care. It is largely from this position that criteria have been developed for who needs family planning. However, as suggested earlier, this viewpoint does not imply that the public also views family planning as preventive medical care. In fact, it seems quite reasonable to assume that most individuals and couples who utilize family planning methods do so primarily for reasons other than health. This is not to say that Americans do not value their health. They do. What is meant is that, first of all, family planning is not necessarily viewed

163

in a health context and, secondly, that reasons other than health have a decisive influence on whether or not and what type of family planning methods are utilized. Consequently, it is contrary to logic for one to assume that those deemed most in need of family planning from a medical point of view will also be most likely to engage in such practices. Indeed, the general notion of preventive health care is foreign to some of the groups that are defined medically as being most in need of family planning.

One implication is that a major task of health professionals is an educational one. It is their responsibility to take the initiative in showing the public and the individual the connection between family planning and health. It has been argued that family planning is a private matter. However, research shows that some clients often wish that health professionals would initiate discussion of family planning.

On a broader level, the notion of preventive health care needs to be made more familiar so that it can become part of the life styles of those most in need of family planning. But even if preventive medical care was a familiar concept to the general public and even if the public was aware of the connection between family planning and preventive health, it is unlikely that those most in need would invariably seek out such services. The reasons are discussed below.

CLIENT'S VIEWPOINT

One may already have concluded quite accurately that in many respects the four factors discussed in the introduction to Part III will be least favorable for those groups in most need of family planning on the grounds of health considerations. Some concrete examples are provided, as follows:

First, there is some evidence that both the subjective and objective availability of medically prescribed family planning methods is less than adequate for the adolescent, the poor, and the nonwhite.

Second, there is substantial social opposition in some quarters to making family planning available to single persons and especially to teen-agers. Thus, in addition to less availability, there is less social support for family planning services directed at these groups. On the other hand, there are those who would like to require welfare recipients to practice contraception as a condition to continued receipt of financial aid.

Third, among the poor and nonwhite there is often positive social support available to the out-of-wedlock mother and child. The reason is that there is a greater value being attached to social definitions of legitimacy as opposed to the legal definitions that appear to be more important to other social classes. Social legitimacy involves the giving of proper parental care and affection to the offspring of a publicly recognized sexual union that lacks benefit of clergy, that is, a common-law arrangement. Hence, in these groups there is not as much stigma attached to having an out-of-wedlock child despite the increased risks to health.

Fourth, for the teen-ager, there is some evidence that his personal values conflict with the use of family planning methods. Notions of romantic love, of spontaneity, or of morality, and guilt conflict with being prepared (by contraception) for sexual activity.

Additional examples could be cited; however, the ones mentioned above should suffice to make two points clear. First, they illustrate that factors other than health considerations play a crucial part in determining whether those most in need are likely to use family planing. Second, there is evidence that some of the groups most in need of family planning are less likely to have access to factors such as positive social support that are critical in determining whether effective family planning methods will be used. A reversal of this situation often exists in the case of illegitimacy in which the goal of family planning may not be pursued because of a relative *lack* of social disapproval for the out-of-wedlock mother. Health professionals need to keep these two points clearly in mind when dealing with their clients.

SOCIETY AND THE PRACTITIONER

The preceding discussion has focused upon the client's lack of awareness of contraceptive use as an aspect of preventive health service, and other characteristics of the client that account for some of the disparity between who needs and who uses family planning. A third explanation that merits consideration is the influence that societal forces exert upon the practice of health professionals in family planning programs.

Health practitioners are most often members of the middle class and possess values that are representative of this group. Professional knowledge and expertise are superimposed upon life styles, attitudes, and beliefs that arise from and are reinforced by the practitioner's position in the social structure. Yet, in the daily activities of professional life he or she deals with clients whose life circumstances may be vastly different. The potential for misunderstanding is enormous in the very situation where the need for information exchange and open communication is greatest. It is not unusual to find that a single word as it is used by the professional and by the patient may have considerably different meanings. The paper by Smith in Part I introduced this point by stressing the need for the physician to determine the precise meaning of "birth control" to the patient when contraceptive information is sought.

In addition to social class, racial and ethnic differences and societal expectations for "appropriate" sexual behavior for different age groups also affect the health practitioner. Nowhere is this more evident than in today's ferment over adolescent sexual behavior and contraceptive use. The changing sexual mores of our society have produced conflict in the adolescent who is struggling with the need for independence but who requires support at the same time. There exists a dire need for understanding counsel from health practitioners and for prescription of contraceptives for the sexually active teen-ager.

The practitioner is frequently unaware of the influence of his own inhibitions and inadequacies in discussion of sexual behavior with patients. There is a need for introspection in order to identify hidden ambivalencies and conflicts on the part of the health professional in order to avoid being insensitive to patient needs because of his own feelings. This advice includes all members of the health team, since patients may seek information from anyone in the practice setting, and no group is immune to difficulties in this sensitive area.

Finally, the physical characteristics of the settings where services are offered may influence the attitudes of both patients and practitioners. Budget limitations, which may result in the use of less than adequate buildings with minimal comfort and little privacy, present the image of "second class" services to those who provide as well as to those who seek service in such surroundings. It is difficult for the practitioner to convey respect for individuals in settings that permit little individualized service and in which overcrowding and long waiting times may be the rule.

The articles in Part IV give detailed attention to numerous facets of the reasons for the disparity between need and use in family planning. The first article (Jaffe and Polgar) delineates what the authors term the "cultural-motivational" and the "accessibility" approaches that have been utilized in the development of family planning programs for the poor. These two strategies involve different perspectives concerning the nature of the potential client and his or her motivation for the use of contraception, as well as the implications for the planning and implementation of family planning programs. Their point is that neither approach alone is adequate for reducing the disparity between need and use; a combination of elements from each seems required.

The article by Fischman points out some crucial reasons why nurses in particular have been slow to take on the task of educating clients as to the relation of family planning to health. This is the case despite the policy statement issued by the American Nurses' Association, which endorsed the responsibility of nursing in this area. Necessary support from health departments and other official agencies has not been forthcoming. Nursing faculty members often lack the necessary preparation, and the lack of programs in many teaching hospitals has meant that practice settings were not available in which nursing students could learn to instruct patients. Fischman also discusses ways in which the physical characteristics of the practice setting may impede the delivery of care.

In "Family Planning Counsel," Lieberman draws upon his clinical experiences and insights to provide practical advice to the health professional in family planning. He cautions for the need to know one's own biases and to counsel on the basis of clinical judgment while leaving personal decisions to the client—whether adolescent, unmarried, or whomever. Wagner et al. continue in this vein but with specific reference to the sexually active adolescent. The unique and, for many adolescents, biologically unrealistic restraints imposed by society are objectively discussed; the needs for understanding, for counsel, and for service are documented with acknowledgment by the authors of the controversial nature of their topic.

In the two remaining articles of Part IV, Kane et al. present findings that illuminate the matter of differences between ethnic groups in motivation for contraceptive use. These findings serve to invalidate the middle-class assumption that the disparity between need and use is attributable to client ignorance or indifferences. Zelnik and Kantner carry this point further in their report on illegitimacy among blacks. A major finding reported by them is that contraceptive use by the unmarried female is seen as rational and calculating; thus, it is disapproved because of the psychic costs involved until the birth of one or more illegitimate offspring prompt its use. In addition to exemplifying an ethnic value, this provides an excellent example of conflicting values within the individual.

17 Family planning and public policy: Is the "culture of poverty" the new cop-out?*

Frederick S. Jaffe
Steven Polgar**

Irene Taeuber has noted that family-planning programs in developing countries raise the issue of whether "birth control, like death control, can be partially separated from those levels and conditions of living that have been its historic accompaniments."[1] The same sort of question underlies the relationship of family planning and poverty in the United States: Under what conditions can effective family planning be introduced successfully to people who have long suffered from deprivation and under-education? To what extent will it accelerate their exit from poverty by enhancing their ability to grasp new economic, education, and social opportunities (if these are actually made available)?[2] The answers to these questions have enormous significance for formulating

public policy aimed at inducing social change, as well as considerable theoretical interest. And even to *ask* these questions implies a particular conceptual framework that is by no means widely shared among analysts and practitioners in the United States family-planning field.

In this paper, we will explore the manner in which the culture of poverty concept has been applied to family planning. The dichotomy between the *cultural-motivational* and *accessibility* approaches elaborated here is adapted from a dichotomy recently formulated by Herbert Gans.[3] If the major purpose of research is the elimination of poverty, Gans suggests that studies of the poor are not the first order of business but rather studies of the economy, the society, and the "persisting cultural patterns among the affluent" which combine to keep people in poverty. He finds the *cultural* approach to poverty deficient because it ignores aspirations of the poor which conflict with behavior and emphasizes obstacles to change; the pure *situational* view which

*Adapted from a paper presented before the American Sociological Association and the Society for the Study of Social Problems, San Francisco, August 29, 1967. The research and analyses on which the paper is based were done 1964-1967.
**Frederick S. Jaffe, B.A., is Vice-President for Program Planning and Development, Planned Parenthood World Population. Steven Polgar, Ph.D., is Associate Professor of Anthropology and Associate Director of Carolina Population Center, University of North Carolina; formerly Director of Research, PPWP.

[1] I. Taeuber, "Toward Resolution of the Problems of Population Growth," *Science,* 152 (June 17, 1966), p. 1612.

Reprinted from *Journal of Marriage and the Family* XXX(2):228-235, May 1968. Copyright National Council on Family Relations.

[2] Cf. H. L. Sheppard, "The Effects of Family Planning on Poverty in the U.S.," in U.S. Senate, Committee on Labor and Public Welfare, Subcommittee on Employment, Manpower and Poverty, *Examination of the War on Poverty,* September, 1967; and A. A. Campbell, "The Role of Family Planning in the Reduction of Poverty," elsewhere in this issue.
[3] H. Gans, "Poverty and Culture: Some Basic Questions About Methods of Studying Life-Styles of the Poor," prepared for the International Seminar on Poverty, University of Essex, April, 1967.

posits instantaneous and uniform response to opportunities he regards as too simple. The prime issue, he concludes, is "to discover how soon poor people will change their behavior, given new opportunities, and what restraints or obstacles . . . come from that reaction to past situations we call culture."

II

The implementation of family-planning programs in the United States has received relatively little systematic study. However, research findings and empirical observations in a number of related areas establish the basic context for development of these programs, principally:

1. The traditionally observed inverse relationship between income and family size. (In 1964, nearly half of all families with four or more children were either poor or near poor, by official standards, and their risk of poverty was almost three times as great as for families with three children or less. Nearly half of the children living in poverty were growing up in homes with five or more children under 18.[4])

2. Studies of fertility attitudes and practices, which show that the poor: want an average of less than three children; make some effort to control family size; must rely more on less effective, non-medical contraceptive methods; and have more excess fertility (in terms of their own preferences) than higher income couples.[5]

3. Studies of the differential distribution of medical services, which show that the poor have access to medical care primarily for emergency or chronic conditions and rarely for preventive services.[6]

4. Cultural studies which confirm the desire of the poor for effective fertility control but elaborate the difficulties many of them have in utilizing coitus-*connected* contraceptive methods.[7]

5. Analyses and observations of pilot clinical programs, which show that the response of poor patients to coitus-*independent* methods—the pill and the IUD—has been considerable where services have been made available with some degree of energy and that the principal source of new patients for these services is patient-to-patient referral.[8]

These findings support the hypothesis that the difficulties of the poor in family planning derive in very large measure from lack of realistic opportunities to achieve genuinely held aspirations for small families. For a systematic test of this hypothesis, family-planning programs can be developed in such a way as to alter this opportunity structure, by creating services where none exist or by removing environmental obstacles where existing services are

[4]M. Orshansky, "More About the Poor in 1964," *Social Security Bulletin,* (May, 1966).

[5]Cf. principally P. K. Whelpton, A. A. Campbell, and J. E. Patterson, *Fertility and Family Planning in the U.S.,* Princeton, New Jersey: Princeton University Press, 1966; R. Freedman, P. K. Whelpton, and A. A. Campbell, *Family Planning, Fertility and Population Growth,* New York, 1959; D. J. Bogue (ed.), *Sociological Contributions to Family Planning Research,* Chicago, 1967; A. A. Campbell, *op. cit.* For data on attitudes and practices from the 1965 National Fertility Study cross-tabulated by income and rurality, see F. S. Jaffe, *Family Planning and Rural Poverty: An Approach to Programming of Services,* National Advisory Commission on Rural Poverty, 1967 (in press).

[6]Cf., e.g., A. F. Yerby, "The Disadvantaged and Medical Care," *American Journal of Public Health,* 56:5 (January, 1966).

[7]Cf. L. Rainwater, *Family Design,* Chicago: Aldine Publications, Inc., 1965; L. Rainwater and K. Weinstein, *And the Poor Get Children,* Chicago: Quadrangle Books, Inc., 1960.

[8]Cf., among others, S. Polgar and W. B. Cowles (eds.), "Public Health Programs in Family Planning," Supplement to *American Journal of Public Health,* (January, 1966); S. Polgar, "U.S.: The PPFA Mobile Service Project in New York City," *Studies in Family Planning,* No. 15 (October, 1966); D. J. Bogue, "U.S.: The Chicago Fertility Control Studies," *Studies in Family Planning,* No. 15 (October. 1966); R. Frank and C. Tietze, "Acceptance of an Oral Contraceptive Program in a Large Metropolitan Area," *American Journal of Obstetrics and Gynecology,* 93 (September 1, 1965), p. 122; and G. W. Perkin, "A Family Planning Unit for Your Hospital?" *Hospital Practice* (May, 1967).

inacessible because of such factors as distance, crowding, eligibility and fee practices, scheduling, lack of accurate information, and the depersonalized manner in which services are delivered. The aim of such programs is, in accord with Gans' suggestion, "to design the opportunities in such a fashion that they can be accepted without requiring an immediate change in strongly persisting norms."[9]

In several communities which have made rapid progress in family planning, such as New York City and Washington, D.C., strategies which maximize *access* to services have in fact been employed (without a conscious effort to test this approach against alternative strategies). The New York City program has been analyzed retrospectively elsewhere.[10] These and related observations suggest that the diffusion of family planning among the poor, in response to the program inputs *currently known,* takes place more or less as indicated in Table 1.

In less than five years, the opening of a substantial number of hospital and neighborhood clinics in New York, plus a moderate informational effort, attracted approximately half the target population, despite conditions which can hardly be regarded as optimal: A recent evaluation of some hospital services, for example, reveals that the average patient must spend two and one-half hours in, typically, a dirty, overcrowded and chaotic clinic before the service is completed.[11] Despite the persistence of such unfavorable institutional factors and the relationship of family planning to deeply internalized attitudes about sex, even a modest improvement in the opportunity structure thus seems capable of bringing about substantial behavioral change.

Since no one has yet served the remain-

Table 1. Estimated response to program inputs

Group	Principal program input	Percent of target population
I	Initial central clinics	15–25
II	Neighborhood clinics	35–50
III	Home visiting, transportation, etc.	20–30
IV	Counseling and supportive measures	10-15

ing half of the target group, it is difficult to estimate the size of Groups III and IV (see Table 1). Nevertheless, it seems reasonable to postulate that further improvements in accessibility—i.e., additional clinic sessions at more convenient times, transportation and baby-sitting help, and information about the service transmitted face to face by neighborhood workers—will help to enroll a sizeable proportion of those still unserved. This would leave only a small group —perhaps 10-15 percent—which requires more intensive counseling and supportive measures (such as the short-term group-counseling services pioneered by Maurice Russell[12]).

The accessibility strategy, of course, necessitates that the priorities of the health and welfare systems be reordered and their budgetary and staff resources either increased or reallocated. It is thus not surprising that very few health and welfare officials have reacted with enthusiasm to this approach. In fact, progress in extending family-planning services has been resisted, step by step, by most of these institutions and has usually come about because of unrelenting pressure from outside, largely from the political community.

---

[9]Gans, *op. cit.*
[10]F. S. Jaffe, "The U.S.: A Strategy for Implementing Family Planning Services," *Studies in Family Planning,* No. 17 (February, 1967).
[11]Unpublished data from Planned Parenthood–World Population Operational Evaluation Unit.

---

[12]M. V. Russell and Lila Swell, *A Demonstration Project in Fertility Control,* doctoral dissertation, Teacher's College, Columbia University, 1964; a summary was presented by Russell at the American Orthopsychiatric Association, Chicago, March, 1964.

Yet, *expressed* public policy on family planning, as reflected in laws, pronouncements, regulations, and public discussion, has changed dramatically during the last decade. *Actual* public policy, however, comprises more than legislation, rhetoric, and ideology and is best measured by the behavior of social institutions and the way in which we allocate financial and professional resources; by this test, the changes have been considerably less spectacular.

In most parts of the country—and in the federal government—public health and welfare agencies have hardly responded to the policy shift with the energy of newly liberated institutions. Less than one-third of local health departments,[13] and one-fifth of hospitals with large maternity services,[14] claim they provide any kind of family-planning services for medically indigent patients, and most of these services are pitifully inadequate. From all available data, the most generous estimate we can arrive at is that only 700,000 poor patients are currently receiving services from all public and private agencies combined, leaving 87 percent of the estimated target population of 5.3 million[15] without access to subsidized services. Despite 41 Presidential exhortations,

no federal agency has yet formulated even a rudimentary plan to overcome this deficit or taken the initiative to seek the appropriations needed to carry out such a plan; on the contrary, an independent review of the family-planning efforts of the Department of Health, Education, and Welfare in 1967 established that the Department's policy declarations on family planning have *not* been perceived by any of the relevant operating agencies as a mandate to give the field any real priority in funds or staff.[16]

One could categorize this discrepancy between word and deed simply as but another example of Howard Becker's dictum that "institutions are refractory. . . . Hospitals do not cure people; prisons do not rehabilitate prisoners; schools do not educate students."[17] One might add that this health system has at its disposal, to finance personal health services for poor people, an estimated 85 percent of the per-capita expenditures for these services of middle-income families,[18] but seems unable or unwilling to deliver equivalent care.

Yet the matter deserves closer scrutiny, particularly because of the way in which social science concepts are being used to legitimize institutional resistance to change. As Lee Rainwater has acknowledged,[19] official resistance has been buttressed by misreading his early pre-pill studies, not as indicating that some of the poor would require a good deal of help in adopting family plan-

[13]1966 American Public Health Association survey of state and local health department family-planning activities.
[14]Derived from *Journal of the American Hospital Association*, Guide Issue (August 1, 1966).
[15]G. Varky, F. Jaffe, S. Polgar, and R. Lincoln, *Five Million Women*, Planned Parenthood-World Population, October, 1967. The target population is calculated by applying the Dryfoos-Polgar formula for estimating need for subsidized family-planning services to a special tabulation by the Census Bureau of the characteristics of women aged 18-44 living in poverty and near-poverty in March, 1966. Campbell (*op. cit.*) employs the same fundamental approach, with slightly different assumptions on some points, to arrive at his estimate of a target population of 4.6 million women at any given time. The minor differences between the two estimates are less significant than their basic agreement on method and on the approximate size of the population in need of services.

[16]O. Harkavy, F. Jaffe, and S. Wishik, *Implementing DHEW Policy on Family Planning and Population, A Consultants' Report to the Department of Health, Education, and Welfare*, September, 1967.
[17]H. Becker, "Which Side Are We On?" *Social Problems*, 14 (Winter, 1967), pp. 242-243.
[18]L. Bamberger, "Health and Poverty: The Community's Viewpoint," *Bulletin of the New York Academy of Medicine*, 42 (December, 1966), pp. 1144-1145.
[19]L. Rainwater and D. J. Pittman, "Ethical Problems in Studying a Politically Sensitive and Deviant Community," *Social Problems*, 14 (Spring, 1967), p. 362.

ning, but as implying that most of the poor did not *really* want to limit their families. The simplistic notion of motivation[20] propounded in many demographic studies, which treat couples' choices between effective and unreliable contraception with marvelous indifference to what we know about the grossly unequal distribution of medical care, is also invoked to justify inaction.

These long-standing ideas have now been linked to the "culture-of-poverty" concept as it is frequently applied—or misapplied —in health and welfare services. At the federal level, for example, DHEW does not have even a simple inventory of which agencies are providing family-planning services with *its* funds or any concrete assessment of the adequacy of existing services. It has not published any professional material or guidelines on how family-planning services should be delivered in hospitals, health departments, or voluntary agencies. Yet the only two Departmental publications[21] purporting to guide family-planning program development reflect in large measure the cultural-motivational approach.

III

Table 2, contrasting the accessibility and cultural-motivational approaches to the major questions of program development in family planning, draws on a number of published and unpublished sources. While we do not pretend to be completely objective and detached, as the previous discussion has made clear, we have attempted to present an accurate picture of the divergent emphases of the two approaches.

It will be evident that the two approaches are very different even in their formulation of objectives and description of the population in need. The cultural-motivational advocates find somewhat insufficient the goal of "simply . . . helping parents to fulfill their aspirations in reference to child-spacing and family size,"[22] which the other group would regard as a not-insignificant accomplishment. Both ostensibly describe "the poor" as the

---

[20]S. Polgar, "Some Socio-Cultural Aspects of Family Planning in the United States," *Human Organization*, 25 (Winter, 1966), p. 321. Simplicism on this question is apparently not unique to family planning. A recent (1967) publication of the American Psychiatric Association and the National Association for Mental Health (R. M. Glasscote *et al., The Treatment of Alchoholishm: A Study of Programs and Problems*) puts the issue in these terms: "In virtually all facilities providing treatment for alcoholic patients, much importance is attached to the issue of motivation, for which we may read sincerity. Often the key screening criterion is the patient's motivation to stop drinking, and few facilities are interested in working with patients whom they define as 'inadequately motivated.' They almost seem to assume that motivation is an all-or-none state: if it is there the patient can be worked with; if it is not nothing can be done until the patient really wants to stop drinking. It is almost as though the motivated patient is 'worthy' and the nonmotivated one is not. Thus, the earlier attitude of rejecting all alcoholics shifts to one of accepting only those who fit a certain image. Frequently, the use of motivation as a screening criterion has been a handy way of excluding people of cultural backgrounds different from the therapists'. Placing the blame for failure on the patient rather than the treatment needs to be replaced by viewing each such occurrence as a challenge to the therapist and the hospital to develop more effective techniques. If current techniques are effective with only a certain proportion of the target group, then further study leading to new techniques is needed. Evidence is accumulating that changes in the way an agency is organized and operated and changes in its treatment philosophy can substantially enhance its ability to work with the supposedly unmotivated patient."

[21]C. Chilman, "Poverty and Family Planning in the United States. Some Social and Psychological Aspects and Implications for Programs and Policy," *Welfare in Review*, (April, 1967); C. Chilman, *Growing Up Poor*, U.S. Government Printing Office, 1966. Dr. Chilman is one of the few DHEW professionals who has diligently attempted to explore the policy and program implications of family planning. Her emphasis, which may be valid for a small percentage of the family-planning caseload, is unfortunately not balanced by other DHEW professional material relevant to the majority of the poor; the result is a serious conceptual distortion in DHEW's overall emphasis.

[22]Chilman, "Poverty and Family Planning in the United States," *op. cit.*, p. 8.

Table 2. Family planning and poverty: Two approaches to program development

	Accessibility	Cultural–motivational
Objective	Reduce discrepancy between desired and achieved family size and birth intervals among those unable to receive family-planning help from private medical sources.	Not "simply" effective fertility control but also improved marital relationships and better guidance for children on sex and family life.
Target group: Characteristics	"The poor," *meaning*: the medically indigent or those who cannot afford private medical care; families of 4 with incomes below roughly $4,150 (nonfarm) and $2,920 (farm); only 14 percent receive public assistance.	"The very poor," *meaning*: primarily the chronically unemployed and underemployed, public assistance recipients, the "hard core poor" or the "multi-problem" family.
Target group: Size	Estimated 5.3 million women at any given time.	No estimate attempted.
Meaning assigned to aspirations for small families, approval of family planning	Reflection of desire for better future for children; held intensely enough to provide basis for directed programs to meet expressed needs.	Aspirations for small family size frequently ignored; when acknowledged, often treated as mere verbal expression or as one of many "unrealistic" aspirations of poor.
Major explanations for failure of target group to adopt modern fertility-control practices	Reliable methods require medical family-planning services which are unavailable or inaccessible because of distance, high fees, inconvenient timing, overcrowding, and/or depersonalized delivery. Lack of accurate information about efficacy, cost, safety, and effects of modern family-planning procedures. Conventional and folk methods are unsuitable to life-circumstances (*not* style) of the poor.	Unidentified "services" and non-prescription methods are available but under-utilized or resisted by the poor because of lack of motivation stemming from life-style patterns; fatalism, apathy, magical thinking, present-time orientation, alienation, poor marital adjustment, excessive sex practices, "machismo," and the "hungry womb."
Major remedies proposed	Make modern voluntary family-planning services available and accessible (incorporating them in existing health services where feasible, developing separate facilities where necessary); create a network of well-publicized hospital and neighborhood services offering free or heavily subsidized care at suitable hours (including weekends, evenings); improve clinic atmosphere and quality of services; and staff clinic so that waiting time is minimum.	"Instill" stronger motivation for fertility control by intensive counseling and by family life and sex education programs designed to bring about less "maladaptive" values and behavior.
	Provide outreach educational (not motivational) programs to dispel misconceptions and inform patients how, where, and when to obtain services; provide help in facilitating clinic attendance.	Develop family-planning services *only* as part of more "comprehensive" health or welfare programs, which include educational, economic, social, and psychological counseling and services.
	Employ trained neighborhood personnel in both clinic and educational programs. Expand research for more suitable methods. Remove welfare rules (e.g., "man-in-the-house") which jeopardize recipient's eligibility for public assistance if she attends a family-planning clinic.	
Primary agencies which should be responsible for family-planning programs	Hospitals, other health agencies, and community-action groups. (Welfare agencies have referral, reinforcement, and reimbursement role.)	Welfare agencies and schools.

Continued.

Table 2. Family planning and poverty: Two approaches to program development—cont'd

	Accessibility	Cultural-motivational
Time envisioned for extension of family planning to most of poor	Five years.	Unspecified, but very lengthy.
Overall strategy and phasing	Serve those readiest to adopt family planning first; utilize chain reaction of successful experience within low-income community to spread information and reinforce direct educational activities; intensify educational and outreach efforts, and develop specific projects for those least ready to adopt family planning, in later stages of program development. Develop professional, community, and political support/pressure for adequate budgetry appropriations and for monitoring extent to which policy is translated into adequate programs.	Emphasize familiarization and orientation programs for health and welfare professionals, particularly sensitivity training in "life styles" of the poor. Otherwise unspecified.
Estimated cost	$100 million annually.	Unspecified.

target group, but, on close reading, the cultural-motivational camp is seen to focus on only a segment whom social workers characterize as the "multi-problem family." Nor have they attempted to estimate the size of the target population. The accessibility approach, by contrast, lends itself to qualification based on objective criteria such as age, income, parity, residence, etc.[23]

There are similar striking differences in interpreting the stated aspirations of the poor for smaller families and in explaining their failure to realize these goals. The accessibility approach views these aspirations as a meaningful basis for program development; until quite recently the cultural-motivational approach largely ignored them or raised methodological quibbles about their validity.[24] Those who stress accessibility explain a large

part (but not all) of the family-planning difficulties of the poor in terms of such factors as realistic availability of services and the prevalence of misinformation uncorrected by successful peer-group experience. The other camp adopts the entire "culture of poverty" package of internalized maladaptive values and, without benefit of investigations specific to modern contraception, asserts that these values lead the poor to resist family-planning services (which are assumed to exist in more or less sufficient quantity but are rarely identified).

Rather different remedies and strategies also emerge from the two positions. The accessibility approach leads to plans for a more or less sequential development of program activities, based on the diffusion strategy cited above which in turn is founded on a solid body of research[25]; heavy emphasis is placed at the outset on changes in the health delivery system to incorporate family-planning services in all appropriate facilities, complemented first by informational

[23]Cf., e.g., Varky *et al., op. cit.*

[24]The most formal critique of these studies has been made, in relation to family-planning programs in the developing countries, by P. M. Hauser, "Family Planning and Population Programs," *Demography*, 4:1. For a response to this criticism, see B. Berelson, "National Family Planning Program: Where We Stand," paper presented at University of Michigan Sesquicentennial Celebration, November, 1967.

[25]E. Katz *et al.*, "Traditions of Research on the Diffusion of Innovations," *American Sociological Review*, 28:2 (April, 1963), pp. 237-252.

and later by more intensive outreach activities which are tied directly to the service network so that tangible assistance is provided, not merely exhortation. The cultural-motivational approach, on the other hand, emphasizes counseling, coupled with family life and sex education intended to restructure values and strengthen the presumably deficient incentive of the poor for family planning. Sensitivity training of professionals in the life-style of the poor is also stressed to bridge the cultural gap, as is the precept that family-planning programs *must* (not *should*) be part of a larger system of comprehensive care, regardless of the different problems of costs, manpower, and time involved in achieving the two goals.

The accessibility advocates regard it as feasible to build, within as little as five years, a reasonably adequate network of services and programs capable of introducing modern family planning to most of the poor. The other group views the process as much more protracted: "Since behavior grows out of a whole lifetime, it cannot be expected to change quickly."[26] The accessibility approach assigns primary responsibility for family planning to hospitals and other health agencies and estimates the cost of providing these continuing services at approximately $100 million a year. The cultural-motivational advocates stress the role of welfare agencies and schools and are silent on costs.

IV

These issues affect quite directly the way in which the program is conceptualized and implemented. For example, a preliminary plan for a "family-planning" program drawn up by one state health department calls for staff of 14 psychologists, social workers, psychiatrists, and genetic counselors, but only five obstetricians! Is it contemplated, as a matter of public policy, that each impoverished woman must undergo a psychiatric, social, and genetic work-up before she is examined and issued a prescription for pills?

Early in 1967, it was seriously whispered in some federal circles that family planning should be soft-pedaled on the grounds that it would further threaten the egos of poor Negro men. Of couse, there exists no evidence that family planning has damaged male pride among the overwhelming majority of American couples, white and nonwhite, who already practice it. But there is research evidence that low-income Negro men desire small families and favor family planning[27] and in Puerto Rico—the one place where it has been scientifically studied—that the underlying "machismo" theory is without substance.[28] Perhaps more significant, the objection reveals the unstated view of the scope of the problem which many cultural-motivational advocates share: They see the problem—and the target group for family-planning services—as primarily among relief recipients and nonwhites, and they cannot correct this view because of their inattention to quantitative matters. In reality, an analysis of a special Census Bureau tabulation of the characteristics of women aged 18-44 living in poverty reveals that less than 15 percent of the target group are public assistance recipients and only 30 percent are nonwhite.[29]

In line with Gans' suggestion, it should also be asked why only the life-style of the poor is perceived as an obstacle to adoption

---

[26]Chilman, "Poverty and Family Planning in the United States," *op. cit.*, p. 10. For similar views relating to overseas family-planning programs, see, e.g., J. C. Cobb, "Technology Is Not Enough," *Harvard Alumni Bulletin* (Spring, 1967).

[27]Cf. B. D. Misra, "Correlates of Males' Attitudes Toward Family Planning," in Bogue (ed.), *Sociological Contributions to Family Planning Research, op. cit.*; and C. L. Harter, "Male Fertility in New Orleans," paper presented at the Population Association of America, April, 1967.

[28]R. Hill, J. M. Stycos, and K. W. Back, *The Family and Population Control*, Chapel Hill, North Carolina: University of North Carolina Press, 1959, pp. 100-107.

[29]G. Varky *et al., op. cit.*

of family planning. For example, evening and weekend clinics, where they exist, are heavily utilized by the poor. Administrators find it difficult, however, to staff these sessions, particularly in the absence of a system which bestows adequate financial and professional incentives for this kind of work. Yet no one attributes these obstacles to adoption of family planning by the poor to the "life-style" of doctors and nurses.

Nor has the endless debate over whether —and under what humiliating conditions— services may be given to those not officially married and living with spouse (41 percent of the target group) been interpreted as an obstacle deriving from ideal norms which the middle class professes.

The cultural-motivational advocates appear unaware that Oscar Lewis himself estimates that only 20 percent of Americans living below the poverty line have characteristics which manifest a culture of poverty.[30] This is of the same order of magnitude as the estimate that only 10-15 percent of the poor would require intensive counseling and supportive measures before adopting family planning.

It is also difficult to understand the apparent faith of the cultural-motivational advocates in counseling and education, which admittedly have achieved limited success in changing cultural values.[31] Nevertheless, as-

suming that these remedies, *applied in the context of a reasonably adequate opportunity structure*, are indeed valid for a small group which has more than the ordinary difficulties in adopting family planning,[32] why should the needs of this residual population determine the shape and content of a program designed to serve all of the poor?

V

It is not exactly unprecedented for institutions to attribute their failures to the inadequacies of the recipients of their services.[33] Yet, given the history of family planning in the United States, it is disconcerting how rapidly a version of the culture-of-poverty concept has been co-opted as the explanation for slow progress—and how closely it reflects the thinking of many administrators and program personnel. Unlike, say, education, family planning is not a field in which the institutions have ostensibly struggled manfully for decades to bring enlightenment to the poor.

Until a few short years ago, virtually the only organized family-planning services for the poor were the sparse clinics operated by Planned Parenthood; they depended on meager private contributions and were treated as outcasts by the health and wel-

---

[30]Oscar Lewis, *La Vida,* New York: Random House, 1966, p. li.

[31]E.g., "Unfortunately, planned changes in culture patterns are extremely difficult to effect." Chilman, *Growing Up Poor, op. cit.,* p. 75. Yet such is the faith that a major professional association, in a draft of a national policy statement on family planning in 1967, included the assertion that "counseling is *essential* to help individuals and families with the economic, social, physical and emotional implications involved in family planning" (emphasis added). The statement was removed only after the drafting committee was reminded that about 80 percent of American families, the vast majority of whom never had any counseling, already practice some form of family planning.

[32]G. Meier, "Unwanted Pregnancies Among a Group of Relief Recipients—A Follow Up on a Persisting Problem," *Eugenics Quarterly,* (March, 1963).

[33]The *N.Y. Times* on July 13, 1967, reports the response of two federal agencies to highly publicized Senatorial demands for action to deal with outright starvation among Mississippi Negro children. The Secretary of Agriculture, decrying the demands as "very intemperate, violent and emotional," suggested a "massive educational effort" to get the poor to improve their diets because, he said, the *real* problem is that most poor people mistakenly believe the food stamp plan "will let them eat as poorly as they always have but for less money." The Surgeon General stated that Americans know much more about hunger in other nations than in the United States. "We don't know the extent of the problem or what needs to be done," he said.

fare system. Even today, after what is widely celebrated as a remarkably rapid transformation in public policy testifying to our society's capacity to meet acknowledged social problems, virtually all existing family-planning services are underfinanced, understaffed, and receive very little priority from health and welfare agencies.

In effect, a health and welfare establishment, which spent a half-century claiming that insurmountable religious opposition prevented it from providing family planning to the poor, discovered, almost as soon as the religious controversy waned, that it is the culture of poverty which prevents the poor from adopting modern family planning. One can easily see the "fit" between the culture-of-poverty concept as applied to family planning today and the distillation of middle-class wisdom on the subject which Margaret Sanger heard from physicians more than 50 years ago: They admonished her that "the people you're worrying about wouldn't use contraception if they had it; they breed like rabbits."[34] The people she was then worrying about were mostly impoverished Jewish immigrants who adopted contraception as soon as it became available to them and whose descendants are today among the most faithful contraceptors in American society; when Mrs. Sanger was prosecuted for opening a clinic in Brooklyn, the district attorney told the jury that "the clinic was intended to do away with the Jews!"[35]

One is also struck by the "fit" between the current situations in family planning in the United States and in the developing countries. Frank Notestein, summarizing the overseas experience, cites as perhaps the "basic reason" for skepticism about the prospects for success the fact that *institutional structures* are too hostile to the very idea of family planning" (emphasis added). The attitudes of the people go in the opposite direction:

Wherever there have been well-organized contraceptive services through which information and supplies are readily available, the response has been large. Where there is indifference, it usually has been to poorly organized services poorly supported by educational effort. *Any lack of interest on the part of the public is less serious than the apathy of the middle classes and the lesser officials who cannot bring themselves to believe that their illiterate peasants are sufficiently intelligent to understand their own problems. Both surveys and the public response to services clearly demonstrate that ordinary people have a much better understanding of their own problems than their lesser officials appreciate* (emphasis added).[36]

VI

In conclusion, we would like to emphasize two policy issues which may well be influenced by the evidence adduced by social scientists and others in the debate between the accessibility and cultural-motivational camps.

First, can our affluent society insure the competent delivery of a relatively simple and inexpensive medical service to a small group of the poor—a service which has support from one end of the political spectrum to the other? If our institutional structure proves impervious to the necessary changes in programming, we had better find this out quickly because it will certainly imply that we are deluding ourselves about delivering

[34]M. Sanger, *Autobiography*, p. 93. Also see J. M. Stycos, "Survey Research and Population Control in Latin America," *Public Opinion Quarterly*, 28 (Fall, 1964), p. 368: "The elite in most societies belive that these people have many children because they want many children. They believe there are deep-seated psychological drives to demonstrate fertility, pervasive cultural and religious norms encouraging maximum childbearing, obsessive sexual patterns, and economic ideologies for the large family. They believe that to run counter to such a profound array of beliefs, drives, behavior patterns and norms would either be political suicide or a waste of time. And indeed, they would be correct if such assumptions were true. But repeatedly surveys demonstrate [throughout the world] that couples want a moderate number of children."

[35]Sanger, *op. cit.*, p. 226.
[36]F. Notestein, "The Population Crisis: Reasons for Hope," *Foreign Affairs* (October, 1967).

much more complex social, educational, and health services. It will also have rather serious implications for our ability to provide developing nations with significant assistance on voluntary family-planning programs.

Second, can these changes be carried out rapidly enough to head off pressures for coercive measures which are being advocated with increasing vigor as public assistance expenditures rise? Bills to make sterilization compulsory for various classes of relief recipients have been introduced in at least eight states[37] and debated in many more. Lower court judges in recent years have increasingly taken it upon themselves to offer welfare defendants a choice of sterilization or jail.[38] It requires little imagination to envision the set of circumstances in which such coercive proposals could be successful,[39] particularly if the implementation of voluntary family-planning programs continues at a glacial pace. Elite reactions to the higher fertility of the poor have always implicitly subsumed the compulsion idea as the "realistic" solution for people who are

regarded fundamentally as irresponsible, immature, and animal-like.[40] The entire history of the voluntary family-planning movement and the increasingly widespread "democratization of birth control"[41] refute this notion. Yet the ancient myths die hard, and it is not difficult to see how the culture of poverty concept might be used to lend ostensible scientific support for a revitalized eugenics movement promising "salvation from 'poor parents' rather than 'poor heredity.' "[42] Social scientists can ignore such perils only at the risk of following in the footsteps of the guilt-ridden fraternity of atomic scientists.

---

[37]Cf. J. Paul, *Three Generations of Imbeciles Are Enough: State Eugenic Sterilization Laws in American Thought and Practice* (unpublished manuscript). Chapter 3, "The Return of Punitive Sterilization: Current Attacks on Illegitimacy and the ADC Program" is scheduled for publication in *Law and Society Review.* (Paul is Research Political Scientist, Division of Neuropsychiatry, Walter Reed Army Institute of Research, Washington, D. C.)

[38]Cf. E. Z. Ferster, "Eliminating the Unfit—Is Sterilization the Answer?" *Ohio State Law Journal,* 127 (1966), pp. 591 ff., particularly pp. 607-613, 619-625.

[39]Cf. D. P. Moynihan, *The Crises in Welfare: The View from New York,* prepared for Governor Rockefeller's Conference on Welfare, Arden House, November 2, 1967.

[40]The contention between the compulsory and voluntary approaches to lower-class fertility has a lengthy and repetitious history which has often resulted in huge ironies. In 1906, for example, Drysdale of the Neo-Malthusian League argued that Parliament should not adopt a legal minimum wage unless it also enacted a legal maximum family so as to prevent the "reckless classes" from excess reproduction. But a few years later, when the League circulated a practical pamphlet on family-planning methods among the "reckless classes" in London's East End, it immediately became a best seller. (See R. E. Dowse and J. Peel, "The Politics of Birth Control," *Political Studies,* 13:2 (June, 1965), p. 179. The interplay is repeated in modern dress in 1967 when the authorities in Prince George's County, Maryland, decided to make a visit to a birth-control clinic mandatory for relief applicants, only to discover that the existing voluntary clinic at the county health department was inadequate to meet the demand for services even before the coercive ruling and could not book appointments earlier than one to two months. (Washington *Post,* June 4 and 7, 1967.)

[41]N. E. Himes, *Medical History of Contraception,* Baltimore: Williams and Wilkins, 1936.

[42]Ferster, *op. cit.,* p. 619.

18 Issues and problems that confront nursing in delivering family planning services

Susan H. Fischman

For the past three years, I have been associated with the family planning program at Harlem Hospital in New York City. As I have become more and more involved in family planning services, the issues and problems that nursing must face in order to be responsive to total patient care have become increasingly evident. But one serious problem seems to loom above all others, one that has a direct influence on many of the other problems confronting nursing—the lack of adequately prepared nurses, knowledgeable in methods of contraception and experienced in teaching and counseling patients on human reproduction and birth control.

Why are students inadequately prepared for this nursing responsibility? The answer is not a single fact but a combination of factors at work in schools, hospitals, the community, and society. For change to take place within the nursing school curriculum, sufficient pressure and demand must be accumulated. Up to now, despite the ANA 1966 policy statement that endorsed nursing's responsibility for family planning education, the pressures for change have not been strong enough. Policy statements that support family planning activities have not

been forthcoming from state, county, and local health departments. In many parts of the country, considerable resistance toward family planning still exists because of religious opposition or fear of religious opposition. Within schools of nursing, faculty members may not be knowledgeable and may feel uncomfortable with this subject.[1] Furthermore, some believe that formal sex education, including family planning, does not fall within their province and should be left to parents, churches, and voluntary groups. Pressures on nursing from many other areas can preclude adding additional material to an already crowded schedule.

Up to the present time, state board examinations have not included questions on family planning. If the board of examiners began to test students in this area, nursing schools might increase their family planning course content.

Perhaps the most important factor inhibiting nursing education in family planning is that many teaching hospitals do not have family planning programs.[2] It follows that the impetus for nursing educators to include family planning in the curriculum will remain minimal if programs requiring such nursing skills are nonexistent and if students have no opportunity to gain practical experience. Why are there no programs? Hospital administrators may be afraid of antagonizing their wealthy contributors who hold opposing religious views. Preferring not to "rock the boat," they maintain the *status*

Reprinted from Edmands, E. M., editor: *A Report on the First National Planning Conference for Nurse Education in Baccalaureate Schools of Nursing,* Carolina Population Center, No. 7, pp. 161-167, 1970.
Reprinted by permission of Carolina Population Center.

quo. But more importantly, the medical profession universally has not taken the lead in family planning program development. Thus, many women, particularly the poor, have not been able to receive the benefits of effective contraceptive methods that have always been available to private patients.[3]

Consequently, many nursing students receive family planning education, not from the faculty, but from Planned Parenthood affiliates. This usually includes a lecture on methods and an observation of a clinic session. Frequently, little effort is made to relate the student's experience at the Planned Parenthood center with the actual patient care given on the obstetric and gynecology floors. Too often, nursing curricula remain unresponsive to issues of the sexual revolution at home and burgeoning populations abroad. Students are not often given opportunities to discuss and evaluate their own sexual feelings and emotions so that they can develop their expertise in talking with patients about matters related to family planning and sexuality.

When thinking about the delivery of health services of any kind, one may visualize a group of runners facing a long series of hurdles with the desired finish line in the distance. As the runners begin to race and jump, the hurdles become higher forcing some runners to drop out of the race. So too, policies and procedures that patients encounter while seeking health care can be regarded as potential hurdles, and as they become more difficult, unrealistic, and demanding, patients "drop out" never reaching the care for which they set out. With planning and foresight some of the "hurdles" that create fragmented, inconvenient health services might be removed or at least lowered to a reasonable "jumping" height.

Because hospitals and health departments have not established programs to meet the family planning needs of women who rely on tax-supported services for medical care, voluntary agencies and anti-poverty groups have attempted to fill the gaps. But, these programs are often separated from a medical setting where other ambulatory maternal and infant care services are obtainable. They operate with limited budgets, have sessions that are infrequently scheduled, and have physical facilities that are less than desirable. Nurses and other staff face many difficulties running clinics that are located in old, drafty buildings waiting to be torn down by Urban Renewal, in mobile units and store fronts that afford little privacy for the patient, in school gymnasiums where the screens in front of the examining tables keep falling down, in office buildings where the only bathroom is way down the hall, and in ghetto locations that are considered unsafe by the patients. More important, what impression does the patient get about contraception if she must obtain her medical care and supplies in undignified, distant, dingy, crowded facilities separate from a medical setting?

Slowly, less adequate family planning clinics will surely close, and medical institutions will assume their responsibility for providing comprehensive maternal health services. As programs move into health departments and hospitals, inservice education will be necessary to inform the graduate nurse of her role in family planning and of developments in the field of contraception. Here again, hurdles appear. Some hospital nurses will regard family planning as an additional task for an already overworked staff, and others will have opposing religious views or misunderstandings about the concept of family planning. In addition, suspicion and hostility may exist toward family planning programs particularly in low-income communities because of sensational news media coverage and/or antagonisms inspired by militant groups or misinformed neighbors. More often than not, the dissident voices are not those of the women who need and want service.

We need to reassure the hospital staff as well as the community that all religions endorse planned families but differ on techniques; that contraception will be provided on a voluntary basis with no pressures applied; that family planning should be offered to all women, not just those with "too many babies"; that medication will be without undue hazard and risk; and that complete medical evaluations precede prescription of any contraceptive. In addition, hospital staffs and community groups should have the opportunity to observe family planning program activities. Through knowledge and discussion, an attitude of cooperation with the family-planning service can be developed. The positive effects that the program can have on the health of women and their babies through decreased infant and maternal morbidity and mortality should be stressed.[4]

As the family planning program is initiated, it is generally advantageous to hire nurses who will be totally responsible to the program, free from the pulls and pressures of nursing service when staff shortages occur in other areas of the hospital. In addition, it will be easier and more economical to provide intensive education to a few nurses rather than an entire nursing staff. The woman who comes to the clinic for the first time may be fearful and embarrassed. The nurse can help her relax by explaining clinic procedures and reassuring her that the examination will be private with minimal discomfort. Opportunities to ask questions about the methods before making a decision will help to alleviate additional anxieties. Contraceptive methods, the essential components of a family planning service, may cause difficulties and unpleasant side effects. A sympathetic, compassionate staff who take time to listen, reassure, and answer questions is of utmost importance. Doctors and nurses must learn the art of communicating in descriptive, rather than medical, terms, using analogies that convey a vivid, mental image that non-medical people can understand.[5]

Undue hardships may be imposed when all methods are not provided in the family planning program. Because of biases toward oral contraceptives or IUDs, physicians may refuse to prescribe one or the other. With contraceptive methods that are less than

ideal, women should be able to shift from one to another as complications, problems, or dissatisfactions arise.

The patient's decision may also be influenced by the fact that in some programs one or several methods are offered free while a charge is imposed for others. Family planning is rarely a one-step service; it requires continuous visits for supplies, consultations, and periodic examinations. Patients have a sense of pride and do not want to owe money for their care or receive free care when others are paying. Free services for medically dependent women eliminate economic barriers and avoid embarassing financial screening.

Family planning clinics that are separate from postpartum or gynecology clinics present additional hurdles. Many potential contraceptors are lost because fragmented services mean another appointment on another day, another carfare and babysitter, another pelvic examination, another record to be filled out, even another staff.[6] Additional inconveniences occur when each method is assigned to a special clinic session. Thus, the woman who wants to switch from one method to another must come back on another day.

Procedures must be flexible and adaptable. Why must all new patients receive group instruction at the same time, only to have to wait several hours more for their physical examinations? With the use of continuously playing teaching films, new appointments can be staggered. Why are clinic sessions like banking hours, from nine to three and closed on holidays? If we want to provide service for all patients, especially the working mother, evening or Saturday sessions are absolutely essential. The clinic must be accessible by direct telephone lines because hospital switchboards are often overloaded. Many are the complaints from patients who have waited in vain for an operator to answer or who were cut off and lost their last dime in the pay phone. Administrative concern can provide efficient medical care and relieve unnecessary burdens from already burdened people.

In any program, one of the biggest problems is the woman who "drops out"—fails to continue with her contraceptive method, eventually becoming pregnant again. From my own experience, in Baltimore, interviewing women who did not return to the clinic, I found their major reasons to be (a) fears about methods, (b) side effects, and (c) improper usage of the method with a resultant pregnancy.[7] I am convinced that nursing support and anticipatory guidance for each patient at each visit can prevent some of these unfortunate apprehensions and failures.

Providing educational and informational services for the male deserves to be mentioned to remind us of an almost untouched area. Currently, the most effective contraceptives are used by the female, and so programs are aimed at her. There is no doubt that men need and want more information about family planning and sex education. A husband may be concerned about the effects that contraceptives will have on his wife's health or on their sexual relationship. Often, his attitude will determine whether his wife will be a consistent, effective contraceptor.

CONCLUSION

There are no easy, prepackaged solutions to the issues and problems of family planning programs. It is clear that nursing education alone cannot solve them for even if all graduating students this year were fully knowledgeable about family planning, they would still confront resistance and opposition from hospital administrators, physicians, and graduate nurses. But nursing educators can help to overcome current apathy and inaction by deciding now to meet their obligation to provide students with knowledge in all areas that affect the health and well-being of patients. Unwanted pregnancies, illicit abortions, battered children, rapid pregnancies with resultant strains upon physical and emotional health are all relevant issues in nursing today, and they deserve to be fully discussed. In this way, the graduat-

ing student will be prepared to help physicians and nurses initiate family planning programs for all women and to fully participate in these programs. And, of no small importance, she may also be much better prepared to understand her own sexuality and to harmonize those aspects of herself with her life goals.

NOTES

[1] Carolyn A. Houser, Elizabeth M. Edmands, and Johan W. Eliot. "The Teaching of Fertility Regulation in Basic Schools of Nursing in the United States," *American Journal of Public Health,* LIX, No. 6 (June 1969), 982-95.

[2] Gordon, W. Perkin, "A Family Planning Unit for Your Hospital?" *Hospital Practice,* II, No. 5 (May 1967); and Frederick S. Jaffe, *Family Planning and Rural Poverty: An Approach to Programming of Services.* Publication No. 5, Center for Family Planning Program Development, The Technical Assistance Division of Planned Parenthood-World Population (New York: PP-WP, May 1968).

[3] President's Committee on Population and Family Planning, *Population and Family Planning—The Transition from Concern to Action* (Washington, D. C.: Government Printing Office, November 1968).

[4] See Note 2. Also, see, Gerald I. Zatuchni, "International Postpartum Family Planning Program," *American Journal of Obstetrics and Gynecology,* C (April 1, 1968), 1028-41; and Susan H. Fischman, Murray D. Batt, Patricia A. Boone, Jean W. Tease, and Donald P. Swartz, "Education for Family Planning in a Municipal Hospital: A 24 Month Retrospective Study of the Program in Harlem Hospital Center, New York," A paper presented at the American Association of Planned Parenthood Physicians meeting, April 1969, San Francisco, California.

[5] Susan H. Fischman, "Choosing an Appropriate Contraceptive," *Nursing Outlook,* XV, No. 12 (December 1967), 28-31; "What Emotional Problems in Family Planning Do You Encounter?—Viewpoints," *Medical Aspects of Human Sexuality,* II, No. 8 (September 1968), 14-21; and Miriam T. Manisoff, *Family Planning, A Teaching Guide for Nurses* (New York: Planned Parenthood-World Population, 1969), pp. 32-42.

[6] See Note 2.

[7] Susan H. Fischman, "Dropouts from a Family Planning Program: A Study of Factors Associated with Failure to Return to an Oral Contraceptive Clinic," *Bulletin of the American College of Nurse-Midwifery,* XIII (August 1968), 82-9.

19 Family planning counsel

E. James Lieberman*

The greatest psychological blessing that can be conferred upon a child at birth is to be wanted by his parents. Conversely, an enviable asset for new parents is to be in a position to welcome wholeheartedly the new addition to the family. This is not to say that all unplanned pregnancies are unwanted or that they turn out badly, but that there is an optimum readiness for parenthood and this readiness is too often neglected in our society at present. This neglect is in part an indictment of medical and public health practice.

There is a striking contradiction—rarely noted—in the way our society regards readiness for the responsibilities of parenthood. There is virtually no interference or even cautionary suggestion against parenthood for married couples who are biologically able to reproduce. Even for the unmarried, social sanctions against pregnancy act chiefly as punishments or threats, without supporting prevention: the prospect of punishment often fails as a deterrent. Even couples who decide that they are unable to rear a child properly have been—and are still being—denied full information and necessary implements to practice birth control. There still exists a medical-social bias that favors pregnancy as the inevitable outcome of sexual intercourse, especially for the deprived segments of our population. In this circumstance of effective, albeit unconscious bias, no attention is paid to the quality of parenthood in store for the child-to-be, or of the wishes of the parents-to-be in regard to their own future, except perhaps to deny the right of conjugal love unless they wish to procreate.

By way of contrast we note the plight of an infertile couple (especially one of mature years, mixed religion or race, or low income) who wish to be parents. For an approved adoption procedure they must be thoroughly evaluated as to their qualifications as parents, and many adoptive couples will testify to the emotional stress involved in presenting oneself for this kind of judgment. Sometimes the adoption procedure is followed with such scrupulosity that people are discouraged altogether, and infants remain unnecessarily long in institutions or in a series of foster homes.

In short, there seems to exist a kind of societal ambivalence which grants unwanted parenthood to many who are not prepared for it, while denying or making difficult the achievement of parenthood for some who are eager and well prepared. Medical-social authorities may not intend this manifest discrepancy in values, but it is apparent that some deliberate rethinking of value positions will be necessary before these dichotomous —illogical but potent—forces can be eliminated. The medical responsibility is clear: the most effective contraceptive methods can be obtained only through medical channels. At the same time, family planning strikes some physicians as alien, perhaps because it is not a part of curative medicine, aside from any religious issues that may be encountered.

It will undoubtedly be helpful for physicians and medical students to discuss family planning as part of medical practice so that whatever ambivalence exists does not remain

*E. James Lieberman, M.D., is Chief of the Center for Studies of Child and Family Mental Health, National Institute of Mental Health, Chevy Chase, Maryland.

Reprinted from *Journal of Marriage and the Family* **30**(2): 308-310, May 1968. Copyright National Council on Family Relations.

183

hidden or become entangled with religious or personal biases. A recent survey of physicians indicates that one-quarter would never prescribe birth control: another study showed that only a minority of physicians who deal with premarital couples will invite a discussion of family planning, in spite of the fact that most couples are concerned with this, and a great many—especially of the ones who need it the most—are too embarrassed to initiate a discussion themselves. Many physicians are incapable of counseling the patients in regard to sexual problems: whether most or all should be able to do so is a matter for discussion within the profession. But it is beyond question that medical men should be informed and able to discuss family planning with appropriate sensitivity to the needs of different individuals. Counseling on sex may possibly be obtained elsewhere, but access to effective family planning is controlled by physicians and must be handled conscientiously and effectively by them.

MARRIAGE AND DIVORCE

A manifestation of social ambivalence toward personal commitment, similar to that seen in regard to parenthood, occurs in regard to marriage. It is generally assumed that individuals of legal age are fully capable of reaching independent decisions to marry, and rarely does clergymen or physician raise any question premaritally about the wisdom of the match. The clergy and the law are known, however, to question the independent judgment of the same individuals should they later decide that they want to dissolve the union. They may be older and wiser, but unless both spouses agree that the marriage is dead it may be impossible for one party to exercise his judgment in regard to his own future. Of course there are social arguments for this constraint. The reason for pointing out the discrepancy is that society does not place proportionate constraints upon young people during the process of deciding to marry.

Parents, of course, have had the child's lifetime to instill a set of values and the capacity for judgment. But we do not know enough about child rearing to specify the causes of an offspring's errant behavior. Parents with misgivings about the imminent marriage of their child are in a notoriously uncomfortable position; in some cases their opposition may even increase the likelihood of an elopement. Physician and clergyman have influence and responsibility here, because they are among the few non-family adults with whom the couple interact about the decision to marry.

Physicians are loath to get involved in questioning the soundness of a relationship and prefer to pass the buck to the clergymen, who do not want to alienate members or potential members of the congregation. While either is understandably reluctant to risk overstepping his bounds, it can be argued that he should exercise whatever capacity he has to assess a relationship on behalf of those involved and their potential offspring. For the most part, society does not provide other disinterested agents with whom young people can soberly examine their decision, free from the constraints and conflicts of the family circle. And for very poor people, marriage often takes place without benefit of either physician or clergyman.

COUNSELLING TEEN-AGERS

Adolescents are often caught between a natural (and probably healthy) psychological barrier to consideration of their own parents as sexual people and hence as sexual advisors, and the absense of any other qualified advisors with whom to consult. Such a youngster may well turn to the physician or other counsellor or may be brought in by a worried parent.

Adolescents who are blocked in their parents' presence can often talk to other adults. Two essentials for the counselling role are an ability to empathize and a willingness, at times an insistence, that the teen-ager makes his own decisions and learn to handle the responsibility for them. Some adolescents will experiment with sex, apparently heedless of consequences such as pregnancy or venereal disease, from a need to reduce deep-seated anxiety about personal identity, peer group status, potency, etc. In cases like these, knowledge unburdened with moralism may be the best deterrent to destructive sexual experience.

On the other hand, there may be young people who are quite sophisticated and engaged in what they feel is a serious relationship, who insist that sexual experience before marriage is not inherently wrong and who want protection against pregnancy. Whereas in the previous case it may have been sufficient to reassure a young man or woman that sexual fulfillment in adulthood does not depend upon experience in adolescence, and may indeed suffer from certain kinds of early sexual experience, this is not the issue with the second hypothetical couple.

At times, otherwise responsible adults will attempt to bolster a moral position by telling teen-agers that all contraceptives have disadvantages and none are to be relied upon. They omit the fact that most contraceptives are far better than nothing and that methods adopted through mutual agreement and experience become very reliable. The chances are that most teen-agers will not use contraceptives during initial experiences, because such planning negates the spontaneity which characterizes young romance. By attempting, however, to scare a determined couple away from sex on technical grounds, the counsellor runs a risk either of appearing dishonest or of convincing young people that contraception is a nuisance and not worth the trouble. Negative attitudes toward contraception may persist—who, after all, will correct them? The result may be a delay of family planning in marriage until all the wanted children are born without benefit of planned spacing. Effective family planning for most couples requires determination and

practice or adjustment and should not be put off until the time when another child would be a disaster. Apart from the pill, which can be prescribed for other than contraceptive reasons and at the same time provide near-perfect contraception, the reliability and suitability of other methods can usually be much better established after marriage than before. This amount of cautionary advice can be given without resorting to scare tactics.

In this connection one should consider the unique advantage of the condom for honeymoon couples. Many girls are sensitive about the initiation of sexual activity and by implication the preparation for it, especially that involved in being fitted for a diaphragm. The condom is as effective as the diaphragm, and its use by the inexperienced couple provides for male initiative and responsibility which may be salutary at this crucial time. I question whether it is wise routinely to recommend either use of a diaphragm from the beginning or dilatation of the virginal hymen, although these should be discussed with the bride-to-be. The counsellor must not disapprove or scorn the preferences of his clients. If he feels that the patients are lacking essential information, he can provide this but should leave matters of taste and convenience to them and encourage further discussion of the factors.

There have been case reports of untoward reactions resulting from the introduction of effective contraceptives. This is more likely to occur where the sexual relationship is unsound already, e.g., where the husband's potency depends in part upon the wife's anxiety. The pill has in some cases led to a disruption in the sexual relationship, because the women no longer fears pregnancy and may have an increase in libido, which is threatening to some men. Conversely, some women will not tolerate the pill or intra-uterine device due to unrecognized guilt about sexual relations free of the risk of pregnancy. In marriages where sex has been regulated to some degree by the fear of pregnancy, the introduction of contraceptives may alter the balance with unexpected repercussions. It is well for the physician to think of this as one possibility in contraceptive failure. He should always discuss attitudes at the time when contraceptives are first being prescribed in order to prevent these undesirable reactions.

THE FIRST CHILD

Too little attention has been given to child-spacing, probably because the burden of "too many" is so much greater than the burden of "too soon." But it is shocking to realize that, as of 1960, two-thirds of United States couples used *no* contraception prior to the birth of the first child, and, of couples with children, 54 percent had at least one born too soon, i.e., timing was unplanned. As mentioned already, family planning takes practice and should not be delayed until a couple is desperate. Equally important is teaching that time intervals are vital for initial marital adjustment and for the establishment of good parent-child relations once offspring come into the home. Unfortunately, the desperation of a young couple trying to cope with one or two children born too soon is overshadowed by the more sensational stories of mothers of six and eight. We need to remedy this gap in foresight starting with teen-agers in high school. The first child is really the crucial event. The onset of parenthood must not be an accident or the result of indifference.

Finally, family-planning education must break down the fiction that the rapid growth of population in this country is due to the poor. Although it is true that individuals living in poverty are still grossly underserved, and have more children than they want, they represent a minority of the population. The more affluent majority, by averaging 3-4 children per couple, are contribtuing most to population growth in this country. We now have over 200,000,000 people, and expect 300,000,000 by the turn of the century. Getting crowded? Those who think so had better get busy persuading the middle class to set the pace at 2.2 children per couple, average!

REFERENCES

Family Planning and Mental Health (booklet), Population Crisis Committee, National Institute of Mental Health, January 13, 1966.

Flowers, Jr., Charles E. "Changing concepts of the premarital examination," *Medical Aspects of Human Sexuality,* 1:4 (1967), pp. 51-55.

Nash, E. M. "Premarriage and marriage counseling: a study of practices of North Carolina physicians," *Journal of American Medical Association,* 180 (May 5, 1962), pp. 395-401.

Whelpton, Pascal K., Campbell, Arthur A., and Patterson, John E. *Fertility and Family Planning in the United States.* Princeton, New Jersey: The Princeton University Press, 1966, p. 243.

20 Sexual behavior of adolescents

Nathaniel N. Wagner, Ph.D.*
Nina Perthou, B.A.
Byron Fujita, B.A.
Ronald J. Pion, M.D.

The sexual behavior of young people is an important issue today, particularly in the controversial areas of sex education and contraception. As many of the taboos surrounding sex and sexuality dissolve, a new openness in depth and range of discussion emerges. The double standard of chastity for females and "look the other way" for males is under attack. Premarital and nonmarital sexual mores are being questioned and challenged. In seeking moral choices, today's teen-agers seem to be searching honestly for answers that will respond to the realities of their lives. They are less accepting and tolerant of traditional responses to their questions about sexuality. To make responsible choices and to better understand sexuality, they want and need honest, frank and wise advice and discussion. They also need factual knowledge about physiology and contraception. Sadly, they often feel they must go to persons other than their parents for this assistance.

*Dr. Wagner is associate professor of psychology and psychiatry and director of clinical psychology training, University of Washington, Seattle.
Miss Perthou and Mr. Fujita are research assistants, division of family planning and education, department of obstetrics and gynecology, University of Washington School of Medicine.
Dr. Pion is director, division of family planning and education, department of obstetrics and gynecology, University of Washington School of Medicine.

Reprinted from *Postgraduate Medicine* 46(4):68, October 1969. Copyright McGraw-Hill, Inc.

ILLEGITIMACY

There are pressing reasons for the physician to reexamine teen-agers' sexual behavior. The first reason is the rise in illegitimacy, a major social problem. The findings of the National Center for Health Statistics show that the illegitimacy rate in the United States tripled during a 25 year period; illegitimate births rose from 89,500 in 1940 to 291,200 in 1965. When the increase in population is considered, the rate of illegitimate births in women of childbearing age (15 to 44) has increased from seven per thousand women to 23 per thousand. One of every 12 children in the United States is born out of wedlock. The concept of out of wedlock appears more rational and less prejudicial than the concept of illegitimacy. Are there really *illegitimate* births and *illegitimate* children?

Statistics on "illegitimacy" are usually incompletely gathered from birth certificates in which the father's name is not given or is different from the mother's name. Obviously the length of time the couple has been married before the child's birth is not considered. In the United States, one of every six women gives birth within eight months after her first marriage and an estimated 50 to 75 percent of teen-age brides are pregnant at the time of marriage.

More than 40 percent of females who give birth out of wedlock are teen-agers. Considering the genuine scientific advances in reliable contraceptives, the widespread sophistication regarding their use, and the assumed increase in their availability in the past 25 years, these out-of-wedlock statistics become particularly distressing. Although clinical evidence suggests that a small proportion of the out-of-wedlock pregnancies are desired, the impressive number of unwanted pregnancies appears to show an unquestioned need to provide sources of accurate information and effective contraceptives. It should be emphasized, however, that all insight regarding sexual activity based on out-of-wedlock rates is inferential at best. Since sexual activity in itself is an important consideration, this defines another reason for the physician to have concern.

FACTORS INFLUENCING ADOLESCENTS

There is a real lack of systematic research on the sexual behavior of young people. However, the few studies conducted on college populations suggest that among females the trend is toward increased nonmarital and premarital sexual activity in intercourse and involvement just short of intercourse. Such activity in males seems relatively unchanged. As a result of this situation and the increasing number of teen-agers, the physician will continue to be consulted for help. Thus it is imperative that he recognize the pressing needs of adolescents—those who seek his assistance and those who would like to or need to obtain it. To meet this responsibility, the physician should familiarize himself with the social, psychologic and physiologic factors at work within adolescents, the external circumstances and pressure that surround them, and the legal and medical considerations in treating them.

To understand the sexual behavior of adolescents, one must be aware of the context within which a teen-ager struggles to find his identity and come to terms with his new physical maturity. All behavior is a personal manifestation or expression that is derived from two basic sources. In the first are the many psychologic, emotional and dispositional factors that affect behavior and are affected by it. Although behavior is one level of "what is," it does not exist in a personal vacuum. The second source is the power, influence, values and expectations that are initially external to the individual and are presented, assimilated and synthesized in a personal way. To the individual, these external yet related sources generally articulate "what ought to be" rather than "what is." Along with the peer group, the traditional institutions usually serve this function; however, these two groups are diverging in their interpretation of values. This schism makes it more difficult for the teen-ager to find consistent, unambiguous sexual standards.

The second context of which one must be aware is that young people present some developmental inconsistencies. Adolescence is the period in which the gap appears between physical and emotional maturity. It is the period when teen-agers are sophisticated enough to understand the proposals that adults are trying to communicate to them, but they do not believe the proposals; they believe only what they learn through personal experience. It is the period when a young woman fully realizes that she must restrain her sexuality but be ready to express it after and within marriage. The many discontinuities pervading adolescence promote the so-called generation gap—a gap that has always existed but which apparently has widened as a result of the broader experience and freer expression of young people today compared with those of the past. The result of the gap between adolescents and parents and traditional institutions is seen in the adolescents' frantic quest for identity, especially in sexuality. There is a marked ambiguity between the meaning of sexuality and "proper" behavior. Sex is fun, it is wrong, it is grown-up, it is cheap, it is sophisticated, it is dirty—these are just a few of the teen-ager's confused ideas about sexual behavior.

If marked ambiguity in attitudes and behavior characterizes adolescence, the growing ambiguity found in the traditional institutions intensifies this characteristic. The problem is particularly acute in sexuality.

Society has increasing difficulty in imposing moral willpower based on fear; it must develop this willpower on a basis of choice, which is a more difficult task. It no longer can expect ignorance of sexual behavior through isolation; it must combat misinformation. Other specific factors that add to society's difficulties are (1) an apparent decline in parental control, due to various reasons, (2) a general decline in community scrutiny of teen-agers, due chiefly to the use of automobiles, (3) an apparent weakening in the church's power and influence in sexual matters, and (4) a growing unwillingness of college authorities to continue the concept of *in loco parentis,* which becomes more important with the growing number of persons of college age, especially girls. These factors have brought an era of change in which moral standards with which the young person may identify are less stable and clear than they were. The adolescent is faced with anomie, an inability to perceive the "norms."

Other sources of ambiguity that express what "ought to be" but clash with the traditional institutions are in the fields of fashion, cosmetics, motion pictures, television and advertising—all project an image that makes precocious and more frequent sexual involvement a goal. We in the United States have been called a seductive society, and we have no real defense against this charge.

Another factor stimulating confusion for the adolescent is the concept of the "new" woman. An important aspect of this concept is the separation of sexual involvement and procreation. The new and improved contraceptives for women have enhanced the possibility of sexual involvement, which complicates the sexuality. The married woman no longer can say No to sexual intercourse because she is supposedly "unsafe." Married couples are forced to reexamine and perhaps reevaluate their sexual relations and often, thereby, their personal relationship. Similarly, young unmarried couples must carefully reexamine sexuality both as an expression of

their feelings toward each other and as a means of possible parenthood.

THE PHYSICIAN'S ROLE

From the preceding discussion, it becomes clear that young people who come to a physician for assistance must be treated as individuals who are in a difficult time of life. When a younger patient has need for a contraceptive, the physician should not refuse this service simply because the patient is young or does not have parental consent. Although the teen-ager should be encouraged to seek parental consent, the physician should try to manage the situation so that the patient's suffering is minimal. We feel that unwanted pregnancy is a disease—a disease with consequences that affect every level of society.

A physician who prescribes contraceptives for a minor without parental consent usually is concerned about the legal aspects. Thus far there has not been a single instance of legal action against a physician who has given this service, although some practitioners openly advocate family planning service for unwed minors (obviously the communication of information about condoms and foams carries no possibility of legal action). If such a case is brought to court, a logical argument can be made for a legal finding that a teen-ager old enough to be sexually involved and to seek medical assistance is old enough to be considered responsible. All this is pure speculation, however, since an enhaustive search has not revealed a single legal action of this kind. The conservatism of physicians who have not had any judicial experience is interesting to note. The dynamics of parents instituting legal action against a physician who has prescribed for their sexually active teen-ager are such that a case of this kind may never come to court.

Regardless of his decision about prescribing contraceptives to a minor patient, the physician has a responsibility to the teen-ager who is in a difficult situation. That responsibility goes beyond dispensing a stern moral lecture. By listening thoughtfully and without quick moral judgment to the young patient's problems, the physician can help him understand his behavior. We have been impressed by the frequency with which teen-agers have restrained their sexual involvement or, sometimes, abstained from it after they have received contraceptives and some supportive counseling. It seems that as long as adult society says, You can't, they feel that they must. But when the teen-ager is asked, Is this what you want? the responsibility for his behavior is returned to him, which is as it should be.

Assuming for a moment that the liberal dispensing of contraceptive information and prescriptions will increase teen-age sexual activity, how does this compare as a moral issue to withholding such information and prescriptions, which in reality is increasing unwanted human beings on this soon-to-be-overcrowded earth? What is really the greater evil? Are our decisions rational ones?

COMMENT

We are acutely aware of the controversial nature of this paper, and we do not expect our readers to agree with all our views. However, if this brief discussion will encourage more introspection and throughtfulness in physicians who deal with adolescent patients, we believe that we will have performed a genuine service.

21 Motivational factors affecting contraceptive use

Francis J. Kane, Jr., M.D.
Peter A. Lachenbruch, Ph.D.
Lee Lokey
Neil Chafetz
Richard Auman
Leo Pocuis
Morris A. Lipton, M.D.

Jaffe and Polgar[1] have, in a discussion of factors influencing contraceptive practice, expressed concern that there has been undue preoccupation with concepts such as "machismo" in the male or the "hungry womb" in the female, which they feel have been used as a rationalization for the lack of provision of easily accessible facilities to provide contraception information for the poor. They argue cogently that, where such facilities have been made available, significant numbers of seemingly unmotivated people consistently have been able to use contraception effectively. However, even they estimate that as many as 15 to 20 per cent of the population may require counseling and supportive services, presumably for their lack of motivation in using the available information and techniques. Even if this modest figure of 15 to 20 per cent of childbearing women is accurate, the large number of women involved is clearly an indication for further research in this area.

There have been many studies in recent years on the knowledge and practice of con-

From the School of Medicine, School of Public Health, and Department of Psychiatry, University of North Carolina, School of Medicine, and Michigan State University.

traception in various levels of our society. Kiser and Whelpton[2] pointed to the importance of socioeconomic differences in affecting the utilization of contraception, but also they comment that they felt that psychological factors were extremely important in the understanding of nonuse of contraception. Blair's study[3] of attitudes toward contraception in urban Negroes showed that, in general, they desire fewer children than Caucasians, but, in fact, continued to have more children than desired. Blair's Negro respondents reported twice as many "accidental" pregnancies. Fifty per cent of nonwhite women reported themselves to have "taken chances" with irregular and careless use of birth control methods.

Kronus,[4] in a study in the rural South, reported less than one third of the population made a change in contraceptive practice to effectively prevent pregnancy, even when free information and contraceptive technology were offered. Misra[5] reported that Negro men described themselves as lacking diligence in using contraception. Less than one third of the men surveyed were seen to have good contraceptive protection. Substantial objection and dislike of available contraceptive means were reported by the men studied. These findings are believed by the author to represent the result of inadequate information and understanding of contraception. These studies on the knowledge of, attitude toward, and practice of

191

contraception support the premise that there are some for whom adequate information and availability are the most crucial variable. They do not provide us with any insight into why there may be inadequate use in the face of available information and technology and do nothing to help us predict who will not be reached by these techniques.

In this country, the group which has changed the least, and continues to be most overproductive in terms of excess fertility, is the southern rural Negro,[6] as concretized in the aforementioned study of Kronus[4] in an Alabama population. The study to be presented is an attempt to describe some of the factors which may contribute to such a phenomenon, in a Negro southern rural population in North Carolina.

METHODOLOGY

The populations to be described are consecutive samples of patients studied on the maternity wards of the North Carolina Memorial Hospital during the summers of 1968-1969. Ninety-five per cent of married and unmarried women who were delivered during this period were interviewed by the principal investigator or specially trained third-year medical students.

The patients were interviewed on the second or third day post partum and were administered a semistructured interview designed to elicit: (1) knowledge of birth control methods; (2) use of birth control methods in this and other pregnancies; (3) consistency of use of birth control methods; (4) number of planned pregnancies; (5) whether their family was larger than desired and the reasons therefore; (6) demographic data relating to age, sex, education, etc. Each patient and subject also completed the Neuroticism Scale Questionnaire (NSQ),[7] which is a brief, 40 item self-rating instrument which gives a total neuroticism score and scores on four other factors. This questionnaire is derived from items discriminating neurotic from normal patients on the 16 PF test[8] and is described as reliable and valid in

Table I

	Negro (126)	Caucasian (132)
Education beyond 12th grade	8%	58%
More than 6 children	32%	4%
Knowledge of contraception	No difference	No difference
Use of contraception	Significantly less	—
Consistent use	Significantly less	—
Men responsible	Significantly increased (threefold)	—
Men contraception	Significantly increased (threefold)	—
Shared responsibility	—	Increased (twofold)

prior testing in normals and neurotics. The four factors are: (1) submissiveness versus dominance; (2) sensitivity versus practicality and/or insensitivity; (3) depression versus happy-go-lucky cheerfulness; and (4) anxiety. Age and education have been shown to cause no significant variance in previous testing of this instrument.

RESULTS

One hundred and twenty-six Negro married women and 132 Caucasian married women completed the full interview (Table I). There were no significant differences in age, but there were significant differences in education. Only 8 per cent of the Negro patients had education beyond high school, while 58 per cent of the Caucasian population showed such experience. Analysis of our own data showed no relationship of NSQ scores to age or education. Thirty-two per cent of the total Negro sample had more than six children versus only 4 per cent of the Caucasian sample. Twenty-three per cent of the Negro sample reported this to be contrary to their wishes, while 3 per cent of the Caucasian sample so reported.

Table II. Neuroticism scale questionnaire

	Negro	Caucasian
Sensitive versus practical	Significantly increased	—
Depressed	Significantly decreased	—
Anxiety	Not significant	Not significant
Submissive	Significantly increased	—
Total neuroticism	Significantly increased	—

Table III. Menstrual data

	Negro (126) (%)	Caucasian (132) (%)
Adequately prepared	Not significant	Not significant
Menarche upsetting	Increased (0.2)*	—
Irritability	39 (0.0001)	70
Fatigue	42 (0.03)	57
Pain	64	63
Headache	25 (0.06)	35
Breast swelling	12 (0.0001)	48
Abdominal swelling	32 (0.0001)	60
Depression	35 (0.002)	55
Anxiety	21 (0.00001)	54

*Level of significance (χ^2).

While there was no significant difference in knowledge about birth control methods in the two populations, Negroes used contraception significantly less often. The Negro population also reported themselves to be significantly more inconsistent in the use of birth control methods. When questioned about who was responsible for contraception in the family, Negro men were reported to be three times as often responsible, while the Caucasian patients reported shared responsibility twice as often as the Negro population. The reported responsibility of the Negro man for contraception was supported by the threefold difference reported in use of male-type contraception, such as condoms and withdrawal. Two thirds of those women with very large families reported overt or covert rejection of contraception on the part of their husbands and felt that continued childbearing was desired by the husbands. When asked whether they would have this baby if they had it to do over again, 46 per cent of the Negro mothers said no, while only 24 per cent of the Caucasian sample so reported.

There were significant differences on four of the five items on the NSQ (Table II). The anxiety factor showed no differences in the populations studied. The psychological test material seems to indicate that, compared to Caucasian women, Negro women scored themselves either as more kindly, gentle, or helpless, or more practical, tough,

hard, and responsible. In other words, they tended to cluster themselves at the extreme of this dimension, in contrast to the Caucasian. On the depressive tendency, they tend to score themselves significantly more often cheerful and extroverted being expressive, sociable, talkative, and impulsive. On the submissive versus dominant component, they seemed to score themselves as strikingly more submissive, obedient, complacent, and dependent. The Negro women were also found significantly higher on the total neuroticism score.

Information collected about the onset of the menstrual function, preparation for menstrual function, and symptoms experienced during the menses are of interest (Table III). The Negro married women reported themselves to have been disturbed significantly more often at the onset of the menses. The ratings of adequacy of preparation for menses for each group were without difference. With approximately one-third having reported this preparation to be adequate in both samples, the Negro women reported more often that they received it from persons other than their mother. There were striking differences with regard to report of menstrual distress between the Caucasian and Negro populations, in that Negro married women reported significantly fewer menstrual symptoms. There were no differences in reported frequency of sexual intercourse and reported frequency of sexual orgasm accompanying sexual intercourse.

COMMENT

The data collected clearly indicate that knowledge of techniques of contraception is generally well diffused in the populations studied. The chief differences relate to use of what they know, and consistency of use when it is used. The data are susceptible of several interpretations. There are those who would contend that the techniques prescribed by doctors are not easily available to the Negro poor in our area, and that the preponderance of use of condoms and withdrawal and other nonmedical forms of contraception reflect this. Unfortunately, in this study we did not specifically ask about whether the patients knew where to obtain these techniques; but in more recent studies in this same population, and in the county hospital serving an urban Negro population, which is staffed in part of the medical school, we have found that, in all but a small minority, knowledge of where to obtain methods of contraception is in the possession of those interviewed.

We believe two other factors are also of considerable importance. The first of these we could not examine directly. About half of the women, who were grand multipara or above, reported significant opposition from their husbands to the use of contraception. This was supported by the reports of an anecdotal nature from medical students, who reported that a community clinic which dispensed contraceptive advice had to be closed down because of the disinterest of those in the area; this, despite the fact that a considerable amount of time was spent making the clinic known to people in the area and that the time schedule of the clinic was convenient to the working poor. The principal reason given to the students was the opposition of the husbands in the

area to the clinic. While we have no data directly from the husbands, the reported use of contraception of the male-type almost exclusively, and the responsibility of the Negro male for contraception in the family, with so little effectiveness, would certainly support these contentions. These findings are in accord with those attitudes and practices reported by Misra[5] in his study of urban northern Negroes. The submissiveness and helplessness reported by these women would also be in keeping with the passive relationships they described. The low self-ratings on the depression factor is described as indicating a tendency toward impulsivity. This tendency toward impulsivity may be represented clinically by the "taking of chances" which seem so often to be reported by those with excessive fertility. This chance taking seems especially to involve procreative aspects of sexuality, since frequency of sexual intercourse and orgasm rate are not different in the two groups.

These findings seem to support the argument of Lerner[9] that the procreative aspect of sexual function is overused among the poor as a means of generating self-esteem and worth. He points out that, in such a setting, contraception may be experienced as a further impoverishment, and to some an unbearable deprivation. Lerner also commented on the strong wishes for dependency in his poor planners, which trait also may be reflected in the high ratings of the submissive dimension of our black population.

There are two other pieces of evidence from the data gathered that indicate that, for these women, childbearing is an important source of self-esteem. The Negro women were significantly different in rating themselves higher on the sensitivity factor than the Caucasian women. This sensitivity factor has been called the masculinity-femininity factor, and, indeed, male homosexuals score significantly higher than the nonhomosexual men on this factor. There is also the finding of the markedly less frequent rate of complaint about menstrual symptoms in the Negro population, a phenomenon reported by other investigators.[10]

Paulson[11] has shown, in a recent study, that women with significant premenstrual and menstrual symptomatology portray themselves as less adequate and less able to fulfill maturely the psychosocial and psychosexual roles which they and society expect. Coppen and Kessel,[12] in a study of 463 subjects randomly selected, showed that high neuroticism scores on the Maudsley Personality Inventory were correlated with a high degree of premenstrual distress (except dysmenorrhea). The lessened incidence of postpartum depression in our group probably reflects this lessened conflict.

Femininity and motherhood seem to be, for the Negro women, less conflicted, and thus more likely a positive source of self-esteem and confirming their role socially and personally. The increased total neuroticism scores clearly indicate that, if femininity and womanhood are sources of self-esteem to the Negro female, these sources of self-esteem are not sufficient to guarantee overall personality adjustment and make it even more likely they will be overused in an effort to achieve some inner peace. Further studies are needed to confirm our preliminary observations, since there were major educational and socioeconomic differences in the sample. Studies are also needed to define and confirm or refute the data about the male member of the Negro marital pair.

The data we have gathered is, in many ways, consistent with other studies reported. The verification of these data, and the sociopsychological characteristics of good versus poor contraceptive users, is the subject of a future study. The women describe themselves as passive in response to contraception, and somewhat impulsive from a characterologic standpoint. These factors, plus the evidence relating to their lack of conflict about femininity and motherhood, suggest that measures aimed at preventing conception in this population must not only include technological advice, but also must be geared to helping these women find alternate modes of gratification to replace that of the reproductive process. In a population such as the one we serve, only massive aid to disrupted families, increased educational opportunities, and vocational training opportunities for men and women are likely to meet this problem. The provision of contraceptive technology may make it possible for these people to use such opportunities if they are available, but one is likely to fail without the other.

REFERENCES

1. Jaffe, F. S., and Polgar, S.: J. Marriage Family 30:228, 1968.
2. Kiser, C. V., and Whelpton, P. K.: Population Studies 7:95, 1953.
3. Blair, A. O.: A Comparison of Negro and White Fertility Attitudes, *in* Bogue, D. J., editor: Sociological Contributions to Family Planning Research, Chicago, 1967, Community and Family Study Center, pp. 1-35.
4. Kronus, S.: Fertility Control in the Rural South: A Pretext, *in* Bogue, D. J., editor: Sociological Contributions to Family Planning Research, Chicago, 1967, Community and Family Study Center, pp. 129-160.
5. Misra, B. D.: Correlates of Males' Attitudes Toward Family Planning, *in* Bogue, D. J., editor: Sociological Contributions to Family Planning Research, Chicago, 1967, Community and Family Study Center, pp. 161-271.
6. Hill, A. C., and Jaffe, F. S.: Negro Fertility and Family Size Preferences: Implications for Programming of Health and Social Services, New York, 1966, Houghton Mifflin Company.
7. Scheier, I. H., and Cattell, R. B.: Neuroticism Scale Questionnaire. Champaign: Institute for Personality and Ability Testing.
8. Institute for Personality and Ability Testing: 16 Personality Factor Questionnaire, Champaign, Illinois.
9. Lerner, B. A.: Contraception and the Poverty Syndrome, presented at American Psychiatric Association Annual Meeting, San Francisco, May 13, 1970.
10. Gottschalk, L. A., et al.: J. Nerv. Ment. Dis. 138:524, 1964.
11. Paulson, M. J.: Amer. J. Obstet. Gynec. 81:733, 1961.
12. Coppen, A., and Kessel, N.: Brit. J. Psychiat. 109:711, 1963.

22 UNITED STATES: Exploratory studies of Negro family formation—factors relating to illegitimacy

Melvin Zelnik
John F. Kantner*

National data on illegitimate births in the United States are both defective and deficient. They are especially hazardous for the purpose of studying trends over time or differentials between subgroups of the population. One difficulty is that not all states require the legitimacy status of a birth to be reported when the birth is registered. Another is the likelihood that, even where data are collected on legitimacy status, there may be variations among different groups in the validity of the information that is provided. Despite these difficulties there can

be no doubt that there has been an upward trend in illegitimacy and also that the number of illegitimate births is greater among nonwhites than among whites.[1] This difference is particularly evident among women under age twenty. In 1967, for example, the estimated *number* of illegitimate births to nonwhite women under 20 years of age was 44 per cent greater than the comparable figure for white women. At that time, there were about six times as many white females 10-19 years of age as there were nonwhite females in these ages (15,970,000 compared to 2,598,000).[2] In 1968, illegitimate births amounted to nearly one-third of total nonwhite births.[3] To some degree this high "illegitimacy ratio" was due to the fact that, while legitimate nonwhite births

*This is the second report by Dr. Melvin Zelnik and Dr. John F. Kantner, both professors in the Department of Population Dynamics at the Johns Hopkins University School of Hygiene and Public Health, on a series of feasibility studies undertaken to develop and test new approaches to the study of fertility among American Negroes. Their research was supported in part by grant number 470 from the Social and Rehabilitation Service, U. S. Department of Health, Education, and Welfare. The group discussions referred to in the report, as well as other related current studies in the field, were conducted by the Institute for Survey Research, Temple University, of which Dr. Aaron Spector is Director. The earlier report on this topic by Professors Kantner and Zelnik, entitled "United States: Exploratory Studies of Negro Family Formation—Common Conceptions about Birth Control," appeared in *Studies in Family Planning*, No. 47, November 1969.

Reprinted from *Studies in Family Planning* 1(48):5-9, 1970. Copyright The Population Council.

[1]In the United States official data pertaining to illegitimacy, as well as to many other characteristics, are not available separately for Negroes. However, since Negroes account for about 95 per cent of the nonwhite population of the United States, statements made in reference to levels, trends, rates, etc., concerning nonwhites are essentially applicable to Negroes also. Beginning with the discussion "Factors in Premarital Conception," we are dealing specifically with Negroes.
[2]U. S. National Center for Health Statistics, *Vital Statistics of the United States: 1967* (Washington, D. C.: U. S. Government Printing Office, 1968) Volume 1, Natality Tables 1–26 and 3–2.
[3]———, "Advance Report: Final Natality Statistics, 1968," *Monthly Vital Statistics Report*, Vol. 18, No. 11, January 30, 1970.

declined fairly regularly during the 1960s, the number of illegitimate births increased. But the illegitimacy rate has also been rising,[4] so that we are dealing here with a change in the behavior of unmarried women and not merely with a statistical artifact.

A similar trend has been evident among whites but the color differential, although not so great as in the past, is still substantial. In 1940 the estimated illegitimate fertility rate of women aged 15-44 was ten times as high for nonwhites as for whites; by 1967 the nonwhite rate was about seven times higher.[5] Part of the difference in the level of illegitimacy results from a greater tendency among nonwhites to carry illegitimacy into the higher birth orders. For example, whereas about 70 per cent of all white illegitimate births in 1967 were first births, this was the case for only 50 per cent of nonwhite births.[6]

These trends are more than a little puzzling, for the rise in illegitimacy has occurred during a period when, partly in response to the availability of highly efficient contraception, the fertility rates of both whites and nonwhites have fallen precipitously.

The differences in levels of illegitimacy between whites and nonwhites also defy easy explanation. Data from two national surveys indicate that, except in the rural South, black wives want fewer births than white wives[7] and, moreover, that blacks exceed

whites in the proportion of first births that are reported as having been "unwanted." Although these findings relate to married women living with their husbands, there is no obvious reason to suppose that women living under less stable arrangements would welcome children more. More to the point perhaps are findings from local studies which generally indicate that Negroes desire a smaller family size than they actually achieve and have a strong interest in fertility control.[8] One study reports that 90 per cent of a group of mothers of illegitimate children who were receiving welfare assistance declared that the child was unwanted.[9]

THEORETICAL PERSPECTIVES ON ILLEGITIMACY

An early advance toward the scientific understanding of illegitimacy was provided by Kingsley Davis in an article[10] first published in 1939 and still being reprinted in the 1960s. Davis distinguishes between a "moral" or "problem" approach to illegitimacy and a "scientific" or "sociological" approach. The prevailing approach had been a moral one up to that time. The theory that Davis advanced is as follows: (1) illegitimacy always arouses moral disapproval and indignation toward both the mother and her child; (2) illegitimacy could be abolished if society approved of universal sex education, free and available contraception and abortion, and legal sanction against those who have illegitimate children. Davis observed that at the time this scheme could not be adopted because a moralistic condemnation of illegitimacy was functionally necessary for the integrity of the social sys-

[4]Reynolds Farley and Albert Hermalin, "Family Stability: A Comparison of Trends between Blacks and Whites," paper presented at the 1970 Meeting of the Population Association of America, Atlanta, Georgia, April 1970.
[5]Ibid., Table 6.
[6]National Center for Health Statistics, "Advance Report: Final Natality Statistics, 1968," op. cit. Tables 1–27.
[7]P. K. Whelpton, Arthur A. Campbell, and John E. Patterson, Fertility and Family Planning in the United States, (Princeton: Princeton University Press, 1966), Table 189; Charles F. Westoff and Norman B. Ryder, "Family Limitations in the United States," paper presented at the 1969 session of the International Union for the Scientific Study of Population, London, September 1969.

[8]For several citations see Adelaide Cromwell Hill and Frederick S. Jaffe, "Negro Fertility and Family Size Preferences," in The Negro American, Talcott Parsons and Kenneth Clark (eds.), (New York: The Daedalus Library, 1965), pp. 205-224.
[9]Ibid., p. 213.
[10]Kingsley Davis, "Illegitimacy and the Social Structure," The American Journal of Sociology, 45 (2):215-233, September 1939.

tem. The scheme, he noted, was unrealistic on two counts: first, it assumes that the abolition of illegitimacy is a supreme goal and second, it assumes that human reproduction can be guided by logico-empirical science. The means necessary to eliminate illegitimacy, he pointed out, are more taboo than illegitimacy and reproductive institutions are lodged well below the surface of rationality. He concluded that if a society were so emancipated as to approve of contraception and abortion, it would not have to worry about illegitimacy.

Many of the premises of Davis' theory no longer hold true. However important the theory might have been in suggesting a functional approach to illegitimacy, it offers little assistance in explaining either recent trends or racial differentials in illegitimacy. Although we do not have data to document our assumption, moral condemnation of illegitimacy, which Davis treats as a sociological given, appears to have lessened. We have moved from moral indignation over the "sin" of the mother to concern with the conditions surrounding the state of illegitimacy—low income, lack of a "male image," poor nutritional standards, the immaturity of the mother. Is the rising trend in illegitimacy to be explained by greater tolerance of it? Are white–nonwhite differentials due to greater tolerance toward illegitimacy on the part of nonwhites? Perhaps so, but at the present time there is no theory which would account for a more relaxed attitude toward illegitimacy.

Also at variance with Davis' theory are the changes in attitude and behavior with respect to sex education, contraception and abortion. These are no longer taboo but are actively promoted by respected groups in society. We do not mean to suggest that all opposition has died out. Indeed, there are significant groups within American society opposed to birth control, and within the Negro community there is widespread opposition to abortion. In general, however, opinion regarding birth control measures has become more relaxed and permissive with no concomitant decline in rates of illegitimacy.

It would seem that we have no theory sufficiently dynamic to account for the changes which have occurred. The one attempt, as we have seen, is deficient in the face of facts. It treats illegitimacy as universal, as something that results because the measure sufficient to prevent it are as morally repugnant as illegitimacy itself. It is perhaps too static and too undiscerning to account for changes over time or difference among populations in the prevalence of illegitimacy. In this paper we shall try to identify the factors that might be related to illegitimacy. We shall give special attention to the explanation of high levels of illegitimacy among Negroes. The published data that we use, however, refer to nonwhites.

ILLEGITIMACY AS A SOCIAL FACT

Illegitimacy is the end product of a behavioral chain involving intercourse, marriage and gestation. As pointed out earlier in the paper, this sequence also involves behavior at the time of registration, i.e., the decision to report an illegitimate birth as much as to conceal it. As a social fact, therefore, illegitimacy is a complex one.

Various students of the problem in the United States have analyzed the illegitimacy sequence and have shown that the approximately one-to-seven ratio between white and nonwhite illegitimate fertility rates is, to a large degree, a compound of differences in out-of-wedlock conceptions and differential tendencies to conceal these through marriage. In a study in Detroit, Pratt[11] found that out-of-wedlock conceptions were three times more numerous among nonwhites than among whites. He also found a much greater tendency among whites to marry before the birth of the child. It would appear from Pratt's findings that as of 1960 the white-

_____
[11]W. F. Pratt, "Premarital Pregnancy in a Metropolitan Community," paper presented at the Annual Meeting of the Population Association of America, April 1965.

Table 1. Proportion of first births assumed to have been conceived outside marriage for whites and nonwhites, United States: 1964-1966

Age	White	Nonwhite
15-19	49.2	83.8
20-24	18.5	56.6

Source: National Natality Survey, 1964-1966. Data presented in a paper by Mary Kovar to the annual meeting of the Population Association of America, April 1970. The estimate of first births conceived outside of marriage is obtained by combining the estimated number of illegitimate first births from registration data with the estimated number of legitimate first births which occurred between 0-7 months after marriage. Data on the interval from marriage to first birth are provided by the 1964-1966 National Natality Survey (NNS) which is a sample of all births registered in those years.

Table 2. Proportion of first births assumed to have been conceived outside of marriage, by legitimacy status at birth for whites and nonwhites, United States: 1964-1966

Age	Legitimate		Illegitimate	
	White	Nonwhite	White	Nonwhite
15-19	68.4	30.0	31.6	70.0
20-24	62.4	47.2	37.6	52.8

Source: Same as Table 1.

nonwhite illegitimacy differential was partially a function of differences in the frequency of both premarital conception and the decision to marry prior to delivery.[12] Similar findings come from the National Natality Survey conducted by the National Center for Health Statistics (Tables 1 and 2).

It is probable that, in addition to differences by race in premarital conceptions (Table 1) and marriage propensities (Table 2) among the premaritally pregnant, there are differences in the use of contraceptives and the incidence of abortion. Relatively little is known about these areas, however, since most of what we know about racial differences in fertility in the United States

[12]Pratt also observes that greater recidivism among nonwhites somewhat inflates the racial differential in so far as the *number of women* is concerned.

is with respect to married women in stable unions.

Having looked briefly at racial differences in some of the major components of illegitimacy, we shall devote the remainder of this paper to a discussion of possible factors underlying these differences. Our object is to formulate the problem more comprehensively[13] and to suggest lines of further investigation. We shall rely upon material abstracted from intensive group discussions with 166 Negro women of different marital and socioeconomic status—discussions which touched upon attitudes toward illegitimacy and the factors surrounding and, presumably, influencing it.[14] We cannot assert that these materials are representative of the views of all Negro women, but since our aim is primarily conceptual and indicative, this limitation is not critical. Unavoidably, we shall be discussing the problem largely as it relates to blacks.

FACTORS IN PREMARITAL CONCEPTION
Intercourse

We have no evidence concerning the incidence or frequency of premarital intercourse. Among the participants in the group discussions, however, most reported having had premarital intercourse. It is not possible to determine from this information

[13]One reason for the failure to comprehend the factors involved in illegitimacy is that most studies have focused solely on the mothers of illegitimate children. Such a procedure is of little assistance in determining the causal factors leading to an illegitimate birth. Doing so involves studying also other unmarried females with respect to the intercourse and gestational components, as well as married women who conceived premaritally. The ideal method would be to follow a cohort of young females over time. We hope to carry out such a study on a national sample of females aged 15-19 who would be contacted periodically over a four-year time interval.
[14]For a description of how these discussions were conducted, see John F. Kantner and Melvin Zelnik, "United States: Exploratory Studies of Negro Family Formation—Common Conceptions about Birth Control," *Studies in Family Planning*, **47**: 10-13, November 1969.

whether there has been a change over time in the extent of sexual activity. Despite general agreement on the part of all women, young and old, married and unmarried, that "times are different today" and that "young girls are going to do it," our impression is that there has been little or no change in the prevalence of premarital intercourse. The appearance of change is due, we believe, to a greater readiness to discuss such matters today than in the past and to a lack of communication between young and old.

Older women apparently are unaware of what the extent of premarital intercourse was among their age peers. Young women state that their mothers and older relatives do not realize the extent of sexual activity in the present generation. The older women, however, do accept the likelihood of a high degree of sexual activity on the part of young women.

Among the never-married women only a few respondents, 15 to 16 years of age, said they had not had intercourse. A majority of the never-married women acknowledged having had intercourse, in some instances with an intended spouse. A few participants were reticent on the subject. Many of the ever-married women reported premarital intercourse. In a number of such cases the male partner subsequently became the husband.

At this point it is worth asking under what conditions young, unmarried Negro women have intercourse. We are not concerned with the reasons why any particular woman does so, but rather with the social context. Aside from the obvious facts of a biological urge, the unchaperoned mixing of the sexes, and the postponement of marriage beyond the age of physical maturation, several points were raised by the participants that received categorical agreement and are relevant to the question of intercourse. First is the general pejorative view of men as sexual animals. As one woman put it—to a chorus of agreement—"Men are 95 per cent dog." Second is the notion that there are always some women who are willing to satisfy this pervasive male lust with

the result that a woman is forced to compete in the granting of sexual favors to hold on to a man in whom she has an interest. To be "interested in" a man does not connote love but may be more in the nature of an option taken on him. The granting of sexual access therefore may be seen as a "holding operation" while the girl resolves the troublesome and evanescent question of the state of her true affections.

This male buyer's market for sex is strengthened further by the general subscription to the idea that every woman wants and expects her husband to be sexually experienced at the time of marriage. Without such experience a man is suspected of homosexuality, impotence, or other sexual deficiency. In a such a context of perception it is not surprising that sexual involvement would seem nearly inescapable—a situation that is but a step removed from acceptance. There is, indeed, an element of the self-fulfilling prophecy here: the belief that sex is pervasive in the world in which the young woman must compete socially leads her to accept the inevitability of it. Given that the system does not provide amply such alternatives as concubinage or prostitution, it is not surprising that the male comes to be regarded as a "sexual animal."[15]

The frequency of premarital intercourse may also be enhanced by the relatively weak sanctions against it or against its possible consequences. As we will discuss later, there appear to be differences between whites and Negroes in the severity of sanctions against illegitimacy and the rearing of an illegitimate child. Unprotected premarital intercourse involves much greater social risks for the white woman.

---

[15]It has been suggested that living arrangements, specifically the doubling-up of families and the presence of "lodgers" in many Negro households, are factors in family instability. See Gunnar Myrdal, *An American Dilemma*, (New York: Harper and Brothers, 1944), p. 934. The relationship, if any, of this practice to illegitimacy has not been explored and no incidental light was thrown on it by our discussants.

In sum, we would expect relatively earlier and relatively more frequent intercourse among Negro women than among white women, because their social environment is more conducive to sexual activity and the penalties for illegitimacy are less stringent.

Contraception

The connection between premarital intercourse and illegitimacy could be weakened by the effective use of contraception. The older women in our group of discussants were predominantly in favor of providing contraceptive service for young, unmarried women. There was general agreement that girls of 16 years were not too young to receive such services. However, the younger participants, although favoring the availability and use of contraception in principle, often opposed its use in the concrete case. Use of contraception, they argued, suggests a degree of sexual readiness or wantonness with which they did not want to be associated. Seemingly it is tinged with the suggestion of promiscuity and this is generally rejected, although selective sex is not. But even in the case where the number of partners is limited, the use of contraception is pictured as "cold and calculating," as too rational, thereby dimming the aura of romance and impulsiveness that is supposed to surround the act of sex. Contraception thus has a psychic "cost" which many young women are unwilling to bear until they have had one or two illegitimate children. That the "cost" is psychic rather than physical is supported by the observation that the romantic objection to the use of contraception applies to pills and IUDs as well as to coitus-related methods.[16]

---

[16]In our earlier paper we noted that for most discussants "birth control" or contraception means "pills." We called attention also to widespread misunderstanding with respect to the risk of becoming pregnant. Relatively short periods of exposure without a resulting pregnancy are taken by many women as an indication that they are reasonably secure and need not use contraception.

Resolution of pregnancy

Early and frequent intercourse combined with a disinclination to use contraception leads inevitably to a relatively high incidence of pregnancy. How, according to our participants, should this situation be handled?

Abortion. In the earlier paper in which we dealt with the subject of abortion, we reported that none of the participants accepted abortion as a way for an unmarried girl to escape the consequences of a voluntary sexual encounter. This rejection of abortion—on moral grounds, although, no doubt, influenced by the common view of illegal abortions as clandestine and squalid—was as definite and forceful among women who had themselves borne illegitimate children as it was among others. There is, it seems, a heavy emphasis on the importance of preserving life once begun. The underlying justification often given is an interpretation of Christian morality akin to that of the Roman Catholic Church. Abortion can be countenanced only under unusual, extenuating circumstances, and not by all even then.

Adoption. The overwhelming advice to a premaritally pregnant woman thus is to "have the baby." A few of the older women advocated giving up the baby for adoption but in general this suggestion was not favored and among the younger women it was almost never regarded as an acceptable resolution. The child is part of the romantic complex, a symbolic fulfillment of love's design. In a case where "love" is one-sided or perhaps becomes a postnatal casualty, the child may be valued as a visible symbol of the love that once existed. When "love" is not involved, the argument against giving up the child for adoption may be the welfare of the child. To "put a child up for adoption" is to abdicate one's humane concern for the innocent and defenseless. It is also seen as threatening the mother with a life of regret and remorse that may affect her as she learns more of the world in which she has abandoned her child. The difficulty of placing black children for adoption was rarely mentioned although this may have contributed to the negative attitudes toward it.

Finally, the birth of a child is a way, as is marriage, for an unmarried girl to gain independence from parental (often matriarchal) control. We need not resort to psychological explanations to understand this. In the social, economic, and political framework of Negro society, the ways of asserting independence are limited. Compared with a white girl of the same age, a black girl finds it harder to get a job that will support her; she lacks the residential options open to whites, and she may be concerned about the discrimination she will encounter on leaving home. For all these reasons she may find that the easiest road to independence is a role change within the family. Her child and her status as a mother help her to achieve this change of role.

Marriage. From data cited earlier in this paper it is clear that nonwhite women resort less often than white women to marriage as a way of concealing a premarital pregnancy. The discussants provided some insight into this phenomenon. Here again "romantic love," a primary rationale for sexual involvement,[17] was given as the only justifiable criterion in the choice of a marriage partner. This position was taken regardless of the age or marital status of the discussant. Mothers agreed that they would not try to force a marriage of a son or a daughter in such an instance. Among the younger women, the "love" criterion was applied bilaterally. Any suspicion that the male partner was not romantically involved with the woman should be taken as sufficient reason for not marrying him even if the woman is in love with him, since this would destroy any possibility that mutual love might develop because the man, it is claimed, would resent his entrap-

ment.[18] To force a marriage is to increase the chances of having a husband who "chases other women," drinks, and beats his wife. There is reason to believe that, historically, "romantic love" has been an important basis for marriage among American Negroes. Jessie Bernard[19] makes this point with respect to the "plantation family" in terms that are wholly consonant with the views expressed by our discussants.

The idea of marriage "to give the baby a name" was mentioned, usually to complete the phrase "a girl shouldn't get married just to give the baby a name." When this course was suggested by one older woman of upper educational and income status, who pointed out that the baby then could be placed for adoption and the couple divorced, it was forcefully opposed by the other discussants. As the discussion subsided even she admitted that she would not have forced marriage on the couple, had such a situation occurred in her family.

ATTITUDES TOWARD ILLEGITIMACY

The configuration of attitudes and behavior with respect to sex, birth control, and marriage is undoubtedly contributory to high levels of illegitimacy. What about attitudes toward illegitimacy itself? It is our impression that, in the black community, whereas ideally childbearing takes place within a marriage based on mutual love, illegitimate pregnancy on the other hand is not the cause for moral condemnation and scorn. The younger women among the discussants indicated that they did not or would not experience any sense of shame at being premaritally pregnant. Only one young woman who had been premaritally pregnant reported having felt some unease about appearing in public at the onset of pregnancy

---

[17]The role of "love" as a rationalization for sex is strong but not exclusive. As noted earlier, innocent love manifested as "having an interest" is enough, given the competitive situation, to lead to sexual involvement.

[18]More commonly among blacks than among whites, a couple continues to see one another after the child is born. On the other hand, more whites marry before the child is born.

[19]Jessie Bernard, *Marriage and Family Among Negroes* (Englewood Cliffs, New Jersey: Prentice-Hall, 1966), pp. 36-37.

and more specifically at the point when her pregnancy first became noticeable. However, within a short period of time, all sense of uneasiness disappeared because she was not subjected to any scorn or ridicule. In fact, her initial concern and self-consciousness may have been no greater or different from that experienced by many young married women at the time of their first pregnancy.

The attitude toward illegitimacy perhaps is best illustrated by what we call the "one mistake syndrome." All of the participants subscribed to the view that "everybody is entitled to one mistake"—in this case to at least one premarital conception. Such a situation is not ideal or preferred, but neither is it deserving of condemnation. A second element in this "syndrome" is the view that the unwed mother has the right to receive, and the parent the responsibility to provide, assistance and care. "What can a mother do? Just because her daughter has a child, they can't be thrown out into the street." The liberal and accepting views reflected by our participants are in perfect agreement with the observations made over 35 years ago by Charles S. Johnson. As reported by Gunnar Myrdal, Johnson noted that: "The Negro community also has the healthy social custom of attaching no stigma to the illegitimate child . . . a high value is placed on children generally and those who mate outside of marriage do not have a tendency to prevent the coming of children . . . Another healthy social attitude . . . is that of regarding a forced marriage as less respectable than desertion after a forced marriage. The erring daughter is forgiven by her parents and is not ostracized by the community."[20]

To illustrate the lesser commitment of Negroes to the norm of legitimacy does not help to explain it. Prior to the Civil War virtually all Negro births in the United States were illegitimate. Subsequently this changed but even after the Civil War a substantial proportion of Negro births were illegitimate.

The increasing trend in illegitimacy shown by the recorded data may be somewhat overstated as a result of improved reporting. Whatever the exact increase may have been, illegitimacy in the Negro population has always been widespread. In an earlier period and continuing up to the recent past, Negroes had little control over illegitimacy. If popular literature is to be believed, the sexual predation of white males abetted by a defenselessness based on fear, resulted in many "good" women, young and old, married and single, bearing children "through no fault of their own." Illegitimacy had to be accepted; it became indeed essentially institutionalized.[21]

The fact that illegitimacy was widespread and often blameless insofar as the mother was concerned is coupled with two other facets of Negro existence.[22] First, the ascribed status as a Negro is a much more powerful determinant of one's place in society and one's chances in life than is legitimacy status. In effect, to the dominant white society, being legitimate or illegitimate is of little consequence where the Negro is concerned—what is important is skin color. To the extent that rewards are allocated (or withheld) "equally" among blacks, regardless of legitimacy, there are no negative

---

[20]As summarized by Gunnar Myrdal, *An American Dilemma, op cit.*, p. 935.

[21]Expressions of opprobrium are a sensitive indicator of which relationships are sanctified in society. We suspect that a study of opprobrious language in the United States would show that Negroes make relatively less use of such terms as "bastard" and other designations of illegitimacy than do whites.

[22]The comments which follow must be qualified to the extent that the status of the Negro in American society is changing. For example, although a Negro college graduate is likely to receive less pay than his white counterpart in the same job, it is unlikely today that he would be relegated to a menial position, a not unlikely event in the past. Because of this change, as well as changes in sexual behavior apparently occurring within the entire society, we cannot anticipate the future direction of illegitimacy among blacks; however, we believe the various changes are of too recent origin to negate our interpretations of past experiences.

sanctions against being illegitimate and no rewards for being legitimate. Such equal treatment would tend, we believe, to neutralize any societal condemnation against illegitimacy.

There is, however, a second condition which we believe may have operated in the direction of increasing the opportunities of the illegitimate black child and his status within the black community, if not within the total society, thereby further serving to reduce societal normative injunctions against illegitimacy. Within the Negro community, activities such as gambling, which are illicit in the eyes of the larger community, are important routes to economic success and to political influence through contacts with the white-dominated legal structure. Economic success and political influences are associated with a life style characterized by patterns of consumption that, against a background of general deprivation, are highly conspicuous and highly admired within the Negro community.[23] We suspect that children born into "poor but respectable" Negro families are less likely than illegitimate children to take such a route. The literature of the American Negro, fictional and nonfictional, is filled for example with accounts of Negro college graduates working at low-paying menial jobs (the only ones open to them until recent years). In a sense, their socialization and the familial emphasis on "honesty

and respectability" may be said to have incapacitated them for activities outside of this domain. Our hypothesis is that the child of an unstable family has a better than average chance of taking the other route and thereby achieving high income and status within the Negro community.[24]

In sum, we would be willing to argue that, given comparable socioeconomic background and holding educational attainment constant, the black female as compared with her white counterpart is more likely to engage in premarital intercourse; less likely to use contraception; more likely to conceive; less likely to attempt to alter or change that condition (through abortion, falsification of legitimacy, or marriage); more likely to bear and raise her illegitimate child; less likely to experience any condemnation for doing so; more likely to experience parental acceptance and assistance together with a more independent status; and better able to feel that her child has as good a chance in life as any legitimate child of her race born into similar economic circumstances. In our view, these considerations, which need to be submitted to further research, provide essential clues to the phenomenon of illegitimacy as it exists among blacks in the United States.

---

[23]St. Clair Drake and Horace R. Cayton, *Black Metropolis,* revised edition, (New York: Harper and Row, 1962), pp. 546-550; and Franklin E. Frazier, *Black Bourgeoisie,* (Glencoe, Illinois: Free Press, 1957), pp. 127-128. Among the older, pre-Depression "respectable" upper-class Negroes as well as among more recent post-Depression upper-class Negroes, some of whom derive their status from the "criminal underworld," light skin-color was a highly desirable attribute. Such coloring, however, implied that the person was illegitimate or could trace his lineage to an illegitimate ancestor, i.e., to an illicit offspring of miscegenation.

[24]This statement may appear to be in conflict with the voluminous literature relating to the undesirable consequences of family instability for the socialization of black children, e.g., the absence of a male image. There are several points to be made here: (1) these consequences have not been demonstrated precisely so that one can say that the socialization of an illegitimate black child differs significantly from that of a legitimate child born to a mother of the same age and of similar economic circumstances; (2) even if the alleged consequences are true, we are concerned here with what the people who are involved, not outside observers, believe to be true; (3) socialization patterns that deviate from those which are culturally prescribed may be associated with particular behavioral anomalies but are not necessarily incapacitating with respect to achievement, especially achievement along certain lines.

PART V
ROLES OF HEALTH PROFESSIONALS IN FAMILY PLANNING

A complex network of roles and functions must be coordinated when health professionals work together in family planning. This is the focus of attention in the final section of this book. Each of the disciplines involved in such efforts assumes the responsibility for defining its unique roles and functions; the coordination of these into an effective program of service occurs at the institutional level, whether this be a private practitioner's office, a postpartal clinic in a hospital setting, a comprehensive health center, or a freestanding facility. The daily activities of the practitioners are shaped by the administrative policies of the agency itself, by state and local laws, by standards of practice formulated within each discipline, and, hopefully, by characteristics of the client group to be served.

Each of the papers in this section addresses in some way the problem of preparing individual practitioners in the several disciplines for effective provision of family planning services. Since organized delivery programs are relatively new, much of the specific preparation up to this time has been at the in-service level; incorporation of relevant material into the formal curriculum for the basic education of health professionals has lagged far behind. The general lack of training facilities, cited earlier by Fischman, has meant that students of medicine, nursing, and social work have rarely had the opportunity to observe and participate in ongoing programs.

Health practitioners rarely have more than fragmentary knowledge of the skills, competencies, and functions of other members of the health team, yet each is expected to provide service to clients in highly complex organizational settings where successful coordination often depends on interdisciplinary effort and understanding. There is need for educators in the health professions to provide opportunities for interdisciplinary courses and clinical experiences in basic programs that prepare for beginning levels of practice.

One area that might be explored in such courses is that of shared responsibility for patient teaching. In some instances, the physician has regarded instruction about family planning carried on by the nurse and the social worker as an intrusion into his relationship with the patient.

When such feelings can be explored within an actual care setting, there is potential for clarification and the establishment of guidelines. Unfortunately, jurisdictional disputes of this type may not always come to the surface, and informal, yet powerful sanctions are sometimes exerted by physicians when other team members are believed to transgress. Frequently, the unfortunate result is the subsequent absence of any type of meaningful instruction for patients.

Appropriate roles, needed expertise, means of coordinating the activities of different disciplines, and sensitization of the professional to the patient or client are among the major concerns of the articles in this section.

Wolf and Ferguson cite a number of studies that report desire on the part of patients for health professionals to initiate discussion of family planning. Embarrassment or fear often prevent the potential adopter of contraception from actively seeking the information needed. Failure to ask questions often leads the practitioner to assume that the patient already possesses the information, or does not wish to discuss contraceptive use. Wolf and Ferguson also note the effect of the over-enthusiastic physician who may alienate the patient by strongly urging a particular contraceptive agent. Although the physician may be merely stressing the effectiveness of a prescription method, the patient may be searching for some hidden meaning to explain the physician's emphasis. This same admonition applies to all practitioners in family planning.

The papers by Edmands and Burnstein also note the potential willingness of the client to receive information that is presented at his or her level of understanding and that permits adequate time to question the nurse or social worker about all of the details considered by the *client* to be relevant.

Edmands cites the importance of the nurse's reception of the patient at the time of the first family planning visit. It is at this time that attitudes conveyed by the nurse toward the patient, as a person who is worthy of respect, may strongly influence future method adoption and continued use.

Burnstein also speaks of the importance of the initial phase of the social worker's contact with the patient. The need to question skillfully while avoiding intrusion into matters that the patient may prefer to regard as private, at least until rapport has been established with the worker, is a vital consideration.

In each of the papers mentioned up to this point, the authors who represent medicine, nursing, and social work have identified professional concerns that are in part unique to each individual practitioner group, but in part commonly shared by all three of the disciplines. The three groups identify the need for the practitioner to be comfortable with his own sexual nature and needs, to be skilled in conveying family planning information that is comprehensible to the patient, and to convey respect for each patient whatever his or her decision about the use of contraception may ultimately be.

The paper by Parrish exemplifies these common professional concerns as they were demonstrated in the planning and implementation of the community family planning program in Lincoln Parish, Louisiana. Parrish stresses the importance of political and organizational preparation adequate to ensure community understanding and acceptance as the initial stage of program development; however, once such initial preparation has been achieved, it is the program in action that sustains and promotes the continued recruitment of clients. Parrish describes the careful selection and training of the staff that involved their own personal security about sexual roles, and the ability to convey information and services to clients in ways that were technically correct, yet warm and respectful in tone.

Werley et al. have recognized the need for more precise information about attitudes toward family planning on the part of health professionals. Students and faculty members in schools of medicine, nursing, and social work were surveyed to determine knowledge, attitudes, and opinions regarding family planning and human sexuality. Preliminary findings are reported from data on the nursing student sample. These reveal general attitudes of this group toward family planning that are favorable, but the authors note that the students perceived a lack of material on family planning in the curriculum of schools of nursing. Documentation of knowledge and attitudes of health professionals is essential, since changes both in the structure of family planning programs, and in the types of workers who function in them necessitate ongoing evaluation of service.

The paper by Rosenfield serves to point out the effect of societal change upon professional roles and functions. The demand for health services has in some instances outrun the supply of traditional health professionals to provide them. Rosenfield points out that the creation of paraprofessionals in the health fields has caused a realignment of functions for the traditionally established professional groups. New kinds of health workers are being effectively trained to perform services once only assigned to the physician or the nurse. For example, in many developing countries (and in the United States; see the Ostergard et al. reference by Smith in Part I) responsibility for the insertion of the IUD rests with paraprofessionals. This raises the matter of expanded educational and supervisory functions for the health professions. It also emphasizes the need for imaginative, adaptable approaches to remedying the short supply of health manpower in general.

23 Survey of health professionals regarding family planning

Harriet H. Werley
Joel W. Ager
R. A. Hudson Rosen
Fredericka P. Shea*

As noted earlier in this volume, most of the health professional organizations, through formal policy statements, have recognized a need for positive action to cope with problems related to family planning. They have based such action upon multiple concerns: the consequences for society of rapid population growth, the rights of individuals to family planning information and services, and the possible results on health and quality of life when such information and services are not readily available.

Concomitant with such organizational action, a number of health professionals have taken additional steps. For instance, a numbers of them have conducted studies about family planning education. These studies have been undertaken in schools of nursing, (Houser, Edmands, Eliot, Dickinson, and Dodge, 1969), medicine (Eliot and Houser, 1967; Tietze, Kohl, Best, and Eliot, 1966), and social work (Council on Social Work

Education, 1970). Some of them have pointed up gaps in curricula and confusion about possible family planning roles for health professionals. In addition, conferences and institutes have been held with health professionals to discuss the population issue, the responsibility of the respective professions in relation to services required, and inclusion of family planning content in their various curricula (Edmands, 1970a; Haselkorn, 1968; Hyde and Bloch, 1969; Rapoport, 1968). Also in recent years there have been increasing numbers of articles on the subject of family planning education in the professional literature of the three health-focused fields (Beasley, 1969; Carter, 1966; Edmands, 1970b; Greenblatt, 1972; Haselkorn, 1971; Lief, 1970; Rapoport, 1970).

So far, however, there has been little information available on the extent to which such perspectives have been incorporated into the thinking and behavior of the bulk of individual health professionals, although this is an important area for investigation. Increasing numbers of workers are needed in the area of family planning. The attitudes and perceptions of health professionals as a whole regarding family planning may be significant in determining the availability and acceptability of such services to clients. In a sense, these professionals serve as the "gatekeepers" of family planning services, since they may render direct care, train, and/or supervise workers in this area.

Because of the pivotal position of health professionals in the family planning area,

*Harriet H. Werley, Ph.D., the senior author, is Professor and Director of the Center for Health Research, Wayne State University College of Nursing. Joel Ager, Ph.D., is Associate Professor, Department of Psychology and the Center. R. A. Hudson Rosen, Ph.D., is Research Associate in the Center and is Survey Project Director for the research reported in this paper. F. P. Shea, M.S., is Assistant Professor and Assistant Director of the Center, Detroit, Michigan.

Original article from research supported by Grant NU 416, Division of Nursing, Bureau of Health Manpower Education, National Institutes of Health, U. S. Department of Health, Education, and Welfare, Washington, D. C.

we decided to study their attitudes toward the topic. We selected faculty and students in schools of nursing, medicine, and social work as the first group for investigation, since they underpin the work of practitioners in the field. We hope to study the practitioners as well, however; tentatively, that will be the next phase of our long-range study.

To get data from a large representative sample of subjects from the three professions, we chose the survey approach, using a questionnaire and designing the research to focus on aspects of family planning that are essential in working with clients.

OBJECTIVES

The major objectives of our research were (1) to assess the attitudes of students and faculty in schools of nursing, medicine, and social work about family planning; (2) to identify their perceptions of appropriate professional roles for the delivery of family planning services and some of the factors related to role performance in family planning programs; (3) to assess knowledge about human sexuality and birth control; and (4) to obtain opinions from students and faculty about preparation in the professional schools with respect to family planning. We planned to use these data as baseline information against which change in the future might be measured.

A major focus of the research was a comparison of the three professions on aspects of family planning that might affect counseling of clients. We were interested in how members of the three professions view their own and other health professionals' roles. For example, does the medical student view the role of the social worker differently from the social worker? We also wanted to examine the relations among the variables pertaining to knowledge, attitudes, feelings about roles, and preparation for roles.

In addition, we needed information about curriculum content in the schools, and we planned to examine the curricular variables in relation to the other variables discussed

above. For example, are there differences and, if so, of what kind between students who have had and those who have not had clinical practice in family planning? We planned to examine similar questions for faculty members in the sample.

DESCRIPTION OF THE RESEARCH

We conducted the research by means of a nationwide survey of health professionals (faculty) and preprofessionals (students) in schools of nursing, medicine, and social work on the topic of family planning. The survey was made throughout the country, in a total of 47 schools of nursing, 11 schools of medicine, and 15 schools of social work.

Pilot study

A pilot study involving schools of nursing, medicine, and social work was conducted in the spring and early summer of 1971. We ran it to help in questionnaire revision, as well as to provide some information about optimal means of gaining cooperation in the schools, and to establish some basic procedures for data analysis. As a result of the pilot study, the questionnaires were shortened considerably and many of the items were clarified.

Instrument

As was noted in our discussion of the pilot study, the data were collected by means of pretested, printed questionnaires. To encourage response, the questionnaires were printed in a small booklet form, making them relatively compact and attractive. Six different questionnaires were used; one each for nursing facility, nursing students, medical faculty, medical students, social work faculty, and social work students. The first six sections of each type of questionnaire were identical. The only variation was in the final section of "Curriculum" where certain items were modified to make them profession-specific and faculty/student-specific.

The questionnaires were coded to protect

the anonymity both of the individual respondents and of the participating schools. They were designed so that key punching could be done directly from them.

The topic areas covered by the questionnaires included attitudes, beliefs, and knowledge about sexuality, contraceptives, and family planning; conceptions of professional roles; and curriculum related to sexuality and family planning. Format of items varied. Some sections of the questionnaire had a traditional checklist format. Other sections included Likert type of items, Porter type of scales (1961); and Guttman facet type of items (1958).

General attitudes toward family planning and population. Items in this first section used a six-point forced-choice scale, which omitted the middle "undecided" category (Rosen and Rosen, 1955a). The response alternatives and their coded values were (1) strongly disagree, (2) disagree, (3) disagree more than agree, (4) agree more than disagree, (5) agree, and (6) strongly agree. To maximize information obtained and to minimize number of separate questions needed, we listed several phrases for each item stem. Respondents indicated extent of agreement (or disagreement) for each phrase. An example of an item can be found in Table 4. A total of 73 attitude items was generated. Attitude areas covered by the items included the population problem, family size, birth control, male and female sterilization, abortion, and sex education.

We were interested not only in responses to the individual items but also in the respondents' overall attitude toward family planning and population. Consequently, we used an empirical keying procedure to devise an overall family planning attitude scale. First, a priori scales for both positive and negative attitudes were constructed, based on pooled judgments of the project staff. The individual items were then correlated with both scales. We retained items for the positive scale that correlated .40 or more with the a priori positive scale or less than

−.30 with the a priori negative scale; for the negative scale we retained those negative items that correlated .40 or more with the negative a priori scale or less than −.30 with the a priori positive scale. Scores for the overall family planning scale were obtained by subtracting the score of the negative scale from the score on the positive scale.

Attitudes toward instructional program. We used 10 Porter type of items to assess student and faculty views about a school's instructional program as it related to family planning. The Porter methodology was developed to study management personnel need satisfaction as a framework for understanding work motivation. This type of item takes the format of asking three questions in combination about a particular aspect: (a) How much is there now? (b) How much should there be? (c) How important is this to you? Responses were made on a seven-point scale, with "1" being the "little or none" anchor and "7" the "much" anchor. While Porter used Maslow's (1943) conceptualization of need hierarchy to estimate need satisfaction in industry and in the military (1961, 1962, 1963a, 1963b, 1967), we assessed program satisfaction as it related to instruction about the female and male reproductive systems, human sexuality, contraceptive methods, female and male sterilization, the population-pollution problem, psychological aspects of birth control, problems related to unplanned pregnancies, and counseling of clients. With this format we could compute a difference score $(b-a)$ for each item that could indicate the perceived need for instruction in a certain area, as well as an importance score that could also be used in combination with the difference score $c(b-a)$ to indicate both direction and degree of dissatisfaction with the perceived existing situation.

The Porter format is similar to an earlier design developed by Rosen and Rosen (1955b) that also used a tripartite question format in a study of members' attitudes toward their union. The Rosen design probed each topic under investigation in terms of standards (what should be done), perceptions (what was seen as being done), and evaluations (the feeling about what was seen as being done). The Rosens tested whether such a design would permit new insights into the bases for evaluations. They reasoned that satisfaction and dissatisfaction are related to the extent to which desires are seen as being met and that dissatisfaction will tend to result either when people see an activity carried on to a greater extent than they want or because they perceive too little being done in terms of their desire.

Knowledge of human sexuality and family planning. Sixteen knowledge items that could be answered in terms of "agree," "disagree," or "don't know" were included. These items pertained generally to sexuality and family planning. In addition, respondents were asked to indicate the perceived effectiveness of 11 contraceptive methods on a five-point scale ranging from "ineffective" to "completely effective." A "don't know" column was available for those who felt they lacked knowledge to make a judgment about these methods.

Views of professional roles relating to birth control. We used a facet approach (Guttman, 1958) to assess perceived appropriateness of professional roles in giving birth control information to various types of clients. This type of item is particularly well suited when, from the subject's point of view, the appropriate response would be a function of a number of conditions. The following four facets were used: (1) type of professional worker, (2) type of client, (3) level of birth control service, and (4) client versus professional initiation of service (See Tables 2 and 3). This facet design generated 3 × 3 × 4 × 2 or 72 items; for each, the respondent indicated whether he or she felt the action specified was appropriate or not appropriate.

Background. The background consisted of 20 items. Questions included such characteristics as age, sex, race, religion, marital status, and number of children. In addition, we asked about the number of children respondents expect to have, the number they consider ideal for themselves and for the average American family, and their involvement in community programs related to the population-pollution problem.

Curriculum. In the section on curriculum, nursing students were asked to indicate type of nursing program and year of enrollment. Some of the questions we asked students were the following: In which *courses* have you received information about family planning or birth control? In which *settings* have you had clinical practice in family planning? About how many actual hours of classroom instruction and clinical practice have you had in family planning? Among other questions, faculty were asked to indicate in which content areas they had received instruction in family planning as a student. They were then asked to indicate on a checklist content areas relevant to family planning that they included in their courses and/or clinical instruction.

Target populations

We defined the populations as follows.

Schools. Only schools with the following criteria were selected: those with more than 50 students, within the continental United States, functioning since 1969, and no present plans for closing. Schools utilized in the pilot study were omitted. Sources for sampling were the listings of approved schools by the National League for Nursing (state-approved schools of nursing-RN, 1971), the American Medical Association (Medical education in the United States, 1970), and the Council on Social Work Education (graduate professional schools of social work, 1970).

Students. All students who were enrolled in the professional school were included.

Faculty. All *paid* full-time teaching and student counseling faculty in residence during the fall of 1971 were included. This left out some categories of personnel such as adjunct professors and agency and clinical supervisors.

Sampling

Sampling of the schools was done as follows.

Nursing. The more than 1,300 schools of nursing in the United States were broken down into subcategories for the purpose of more precisely controlling the sampling. The variables on which the breakdown was made were (1) type of program (diploma, associate degree, and baccalaureate degree), (2) religious affiliation (Catholic versus non-Catholic), (3) size of school (over 150 and under 150 student enrollment), and (4) size of community, using Standard Metropolitan Statistical Areas criteria for classifications of over and under 50,000 (Bureau of the Budget, 1967). Because of the small number of schools in some of the possible cells, certain cells were collapsed.

Random sampling of schools was done within the subcategories discussed above and resulted in selection of 47 schools.

To simplify the sampling of students within schools, we took all students, and also all faculty, within a selected school regardless of enrollment. We planned to make adjustments in the analysis for the relatively greater contribution of the larger schools to the sample.

Medical and social work. Sampling was simpler for the medical and social work schools, because there were far fewer schools in the total, and they were less diverse than nursing schools in terms of the variables being considered. Twelve medical schools were randomly selected from the list of non-Catholic schools (90 in all); three of the four Catholic medical schools also were included, for 15 medical schools in all. Similarly, 12 non-Catholic schools of social work were selected randomly from a population of 60 schools. Three Catholic social work schools were selected from the total of seven such schools. The total of social work schools in the sample therefore was 15.

All students and faculty who were part of the population as defined above were included in the sample for both medical and social work schools.

Procedure

The field work phase of the survey began on October 11, 1971. Prior to that date, we contacted a number of schools, first by telephone and then by letter, to obtain cooperation and to work out dates and procedures. Such contact with schools continued through November.

Of the 47 nursing schools in the initial sample, one was unable to participate and was replaced by the first alternate school randomly selected within that cell. The picture with the medical schools was quite different. Of the three Catholic schools, one refused and was replaced with the other Catholic school of medicine. Of the 12 non-Catholic medical schools randomly selected for the sample, six were unable to participate. We approached five alternate schools. Of these, two agreed to cooperate and three refused. At this point, we decided to use only the eight non-Catholic schools that had agreed to participate, because of time demands to complete the project. Thus, 11 medical schools were included in the study. Of the 15 social work schools approached initially, two non-Catholic schools refused and were replaced with the first two alternate schools on the list of randomly selected schools.

Once cooperation from the various schools had been obtained, dates were set up for administration of the questionnaires, and trained data collectors went to each school to conduct the survey. The data collectors had been given a week's orientation about all phases of the research before going into the field.

Across nursing schools sampled, the average response rate was 78% for students and 84% for faculty. Complete data on percentage of questionnaires returned for the medical and social work schools are not yet available. However, at present the average across medical schools was about 56% for students and 42% for faculty. Among social work schools the average rate of response was about 60% for students and 73% for faculty.

PRELIMINARY RESULTS

Because not all the data have been processed as this is written, the results reported here must be limited to a preliminary analysis of selected items. These results will deal only with student responses from the 47 schools of nursing, and primarily with the basic descriptive information as expressed in percentages and means. Similar data will be available later for medical and social work students and faculty, as well as for nursing faculty. In addition, we will make comparisons across professions and between faculty and students within professions.

Further analyses will also include an investigation of relationships among the items and scales, including the curricular and background variables. Correlations or chi-square will be used as appropriate. Also, factor analysis of selected item and scale sets will be done.

Background

It may be useful in understanding the results to have some background about the characteristics of the people in the sample. The 6,333 nursing school students as a group were generally white (93%), women (96%), and between 18 and 25 years old (82%). Most of them were single (76%), although 20% were married. Most of them also had some religious affiliation and activity. Fifty-eight percent described themselves as Protestant, 36% as Catholic, 1% as Jewish, 2% as some other religious classification (such as Moslem, Buddhist), and 3% said that they had no religion. All but 13% attended church at least occasionally, and almost half (48%) attended once a week or more. A quarter (25%) of them were studying for an associate degree, 40%

for a diploma, and a third (34%) for the baccalaureate degree in nursing. One percent were in a graduate nursing program. They were full-time students (96%). A third (33%) were in their first year of the nursing program, and almost a third (30%) in the second year. About a quarter were third-year students (13% in diploma programs and 11% in baccalaureate), 12% were fourth-year baccalaureate students, and 1% were in a fifth-year baccalaureate program.

Attitudes toward instructional program

Let us look first at nursing students' views of their school programs concerning family planning. Table 1 shows the means for their judgments on selected aspects of their programs. Dissatisfaction is operationally defined here in column E in Table 1, that is, the discrepancy between what respondents said should be done and what they said was being done, multiplied by how important they stated such activity was.

Looking at column E, we see that most dissatisfaction occurred with respect to discussion in school programs of psychological aspects of birth control and of problems related to unplanned pregnancies. Although these were not generally considered to be the most important areas of family planning instruction (column C), they were areas of greatest disparity between the students' standards and perceived teaching (column D).

Least dissatisfaction was evident with regard to instruction on female and male reproductive systems (column E), even though these subjects were of maximum importance (column C). Most respondents saw their school programs meeting their standards quite successfully on these topics (column D).

Looking at all items, we can see that school programs tended to be considered most adequate in the basic, clearly defined, and well-understood subject areas. As less clear-cut and more complex material was considered, satisfaction with programs tended to decrease.

Table 1. Means for nursing students on three-part items assessing some aspects of instructional problems relevant to family planning

Item	Content	A (Is now)	B (Should be)	C (Importance)	D= (b—a)	E= c(b—a)
1	Instruction on female reproductive system	5.40	6.48	6.30	1.08	6.80
2	Instruction on male reproductive system	4.98	6.43	6.22	1.44	9.03
3	Instruction on human sexuality	3.56	6.08	6.05	2.52	16.07
4	Instruction on contraceptive methods	3.76	6.20	5.89	2.44	14.95
5	Instruction on sterilization for the woman (tubal ligation)	3.45	5.70	5.13	2.24	12.43
6	Instruction on sterilization for the man (vasectomy)	3.19	5.65	5.06	2.46	13.65
7	Opportunities for students to observe and/or counsel clients in family planning	2.91	5.54	5.40	2.64	15.34
8	Instruction on population-pollution problem as related to family planning	2.93	5.65	5.53	2.72	16.54
9	Discussion of psychological aspects of birth control	3.25	6.13	6.01	2.88	18.15
10	Discussion of problems related to unplanned pregnancies	3.22	6.06	5.78	2.84	17.25

Note: Responses were made on a seven-point scale, with "1" being the "little or none" anchor and "7" the "much" anchor

For all items, dissatisfaction of most respondents sprang from their perception that too little, rather than too much, was being provided. Remedial action, therefore, would need to focus on increasing the scope of family planning instruction in the curriculum, rather than decreasing or discontinuing any existing emphases on it.

It is important to remember, however, that the amount of instruction that respondents saw being given was not the only important consideration. For instance, from column A, we can observe that nursing students saw the least instruction being given with respect to actual practice in, or observation of, counseling on family planning, and on the relation of population-pollution to family planning. Although dissatisfaction was high for these content areas, it was less than for psychological aspects of birth control and for problems of unplanned pregnancies (column E). This was the case both because the former content areas were considered less important than the latter (column C) and because the discrepancy between their own standards and perceived instruction was less for them (column D).

Facets of professional role views

Generally speaking, the facet items on appropriateness of professional role yielded a predicted pattern of results. In Table 2 the levels of each facet are given in the order of judged appropriateness. For example, for the client facet we expected the largest percentage of "appropriate" responses for married women, followed by unmarried women 18 years old or over, and the lowest percentage endorsement for unmarried women under 18 years. It can be seen that, as we move from a higher to a lower level for any given facet, the percentages, for the most part, do indeed decrease.

All four facets seem to make a difference in response (Table 3). The fact that there is a relatively small difference between the

Table 2. Percent of "appropriate" responses for facet combinations for nursing students

	Physician			Nurse			Social worker		
	Married woman	Unmarried woman 18 or over	Unmarried woman under 18	Married woman	Unmarried woman 18 or over	Unmarried woman under 18	Married woman	Unmarried woman 18 or over	Unmarried woman under 18
Client requests									
General information	97	96	94	95	91	83	91	89	80
Specific information	98	96	90	68	64	52	49	48	40
Demonstration of devices	95	91	81	70	60	45	32	29	24
Help in obtaining contraceptives	97	89	76	57	48	54	54	45	31
Professional initiates									
General information	97	95	94	91	89	85	88	87	82
Specific information	94	92	89	65	61	54	50	46	41
Demonstration of devices	89	85	80	59	52	44	30	27	23
Help in obtaining contraceptives	89	83	75	50	42	32	44	38	31

Table 3. Average percent of "appropriate" responses for each level of the four facets for nursing students

Professional	
Physician	90.0
Nurse	62.0
Social worker	49.9
Client	
Married woman	72.8
Unmarried woman 18 or over	68.4
Unmarried woman under 18	60.7
Level of service	
General information	90.2
Specific information	66.5
Demonstration of devices	56.4
Help in obtaining contraceptives	56.3
Initiation	
Client requests	68.8
Professional initiates	65.9

client requests and *professional initiates* levels on the initiation factor, may be due to some ambiguity in the wording of the *professional initiates* items.

The following conclusions can be drawn from Tables 2 and 3. First, although nursing students saw all three professions as having a role to play, physicians were accorded by far the greatest role. Roles of nurses and social workers were restricted in great part to particular but differing kinds of activity; for example, it was viewed as more appropriate for nurses to demonstrate the use of birth control devices than to help clients obtain them. The reverse was true for social workers (Table 2).

For all professions, however, and particularly for the nurses and social workers, conducting a general discussion of family planning was viewed as more appropriate than giving specific information, demonstrating devices, or giving help in obtaining devices. This might be interpreted as a less-than-whole-hearted endorsement of professional roles in family planning, as it is presumably the professionals who would be the most qualified to render the more specific kinds of services.

Table 4. Percent of nursing students who agree or disagree with selected attitude items

Attitude	Disagree	Agree
1. I feel that the population increase is:		
a. the most serious problem facing mankind.	39.6	60.4
b. one of several worldwide problems.	7.5	92.5
c. a problem that has been greatly exaggerated.	77.1	22.9
2. I feel that a couple should:		
a. have as many natural children as they wish.	62.8	37.2
b. have as many natural children as they can support financially.	24.0	76.0
c. have *no more* than two natural children.	62.0	38.0
3. Under certain circumstances, I would aid a client in obtaining an abortion:		
a. if it could be arranged legally.	28.1	71.9
b. even if it had to be illegal.	81.0	19.0
4. Family planning should be an integral part of health counseling.	4.7	95.3
5. Physicians should decide the role of other health professionals in the area of family planning.	57.3	42.7
6. It is appropriate for a nurse to insert an intrauterine device (IUD), either loop or coil, for a client.	79.7	20.3
7. Abortion should be performed to terminate pregnancy:		
a. under no circumstances.	80.5	19.5
b. when bearing a child would be detrimental to the health of the mother.	7.5	92.5
c. to prevent the birth of an illegitimate child.	60.9	39.1
d. whenever a *couple jointly* desires it.	44.7	55.3
e. whenever a *woman* desires it.	57.0	43.0

Attitude	Birth control		Vasectomy		Tubal ligation	
8. Birth control, vasectomy, and tubal ligation should be encouraged:	Disagree	Agree	Disagree	Agree	Disagree	Agree
a. under no circumstances.	91.7	8.3	86.5	13.5	87.3	12.7
b. when prevention of conception is desired for *health* reasons.	2.8	97.2	10.4	89.6	7.5	92.5
c. when prevention of conception is desired for *economic* reasons.	7.7	92.3	21.6	78.4	25.4	74.6
d. when prevention of conception is desired for *any* reason.	19.0	81.0	35.3	64.7	41.0	59.0
e. among people in general to restrict population growth.	27.6	72.4	48.9	51.1	54.3	45.7

Turning to type of client, it is clear that age and marital status make a considerable difference in how appropriate professional birth control assistance was judged to be. The widest range of services was considered appropriate for married adults, as expected. However, the greatest need for birth control is considered by many to be among sexually active teen-agers, the group for whom nursing students felt the provision of such services was least appropriate.

Such findings have practical implications for questionnaire design. That is, attitude questions that do not spell out contingencies are limited in the information they yield. For example, responses to the question "Does nursing have a role to play in family planning" would give us no information as to the perceived nature of the role or the conditions under which it is viewed as appropriate.

General attitudes toward family planning and population

Results for selected items are given in Table 4. The six-point response categories have been collapsed into "disagree" and "agree" percentages, for simplicity, since variations within these two types of responses are not discussed in this chapter. Also the wording of items in the table has been altered from that in the questionnaire when necessary for clarity.

Clearly, nursing students as a whole, as represented by the sample studied, thought that population growth was a serious problem, although almost a quarter of them indicated that it has been exaggerated (question 1). They were not sufficiently disturbed by the implications of such growth, however, to feel that the zero population growth philosophy is necessary; that is, almost two thirds of them disagreed with the proposition that couples should have no more than two natural children (question 2). Also, only about half of them supported such measures as sterilization in order to restrict population growth (question 8e), although nearly three fourths of them felt that birth control should be encouraged for that purpose. Possibly a concern for individual rights underlay their hesitancy to generalize with respect to behaviors that might infringe on such rights.

There is no doubt about the nursing students' favorability toward family planning and birth control in general. The majority saw family planning as an integral part of health counseling (question 4). And looking at question 8, we can see that most of them felt birth control should be encouraged when prevention of conception is desired for any reason. Less than 10% of them were opposed to any encouragement of birth control. In the student's view, however, the most important bases for any type of fertility regulation were, first, health needs and, second, economic needs. This is especially clear when one examines their responses to questions about male and female sterilization, as well as question 7 on abortion. They had much more stringent limitations on the appropriateness of these actions than on other forms of birth control, but generally

supported them when necessary for health and, to a lesser degree, for economic reasons. Although not explicit, it is probable that the "certain circumstances" being considered by the nursing students in question 3 were health, or possibly financial, reasons. The importance of financial factors is also evident in question 2b, where slightly more than three fourths of them agreed that couples should have as many children as they could support financially.

We perhaps should note briefly some items that focused on nursing roles in family planning. Most of these students did not think that it was appropriate for a nurse to insert an IUD for a client (question 6), and a sizable proportion of them deferred to physicians' decisions on what the nursing role in family planning should be (question 5). These judgments of the nursing students were compatible with their answers about roles as discussed previously and shown in Tables 2 and 3.

SUMMARY AND CONCLUSIONS

Basic questions asked by the survey may be summarized as follows:

1. How favorable are the general attitudes of professionals and preprofessionals in nursing, medicine, and social work toward family planning? What are the bases for their attitudes?
2. What roles do they believe the various professions should assume in the delivery of family planning services?
3. How satisfied are they with the amount of instruction related to sexuality and family planning in their school programs?
4. How much classroom instruction and clinical experience do the students say they actually receive in the areas of family planning, birth control methods, and human sexuality?
5. How much knowledge do they have about selected items in the areas of sexuality, family planning, and effectiveness of various contraceptive methods?

Further, we were interested in differences between faculty and students, and among the three professions on these variables. Finally, we were interested in the extent to which attitudes toward family planning, satisfaction with curriculum, knowledge, and perceived roles are correlated with each other and with demographic and biographic variables.

Preliminary results for the nursing student sample suggest answers to some of the above questions. General attitudes of the nursing student group toward family planning were favorable. The attitudes toward abortion, however, depended heavily on particular circumstances, such as the reason for the abortion and whether it was legal. Although it was believed that all three professions have a role to play in family planning, again the views on specific roles depended on a number of conditions, among which were type of professional person, type of client, and type of service to be rendered. In so far as satisfaction with curriculum is concerned, students generally felt that not enough instruction was given in all areas covered, particularly in those dealing specifically with family planning.

Many of the problems related to the quality of life in today's world grow out of the numbers of people. Family planning services are, therefore, vital services for humanity from the standpoint of child spacing and limiting family size. The professionals who provide or direct these services, or who train others to do so, make a contribution toward resolving some of society's problems. If we are to learn how we may best meet society's needs in a specific area, we must periodically assess how we are doing in that area, with respect to both service and preparation of individuals to provide the required services. Through this national survey we attempted to do the latter; that is, we looked at factors related to preparing health professionals for service in the area of family planning. Once all the data are analyzed for the three professions (nursing,

medicine, social work), we will be able to share student and faculty findings with respect to the topic of family planning. We trust that these findings will be helpful to educators throughout the country, as well as to others working in the area of family planning.

REFERENCES

Beasley, J. D.: A medical educator's point of view. In Hyde, H., and Bloch, L. S., editors: Family planning and medical education, J. Med. Educ. 44(part 2, special issue), 1969.

Bureau of the Budget: Standard metropolitan statistical areas, 1967. Washington, D. C., 1967, United States Government Printing Office.

Carter, D. M.: Family planning in nursing education, Nurs. Outlook 14(1):62-64, 1966.

Council on Social Work Education. Summary of current status of education for social workers in family planning. Appendix II to background papers for Conference on Social Work Education, Population, and Family Planning, Honolulu, March 1970.

Edmands, E. M.: A report on the first national family planning conference for nurse educators in baccalaureate schools of nursing. Chapel Hill, Carolina Population Center, Univeristy of North Carolina, 1970, University of North Carolina Press. (a)

Edmands, E. M.: Nursing. In Calderone, M. S., editor: Manual of family planning and contraceptive practice, ed. 2, Baltimore, 1970, The Williams & Wilkins Co. (b)

Eliot, J. W., and Houser, C. A.: Teaching about human reproduction, sexuality, and family planning in 26 middle North American medical schools, Ann Arbor, Michigan: Report prepared for the Fourth Regional Macy Foundation Conference, mimeographed paper, 1967.

Graduate professional schools of social work. New York, 1970, Council on Social Work Education.

Greenblatt, B.: Family planning goals and social work roles. Family Planning Perspect 4(1):54-59, 1972.

Guttman, L.: What lies ahead for factor analysis? Educ. Psychol. Measurement 18:497-515, 1958.

Haselkorn, F., editor: Family planning: The role of social work, Garden City, N. Y., 1968, Adelphi University Press.

Haselkorn, F., editor: Family planning: Readings and case materials, New York, 1971, Council on Social Work Education.

Houser, C. A., Edmands, E. M., Eliot, J. W., Dickinson, K. S., and Dodge, M.: The teaching of fertility regulation in basic schools of nursing in the United States, Amer. J. Public Health 59: 982-995, 1969.

Hyde, H., and Bloch, L. S., editors: Family planning and medical education, J. Med. Educ. 44 (part 2, special issue):11, 1969.

Lief, H. I.: New developments in the sex education of the physician, J. Amer. Med. Ass. 212: 1864-1867, 1970.

Maslow, A. H.: A theory of human motivation, Psychol. Rev. 50:370-396, 1943.

Medical education in the United States, J. Amer. Med. Ass. 214:1483-1549, 1970.

Porter, L. W.: A study of perceived need satisfactions in bottom and middle management jobs, J. Appl. Psychol. 45:1-10, 1961.

Porter, L. W.: Job attitudes in management: I. Perceived deficiencies in need fulfillment as a function of job level, J. Appl. Psychol. 46:375-384, 1962.

Porter, L. W.: Job attitudes in management: II. Perceived importance of needs as a function of job level, J. Appl. Psychol. 47:141-148, 1963. (a)

Porter, L. W.: Job attitudes in management: III. Perceived deficiencies in need fulfillment as a function of line versus staff type of job, J. Appl. Psychol. 47:267-275, 1963. (b)

Porter, L. W., and Mitchell, V. F.: Comparative study of need satisfactions in military and business hierarchies, J. Appl. Psychol. 51:139-144, 1967.

Rapoport, L.: The social work role in family planning. In Haselkorn, F., editor: *Family planning: The role of social work,* Garden City, N. Y., 1968, Adelphi University Press.

Rapoport, L.: Education and training of social workers for roles and functions in family planning, J. Educ. Social Work 6(2):27-38, 1970.

Rosen, H., and Rosen, R. A. H.: The validity of "undecided" answers in questionnaire responses, J. Appl. Psychol. 39:178-181, 1955. (a)

Rosen, R. A. H., and Rosen, H.: A suggsted modification in job satisfaction surveys, Personal Psychol. 8:303-314, 1955. (b)

State-approved schools of nursing—RN, ed. 29, New York, 1971, National League for Nursing.

Tietze, C., Kohl, S., Best, S., and Eliot, J.: Teaching of fertility regulation in medical schools. J. Amer. Med. Ass. 196:20-24, 1966.

24 Nursing

Elisabeth M. Edmands

A nurse with a good sense of values is able to cope with the fact that the inconceivable of one age becomes the commonplace of the next.[1]

In the very brief time during which family planning programs have become active, nurses in the United States and throughout the world have been called upon to adapt their basic knowledge for taking an active part in the educational and service aspects of these programs. In many areas this has been a natural outgrowth of their work with women in the childbearing years. In others, it has required a new awareness of the relation of family planning to comprehensive health care for individuals and families.

Perhaps no other health profession has quite the same opportunity for disseminating knowledge of family planning. The nurse is everywhere—in hospitals, clinics, schools, industry, health departments, private physicians' offices, and private homes, and also as a citizen in her own community. She knows the problems of affluence and the frustrations of poverty. By tradition she has been one to whom people turn in times of stress. Quality nursing skills which are given with warmth and compassion have been the stated goals of her profession. In the era of emphasis on preventive medicine, new elements have been added to her responsibilities: she has had to become an educator, a case finder, a counselor, a supporter, and an implementer of programs designed to strengthen the health of the people. She seeks out those in need, informs them of services available, provides basic knowledge, refers them for care, interprets and explains

Reprinted from Calderone, Mary S., editor: *Manual of Family Planning and Contraceptive Practice*, ed. 2, Baltimore, 1970, The Williams & Wilkins Co., pp. 53-61.

physicians' orders, and assists in carrying out their treatments. No nurse, whether in the hospital, the health department, or the community, can fail to observe the relationship between physical health and emotional and social welfare. There is no nurse who has not at some time cared for a woman who either did not want to be pregnant or for whom it was a medical or social tragedy; such nurses are fully aware that the products of these pregnancies, the unwanted children, frequently have—and present—more than their share of problems.

OPPORTUNITIES AND RESPONSIBILITIES
Case finding

Much has been written about the components of good maternal health services—premarital medical examination and counseling, preconception evaluation, prenatal care, delivery and intrapartum care, postpartum care, and family planning. Many private physicians and modern hospitals are cognizant of the interrelatedness of these components and, if they cannot provide all of these services themselves, will refer patients to competent resources for them. This means that all professionals responsible for maternity care must be in constant communication with women who are potential recipients of family planning advice and must advise them about available resources for services. In maternal health programs, nurses have multiple opportunities to find the opportune time for initiating discussion, to determine the readiness and the knowledge levels of patient, and to correlate their teaching with that of the physician or other health workers who are in contact with the patients.

One study[2] found that physicians and nurses were reluctant to initiate the subject of family planning for fear of offending the patient. A study[3] in another location queried mothers about their opinion of who should initiate the subject; overwhelmingly, their answers (92 per cent of 181 women) were that physicians and nurses should bring it up because most women were shy and embarrassed and there were many who did not even know enough to ask. Fortunately, although there is less and less reticence on the part of both professional worker and patient in approaching the subject, many nurses ask for guidelines. This prompted one nursing consultant in a large state health department to set up a series of in-service classes on interviewing for family planning. She found that nurses needed an appropriate vocabulary, communication adapted to the patient's level of understanding, and practical information useful to the individual. There are many approaches that are natural and can be adapted to the situation at hand. During the prenatal period information can be included in a general conversation about many kinds of planning—for medical care, for delivery, for the baby's return home, and for the ultimate number and spacing of children.

Experience has shown that the period after delivery but before the mother leaves the hospital has been one of the most productive for sensitizing patients to family planning. When the hospital stay is short, this must be done within 1 or 2 days, but opportunities present themselves to the nurse when caring for the mother or admiring the baby, or when the husband visits. In addition to bringing up the subject, the nurse can discuss and display the various methods available, point out the health benefits of a suitable period of time between pregnancies, and ensure that the couple has the means and knowledge to follow through on whatever plans the hospital or physician has provided for postpartum and family planning care. In many hospitals this is also in-corporated into a group teaching session on mother and baby care before the mother is discharged. Some physicians, feeling that it is not wise to wait for the postpartum visit, give patients an interim method or insert an intrauterine device before discharge. Whatever the means, it is the nurse who has the responsibility to ensure that the patient understands and has some place to turn to when she has any difficulty.

The pediatrician's office and the well baby clinic are other places where family planning information can be offered, because, when the mother is giving major effort to cope with a new baby, she is highly motivated to wait for her next one.

As important as are the traditional maternal and child health services for case finding, other programs also need to include this information and make resources available; if a parent has cancer, heart disease, mental illness, tuberculosis, venereal disease, or other disabling conditions, the postponement of pregnancy can be as important to his progress as medical treatment is. Because a community public health nursing program is family centered, the nurse can find many opportunities to offer information about family planning as she evaluates the total needs of the families she visits.

Nursing care and counseling in the family planning clinic visit

One of the most critical points of contact for a patient is the first person whom she meets on her first family planning clinic visit, when attitudes and behavior set the stage for acceptance or rejection, comprehension, and the feeling that someone cares about her as an individual. For the nurse to greet each patient before she is registered may not be feasible in busy overloaded clinics, but the nurse can at least see that this first contact is a warm and meaningful one.

Patients making their initial visit for family planning services are embarking on an educational experience. Some who come well prepared will need little more than encouragement and reassurance from the nurse, but others will come with little knowledge and considerable discomfort or apprehension. In the first interview with such a patient, the nurse can evaluate her knowledge and her cultural, ethnic, and religious values and try to judge her degree of motivation. At this time she may need to give basic information about the physical and emotional aspects of reproductive physiology in suitable terms easily understood by the patient. Often, too, the nurse can skillfully supply the words that patients need to enable them to ask their questions, as well as the reassurance that it is all right to ask them. This is also the time for presenting information to enable the patient to make a choice of contraceptives, clearing up points of misunderstanding, and explaining the clinic procedures.[4] Next can come a group session with new patients, conducted by nurse, health educator, or social worker, or sometimes by lay workers under good supervision. Group sessions are valuable for communicating knowledge to a large number of people in a short period of time, exposing patients to others interested in planning their families, and helping the shy or reticent woman to have her questions asked and answered by others without revealing her own lack of knowledge.

Discussion of the need for pelvic examination also falls within the responsibility of the nurse. Although patients may already have experienced this in connection with delivery, there may be some who do not understand why it is necessary. Explanation about the pelvic examination should also include information about the Papanicolaou smear, since, unless the patients understand the purposes of such procedures, they often conclude that their chosen method of contraception may produce cancer or other diseases. During the examination, the nurse, in addition to supervising the arrangements and assisting the physician, also listens for communication between the physician and the patient, so that she can later interpret and reinforce his instructions.

After the educational process, laboratory work, medical counseling, and physical examination are concluded and the patient has chosen her contraceptive, most clinics provide for an exit interview with the nurse, during which the nurse can review all that has happened since the patient entered the clinic. Instructions should be clarified and amplified when necessary, provision should be made for follow up, and supplies should be given.

When possible, a postclinic conference between physician and nurses is valuable for review of patients seen that day; such discussion should also be related to the need for follow up or referral of patients.

Follow-up responsibilities for the nurse

Intervals for follow up may be governed by such factors as the number of professional personnel available, the resources of hospital and clinic, the type of contraceptives chosen, the distance a patient must travel to return, or other variables. Some clinics provide for a routine follow-up clinic visit after the first one or for a home visit by the family planning clinic nurse, the public health nurse, or supervised indigenous personnel, the purpose being to help the patient before she has encountered serious difficulties. Many clinics provide a "hot-line" telephone service available 24 hours a day including weekends. Although this may be manned by a lay worker provided with pertinent data about each patient, the important aspect of this service is to have professional assistance continually available. Some have estimated that 60 per cent of such calls can be handled by a well trained lay worker and 30 per cent by the nursing staff, leaving only 10 per cent for medical referral.

Follow-up home visits should also be made to patients who fail to keep clinic appointments, since, if a patient is motivated enough to come in for a first visit, there is usually some good reason for her failure to keep the second or third appointment; such a reason may be far removed from family planning, for example, transportation, baby-sitting costs, inconvenient clinic hours, objection of husbands or other family members, or disapproval by peers. A reason related to the medical aspects of family planning may be fear caused by such complications as bleeding, nausea, vomiting, weight gain, and chloasma. The benefits of finding out why a patient has not returned are three-fold: first, serious medical complications may be averted; second, the clinic may need to change some of its procedures or methods; and third, the patient is made to feel that someone is genuinely interested in her welfare. In any case she should not be made to feel guilty, delinquent, or uncooperative.

Sensitive areas and controversial issues

With the explosion of new knowledge, new ideas, and changing concepts, subjects once taboo are becoming acceptable for open discussion. Traditional procedures are demanding reassessment to meet the demands of today's realities. Nurses encounter such challenges in all aspects of their service, with nursing in family planning standing as a primary example.

Religious concerns dominated the medical picture at the beginning of this decade, not only in the United States but in many Catholic countries abroad. A Catholic nursing sister, however, stated: "Definition of the nurse's role can be the same for all nurses regardless of their religion. All religions favor responsible parenthood, solidarity of the home and family, and the health and welfare of family members."[5] Another nurse writing on the religious aspects of family planning stated that "it is not the nurse's role to make the decision to use or not use a contraceptive, nor is it her decision regarding which method is chosen. That decision belongs to the patient."[1] A nurse, however, has the responsibility to share public knowledge in the matter of fertility regulation;

she may open up the topic in general terms when circumstances make it apparent that some method of family planning is needed and she may act in a subordinate role to the doctor by assisting him in the fitting of contraceptive devices and giving instructions under his direction. She may also inquire about how the patient is getting along with a particular method.[6] By putting the patient's needs first, all nurses can, in good conscience, truly serve the needs of family planning.

The problem of illegitimacy has been increasing rapidly within the last few years. Some nurses find it difficult to give impartial care to the unwed mother, who may, nevertheless, be most greatly in need of kindness, understanding, and acceptance as a human being; under such circumstances nurses may also find it difficult to give explicit instructions for the care of the mother and her baby. Some nurses find it even more difficult to accept the unwed mother's need for contraception. In an effort to turn the tide of illegitimate pregnancy, efforts are being made in some areas to provide contraceptive services to the sexually active, nulliparous adolescent, and such programs are meeting with resistance from some nurses who wonder whether such a policy may aid in promoting promiscuity or a complete breakdown in sexual prohibitions. If the nurse will reexamine her role in the light of her professional training, she can see that this decision also is not hers. Her decision can be determined in relation to the health needs of each individual; on this premise she should be able to operate.

Indications for sterilization are closely allied with family planning programs and cultural and religious factors play dominant roles in this area as they also do in contemporary efforts to change abortion laws. Hospital policies and state laws govern such procedures in most instances and the decisions to participate or not in such surgery is generally left to the individual.

A number of procedures which were

formerly considered to lie only within the competence of the physician are now being opened up to nurses. Vaginal examinations, Papanicolaou smears, and intrauterine device insertions are among those that nurse-midwives in this country and abroad have been doing for a number of years. In view of the relatively small number of well prepared nurse-midwives and the magnitude of the need for such services in urban and in rural areas, the questions now being raised are whether the nurse can safely perform these procedures and whether it is appropriate that she do so; these questions raise a number of issues to be resolved. Some physician groups believe that this is safe practice provided that it is carried out under medical direction. Some nursing groups agree, but others feel that this is outside the responsibility of nursing and should not be attempted. A few small studies have shown that the nurse-midwife has performed these functions efficiently and without danger,[7] but to date no study has been done in this country using nurses without midwife preparation. In other regions of the world where nursing personnel are extremely limited, experimental programs are under way, teaching young women with a high school education and about 1 year of preparation to do these procedures. A study of 111 baccalaureate nursing education programs showed that instructors of maternity nursing were seriously concerned as to whether to teach skills in rectal and vaginal examinations, and only 9 of them were doing so, all giving such reasons as: "The nurse is expected to do this as a graduate" and "to understand the progress of labor." One instructor reported that her faculty was convinced that vaginal examinations will become a nursing function and thus will have to be added to the nursing curriculum.[8]

In many family planning programs a new category of personnel has been introduced: indigenous workers brought in for training and supervision. In many areas the responsibility for their training has fallen on the nursing service. Depending on the quality of selection and the training of these workers and on administrative structure and supervision, some such programs have been extremely successful. These workers are used in case finding, clinic activities, and follow-up. The "satisfied user" of contraceptives has been very successful in such work because she can talk with her neighbors and her peers from personal experience. Some public health nurses are challenging this role and see it as an interference with their ongoing relationship with families in the community. Other nurses see it as an extension of nursing care to a group of people who might otherwise be inaccessible to them.

Such contemporary issues directly concern the nursing profession. Although some guidelines will be derived from research findings, others will remain controversial because of their complexity.

Nursing in interdisciplinary action

Because of the heavy involvement of nursing in the educational and service aspects of family planning, it is imperative that nursing representation be included from the beginning in program planning committees. Hospital-based nurses contribute knowledge of inpatient and outpatient services, of numbers and backgrounds of nursing personnel needed to staff clinics, and of opportunities available for integration of family planning counseling into other hospital services. Public health nurses contribute awareness of local resources or problems in the community, experience with interagency referral systems, and often know key people in health and social welfare programs, as well as the cultural, ethnic, and religious influences in the community. Nurses can contribute as objectives are defined, policy is determined, target populations are identified, staffing needs are discussed, and educational and service programs are created.

Equally important to *planning* is *program evaluation.* Frequently it is the nurse who knows community reaction, *i.e.,* reasons why programs do or do not go well. Often she senses lack of communication and suggests new approaches. Perhaps the problems are timing and location of clinic services, lack of transportation, or unfavorable rumors spreading throughout the community. Although nursing representatives on such planning and evaluation committees should come from the administrative levels of local nursing services, some means should be found to enable nurses at the clinic or public health district levels to contribute by communicating the practical everyday problems that they encounter.

The growth and development of nursing attitudes

Underlying all activities and functions of a nurse in family planning are her attitudes toward the role of women in society and her awareness and acceptance of her own sexuality and her environment as well as of the environment in which she works. Her early environment and later her peer groups, school companions, and teachers will influence her awareness and changing ideas. Today many students are married before they enter schools of nursing and thus they may bring this experience to their early basic education in nursing. Nevertheless, even in this free society where social experiences have been accelerated, many nursing students experience shock in relation to some aspects of patient care, sometimes in relation to obstetrical and gynecological services. Wise teachers try to anticipate such confrontations with the realities of life.

Ideally, the nurse who works in a family planning program or who recruits patients for it is visualized as a warm sensitive person who can approach all areas of discussion of the reproductive process with ease, lack of embarrassment, empathy, and understanding of the patient's needs and right to information. Realistically, each nurse brings the flavor of her personality, her beliefs, her experience, and her skills to the task at hand. She can also bring negative attitudes which, however, can be modified by reading, purposeful discussion, thought processes, and life experiences shared with peers. Even if deep-seated basic attitudes are not changed, a nurse can be helped to recognize her own biases, to evaluate her opinions, and to adapt her behavior in a professionally appropriate manner so that her capacity to serve will not be inhibited. Through in-service education, case conferences, and expert guidance from her supervisor, each nurse can find opportunities for personal growth. The profession of nursing draws from many sources—medicine, psychology, social sciences, and others. Nursing research develops information, insights, and materials.

Guided by her desire to provide the best possible care to the patient for whom she is responsible, as well as by the patient's right to have confidence in those who care for her, the nurse, through her skills, knowledge, training, and understanding, will make an effective contribution to family planning programs wherever they are found. More effective and acceptable methods of contraception and new understanding of family interaction, of the relationship of health to socioeconomic development, and of many other factors will enable the nurse to increase her capacity to serve.

REFERENCES

1. Chesterman, H. The public health nurse and family planning. Nurs. Outlook, **12**:32, 1964.
2. Siegel, E., and Dillehay, R. C. Some approaches to family planning counseling in local health departments: a survey of public health nurses and physicians. Amer. J. Public Health, **56**:1840, 1966.
3. Edmands, E. M. A study of contraceptive practices in a selected group of urban Negro mothers in Baltimore. Amer. J. Public Health, **58**:263, 1968.
4. Manisoff, M. T. Counseling for family planning. Amer. J. Nurs., **66**:2671, 1966.
5. Sister Mary Helen. Family planning within the curriculum. Nurs. Otulook, **15**:42, 1967.
6. Avellar, G. R. Nurses, family planning and conscience. The Catholic Nurse, **14**:38, 1966.
7. Beasley, W. B. R. The nurse-midwife as a mediator of contraception. Amer. J. Obstet. Gynec., **98**:201, 1967.
8. Simmons, M. P. Is this maternity nursing? Nurs. Outlook, **14**:66, 1966.

25

The physician's influence on the nonacceptance of birth control

Sanford R. Wolfe, M.D.*
Elsie L. Ferguson, Ph.D.

Increasingly, in recent years, money and effort have been expended in developing newer and more effective contraceptive agents and in attempting to make these agents more available to patients. With the growing knowledge and interest in the field of population, much attention has gone into the demography of contraceptive usage; scant data, however, have been gathered on the interpersonal transactions between doctor and patient which very often determine whether the subject of birth control will be brought up at all, and if so, whether it will be accepted.

Clinical experience during psychological evaluation has impressed upon us the marked degree to which the physician's attitude, whether positive or negative, can influence the patient's decision to adopt a contraceptive method.

The observations gathered in this pilot study are from two sources: (1) observations of transactions between doctors and patients in the Prenatal Clinic of a large metropolitan hospital, together with frequent "spot" interviews of these same patients (toward the end of this pilot study,

*From the Department of Psychiatry, Psychiatric Liaison Service, Department of Gynecology and Obstetrics, Johns Hopkins University School of Medicine.

Reprinted from *American Journal of Obstetrics and Gynecology* 104(5):752-757, July 1, 1969. Copyright The C. V. Mosby Company.

a series of 12 intensive interviews of randomly selected prenatal patients were tape-recorded and analyzed) and (2) the records and follow-ups of over 300 clinical psychiatric interviews conducted on obstetric and gynecologic clinic patients over the past 2 years in the same hospital.

The patients served by this prenatal clinic are largely from the Baltimore inner city area, and the vast majority are from the lower socioeconomic classes. Approximately three quarters of the clinic patients are Negro.

REVIEW OF PREVIOUS NOTED PHYSICIAN INFLUENCES

This report deals only with those subtle factors, nearly all unconscious, which operate seemingly outside of the physician's awareness. There are, of course, very definite, overt instances in which the physician's beliefs and his professional manner contribute strongly to the patient's nonusage of contraception. In these cases, it is nearly always the personal religious or moral beliefs of the physician that give rise to this behavior. Reports of religious attitudes[1,2] entering into the doctor-patient relationship in the context of contraceptive usage show a wide variation ranging from the straightforward opposition to birth control of some hospital boards to an instance of a nurse sabotaging contraceptive prescriptions. The relationship of the religious and moral beliefs of the physician and the resultant behavior in regard to the prescription of birth control methods is usually conscious and will not be dealt with in this study.

Lehfeldt and Guze[3] have noted the difficulties that may be involved in the transmission of birth control information from doctor to patient. "The physician's manner of dealing with the patient may also be a subtle component in contributing to failure. Thus, the hostile physician may arouse infantile resentment on the part of the patient."

Van Emde Boas[4] studied five Dutch birth control clinics serving identical populations and correlated a higher failure rate at certain clinics with a tendency to prescribe diaphragm sizes that differed from the other clinics. He concluded an iatrogenic factor leading to this higher failure rate.

Bakker and Dightman[5] have described the "ambivalence" with which physicians approach birth control. They surveyed a cross section of general practitioners and specialists in obstetrics and gynecology as to their adequacy of training concerning birth control. Their conclusion was that medical schools and internship programs have not responded to the necessity of teaching birth control, and only obstetric-gynecologic residency programs seemed adequate in this respect. The authors also surveyed 100 women who were utilizing oral contraceptives as to their perception of the doctor's helpfulness in prescribing and furnishing information on birth control. Of the total women surveyed, only 3 per cent felt that they had received their most useful information on birth control from a physician, as opposed to other sources. It was the conclusion of the study that these findings represented the "ambivalence" with which most of the medical profession approached birth control.

The conclusions reached in the above study[5] may be open to some dispute; it was conducted prior to 1964, and it is likely that many of the physicians that were surveyed were educated at a time when the more effective birth control devices were not yet widely available. At that time, birth control was much less the physician's than the patient's concern. Recent studies[6,7] have revealed that medical students' knowledge of normal as well as abnormal sexuality is very often deficient. It may be that the "ambivalence" toward birth control that Bakker and Dightman refer to is part of a larger uncertainty toward human sexuality due to the inadequate teaching of that subject in most medical schools.

In a descriptive study of birth control practices among the poor, Rainwater and Weinstein[8] described many instances in which both sexual intercourse and contraception were exploited by both husbands and wives in their interpersonal struggles. In the interactions that are described, one or both partner's fear of pregnancy is utilized to punish, reward, or otherwise manipulate the marital partner for some desired end. This study also illustrates many instances where distortions and unreal fears concerning contraception may be perpetuated through a lack of communication between a middle-class physician and a lower-class, and often uneducated, patient.

RESULTS

The analysis of the observed and recorded data as it pertained to the physician's role in birth control revealed the following repetitive patterns in which the patient's resistance to birth control seemed to be increased by the interaction with the physician. In nearly all cases the physician was unaware of his contribution to this resistance.

1. Certain physicians, and ironically often those motivated by their understanding of the importance of birth control to the patient's mental and physical health, tend to be overenthusiastic and somewhat authoritarian in urging some birth control method on the patient. The clinic population is accustomed to being told what to do by a great many people in the community. Between workers from various agencies, bill collectors, and unannounced "welfare in-

spections," these patients undergo a great deal of intrusion into their lives, and as a result are often suspicious of anyone with a specific message to give or a cause to proselytize. They may wonder why the physician is so enthusiastic over a particular method and many find it difficult to conceptualize why such enthusiasm is generated in convincing such unimportant people as themselves.

2. We have encountered instances where the patients were alienated from the idea of birth control when, on discussing the matter, the undertone of the conversation conveyed to the patient the advisability of contraceptive usage because of broad social needs—such as the need to control the world's population problem. Clinic patients seldom think in global perspectives. When birth control information is couched in the phraseology of a broad social problem, it is difficult for the patient to identify this issue with their own personal lives. Also, the patient may see the physician as being more interested in the social problem than in her as a person.

3. Misunderstanding often takes place when the physician waits for the patient to bring up the subject of birth control; the physician may feel that if the topic is not raised, it is a sign that the patient understands it. Herndon and Nash[9] found that only 11 per cent of the physicians in their survey routinely discussed contraception 6 weeks post partum. Contrary to general belief, these patients are usually much more modest in matters relating to sexual affairs than their middle-class sisters and may be timid in discussing such subjects. Also, their passive nature and tendency to avoid any possible conflict with the powerful physician figure may lead them to discuss only topics that the physician has mentioned.

In interviewing a sample of low-income Negro women in the Baltimore inner city, Edmands[10] poses the question: "Do you think that doctors and nurses should wait until mothers ask them about birth control before they talk about it?" Only 2.4 per cent of the sample indicated that doctors and nurses should wait until asked by mothers before initiating birth control information. The dominant reason given by the women in explaining this view was embarrassment or fear. In response to a similar question, Rainwater[11] found that patients from all socioeconomic classes, but especially those from the lower classes, agreed that the physician should volunteer family planning information to his patients. Embarrassment was again given as the reason.

4. Stemming from an attitude of earlier times, and usually in regard to condoms, patients may think of contraceptive devices as illicit and dirty; it is easier to deal with this factor if it is alluded to and discussed by the physician. The sale of condoms in shabby places, in coin dispensers and at low price, conflicts with the value system of the lower class person, which questions the possible effectiveness of cheap things. This factor was alluded to by a number of patients; one patient at a time of minor conflict over the use of a condom by her boyfriend, told him to remove it because she felt that "anything that cheap couldn't be much good." For some patients, the condom may be the optimal method of contraception. In these instances, its use should be supported. Many physicians, however, quickly relegate the condom to an unimportant level and concentrate their conversation on "more sophisticated" contraceptive methods.

5. The incidence of gonorrhea among the teen-age population is high and is increasing rapidly. It is interesting to note that many patients, during episodes of gonorrhea occurring in adolescence, were taken aside at the time of diagnosis by their physician, and in a well-meaning way were lectured on the dangers of becoming sterile from gonorrhea. A surprisingly large number of the women grew up wondering whether they could become pregnant. In 3 of the 12 intensive interviews, the patients considered themselves unable to become pregnant due to an earlier gonorrhea infection and were quite

surprised when the signs of pregnancy became evident. It is impossible, of course, to note what the physician actually said at this time, but in the patients' perception they believed themselves to be sterile and thus no longer in need of birth control.

6. In a number of the psychiatric interviews of obstetric and gynecologic patients, and in one of the prenatal intensive interviews, the patient related a history of a genital injury at an early age; this was usually ruptured hymen due to trauma. In these cases, especially if bleeding occurred, the patients often incorporated the idea that they would be unable to have children in the future. One patient that was interviewed intensively related her self-concept as "sterile" to the memory of a conversation that occurred at the time of early genital trauma between the attending physician and her mother; in this conversation the physician had said that it was likely that the patient might not have children later on in life.

COMMENT

It is very important that the discussion of birth control between the clinic patient and her doctor be a meaningful one. There are a number of reasons. First, and foremost, this population usually has no other place to turn. In most inner city hospitals, the population is increasingly Negro as well as poor. These mothers must depend upon the clinics of voluntary hospitals and upon municipal hospitals for both childbearing and birth control advice. Hill and Jaffe[12] have noted that the majority of nonwhite mothers do not have ready access to private physicians in the childbearing period. A study in New York City[13] showed that 82 per cent of married nonwhites, compared to 14.5 per cent of white mothers, between 1955 and 1959 were delivered of their babies in municipal hospitals or in the ward services of voluntary hospitals. A study done in Washington, D. C., in 1961[14] showed that 75 per cent of nonwhite births were staff cases. A report of the Obstetrical Statistical Cooperative[15] based on 66,000 discharges at 20

major hospitals from New York to San Francisco showed that nearly 94 per cent of nonwhite deliveries were on ward services compared to 35 per cent of whites. Rainwater[11] has noted that while lower socioeconomic class white women may use general practitioners or the clinic services of voluntary hospitals, the majority of similar Negro women tend to be the passive recipients of birth control advice in municipal hospital clinics.

In dealing with obstetric patients in a public municipal hospital or on the ward service of a voluntary hospital, a number of factors are introduced which make the transactions in the doctor-patient relationship differ from those in the relationship of a doctor with a middle class patient. The patient is very often a "captive subject." She may have been referred by one of the public or private welfare services in the community which seek to encourage maternal care. Or she may, in keeping with her life habits, return again and again to the same hospital for medical care; in the latter instance the patient will be referred here and there according to those symptoms with which she presents. In any event, it is unlikely that she has actively chosen the doctor or doctors who will care for her, and if she should come in conflict with these doctors, it is unlikely that she will know of an alternative source of care during her pregnancy. She will thus be more passive, helpless, and less likely to offer any resistance or argument to anything that is told to her in the clinic. If she disagrees with some part of the birth control advice given to her, she is likely to be silent, then simply not carry out whatever method was prescribed. Even though the clinic patient may often feel a good deal of anger at the physicians attending her because of long waits, hard benches, etc., she is often an uneducated and impressionistic woman who is frightened of asking questions of the whitecoated physician confronting her; she may distort his words without the physician being aware of this.

In interviewing these patients and in

studying their records, it is somewhat astounding to note the wide variety of rumors and distortions concerning birth control with which they are bombarded by their friends, relatives, and the communications media. It is quite evident to most of these patients that doctors disagree about the effectiveness and safety of some of the contraceptive methods, especially the oral contraceptives. They may wonder whether these pills will lead to cancer, sterilization, or deformed pregnancies in the future. On the topic of intrauterine rings, the patients worry about the physician's ability to get the ring out once he puts it in. The patients may fear that an intrauterine device or diaphragm may get lost inside of them, or somehow change their sexuality. The nature and degree of such fears and distortions differ from woman to woman, and if opportunity to discuss them is not allowed, the patient may omit mention of them because of her passiveness or because she is ashamed that someone else might think her ideas are foolish. Very often the patient's simple fears or distortions are easily corrected.

When the subject of birth control is brought up, a good deal depends upon the manner with which it is dealt; this point is especially significant in that the concept of birth control must be seen by the patient as fitting into her goals and needs. Thus, the timing and wording of the subject of birth control may be crucial. The doctor's attitude and his ability to discuss the subject in an intuitive manner which allows the patient to feel that she may discuss her fears, suspicions, and expectations of birth control will be of vital importance.

It is unfortunate that the interpersonal transactions between the clinic staff and the patient on so important a topic have received little attention. It would be useful to research this subject systematically in the future. It would be interesting and important to note how the physicians at various levels of training differ in their transactions with patients on this subject and whether duration

of training is of importance in the doctor's ability to communicate with his patient on birth control.

In summary, a large part of the clinic population consists of poorly educated, superstitious, often frightened, and usually passive patients who are used to thinking concretely as they follow their way from clinic to clinic through the hospital without openly questioning any physician's words. In dealing with this population it behooves the physician not only to realize the birth control needs of the patient, but also to anticipate the fears, superstitions, and preconceptions which may keep the patient from utilizing a very much-needed contraceptive method.

REFERENCES

1. Eliot, J. W., and Meier, G.: Obst. & Gynec. 28:582, 1966.
2. Meier, G., Eliot, J. W., and Hoffman, S.: Michigan Med. 66:1071, 1967.
3. Lehfeldt, H., and Guze, H.: Fertil. & Steril. 17:111, 1966.
4. Van Emde Boas, C.: Excerpta Medica International Congress Series No. 46, Amsterdam, 1960.
5. Bakker, C. B., and Dightman, C. R.: Obst. & Gynec. 25:279, 1965.
6. Woods, S. M., and Natterson, J.: Am. J. Psychiat. 124:323, 1967.
7. Lief, H. I.: In Calderone, M. S., editor: Manual of Contraceptive Practice, Baltimore, 1964, The Williams & Wilkins Company, pp. 104-119.
8. Rainwater, L., and Weinstein, K. K.: And The Poor Get Children, Chicago, 1960, Quadrangle.
9. Herndon, C. N., and Nash, E. M., J. A. M. A. 180:395, 1962.
10. Edmands, E. M.: Am. J. Pub. Health 38:263, 1968.
11. Rainwater, L.: Family Design, Chicago, 1965, Aldine.
12. Hill, A. C., and Jaffe, F. S.: In Clark, K., and Parson, T., editors: The Negro American, Boston, 1966, Houghton Mifflin Company, pp. 205-224.
13. Pakter, J., Rosner, H. H., Jacobziner, H., and Greenstein, F.: Am. J. Pub. Health 51:683, 1961.
14. Oppenheimer, E.: Am. J. Pub. Health 51:208, 1961.
15. Obstetrical Statistical Cooperative — 1961 Combined Report, Table IV.

26 Social work practice toward enhancing competence in family planning

Margaret J. Burnstein

Competence in family planning literally means the state of having the requisite ability to limit conception so that children are produced by choice. Our humanistic value orientation assumes the democratic right of the individual to participate in decisions affecting his welfare. The right to plan the number and timing of children is consistent with our commitment to the value of self-determination. That family planning is encompassed in the core concerns of social work is affirmed in the 1967 policy statement of the NASW which says, "We believe that potential parents should be free to decide for themselves, without duress and according to their personal belief and convictions, whether they want to become parents, how many children they are willing and able to nurture, and the opportune time for them to have children."[1] The statement goes on to note that, "Along with the other professions responsible for enhancing family life, social work has to a large extent neglected to include birth control services as part of its over-all task."

This is hard to understand in the face of the fact that records of both family and children's agencies show evidence of concern about the possible relationship between unwanted children and disturbances in parent-child relations. This is also hard to understand in the face of the evidence that excess fertility is a health hazard for mothers and infants. It is equally hard to understand in the face of the cumulative evidence of the relationship between family size and poverty, and in the face of the fact that many social workers practice in health settings that include family planning clinics.

Our relative non-involvement is reflected in the NASW *Abstracts,* which list only thirteen articles on the subject of family planning out of some 2,000 classified from 1965 to 1967. In a review of articles in social work literature from 1950 to 1965, only two on family planning or related material were found.[2]

In view of social work's traditional interest in the family, attention must be directed toward family planning as directly related to family welfare. My task is to identify the implications for practice for enhancing competence in family planning.

Family planning, or fertility control, involves a decision either of omission or commission made by every adult engaging in heterosexual relationships. Only those who know they are sterile do not have to make such decisions. The right to available knowledge about family planning enhances responsible parenthood. Only as people are informed and have appropriate resources can

[1]Statement of NASW Delegate Assembly, Detroit, April 9-13, 1967.

Reprinted from Haselkorn, F., editor: *Family Planning: The role of Social Work,* 1968, pp. 136-143. By permission of the editor and Adelphi University.

[2]Jennie F. Scheller, "The Implications of Family Planning for Social Work Intervention," 1965 research essay, Adelphi University School of Social Work.

they make appropriate choices. Decisions concerning conception control involve multiple intricate questions related to subcultural and religious beliefs, socio-economic status, and psychological factors. Studies of the relationship between birth control practices and sexual behavior and attitudes have concluded that we are just beginning to understand the complexity of these interrelated factors.

Social workers neither recommend methods of contraception nor preempt the role of religious advisers. They can and should, however, use their professional competence to help people know how conception control might help toward prevention of family problems and promotion of family health. Counseling techniques of anticipatory guidance, logical discussion, education, and support can be effectively employed to help people think through decisions about family planning and make use of family planning services.

A natural opportunity exists to learn about a couple's experience with family planning in the initial phase of our contact. As we learn about the number and spacing of children in the family, it is invasive to ask, "Did you and your husband plan it that way?" or, "It would be helpful to know whether you and your husband have practiced birth control," or, "Have you and your husband ever taken any precautions to prevent pregnancy?" We obviously cannot conclude, from the number of their children, that a couple has or has not practiced birth control. It has been proposed that we ask these questions as a matter of routine of all adult clients. Most adults, and even teenagers, in our society are aware of birth control, and it is conceivable that they may have less feeling about invasion of privacy in this area than we have. We need, however, to learn how to initiate such discussions. Immediate referral to a family planning clinic is rarely indicated, except when specifically requested; for example, a woman whose younger sister had recently arrived in New York City in the company of a fiancé with whom she was having relations requested information about resources; another request was made by the mother of a retarded girl. In such instances the information can be given appropriately and an attempt made simultaneously to engage the client in considering how best the information can be transmitted. Generally, however, one would need sufficient exploration to understand how such a referral would be perceived and what reality and feeling considerations might need to be worked through. In most instances, only as the worker has established a relationship of trust is it appropriate and helpful to initiate consideration with the client of family planning services.

With couples seeking help with marital difficulty, a natural opportunity exists for opening the subject of sexual adjustment, which then directly or indirectly opens up discussion of contraception. Our case records and our literature suggest that we know too little about clients' sexual patterns. One of our hypotheses has been that we need not directly discuss sexual functioning because improvement will spontaneously occur as interactional problems are resolved. In our concern for psychosexual maturity, we have perhaps given insufficient attention to the physical aspects of sexual functioning. There are many possible ramifications of birth control in relation to sexual functioning. For many couples there is a relationship between method of contraception and sexual gratification.

Another consideration is the way in which decisions are made by couples regarding family planning. Does one partner take primary responsibility? Although newer methods of contraception have exaggerated the responsibility of the female, we need to be sensitive to how this may operate to depreciate the role of the male in responsible parenthood. With couples experiencing marital conflict, a frequent theme is submission-dominance. Change in contraceptive practice may then have relevance for perceptions of responsible performance of family social roles. One can, for example, as a way of approaching more generalized disparities in role expectation as between husband and wife, focus on responsibility in family planning. The helping process directed toward enabling clients to carry their social roles as husbands and wives cannot ignore behavior related to sex and birth control.

In order to help people achieve competence in family planning, the worker must be knowledgeable about and comfortable with human sexuality. For most men the ability to impregnate, and for most women the ability to become pregnant, are significant factors in their lives. A worker must be capable of teaching clients a vocabulary to facilitate communication in this area. When a client, for example, struggles for a word, the worker can help by volunteering questions, such as, "Are you referring to your husband's penis?", or, "Do you mean your vagina?" The worker must also become familiar with the client's vocabulary and be able selectively to use it: for example, "protection" instead of "contraceptive," "rubber" instead of "condom." There is a significant educational component, in addition to the open, non-judgmental attitude, in a worker's use of himself as a role model in frank discussion. Educational techniques in the sexual area serve not only to provide information, but in effect to sanction sexual activity and pleasure.

It may often be necessary to review with a client previous experience with methods of contraception. This may well lead to considering contraceptive methods that require minimum adaptation. Such exploration requires that workers have knowledge of the physiological and psychological advantages of alternative methods of conception control for a particular couple. Many clients report that the condom, suppository, and diaphragm impose a curb on spontaneity. Delayed reactions to the use of the pill and IUD are fairly commonly reported, and complaints of depression, fatigue, nausea,

weight gain, and other symptoms should of course be discussed with the physician despite the fact that, with some frequency, these symptoms may be psychogenic. The pill is rejected by some women because it requires long-range planning and commitment to sexual relations plus daily medication. Some indications that the pill may tend to develop an anti-male attitude in some women need to be further investigated. Despite the "liberation" afforded by the pill and the intrauterine device, future studies may find that women have developed resentment toward men for possible exposure to physical complications. Although, according to our current knowledge, incidence of complications for both methods appear not to be significant from the general health point of view, these are troublesome and fearsome questions for many women that parallel earlier fears about becoming pregnant. One has only to listen to casual conversation in a family planning clinic to be aware of the degree of concern that patients have in these matters.

Both client and worker should be aware that any change in the sexual pattern of a couple must be thoughtfully considered. Any expectation of change to be realistic must not be projected lightly. "Referral to family planning clinic" is never enough. Decisions with regard to family planning and a change in contraceptive practice should be initiated only after careful discussion, if possible with both husband and wife. Wherever possible, referral should be made to a medical resource that can advise in alternative methods of family planning. For Catholic couples, referral to a resource where the rhythm method is carefully and respectfully taught is obviously indicated. Women should be prepared for clinical and medical procedures, including vaginal examination. Use of anticipatory guidance to prepare clients for the kinds of questions they may want to put to doctors and nurses is highly useful. Follow-up after the clinic visit might well include exploration of the client's experience, her feelings, and her husband's reactions. Associated medical problems are, of course, referred back to the physician or clinic.

One must avoid encouraging a woman to take initiative in this area lest this be perceived as a threat to the husband's masculinity if contraception has traditionally been his domain. This is especially important when the husband is a poorly-paid marginal employee or a member of a minority group. With low-income families of Puerto Rican origin, whether or not the marriage is legal, experience has demonstrated that the men want to be involved in, or at least knowledgeable about, birth control efforts. Men who have been excluded from such decisions have been known to react violently. In one instance, when a man learned that his wife was using a diaphragm, he was certain she intended to use it with other men. Some men expressed fears that their wives were going to destroy them when they learned about the coil a clinic had prescribed, assuming it was a metal spring that could injure the penis. One obvious way of involving males more directly is through scheduling evening hours, providing babysitters, and utilizing male social workers.

This does not imply that we should respond automatically to the first suggestion made by a woman that she bring her husband into the office to have us "tell him about it." Such a suggestion might be significant of problems involving the woman's acceptance of her own sexuality that might well bear examination.

Some women tell in considerable and explicit detail about the sexual appetites of their husbands. This seems to occur with frequency among, but is not limited to, clients of Latin origin. These women may perceive the passion with which they are approached by a man as a reflection of their own adequacy and desirability as women. An upper middle-class client with a functional infertility problem applying for adoption had for many years believed that, had her husband really loved her, he would not have been so

meticulous in the early years of their relationship in his use of condoms. The social worker was able to offer help in clarifying some of the client's misconceptions and subjective distortions, some of which centered around her damaged self-respect as a woman.

One must obviously never assume that an unplanned pregnancy, even when abortion has been attempted, results in an unwanted child.

Some women openly express the gratifications of childbearing. Dr. Robert Coles quotes one such woman as saying:

> . . . to me having a baby inside me is the only time I'm really alive. I know I can make something, do something, no matter what color my skin is, and what names people call me. When the baby gets born, I see him and he is full of life, or she is; and I think to myself that it doesn't make any difference what happens later—at least now we have a chance, or the baby does . . . The children and their father feel it too. Just like I do. They feel the baby is a good sign, or at least he is some sign. If we didn't have that, what would be the difference from death? Even without the children, my life would still be bad. They are not going to give us what they have—the birth control people. They just want us to be a poor version of them. Only without our children, our faith in God and our tasty, fried food or anything.[3]

These women pose a problem not easily resolved. The issues related to the disadvantaged in our society are contained elsewhere in this volume, and we need not go into them here. Until such women and their husbands have a better share in the social and economic goods of society, it is understandable that many will cling to procreation as the only source of pleasure in life. In general, counseling around family planning with low-income clients is often acceptable only after reality needs of the family have been met. The extent to which a person has other gratifications in life may influence his or her

---

[3]Robert Coles, M.D., *Children of Crisis* (Boston, 1967), pp. 368-369.

ability to tolerate interruptions in conception.

While these are generic principles, the particular agency or field of practice exerts specific influence on the need and timing of family planning discussions. Family planning decisions should be included in preventive work with natural parents considering foster care or adoption placement. Also, exploring the attitude of foster parents or adoptive applicants toward birth control may reveal much about their ability to cope with sexual interests of children or the help they can be expected to give a child in relating to his natural parents. Certainly, counseling and available contraceptive help would be important to adults being released from mental hospitals—or for any patients under psychiatric care.

The purposeful inclusion of such social work responsibility would be better assured if an agency's interest in family planning were a matter of policy and if supervisors gave workers the necessary support in learning to effectively involve their clients in such discussions.

In health settings, social work should assume the advocacy role with other institutions in the client's network regarding concrete needs. In the health facility itself, social work can contribute toward building a therapeutic environment. It can bring to bear its insights about human needs to make delivery of services more humane and adequate. Provision of evening sessions with social work services available is an obvious way of meeting the needs of the population group we seek to serve. Clinic visits by appointment, a coat room, attractive reading materials, play equipment, or a supervised play area for children are ways of humanizing services. It is only as such arrangements become more prevalent that we can anticipate that clients will accept preventive health services, including family planning. Social work can and must bring its knowledge and skills to bear to introduce these services in medical care facilities.

The subject of birth control can serve as a focus of discussion in educational and problem-solving groups. Increasingly, hospitals and clinics are using groups for orientation, education, and problem-solving.

The subject of family planning can flow naturally in many adolescent group discussions. Youth-serving agencies could well adapt their programs and practice to increase opportunities for consideration of the complexities and ramifications of family planning. If so, we may find that future studies will no longer reveal, as suggested by Schwartz, that "the ages of 11-13 are optimal for membership in organized groups, . . . that organized group participation decreases progressively as age increases . . . There is evidence that some community centers frown on programs geared to meeting the courtship needs of young adolescents."[4] Groups provide a growth-promoting opportunity for adolescents coping with the task of achieving sexual identity. Sex education and birth control discussions are logical topics for such groups. The group-work method with adolescents and adults can also encourage thoughtful discussion, fact-finding, and consideration of social action around important problems, including poverty and population, public and private morals, etc. Frequently, the group work goal to maximize the decision-making capacity of group members can have a natural flow-over in helping individuals with decision-making around family planning.

Planned programs of visual education in family planning have not been sufficiently exploited by most social agencies. Visual aids can be used for stimulating consideration by staff, clients, patients, and boards of the complex factors, new developments, and conflicting points of view regarding birth control, as well as problems of poverty. A

---

[4]William Schwartz, "Neighborhood Centers," *Five Fields of Social Service: Reviews of Research,* ed. Henry S. Maas (NASW, 1966), especially pp. 148, 149.

bulletin board with current clippings from newspapers and magazines is an obvious device. Items could be displayed to reflect the methodological advances in contraception. Differences in philosophical views of national and religious groups could be illustrated by featuring opposing views simultaneously. Displays highlighting the abortion problem and developments toward legalizing abortion might be included. Printed material with some appropriate annotation might be displayed and distributed. Films can be used to stimulate discussion of responsible behavior, planned parenthood, out-of-wedlock pregnancy, and birth control. A film such as "A Taste of Honey" could be used profitably to help group participants explore these areas.

There is much as yet unknown to which social work might direct some of its research activity. Studies of family planning clinic dropouts might point the way toward enhancing services. Investigations directed toward understanding the experience of patients who enter a hospital following probable extramural abortion might yield clues to the organization of more effective family planning clinics as well as a rational policy toward abortion. We need follow-up studies of patients who have had tubal ligations or vasectomies to understand the effect of sterilization procedures on marital and parent-child relationships.

Many opportunities exist in a variety of social work settings to initiate discussion of birth control. We are as yet only on the threshold of developing professional approaches that will contribute our unique competence to the other health professions concerned with family planning. It would appear that no major modifications of our traditional repertoire of techniques is indicated. We have been slow as a profession to respond to and participate in this new era in conception control. Family planning has much to contribute to social work goals in work with individuals and groups. Family planning is consistent with our value system and our theoretical assumptions and knowledge about man and his social environment. We have the competence as a profession to make a substantive contribution to family planning as a preventive health measure. Furthermore, as social work practice incorporates family planning content, social work will become a more effective helping profession.

27 Development of a community-focused family planning program: Agency and interpersonal relations

Vestal W. Parrish, Jr.*

During the last decade there has been increasing agreement that society and the health professions bear the responsibility for providing family planning services to all in need. "Need" is a vague and debatable concept. In general, it has been defined in the United States as referring to women from 15 to 44 years of age who cannot afford the services of a private physician and who desire, but lack access to, the means of preventing unplanned pregnancies.

The task for society has been largely that of assuming the economic costs of meeting this need. In turn, the task for the health professions has been to determine *how* best to meet this need and to develop programs directed toward that goal. The questions of how best to meet the need or, of what delivery strategies to use, has been and continues to be an object of debate, of trial and error, and of deliberate experimentation. Progress has been made, but we do not yet have final answers.

The purpose of this paper is to describe a pilot community family planning program that was established in order to gain experience in how to deliver services to the rural and urban poor in Louisiana. The general focus is upon how individuals, groups, and agencies at the state, regional, local, and staff levels were involved in this effort, an effort in which health professionals worked in concert with behavioral scientists. The emphasis is upon the involvement approaches used, questions faced, decisions made, and some reflections based on the results of the first 5 years of operation.

STUDY AREA

The pilot program is in Lincoln Parish, a semirural county about 20 miles wide and 40 miles long located in northern Louisiana some 300 miles from New Orleans. The total population includes approximately 34,000 persons of whom about 40% are black. Approximately 50% of the population live in Ruston, the county seat. In 1960, the crude birth rate was 21.1 per 1,000 population, the median annual family income was $3,477, and almost 44% of the families had annual incomes of less than $3,000. Initial examination of the demographic characteristics of Lincoln and of the four surrounding parishes (counties) revealed that they were sufficiently similar to each other and to other rural counties in the southern United States, to serve as a reasonably representative location for a pilot research and demonstration program. Therefore, Lincoln Parish was designated as the study parish and the four surrounding parishes as control areas against which the ef-

*Vestal W. Parrish, Jr., D.Sc., is Assistant Professor of Applied Health Sciences, School of Public Health and Tropical Medicine, Tulane University of Louisiana, New Orleans, Louisiana.

Original article.

fectiveness of the delivery efforts could be evaluated (Beasley and Parrish, 1968, 1969). The program was begun in September 1965, but only after a great deal of necessary background preparation by the directors of the program.

POLITICS AND PRACTICE

The goal for the Lincoln Parish Family Planning Program was to provide medically indigent mothers with the information and services needed to plan family size. Drawing upon findings from research based in New Orleans and in Lincoln Parish, the overall design of the program was based on the hypothesis that the provision of adequate information and services would result in a high level of utilization by indigent women. The strategy for delivering adequate information and services involved the need for identification of the individual indigent women, contacting them through the use of program staff personnel and referrals from other agencies, offering services, providing education, and maintaining contacts to encourage follow-up patient continuation. The program was to be housed in existing local public health facilities.

The program goal was and is socially and professionally respectable; the hypothesis is reasonable; the components of the general strategy are clear cut and relate logically to each other. But, *implementation* of such a program requires the involvement and support of a variety of individuals, groups, and agencies. How was this obtained?

PART I: AGENCY RELATIONS
State and regional level

The individuals, groups, and agencies whose involvement and support was sought at the state and regional levels included the state governor, state attorney general, State Board of Health, State Department of Hospitals, State Department of Welfare, State Medical Society, Tri-Parish Medical Society, and regional charity hospitals.

In order to open a public-supported family planning clinic, the first priority was to prepare the way legally. Section 14:88 of the Louisiana Criminal Code had been interpreted by two previous attorney generals to the effect that it was a felony to disseminate information about any form of birth control device or provide this type of service. Working as a team, representatives for the Tulane University School of Public Health and Louisiana State Board of Health obtained from the attorney general's office on July 16, 1965, a reversed opinion of Section 14:88. This provided the legal basis for proceeding with the Lincoln Parish Program. The Lincoln Parish proposal was then reviewed by the State Board of Health on July 23, 1965, and this body unanimously adopted a resolution to cooperate with and assist Tulane University of Louisiana School of Public Health in the proposed program if the governor of the state approved.

After the sanction of the State Board of Health, the proposal was submitted to Governor John J. McKeithen for his approval regarding (1) the use of federal funds and the facilities of the State Board of Health in cooperation with the Lincoln Parish Program and (2) plans for a statewide family planning program as outlined in the resolution by the State Board of Health. The governor's letter approving both propositions was dated July 27, 1965.

With this base to work from, other groups and agencies then were approached for various reasons. For example, about 95% of our target population delivered their babies at one of the three public hospitals in a 70-mile radius of Lincoln Parish and a large portion received assistance from welfare. Our program design called for a patient contact system involving as referral agents the personnel of agencies in daily contact with a large segment of the target population. Therefore, the endorsement by the State Department of Welfare was necessary in order to develop a working relationship with the regional public hospitals and the local welfare agency. A medical program of this type also needs physician coverage. Even though the State Medical Society, the Tri-Parish Medical Society, and individual physicians can function autonomously, the endorsement of a program by the higher level strengthens the endorsements at lower levels. Formal support was sought and obtained at each level.

Questions of major concern to persons at the state and regional levels were: (1) What would be the possible influences of the program on costs for tax supported agencies? (2) What were the attitudes of religious and racial groups in the total population concerning a couple's right to determine the size of their families? (3) What were the attitudes of these religious and racial groups concerning publicly supported family planning services for the indigent? (4) What were the desires of the indigent segment of the population for family planning services? (5) Would the practices conform to accepted medical standards? (6) Would patients financially able to pay for care be eligible for services in the Lincoln Parish Program? And (7) would guidelines be formulated that could be acceptable to all involved groups and agencies at each level?

As these questions indicate, the primary concern at the state and regional level was political. The need was to avoid basic disagreements between established agencies and various vested interest groups. Years later, after the success of the Lincoln Parish Program had received national and international recognition and the more inclusive Louisiana State Family Planning Program was being developed, it became possible to obtain cooperation from other groups because of their likelihood of receiving funds or other forms of direct reward. These inducements did not exist at the outset; rather, convincing answers to the questions raised had to be provided. More specifically, it was necessary to allay concern over possible negative consequences and provide positive justification.

Drawing again upon findings from research in New Orleans, Lincoln Parish, and elsewhere, one is able to show that more than 90% of the total population, irrespective of race or religion, held the opinion that couples had a right to determine their own family size. Over 90% of the total population endorsed publicly supported family planning services for the indigent, and more than 80% of the lower socioeconomic group expressed a desire for more information about family planning methods. Although 43% of the women in Lincoln Parish were in the lowest income range, these women produced 70% of the unplanned pregnancies, 59% of the live births, 50% of the stillbirths, 58% of the miscarriages and/or abortions, and 94% of the live births out of wedlock. It was further pointed out that the ratios for unwed mothers to married mothers were approximately 4 to 1 for maternal mortality, 2 to 1 for infant mortality, 2 to 1 for fetal deaths, and 2 to 1 for premature births (Harter et al., 1965; Parrish et al., 1965; Pakter et al., 1961).

Research findings such as these provided compelling answers to the questions that had been raised. They provided the basis for a positive argument on political, economic, medical, and humanitarian grounds. For example, health and welfare costs were likely to be reduced by providing the indigent with the means to choose the size of their families and thus to decrease family size and improve the health of mothers and infants.

The development of explicit principles of operation and of patient eligibility criteria for the program served to satisfy the remaining major concerns (Beasley et al., 1969). Guidelines acceptable at all levels were developed. Before these were finalized and endorsed, discussions and meetings took place at all levels. This, of course, meant some give and take on both sides. Guidelines related to the above concerns were then made final: Only persons who met the financial eligibility requirements for services in the state hospitals and public health units would be eligible for family planning services in the program, and medical supervision would be sufficient to ensure that all practices conform to accepted medical standards. In other words, this would be a medically sound program and patients with "adequate funds" to see a private physician would not be eligible for tax-supported care.

After years of operation and a great deal of publicity concerning Lincoln Parish and the subsequently expanded efforts throughout Louisiana, most of the questions originally raised on the state and regional levels remained as objects of concern. There were, however, some major additional changes that program success seemed to have caused. For example, there was a greater willingness to accept and use federal funds, and greater optimism concerning the positive impact of family planning services on other medical and social problems. Many agencies became more aggressive in their desire for greater involvement in family planning. It should be noted that "more involvement" because of program success can be negative or positive. A negative involvement would be a struggle between groups or agencies for more control; a positive involvement would be a stronger effort to function as a team to more adequately deliver family planning services. Thus far, the latter has been true and only observation over time will reveal future trends.

Local community level

The reinterpretation of a state law, support from the state and regional levels, and the respect normally accorded to the Tulane University School of Public Health and Tropical Medicine would have been of little value in establishing a family planning program in Lincoln Parish without internal or local support. Leadership in obtaining this support was furnished by a highly respected local private physician and a public health nurse. Through their support and introductions, contact was made with the local police

jury (elected officials), public health unit staff, welfare agency staff, and medical, religious, civic, and educational groups.

Why involve these groups and agencies? Earlier in this paper I stated that the program design included the use of the local public health facilities and cooperation with local agencies that were in direct daily contact with the indigent population for referral purposes. To accomplish this, it was necessary to obtain the police jury's permission to use the public health unit's facilities as well as to involve the staff members of the public health unit and welfare agency. For physician coverage of the clinic, the active cooperation of the medical group was needed. Involvement and support of the religious, civic, and educational groups at all socioeconomic levels was needed to ensure that the program and its guidelines would be acceptable to the community at large. Their involvement also meant that there had been created an internal educational and communication agent to the target population concerning the availability of services. (One should note that Lincoln Parish is almost 99% Protestant [Parrish et al., 1965] and that the guidelines had been developed for later use in the state program with areas including a large Catholic element. Therefore, the Protestant and Catholic leadership in New Orleans was consulted during the initial stage of the Lincoln Parish Program.)

The primary questions raised at the local level included all of those raised earlier at the state and regional levels plus such additional concerns as genocide, coercion, fear that family planning services would be a prerequisite for the receipt of other benefits financed by tax revenue, the need for confidentiality of clinic information, the possible condoning of promiscuity, freedom of choice of contraceptive methods, abortion and sterilization, and staffing of the clinic on the basis of merit irrespective of race. As would be expected, the local level is the meeting point for concern about relationships between groups and between groups and individuals. The local agencies and groups are closer to the "grass-root" level of the population than is true for the state or regional levels.

Extreme care was taken to provide satisfactory answers to these questions because of the complexity of attempting to initiate a community-focused and supported family planning program in Louisiana during late 1965. The program was established as a medical program where services were offered on a voluntary, racially integrated basis to those financially eligible women who had been married or had at least one pregnancy.

After 5 years of operation, there was a strong positive response to the program by the eligible indigent population and equally strong cooperative community effort. Some of the local political and social attitudinal changes were interesting. For example, the family planning program is identified throughout the community as "our" program as opposed to "Tulane's program." There is less criticism of the indigent population as being irresponsible and having babies in order to receive welfare assistance. The earlier concern that the offering of family planning services might be tantamount to condoning promiscuity is being replaced with acknowledgement of sexual activity and the desire for more emphasis on the prevention of unwanted pregnancies. Local groups as well as agencies are eager to move toward an even more comprehensive program with emphasis on eliminating gaps and areas of duplication in this cooperative community effort.

PART II: INTERPERSONAL RELATIONS
Local staff level

Thus far the discussion has focused on the state, regional, and local community levels from which support must be forthcoming in order to set the stage for a successful family planning program operation. Political and social attitudes were of neces-

sity involved in formulating program guidelines for this first family planning program in Louisiana. The ultimate test, however, resides with the local staff of health personnel. This is the foundation of the entire pyramid, which determines success or failure of a program. Programs on paper are quite different from programs that adequately involve patients over a long period of time. The amount of political concern over this program resulted in close scrutiny of the clinic program by interests at the state, regional, and local levels. The staff members felt the weight of this close observation, knowing that they were the personification of program guidelines in action. Close observation is unusually intense in a nonurban community where communication is extremely rapid. For example, the first case of pregnancy with an IUD in place was reported to the clinic staff by three other patients before the pregnant woman herself could get to the clinic or telephone.

During the first 5 years of the Lincoln Parish program, the clinic staff included two part-time local physicians, and a registered nurse, two licensed practical nurses, and a clerk, who were on a full-time basis. The first 6 months were spent in making final a patient record system and in the careful selection and training of staff members. Individually and as a group, they had many of the same questions that characterized the community and other levels. In addition, however, the staff's direct involvement with patients stimulated questions and attitudes that required a more in-depth introspective evaluation of their own personal values. This was necessary and important for at least three reasons: (1) the staff needed to function as a tightly integrated, cohesive team in a program with a community focus, (2) during the early years of operation in this nonurban area, staff members were closely observed by many liberal and conservative community groups, and (3) staff members are involved in the actual delivery of services as opposed to those who have only opinions concerning these matters.

Since the staff members were faced with the task of implementing the program guidelines and goals, their primary questions and concerns can be clustered around their readiness for two program components: education and service.

Education. The educational component includes a clinic class on reproductive physiology and contraceptive methods as well as home visits involving initial patient contact and follow-up on missed appointments. Thus, a first necessary task was to teach the nonmedical staff the basic facts related to reproductive physiology and contraceptive methods.

But more was demanded of the staff member than just verbally passing on information in an educational role. She was to function as a person in a professional role relating to another person in a patient role. In other words, the educational process concerning some of the more sensitive and intimate parts of a patient's personhood requires nonverbal as well as verbal communication. This, in turn, requires a great deal of sensitivity on the part of the nurse.

Communication with a patient begins at the level of the patient's understanding with the hope and goal of moving upward. Since the patient's understanding is at a lay level, a common meeting ground for staff and patients was sought. Both patients and nurses were female, but the nurses were also professionals. How might this difference be bridged? The common meeting ground was found through sensitizing the nurses to function comfortably themselves as females in the often delicate areas of consideration that are involved in providing professional family planning services.

In training the staff members (including the clerk), each readily admitted how little they had previously been encouraged by professional educators to apply professional knowledge to their *own* individual lives as a person who is female. For example, very

little concrete thought had been given to their knowledge about and personal attitudes toward their own reproductive organs and their functions. Yet, a major component in their professional role and goals as a staff member in a family planning program was to teach indigent patients the location, functions, and respect for their reproductive organs.

The staff members became aware of how easy it is to compartmentalize new factual information (such as reproductive physiology, contraceptive technology) that is related to their professional roles to the point that it may not influence their personal attitudes. From this, they came to feel that they had been pushed toward a kind of "professional robotism" in their earlier professional training. Very little, if any, attention had been given in their prior training to their own attitudes as a person who is female and what diverse influences help to formulate these attitudes.

This type of "professionalism" would cause the professional to ignore the fact of and reasons for his like or dislike for a specific contraceptive method or method in her own life behavior. The effects of this sort of training had to be overcome since they were to communicate verbally and nonverbally with indigent women in a family planning program while trying not to influence the patient's choice of a method. This requires understanding of oneself, especially in order to control nonverbal communication. For example, a specific goal of the training was for the nurse to learn to be able to hold each type of contraceptive in her hand and to discuss it with a patient without embarrassment or distaste or projecting the impression that she regarded it as dirty, bad, or unladylike.

In view of the preceding, staff training related to the educational component of the program was primarily focused on factual information and the identification of influences that may have had an impact on attitudes of the staff toward reproduction, the human body (including their own), and selection of a contraceptive method. Such factors as age and life situation as well as attitudes toward sexuality, pregnancy, childbirth, and parenthood were recognized as possible influences on the decision-making process for women in a family planning program. Even as attitudes and decisions of various staff members differed, the same would be true with staff-patient and patient-patient comparisons. It was concluded, therefore, that what works for one person may not have comparable results for another. To apply this in the educational component of a family planning program means that both verbal and nonverbal communication focuses on facts but with awareness of the valid differences in the decision-making process for other people.

Service. The program includes both a physician clinic and a nurse clinic. These are held on different days and the patients are scheduled according to their needs. During the physician clinic, the nurses prepare the patients for the physician's physical examination, insertion of the intrauterine contraceptive device (IUD) when selected by the patient, or care for a patient's medical complication or complications. After the patient's choice of contraceptive method is discussed with the doctor, a nurse gives the patient more detailed instructions concerning the selected method. The nurse clinic focuses on patients' picking up contraceptive supplies, examination of the IUD patient by a nurse to determine if the device is in place, and reinforcing the patient's understanding of the correct usage of the contraceptive method chosen by the patient.

The primary staff concerns related to the service component were a continuation and intensification of what has been discussed concerning the educational component. Whereas the educational component deals with "talking" about the most intimate parts of a woman's being, the service component focuses on "showing" and "touching" some of these same parts. It was con-

cluded that respect for the patient as a person by means of verbal and nonverbal communication is intensified in the "showing" and "touching" processes. It was further concluded that for health professionals to act as if they conceive of patients as objects without sex, feelings, or a mental capacity to understand does not mean the patient agrees. The patient does not forget the sex of the examiner, nor does she necessarily believe that the person doing the examination forgets it either. A desexualized view of the patient can, of course, act as a defense mechanism for the health professional to protect her or him from personal fears or insecurity. In its extreme form, this view may result in the patient's being regarded as a "thing" or a "vagina." This may make it impossible to lead the patient toward a higher respect for herself or to help her become an effective user of medical services.

How can nurses deal with their own fears and prepare themselves as professionals, who are at the same time females, to communicate with patients who are also females? One basic way used by each of our professional staff members was to recall how *she* feels when in a patient role. With this in mind, the staff members were reminded that some persons have little body modesty, whereas others are embarrassed by their own nude body within the privacy of their own bedroom. Some women have problems touching their sexual organs, whereas others have little concern with this. Another problem recognized by the staff was how the presence of the nurse could and should give the patient support while the physician (a male) looks at and physically examines what to the patient is her more intimate biological organ but what to the physician may simply be a pelvic examination. Still another problem was how comfortable the nurse feels when she touches her own sexual organs or those of a patient, while recognizing herself or the patient as a woman.

It was concluded that all of the above questions were of prime importance, because the nurse frequently serves as the main source of support for the patient throughout the entire clinic experience. For example, the staff nurse must not only prepare the patient for the physician's examination but also serve as a female supporting agent. Physicians occasionally differ in their approach to patients; the nurse should be capable and ready to serve as a buffer, if necessary, between the patient and the physician.

The nurse also teaches the patient how to check for the presence of the IUD when one has been inserted to see if it is in the proper location to prevent pregnancy. This often requires the nurse to take the patient's hand and show her how to properly insert her finger into the vagina while telling her what to feel for in making the IUD check. The nurse watches the patient as she goes through the procedure without the nurse's assistance. A shaky hand or aggressive movements on the part of the nurse can block this educational process; plus, it may produce a patient who will not return to the clinic. The need is to communicate to the patient that touching her sexual organs not only is acceptable but that it is required for effective use of the IUD.

Much of the patient's success as a contraceptive user depends on the nurse's empathy as a professional who functions from a human point of view. This involves the recognition that people are different, that they have a right to be different, but that all have some things in common. Both the professional and patient are females and have some fears and insecurities. One requirement for a professional to function effectively in a family planning clinic is to recognize *her* fears and seek to overcome them in order to relate to the patient on a human as well as professional level. Once our staff members began to understand the communication process and related to patients with empathy, very intimate information could be obtained without any resentment from the patient.

At the end of the 5-year study period, all of the staff had been part of the program for the entire period with the exception of one nurse and a clerk, both of whom had been involved for more than 3 years. Some of the more significant attitudinal changes on the part of the clinic staff included awareness of the following:

1. Politics and social attitudes at different levels may form the initial guidelines for a community-focused family planning program, but only human warmth through a staff member—patient relationship will make the program work.
2. The poorly educated can be taught how to effectively use the IUD and contraceptive pills.
3. The poorly educated will avail themselves of family planning information and services when these are provided within a humane context of mutual respect.
4. Service statistics and attitudinal information can be used effectively in changing negative attitudes with the community.
5. Community agencies and groups will support a staff who are perceived as doing a good job in a sensitive area.
6. The sensitive areas involved in family planning education and service can be constructively dealt with if approached in an intelligent and genuinely empathetic manner.
7. It is amazing how much a professional can learn about life and how to better do her job, when she listens to the "lay wisdom" of the patients.

CONCLUSIONS

The concern of this paper has been to describe how individuals, groups, and agencies on a state, regional, local community level, and local staff level were involved in a community-focused family planning program. The conclusion is that political and social attitudes may have a strong influence on formulating acceptable guidelines for a community-focused family planning program and that political and social attitudes may have a strong influence on formulating acceptable guidelines for a community-focused family planning program, but staff-patient relationships determined success or failure of the program.

On the state and regional levels, specific questions were generally focused on economic and politically sensitive concerns with emphasis on group-to-group relationships. The specific focus of questions on the local community level emphasized a group-to-group as well as group-to-person relationship. The primary concern at the staff level, quite reasonably, was focused on questions concerned with person-to-person relationships and secondarily upon person-to-group relationships.

After 5 years of operation, attitudinal changes on all levels include endorsement of a more comprehensive family planning program. Any major changes in attitudes on all levels are interpreted as being caused by the operational success achieved by the local staff. This fact is not unique to our program and serves to underscore the need

for careful selection, training, and supervision of personnel in programs elsewhere.

REFERENCES

1. Beasley, J. D., and Parrish, V. W., Jr.: Family planning and the reduction of fertility and illegitimacy: A preliminary report on a rural Southern program, Social Biol. 16(3):167-178, September 1969.
2. Beasley, J. D., and Parrish, V. W., Jr.: A progress report on a Southern rural family planning research program conducted in Lincoln Parish, Louisiana. Advances in Planned Parenthood, III. Proceedings of the Fifth Annual Meeting of the American Association of Planned Parenthood Physicians, New York, 1968, Excerpta Medica Foundation.
3. Beasley, J. D., Parrish, V. W., Jr., Bennett, B., and Mayers, A. E.: Lincoln Parish family planning research program: Policy and procedure manual. 1969. (Mimeographed.)
4. Harter, C. L., Ktsanes, V., Fischer, A., and Beasley, J. D.: Family survey of metropolitan New Orleans: Instruction manual, 1965. (Mimeographed.)
5. Pakter, J., Rosner, H. J., Jacobziner, J., and Greenstein, F.: Out-of-wedlock births in New York City: Medical aspects, Amer. J. Public Health 51(6):846-865, June 1961.
6. Parrish, V. W., Jr., Kaplan, J., Harter, C. L., and Beasley, J. D.: Family survey of Lincoln Parish: Instruction manual, 1965. (Mimeographed.)

28 Family planning: An expanded role for paramedical personnel

Allan G. Rosenfield, M.D.*

One of the most critical issues of the second half of the Twentieth Century is, and will continue to be, the rapid rate of population growth, which carries such dire consequences to the future of mankind. Many of the more visible world problems today, including pollution, urban decay, crime, malnutrition, and starvation, are related, in varying degrees, to the unprecedented rate of population growth. At the same time, this growth rate seriously interferes with efforts aimed at social and economic development.

As one studies the problem, the enormity of the task becomes apparent. Growth rates of 3 per cent, so prevalent in countries in the developing world, will produce a doubling of the population in 23 years. Even in the Western nations, with growth rates in the range of 1 per cent, the population will double in only 69 years. It is obvious that such rates of growth cannot continue for very long without catastrophic effects. Several authorities ask what can be done to hasten the fall in growth rates, with some stating that family planning programs alone take too long and may, in fact, be inadequate.[7,13] Many of the proposals may be unrealistic or impractical at the present time,[5] but there seems to be agreement that we are not yet moving fast enough.

---

*From The Population Council, Medical (OBGYN) Advisor, Family Planning Project, Ministry of Public Health, Bangkok, Thailand.

Reprinted from *American Journal of Obstetrics and Gynecology* 110(7):1030-1039, August 1, 1971. Copyright The C. V. Mosby Company.

Modern contraceptive technology has dramatically changed the family planning field. The development of hormonal contraception and the rebirth of intrauterine contraception has made the inconvenient coitus-related practices such as coitus interruptus, rhythm, or abstinence and methods such as the condom, diaphragm, or foam tablets less important. While the developments represent major advances, they still suffer serious disadvantages because of the high discontinuation rates and the medical controversies related to the long-term effects. Forecasts of the immediate future in contraceptive technology are not encouraging,[50] and many believe that the search for improved methods of contraception should have the highest priority.[9]

Whatever the future holds, both in contraceptive technology and in social change, it is suggested that more can be accomplished with present technology and within the framework of family planning than is being done at present. A major problem in the provision of modern contraceptive services has been the extreme shortage of physicians in many areas of the world, most critically in the rural regions of the developing nations. Dr. Candau, the Director-General of the World Health Organization, has been quoted as saying, "Let us recognize that, at the present rate of development, a major part of the developing world will not be able, in this century, to supply enough 'conventional' physicians for their barest needs. We need a new approach. . . ."[54]

Thailand, a nation of 35 million people in Southeast Asia, with a growth rate of approximately 3.2 per cent,[41] can well serve to illustrate the problem. Approximately 80 per cent of the population is presently employed in agricultural pursuits, and 87 per cent live in what is considered rural Thailand.[38] There are, at the present time, fewer than 5,000 doctors, or one doctor for approximately 7,000 people (as compared to one doctor for every 700 people in the United States). But even this figure is misleading because over 50 per cent of all Thai physicians live and practice in the capital city of Bangkok where the ratio is 1:1,000. This results in only one doctor for approximately 13,000 people outside the capital city. Furthermore, if one subtracts the physicians working in the other urban centers, the figures are significantly worse, perhaps in the range of one doctor for 110,000 people living in truly rural areas.

It is suggested that adherence to rigidly set medical standards in rural areas (or in urban slums) will adversely affect the majority of those most in need of contraception by depriving them of easy accessibility to services. The production of new graduate physicians does not hold promise of improving the doctor:patient ratios, primarily because of the rapidly increasing population size,[40] as well as the desire of most graduates to live in urban areas.[30]

There is much evidence available to suggest that many women who are not practicing contraception actually do not want more children, the most striking example being the large numbers of married women throughout the world who submit to criminal abortion attempts. Similarly, a common feature to KAP (knowledge about, attitudes toward, and practice of) surveys in many countries is the fact that the number of women who state that they do not want further children far exceeds those who are currently practicing contraception or who come to a clinic when services are made available.[44] The use of paramedics, located as close to the village as possible, might sig-

nificantly raise acceptance rates, as well as improve continuation rates.

A question of central importance, therefore, in the field of family planning is: Must a physician examine a woman before an oral contraceptive is prescribed or an intrauterine device is inserted? This paper will examine and attempt to reassess the role of the physician in the delivery of family planning services today. Emphasis will be placed on comparative risks of providing contraceptive services with or without physician participation. To evaluate this question properly, it is necessary to review the pertinent methods of contraception and to discuss the general problems faced in providing adequate family planning services.

METHODS OF CONTRACEPTION

Discussion will be limited to intrauterine and hormonal contraception, the two general types of contraception of importance to the issue raised in the title of this paper.

Intrauterine devices (IUD's) for human beings (small steel rings) were first developed in Germany about 40 years ago.[18] There were problems (primarily of sepsis) with these rings, and the method did not attain popularity until after World War II, when the use of the Ota ring spread in Japan.[42] But the major developments came in the past 10 years with the development of inert plastic devices.

The major concern when the IUD was reintroduced was the possibility of a high rate of perforation or of infection. Neither has proved to be of major importance, although the problem of perforation did significantly affect the IUD program of one country.[56] Severe hemorrhage has similarly proved to be rare, although menstrual problems are, along with pain, the most significant of the side effects noted with intrauterine contraception. Contraindications to the use of intrauterine device include acute pelvic inflammatory disease, genital tract cancer, and large myomatous uteri.

The method at first seemed ideal to many

planners in the field of family planning[23] because of its simplicity and reversability, and because nothing was required of the patient or her busband after insertion. With experience, however, it has become apparent that the IUD is not the perfect method, primarily because so many women (40 to 50 per cent) discontinue its use within two years of insertion.[2,29,51,55,62,64] Nonetheless, it still remains a most important method in national programs, particularly in the developing world. It is hoped that current research efforts will result in the development of an improved intrauterine device.

In 1965, reports were first published on the use of an estrogen-progesterone combination that inhibited conception by interfering with ovulation.[46] This discovery has proved one of the most important of the Twentieth Century. In the United States and in other Western nations, millions of women have used "the Pill."

At the present time, however, there is much discussion about the potential hazards of oral hormonal therapy. The controversy has centered primarily on reports from England[19,59,60] and the United States[48] which relate the Pill to thromboembolic disease and on a report published in 1969 which attempted to show a possible statistical relationship of the Pill to carcinoma in situ of the cervix.[33] The debate has been intensified by the recent, widely publicized hearings on the safety of the Pill conducted by the United States Senate. Other important complications reported include various metabolic and vascular changes and jaundice. Extensive reviews of the over-all risks of oral contraception, by a United States Government Advisory Committee[1,3] and by the World Health Organization,[63,65] however, have concluded, from the evidence available at the time of the reports, that the benefits of oral contraception outweigh the risks in properly screened patients. We shall return to a discussion of the concept of the properly screened patient below.

While studies must continue and all potential hazards must be carefully investigated, sight should not be lost of the basic purpose of oral contraception. First and foremost, it prevents pregnancy, a condition which carries a far greater risk than does the Pill, particularly to rural women in the developing world. The reports from England suggest that the risk of death from the Pill due to thromboembolic phenomena is 3:100,000 users.[18,19,20] On the other hand, the risk of death from pregnancy in Thailand, for example, is approximately 400 to 500 per 100,000 live births,[34] the figure undoubtedly being higher in the rural areas, where 85 to 90 per cent of women are delivered at home without trained personnel in attendance.

To date, the Pill has been most widely used in the developed nations of the world, where continuation rates at two years, among well-educated and motivated women, vary between 53 and 71.7.[20,61] It remains to be proved as to whether rural, relatively uneducated women will take such medication regularly.[20] There have been pessimistic reports from Korea and Taiwan,[27,52] but more optimistic ones came from Malaysia and Thailand.[28,53] It is suggested that one possible explanation for the poor continuation rates may be the inconvenience secondary to the requirement that the patient return to a physician's clinic for resupply. Nurses and nonmedical personnel prescribe initially and give resupplies in Malaysia, where the continuation rates appear to be higher than in other developing nations.[53]

Another form of hormonal contraception is presently of interest: long-acting injectable progestational compounds.[35,68] While these have not yet been used widely in national programs, menstrual difficulties remain a problem, and other questions, such as reversability and hypoestrogenism, have not yet been satisfactorily answered, this method of contraception is potentially a most popular one in those cultures where an injection is a highly desired form of medical treatment.[10,31] The discussion below concerning oral contraception would apply here as well, if this form of medication is approved for widespread contraceptive use.

Traditional contraception will be omitted from discussion in this paper. Suffice it to say that, in the opinion of the author, these methods, with the debatable exception of the condom, will not play an important role in lowering birth rates in the rural areas of the developing world.

THE PHYSICIAN EXAMINATION

"Good medical practice" generally requires that a physician take a medical history and perform a general physical examination and a pelvic examination prior to the prescription of hormonal contraception or the insertion of an IUD. Three questions that must be answered are: Is a pelvic examination necessary and does it significantly reduce the risk of complication in a patient taking oral contraceptives? When pelvic examinations are required, can paramedics be taught to do them as safely as those conducted by a physician? Can a simple checklist be prepared that paramedics can use to elicit a satisfactory medical history? These questions will be considered, with particular attention to the contraindications to the use of the two methods of contraception being discussed in this paper.

Is a pelvic examination necessary? In discussing the importance of the pelvic examination, it is worth reviewing the general benefits of such an examination. Unquestionably, there are significant benefits to be gained from routine cytologic screening for carcinoma of the cervix, if facilities and personnel exist to conduct mass screening programs. An early report on cytologic screening[67] reported that 17 women per 1,000 of 108,000 women screened for the first time had suspicious or positive smears. Of the 79 per cent of the patients with a positive report who could be followed, half were found to have carcinoma in situ or invasive cancer, and another 2 per 1,000 had borderline lesions. Similarly, in a care-ful study conducted in Barbados, in the West Indies,[57] among the first 5,000 women screened, 0.5 per cent had invasive carcinoma, 0.8 per cent had carcinoma in situ, and 4.2 per cent dysplasia.

The long-term results of mass screening programs are dramatic. In British Columbia, after 6 years of a program in which a third of all women over the age of 20 were screened, the incidence of invasive carcinoma of the cervix decreased by 30.6 per cent.[17] Most striking has been the fall in death rates due to cervical cancer in those countries in which mass screening programs have been in effect for some time. The cervical cancer death rate has fallen from 19.7 deaths per 100,000 population in 1950 to 14.2 in 1963 in Japan, and from 19.2 in 1950 to 1951 to 13.4 in 1962 to 1963 in the United States.[22]

Thus it is fair to say that cytologic screening programs are beneficial even if there were not concern regarding the possible carcinogenic effects of oral contraceptives. In fact, family planning acceptors present an ideal group in which to begin mass screening programs.

The major limiting factor in most areas of the developing world is the lack of sufficient facilities and trained personnel to handle the smears in a large-scale program. The numbers of available pathologists are small in these countries, and many countries have not yet developed training programs for cytology technicians. Facilities usually do not exist outside the larger urban centers. The introduction of a widespread screening program is costly, although the actual figures will vary from country to country. It is the opinion of the author that one must carefully study the health needs in any given country and make an attempt to establish priorities before committing a sizable budget to a mass screening program for cervical carcinoma. It is felt that, in many countries, the priority for such a program may be relatively low compared to other pressing health needs.

In addition to the diagnosis of cervical pathology, routine pelvic examination is recommended as a means of detecting early ovarian pathology. Preventive measures for ovarian carcinoma, however, have been most unsuccessful, even in those areas of the world where routine pelvic examinations are performed regularly. Several studies from the United States have shown that between 70 and 90 per cent of all patients with ovarian malignancy seek advice late with complaints of abdominal distention due to tumor and ascites rather than any other early symptoms.[37] Early detection by routine examination contributes only a very small percentage of all diagnoses of ovarian malignancy, and even twice-yearly examinations have not been found effective in lowering the death rates from this disease.[11]

Routine pelvic examination adds little to the early detection of endometrial carcinoma, since these patients generally present with abnormal vaginal bleeding before significant changes are noted on pelvic examination. Rather, careful history-taking is of primary importance in the early diagnosis of endometrial disease.

It might seem from this discussion that, aside from the information learned from a Papanicolaou smear, there is little benefit to be gained from a routine pelvic examination. This is not the case, and it is not the purpose of this discussion to reach such a conclusion. Rather, the purpose is to place the benefits in proper perspective when one compares them to the hazards of pregnancy, and the possible hazards of oral contraception, particularly in relation to available medical personnel.

It is the opinion of the author that the logical conclusion to be drawn at this point is that a routine pelvic examination, where facilities and personnel to conduct cytologic screening are not available, while desirable, need not be required prior to the prescription of oral contraceptives. Routine pelvic examination will not increase the chances of diagnosing the other conditions that contraindicate the use of oral contraceptives or reduce the incidence of complications to their use.

Paramedic pelvic examination. When a pelvic examination is indicated, the next question is can paramedics be taught to do it as safely as physicians? There are, in the author's opinion, two major opportunities for the use of paramedics to perform pelvic examinations. The first is to obtain cervical smears for cytologic examinations, in those areas where personnel and facilities are available. The second, and probably more controversial, opportunity is to use them to insert IUD's.

There should be little opposition to the use of a paramedic, such as a nurse, to obtain Papanicolaou smears. In the Barbados study mentioned previously, nurse-midwives, specially trained, took almost all the smears in the project, obtaining very satisfactory results.[57] There are studies being conducted in which patients actually take their own smears (with a different technique, called the irrigation smear).[12,22] It is suggested that nurses or auxiliary health personnel can be given a brief training course so they can play a major role in a mass screening campaign.

The question of the utilization of a paramedic to insert intrauterine devices, while subject to much debate, should actually not be controversial, because it has already been done, in several places, with success. Furthermore, it is suggested that the procedure is easier and less hazardous than the delivery of a baby, which auxiliary midwives are allowed to do in many countries throughout the world.

An interesting project was conducted in Korea in which three groups were studied.[66] In one, IUD insertion was performed by an obstetrician; in the second, by a nurse-midwife supervised by the same physician; and in the third, the insertion was done by a specially trained nurse-midwife without direct supervision. There were no differences in terms of perforation, expulsion, or incidence of other complications. The only difference found was that the unsupervised nurse rejected slightly more patients than the others, referring patients about whom she had any reservations to a physician for a check prior to insertion.

In Pakistan, female lay personnel were given an intensive training course and then allowed to insert IUD's without direct supervision.[21,49] During 1967 and 1968, 600,000 IUD's were inserted by these personnel, accounting for approximately 75 per cent of all insertions in that country. The use of paramedical personnel was attempted in part because of the cultural demand that pelvic examinations be performed by females, in a country with an inadequate supply of female physicians available. A conclusion from this large study was that "IUD performance of paramedical personnel is reasonably comparable to that of medical personnel."[21] A further important point was made: "Full-time family planning personnel, whether medical or paramedical, generally give better services, as far as sterile technique, clinic organization, record-keeping, and follow-up procedures are concerned, than do those personnel, medical or paramedical, who do family planning on a part-time basis."

Use of the paramedic has been tried elsewhere as well. Nurse-midwives were trained to do IUD insertions in the Kentucky Frontier Nursing Service program conducted by the United States Public Health Service.[4] Here again, the program was successful and the results were no different from those of other medically supervised programs. Similarly, in addition to the study on cytologic screening, the group in Barbados successfully utilized trained nurse-midwives to perform IUD insertions.[58] In New York City, an excellent family planning training program for nurse-midwives is conducted at the Downstate Medical Center, which includes training in the techniques of pelvic examination and IUD insertion. Thus, the concept of utilization of personnel other than physicians is beginning to be accepted worldwide.

The key to the success of a paramedic IUD insertion program is an effective training program, which must be tailored to the needs of the job and of the trainee. While there are many other aspects of the training, including population dynamics, review of all methods of contraception (including contraindications, complications, and side effects), techniques of motivation, importance of follow-up, etc., the discussion here will be limited to the actual technique of IUD insertion.

The first step is to learn how to perform a pelvic examination. This entails a good deal of practice, so that one can learn to recognize the position of the uterus and to recognize any pelvic abnormalities that would be a contraindication. Pelvic examination is not difficult; it simply requires practice. Once the skill has been learned, the actual technique of a sterile IUD insertion is easy to teach. The paramedic may receive better training than the average physician because the paramedic's training is both more specific and more closely supervised. It is generally assumed by trainers that the physician already knows how to do a good pelvic examination, and thus little time may be spent supervising physicians during their training.

Thus, the answer to the second question is an emphatic "yes"; the paramedic can perform pelvic examinations to obtain cervical smears for cytologic examination, to rule out pelvic abnormalities, and to insert intrauterine devices. It is important, of course, that the paramedic be effectively supervised.

A paramedic checklist. The third question is: can a simple checklist be prepared that a paramedic can use to screen potential receptors? Table I presents just such a checklist which Thai auxiliary midwives have been using to prescribe oral contraceptives on a trial basis.[47] A series of short questions is asked, and a simple examination is performed. If there is a positive answer to any of the questions or in the examination, the Pill may not be prescribed, but rather the patient must be referred to a physician for further evaluation.

Table I. Questionnaire for midwives prescribing oral contraceptives

	Yes	No
History: ask if the patient has had a history of any of the following:		
Yellow skin or yellow eyes		
Mass in the breast		
Discharge from the nipple		
Excessive menstrual periods		
Increased frequency of menstrual periods		
Bleeding after sexual intercourse		
Swelling or severe pains in the legs		
Severe chest pains		
Unusual shortness of breath after exertion		
Severe headaches		
Examination: check the following:		
Yellow skin and yellow eye color		
Mass in the breast		
Nipple discharge		
Varicose veins		
Blood pressure (yes = above 160)		
Pulse (yes = above 120)		
Sugar in urine		
Protein in urine		

Instructions: If all the above are answered in the negative, the patient may receive oral contraceptives. If any of the above are answered in the positive, the patient must be seen by a physician before oral contraceptives may be prescribed.

If the contraindications and major complications listed in a previous section are reviewed, it can be seen that there is really little the physician can do that the paramedic cannot do, in terms of initial screening. The major concern at present, throughout the world, is the increased incidence of thromboembolic phenomena, documented in both the United Kingdom and the United States. As yet the physician is unable to predict which patient is likely to develop this condition. All that can be done is to check for varicose veins or phlebitis and to ask about any pertinent history. This can also be done, as well, by a trained paramedic.

In both the United Kingdom and the United States, the risk of thromboembolic disease during pregnancy and the puerperium is higher than that seen after use of oral contraceptives.[14] In the developing world, accurate statistics on complications such as thromboembolic disease are generally not available, but it is the impression of well-trained physicians in many of these countries that the condition is extremely rare as a complication of surgery or of pregnancy. This has also been the experience of the author, who has taught obstetrics and gynecology in both Nigeria and Thailand. In hospital statistics in Thailand, thromboembolic disease and pulmonary embolism are rarely found listed.[34] The hypothesis is proposed that if the condition is rare after pregnancy it will also prove rare after use of oral contraceptives, since the etiology in both situations is probably related to change in hormonal levels. A similar hypothesis has recently been proposed elsewhere,[45] but careful study over time will be necessary to test it.

Experience in Thailand over the past year has shown that auxiliary midwives, who have only 10 years of basic education, followed by an 18 month midwifery training program, can be taught to use the checklist effectively.[28] One tentative conclusion of this study was that, in many cases, the midwife is more conscientious in using such a checklist than the average busy physician.

If cytology capabilities are not available, it is suggested that the checklist presented in Table I is adequate for oral contraceptive users and that a routine pelvic examination is not required. The Malaysian National Family Planning Program is almost entirely a Pill program, with over 90 per cent of all acceptors using oral contraception.[6] The majority of prescriptions are given by nurses or, in some cases, by lay personnel, after taking a brief history only. After three years of experience, there has been no indication that a change is needed in this policy.

It is felt by some that a pelvic examination may well be a deterrent to the acceptance of contraception. In a successful large scale project in which Depo-Provera is given to patients after eliciting a careful history, but without requiring a routine pelvic examination,[31] the physician in charge attributes much of the success of the project not only to the popularity of injection as a form of treatment but also to the absence of a required preliminary pelvic exam.[32]

CONCLUSIONS

Much has been written about the critically high rates of population growth prevalent in many parts of the world, with some arguing that improved technology is the only hope or that the problem cannot be solved by family planning programs alone. While the concerns are real, it is argued in this paper that it is still possible to do more within the confines of family planning, with the use of existing methods of contraception, than is being done today, by reviewing and revising overly restrictive medical practices. Modern science has made major strides in recent years in the field of contraception, but it is clear that the ideal method has not yet been found. Intensive research efforts are presently being devoted to the development of improved methods, and there is hope of major advances in the foreseeable future. There is, however, no need to sit back and await these developments; it is necessary, instead, to utilize what is presently available as effectively as possible.

While oral hormonal contraception and intrauterine contraception are two of the most significant developments in modern medicine and remain the most effective contraceptive methods presently available, both have been disappointing because of the incidence of side effects and complications and the high discontinuation rates. Peel and Potts[43] have attempted to compare the mortality rates secondary to pregnancy and to the various methods of contraception. If the expected number of pregnancies through method failure are taken into consideration, their calculations suggest that oral contra-

ceptives and IUD's produce fewer deaths than any of the traditional methods of contraception. Similarly these two methods are shown to be far safer than the risks of either criminal or induced abortion, as well as uncontrolled fertility.

Because of the increasing awarness that there are insufficient numbers of physicians available presently and in the near future, particularly in the face of a rapidly expanding population, there is an urgent need for innovative thinking on the part of the established medical community. Problems must be evaluated rationally, and practical, not theoretical, solutions must be developed.

The use of paramedics to deliver health care is not new. Nurse-midwives do a large number of deliveries in both developed and developing nations. In the West, Britain has had a well-developed nurse-midwifery program for many years. Recently, in the United States, where most deliveries are done by physicians, there has been a call for the development of nurse-midwifery services.[36] In many countries, including the United States, nurses are allowed to give general anesthesia, potentially an extremely hazardous branch of medicine. Of particular interest has been the successful use of auxiliary personnel to provide basic health services in Kenya.[15,16]

Thus, the use of paramedics to prescribe oral contraceptives or to insert IUD's is not really a dramatic departure from "good medical practice," but rather an extension of present accepted practices. We, as physicians, must be willing to do away with rigid standards which tend to imply that only physicians are able to evaluate patients and prescribe treatment. We must be willing to adapt to the needs of society.

Thus, arguments are presented in this paper in support of paramedical prescription of oral contraceptives and insertion of the IUD. It is argued, based on an assessment of the benefits and risks, that omission of a pelvic examination is justified unless cytologic examination is possible. Based on experience elsewhere, it has been demonstrated that, where smears can be read, paramedics can be taught to obtain them. Similarly, there is good evidence that paramedics can be taught to do IUD insertion. A checklist that can be used by paramedical personnel is presented, which includes a series of questions and a simple examination to rule out a history of disease which contraindicates the use of a method of contraception.

The present controversy over oral contraception is an extremely important one, and no attempt is made to belittle the very serious concern of many scientists and lay people alike. It should be stressed, however, that the controversy need not affect the arguments used herein to support the use of paramedics to prescribe hormonal preparations. So long as oral contraception is allowed to remain on the market, it is the contention of the author that prescription by trained paramedics is as safe as by physicians, and perhaps safer in those areas in which there exists a critical shortage of doctors.

It is hoped that through the widespread use of paramedics acceptance rates for effective methods of contraception will rise, as will, hopefully, the continuation rates. Moving such contraceptive services closer to the patient, particularly in the vast rural areas of the world, should have a dramatic effect in showing that more can still be done within family planning.

The time to find solutions is short. It has been estimated that the total world's population will almost double in the next 30 years, an increase of more than 3 billion people, and 85 per cent of this total will be in the developing countries.[24] We cannot simply await further technologic development. It behooves the medical profession to remove unnecessary and unrealistic roadblocks from improved delivery of presently available contraceptive services.

SUMMARY

It is widely accepted today that the world is faced with an extremely critical problem in terms of the high rates of population growth that presently exists in a large part of the world. While some argue about the limits of family planning and present methods of contraception, this paper presents the case for a more rational approach utilizing existing technology.

Three questions are asked: Is a pelvic examination necessary prior to the prescription of oral contraceptives and does it significantly reduce the risk of complication of oral contraception? If pelvic examination is necessary, are there significant differences between examination conducted by a physician as compared to one by a paramedic? Can a simple checklist be prepared for use by the paramedic? It is concluded that the major indication for a pelvic examination is to take a Papanicolaou smear, and, if facilities for reading smears are available, paramedics can easily be taught to obtain the smear. When cytologic examination is impossible, an argument is developed that there is no significant increased risk in the omission of a pelvic examination altogether. Evidence is also presented to suggest that paramedical personnel with proper training and supervision can insert the IUD as safely as insertion by most physicians. Finally, a simple checklist is presented for use by the paramedic. It is argued that the present controversy concerning oral contraception does not affect the rationale for the prescription by personnel other than physicians. A plea is made to the medical profession to be more realistic and practical in setting standards of good medical practice.

REFERENCES

1. Advisory Committee on Obstetrics and Gynecology (Hellman, L., Chairman), Food and Drug Administration: First Report on the Oral Contraceptives, 1966.
2. Advisory Committee on Obstetrics and Gynecology (Hellman, L., Chairman), Food and Drug Administration: Report on Intrauterine Contraceptive Devices, 1968.
3. Advisory Committee on Obstetrics and Gynecology (Hellman, L., Chairman), Food and

Drug Administration: Second Report on the Oral Contraceptives, 1969.

4. Beasley, W. B. R.: AMER. J. OBSTET. GYNEC. 98:201, 1967.
5. Berelson, B.: Studies Family Planning, 38:1, 1969.
6. Bin Marzuki, A., and Peng, J. Y.: Paper presented at Combined Conference on Evaluation of Malaysia National Family Planning Programme and East Asia Population Programmes, March, 1970.
7. Blake, J.: Science 164:522, 1969.
8. Bryant, J.: Health in the Developing World, Ithica, Cornell University Press, 1970, p. 75.
9. Bundy, M.: J. Med. Ed. 44(Part 2): 7, 1969.
10. Cunningham, C.: Social Science and Medicine, 1970. In press.
11. Danforth, D. M., editor: Textbook of Obstetrics and Gynecology, New York, 1966, Harper & Row, Publishers, p. 1000.
12. Davis, H. J., and Jones, H. W.: AMER. J. OBSTET. GYNEC. 96:605, 1966.
13. Davis, K.: Science 158:730, 1967.
14. Editorial: Brit. Med. J. 1:249, 1970.
15. Fendall, N. R. E.: Public Health Rep. 78:977, 1963.
16. Fendall, N. R. E.: Public Health Rep. 82:471, 1967.
17. Fidler, H. K., Boges, D. A., Aversperg, M., and Lock, D. R.: Canad. Med. Ass. J. 86: 779, 1962.
18. Grafenberg, E.: In Sanger, M., and Stone, H. M., editors: Practice of Contraception: An International Symposium and Survey, Proc. Seventh Int. Birth Control Conf., Baltimore, 1932, The Williams & Wilkins Company.
19. Inman, W. H. W., and Vessy, M. P.: Brit. Med. J. 2:193, 1968.
20. Jones, G. W., and Mauldin, W. P.: Studies Family Planning 24:1, 1967.
21. Kaul, S. J.: Pakistan, J. Family Planning 3: 75, 1969.
22. Kawashima, Y., Ino, S., Tashiro, K., Tachibano, M., and Masukawa, T.: Obstet. Gynec. 32:17, 1968.
23. Keeny, S. M.: Studies Family Planning, 6:1, 1965.
24. Kirk, D.: In Behrman, S. J., Corsa, L., and Freedman, R.: Fertility and Family Planning, Ann Arbor, 1969, University of Michigan Press, p. 75.
25. Kistner, R. W.: AMER. J. OBSTET. GYNEC. 75:264, 1958.
26. Kistner, R. W.: Gynecology, Principles and Practice, Chicago, 1965, Year Book Medical Publishers, Inc., p. 552.
27. Korea, Population Council Office Monthly Report (mimeographed), November, 1969.
28. Limcharoen, C., and Rosenfield, A. G.: In preparation.
29. Mauldin, W. P., Nortman, D., and Stephan, F. F.: Studies Family Planning, 18:1, 1967.
30. Maxwell, W. E.: Mimeographed report, 1967.
31. McDaniel, E. B.: Paper presented at the Third National Population Seminar, Bangkok, Thailand, April, 1968.
32. McDaniel, E. B.: Personal communication.
33. Melamed, M. R., Koss, L. G., Flehinger, B. J., Kelisky, R. P., and Dunbrow, H.: Brit. Med. J. 3:195, 1969.
34. Ministry of Public Health, Thailand: Statistical Reports, Department of Medical Services and Division of Vital Statistics.
35. Mishell, D. R., El Habashy, M. A., Good, R. G., and Moyer, D. L.: AMER. J. OBSTET. GYNEC. 101:1045, 1968.
36. Montgomery, T. A.: AMER. J. OBSTET. GYNEC. 105:309, 1969.
37. Moore, D. W., and Lankley, I. I.: AMER. J. OBSTET. GYNEC. 98:624, 1967.
38. National Economic Development Board of Thailand: Factbook on Manpower in Thailand, 1967.
39. National Economic Development Board of Thailand: Population Policy for National Economic and Social Development, 1970.
40. National Economic Development Board, The Institute of Population Studies and the Ministry of Public Health, Thailand: Population Growth in Thailand, pp. 34-35, 1970.
41. National Statistical Office of Thailand: The Survey of Population Change, 1964-1967.
42. Ota, T.: Jap. J. Obstet. Gynec. 17:210, 1934.
43. Peel, J., and Potts, M.: Textbook of Contraceptive Practice, London, 1969, Cambridge University Press, p. 253.
44. Peng, J. Y., Asavasena, W., and Vimuktanon, S.: Med. Gynaec. Sociol. Vol. 2 (No. 7:5 and No. 8:7), 1967.
45. Potts, D. M.: Oral Contraceptive Survey, IPPF Medical Bulletin, Vol. 4, No. 1, 1970.
46. Rock, J., Pincus, G., and Garcia, C. R.: Science 124:891, 1956.
47. Rosenfield, A. G.: Paper presented at the Fourth Asian Int. Congr. Obstetricians and Gynecologists, Singapore, November, 1968.
48. Sartwell, P. E., Masi, A. T., Arthes, F. G., Greene, G. R., and Smith, H. E.: Amer. J. Epidem. 90:365, 1969.
49. Satterthwaite, A. P.: Training and Performance of Paramedical Personnel in the Pakistan Family Planning Programme, in Proceedings of the Pakistan International Family Planning Conference at Dacca, January, 1969.
50. Segal, S. J., and Tietze, C.: Contraceptive Technology: Current and Prospective Meth-

ods, Reports on Population/Family Planning, October, 1969.

51. Southam, A. L.: *In* Segal, S. J., Southam, A. L., and Shafer, K. D., editors: Intrauterine Contraception: Proc. Second Int. Conference, New York, 1964, International Congress Series No. 86, Excerpta Medica Foundation, Amsterdam, 1964, p. 3.

52. Taiwan, First Island-wide Pill Acceptor Follow-up Survey, 1968 (mimeographed, preliminary report), 1969.

53. Tan, B. A., and Takeshita, J. Y.: Paper presented at the Combined Conference on Evaluation of Malaysian National Family Planning Programme and East Asia Population Programmes, March, 1970.

54. Ten Have, R.: Paper presented at Proceedings of the First National Family Planning Seminar, Kuala Lumpur, Malaysia, June, 1968, p. 85.

55. Tietze, C.: Studies in Family Planning, Nos. 3, 7, 12, 18, 25, 36, 47, and 55, 1964-1970.

56. Tow, S. H., Goon, S. M., Lean, T. H., Ratnam, S. S., and Wolfers, D.: Paper presented at Second Int. Postpartum Family Planning Program Meeting, New York, 1967.

57. Vaillant, H. W., Cummins, G. T. M., and Richart, R. M.: AMER. J. OBSTET. GYNEC. 101:946, 1968.

58. Vaillant, H. W., Cummins, G. T. M., Richart, R. M., and Barron, B. A.: Brit. Med. J. 3: 671, 1968.

59. Vessey, M. P., and Doll, R.: Brit. Med. J. 2: 199, 1968.

60. Vessey, M. P., and Doll, R.: Brit. Med. J. 2:661, 1969.

61. Westoff, C. F., and Ryder, N. B.: Public Health Rep. 83:277, 1968.

62. World Health Organization: Basic and Clinical Aspects of Intra-uterine Devices, Technical Report Series, No. 332, 1966.

63. World Health Organization: Clinical Aspects of Oral Gestogens, Technical Report Series, 1966.

64. World Health Organization: Intra-uterine Devices: Physiological and Clinical Aspects, Technical Report Series, No. 397, 1968.

65. World Health Organization: Hormonal Steroids in Contraception, Technical Report Series, No. 386, 1968.

66. Yang, J. M., Bang, S., S. W.: Studies Family Planning 27:4, 1968.

67. Young, P. A.: Obstet. Gynec. 10:469, 1957.

68. Zanartu, J., Rice-Wray, E., and Goldzieher, J. W.: Obstet. Gynec. 28:513, 1966.